WEYERHAEUSER ENVIRONMENTAL BOOKS

WILLIAM CRONON, EDITOR

Weyerhaeuser Environmental Books explore human relationships with natural environments in all their variety and complexity. They seek to cast new light on the ways that natural systems affect human communities, the ways that people affect the environments of which they are a part, and the ways that different cultural conceptions of nature profoundly shape our sense of the world around us. A complete listing of the books in the series can be found at the end of this book.

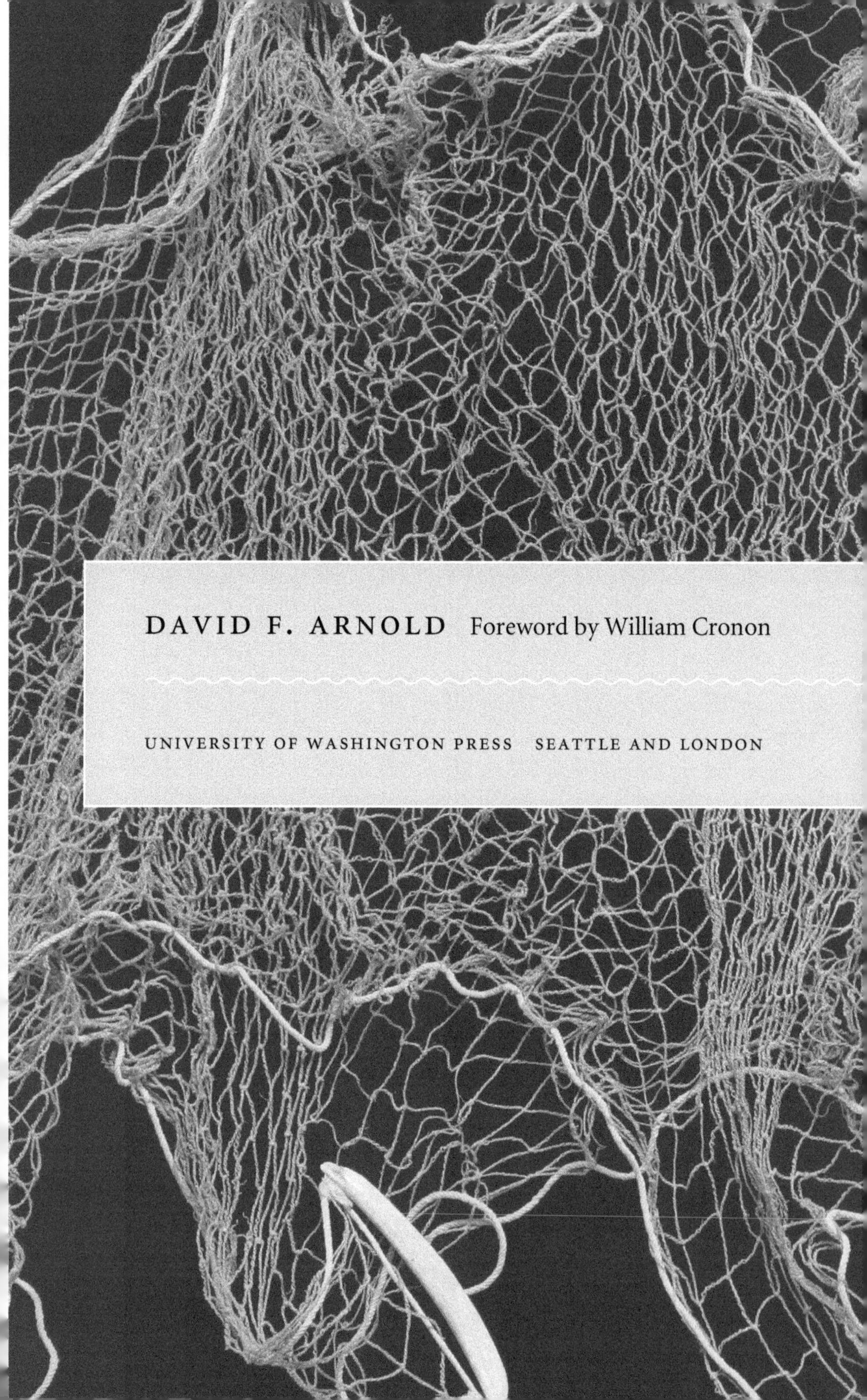

DAVID F. ARNOLD Foreword by William Cronon

UNIVERSITY OF WASHINGTON PRESS SEATTLE AND LONDON

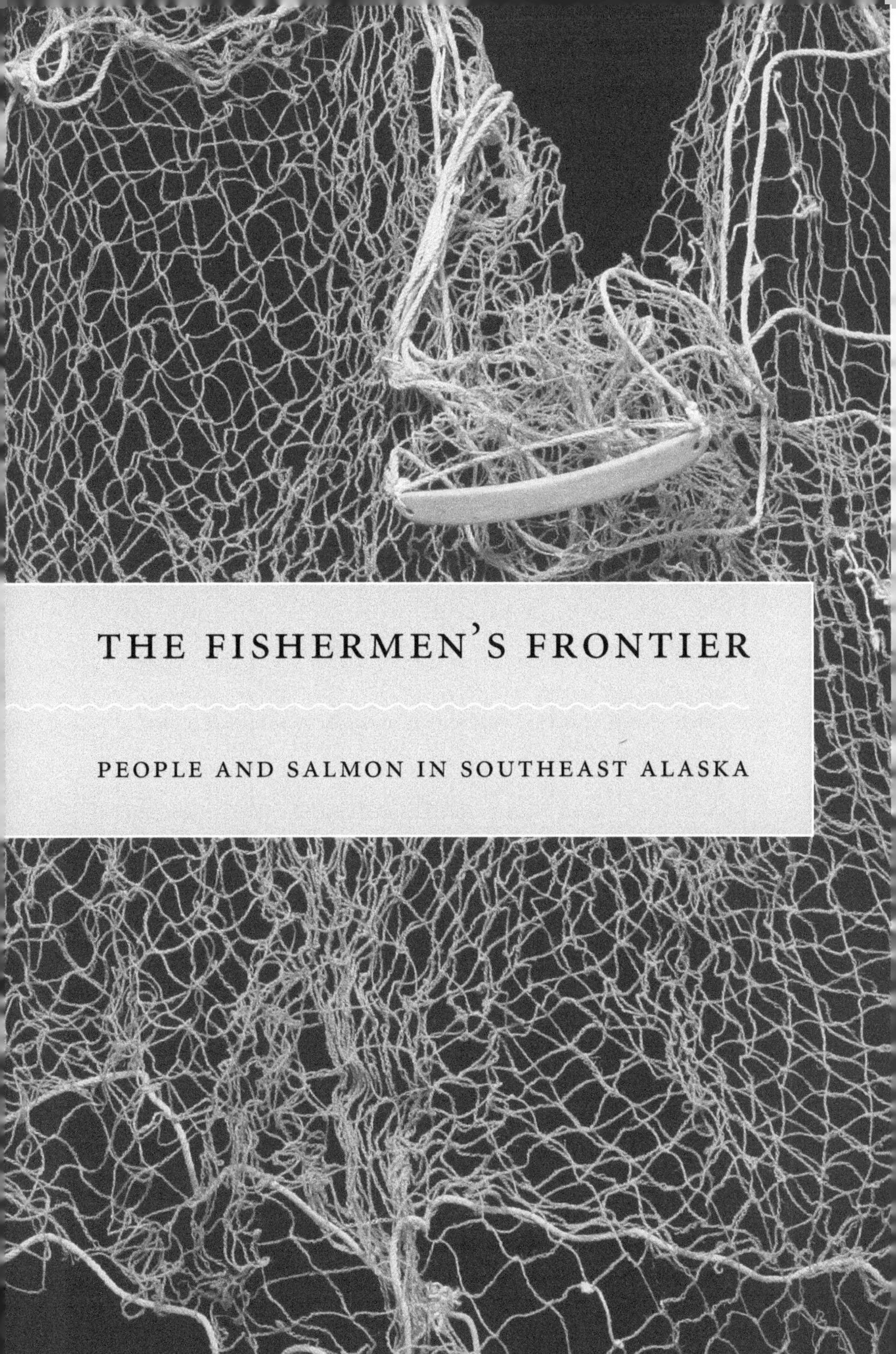

THE FISHERMEN'S FRONTIER

PEOPLE AND SALMON IN SOUTHEAST ALASKA

The Fishermen's Frontier *is published with the assistance of a grant from the Weyerhaeuser Environmental Books Endowment, established by the Weyerhaeuser Company Foundation, members of the Weyerhaeuser family, and Janet and Jack Creighton.*

First paperback edition, 2011
Printed in the United States of America
Design by Pamela Canell
16 15 14 13 12 11 6 5 4 3 2 1

University of Washington Press
P.O. Box 50096, Seattle, WA 98145 U.S.A.
www.washington.edu/uwpress

pp. ii-iii: A Yup'ik sinew net. From *Yuungnaqpiallerput / The Way We Genuinely Live* (University of Washingon Press, 2007).

Library of Congress Cataloging-in-Publication Data
The fishermen's frontier : people and salmon in Southeast Alaska /
edited by David F. Arnold ; foreword by William Cronon
p. cm. — (Weyerhaeuser environmental books)
Includes bibliographical references and index.
ISBN 978-0-295-99137-5 (pbk. : alk. paper)
1. Pacific salmon fisheries—Alaska, Southeast—History.
2. Fishery management—Alaska, Southeast—History.
3. Tlingit Indians—Fishing—Alaska, Southeast—History.
4. Haida Indians—Fishing—Alaska, Southeast—History.
5. Traditional ecological knowledge—Alaska, Southeast—History. I. Title.
SH348.A76 2008 333.95'65609798—dc22 2007048977

The paper used in this publication is acid-free and 90 percent recycled from at least 50 percent postconsumer waste. It meets the minimum requirements of the American National Standard for Information Sciences—Permanence of Paper for Printed Library Materials, ANSI Z39.48–1984.♾♻

FOR ARIENNE, SAMUEL, AND GRACE

Contents

Foreword

ON THE SALTWATER MARGINS OF A NORTHERN FRONTIER | William Cronon

It has long been almost a cliché to refer to Alaska as America's "last frontier." Many of the attributes that characterized other frontier regions have persisted longer there than almost anywhere else in the nation. As with so many other frontiers, waves of immigrants have mingled with, exploited, and sometimes displaced the indigenous populations who have inhabited these far northern environs for millennia. Natives and newcomers for the past three centuries have found themselves enmeshed in colonial trade networks devoted mainly to extracting natural resources from Alaskan environments for shipment hundreds and thousands of miles away. Like most such peripheral economies, Alaska has undergone periods of intense boom and bust as external demand for its resources has waxed and waned and as the supply of those resources has risen and fallen in turn.

Alaska's population has long been dispersed in small, remote communities and a few larger towns tied to metropolitan centers (places such as San Francisco, Seattle, and eventually Anchorage) with disproportionate influence over the life of the region. Alaskan history can easily be organized according to a series of "resource frontiers"—furs, minerals, oil, fish—whose changing fortunes have mirrored those of the state as a whole. Much of Alaskan politics has revolved around who should chiefly benefit from these resources: natives, local workers and communities, or the capitalists, corporations, and government bureaucrats (many located thousands of miles away) that have exercised control over them. Add to these other phenomena the intense individualism so characteristic of American frontier mythology, along with suspicion of government power coupled with deep reliance on government largesse, and it is not at all hard to see why so many people have so easily seen Alaska as the final and most intense expression of American frontier history.

Certain episodes of the Alaskan past loom large enough to have become part of standard textbook accounts of American history more generally, though rarely at much length. The original decision to purchase Alaska from Russia in 1867—mocked as Seward's Folly—gets a brief notice. Perhaps because the photographic record is so extraordinary and the tale-telling of Jack London and Robert Service so compelling, the Klondike Gold Rush has become a set piece as well. (Its story has most recently been retold by Kathryn Morse in her wonderful *The Nature of Gold*, another volume in this series.) Debates over statehood and the role of Alaska during the Cold War sometimes make it into the textbooks, as do the discovery of North Slope oil and the subsequent controversies over how best to conserve and develop resources on the public lands of this largest of all American states.

But if one had to pick a single feature of Alaskan history that has been most important to the largest number of people for the longest time and in the most ways, there cannot be much doubt about what it would be: *fish*. This is true for many more places than just Alaska, yet somehow the oceans and their many gifts to humanity have almost never received the attention from historians that their intrinsic importance merits. If mentioned at all, the watery two-thirds of the planet enters historical narratives as a relatively uninhabited liquid expanse that both divides and connects human beings whose activities—voyaging, exploring, navigating, trading, raiding, warring, and so on—have led them across it. The sea carries spice traders to distant corners of the planet; it floats the armadas of navies for great military encounters; it transports commodities hither and yon; it poses scientific puzzles for navigators, mapmakers, and engineers . . . but rarely for more than a few paragraphs. Even the harvested bounty of marine creatures that the sea has so abundantly yielded since time immemorial receives little more than passing mention. Despite their importance, the oceans have almost always been relegated to the saltwater margins of human history.

Surprising though it may seem, environmental history has been slow to correct this scholarly blind spot. Arthur McEvoy's classic *The Fisherman's Problem*, which traced the story of California's fisheries across the nineteenth and twentieth centuries, stood almost alone in the field for nearly a decade after its publication in 1986. More recently, important new studies have explored the salmon fisheries of the Pacific Northwest, which are among the most defining environmental features of that region: Richard White's

The Organic Machine, Matthew Evenden's *Fish Versus Power*, and (again in this series) Joseph Taylor's *Making Salmon*. These, along with a few extraordinary works of oceanic history by Greg Dening and other scholars, have begun to demonstrate how important it is to write histories that do not end at water's edge.

Now, with the publication of David F. Arnold's *The Fishermen's Frontier: People and Salmon in Southeast Alaska*, we see the full promise of an environmental history that straddles the shoreline to weave together water with land, fish with fisher, native with newcomer, saltwater with fresh, nature with culture. Arnold has set himself the ambitious task of tracing the story of salmon fishing in Alaska across more than a quarter millennium of human history. Those unfamiliar with the history or geography of this far northern region might be tempted to think that a book focused on the harvest of a single family of fish by a single industry in a single coastal region of the largest and least well-known of American states could hardly be of much general interest. But they would be wrong indeed.

Because salmon spend their adult lives feeding in the open ocean but then swim dozens or even hundreds of miles up freshwater streams to spawn in the interiors of continental watersheds, their lives integrate the ecologies of terrestrial and marine environments as few other organisms ever do. Because this far-flung reproductive journey means that salmon can be harvested either at sea or on land, radically disparate technologies have been devised for fishing these amazing creatures. And because those technologies have been used by diverse human groups and cultures in response to quite different political economic systems, it would be hard to imagine a more revealing tale of ecological, economic, technological, and cultural change than that of salmon fishing in southeastern Alaska. It is this story of people and fish transmuting each other through time that David Arnold tells so brilliantly in *The Fishermen's Frontier*.

As Arnold points out in his introduction, one of his goals is to tell the story of salmon fishing as much through the lens of labor history as of environmental history. Although scholars like Richard White, Alan Taylor, Gunther Peck, Thomas Andrews, and others have been calling for an integration of labor and social history with environmental history for more than a decade, Arnold's is one of the first books to achieve a full synthesis of these very different historiographical traditions. A central concern of environmental historians is the impact of human beings on the lives of non-human organisms and environments—so that the alteration of natural systems often gets told as a negative story in which powerful human actors (often workers) make the world worse through their actions. A central concern of labor and social historians, on the other hand, is the exploitation of workers and other less privileged people by those with greater wealth or power—so that the harvesting of natural resources often gets told as a negative story in which powerful human actors expropriate and exploit the labor of others to amass their fortunes. It is not at all hard to see how easily these stories can have different endings and moral implications—and why it might be difficult to integrate and bring them into a single frame. Yet that is what David Arnold has accomplished in this book.

In prose that is always clear and compelling and with research that is wide-ranging and persuasive, Arnold begins by examining Tlingit and Haida fisheries as they existed before Europeans began to alter the cultural and ecological landscapes of coastal Alaska. He pays close attention to the particular ways people fished, harvested, and processed the salmon they caught. Especially important to his argument are land-based fish traps, which during spawning runs could be used to harvest much larger numbers of animals than would typically be true of offshore fishing at other times of the year. One of Arnold's most striking insights has to do with the carefully controlled property rights that native Alaskan communities used in aboriginal times to reduce intergroup conflict and regulate levels of fishing in ways that maintained salmon harvests at sustainable levels.

With the coming of the Russian colony in Alaska in the eighteenth century, labor relations and the harvest of marine mammals were drastically transformed as natives were conscripted to increase the slaughter and trade of seals, sea otters, and other fur-bearing animals. Arnold traces the evolution of salmon harvests across this earliest frontier period as the Alaskan economy began to enter a European colonial orbit. But the industrial transformation of salmon fisheries awaited the arrival of Americans in the second half of the nineteenth century, with their new fishing vessels, shoreline packing plants, and mechanical fish traps. As had already happened in other parts of the United States, an enormous increase in the salmon harvest accompanied these new economic, technological, cultural systems.

Perhaps most intriguingly, Arnold argues that the advent of the American fisheries brought a new system of unregulated property rights that opened up individual access to fishery resources. At the same time, packing companies came to dominate the economic and political life of Alaska to a degree rarely appreciated by outsiders. Conflict and competition increased in parallel with the size of the harvest, and the growing capitalization of both the fishing fleet and the packing plants brought new forms of labor activity that culminated in the formation of unions seeking to protect the rights of workers. Unsurprisingly, organized labor saw different fishing technologies as having quite different implications for corporate profits and the ability of workers to share in the fruits of their own labors. Mechanical fish traps in particular were seen as labor-saving devices that benefited capital very much at the expense of workers, so that protests over their use became a recurrent feature of Alaskan politics across the first half of the twentieth century. At the same time, conservationists both inside and outside the federal government expressed growing concerns about whether the scale of the harvest was sustainable and whether the Alaskan fisheries might experience the same kind of collapse that had already occurred in comparable fisheries elsewhere in the United States.

With statehood in 1959, Alaska gained significant control over its own fisheries, reducing the influence of federal managers and instituting a radical new form of state regulation that reversed the practices of a half century. Whereas the decades following American acquisition of Alaska had seen a system of collective indigenous property rights replaced by an individualistic common property regime open to all comers, the Alaskan state government after 1960 created a strict licensing system that essentially privatized access to the salmon harvest under the watchful eye of professional fishery managers and conservationists. The fortunes of the industry waxed and waned under this new system, only to be confronted in the late twentieth century by the world-wide challenge of industrial fish farming, putting the Alaskan fisheries—which had always relied primarily on the harvest of wild fish—more at risk economically than ever before. That is where things stood in the early twenty-first century as the story told in this book draws to a close.

I cannot hope to summarize such a complex history in this brief foreword, and fortunately I don't need to do so. It has never been better narrated than in the pages that follow. All that is left for me is to praise the subtlety and generosity with which David Arnold tells this story. Among the most remarkable features of his fine book are the fairness and sympathy with which he seeks to understand the very different perspectives of the human actors in this drama, no matter how much in conflict with each other those actors might be. If you follow the twists and turns of this tale to its end, you will gain a much richer understanding not just of the difficulties facing salmon fisheries in modern Alaska, not just of the dilemmas associated with devising technologies and property regimes to protect ecosystems while assuring sustainable harvests of natural resources, but of the equally vital task of sustaining human communities and ways of life as well. In truth, there are few more compelling challenges in the world today. We can be grateful to David Arnold for demonstrating in such a rich and nuanced way the kind of history we must recover and understand if we hope to attain the wisdom we will need to serve fish and people alike.

Acknowledgments

We live in a postmodern world. As consumers of television, of processed food, and even of nature, we experience much of life as spectators. Corporations—what agrarian writer Wendell Berry calls "proxies"—produce our food, our shelter, our clothing, our entertainment. The postmodern mentality suggests that one reality is never superior to another. All realities simply reveal different contexts: a weed in the Disneyland parking lot and a giant sequoia are both "nature"; fishing for salmon and entering data in a corporate cubicle are both forms of "work." I would not deny this. Yet I am glad to know that somewhere out there, setting out on the ebb tide, someone is doing work that dissolves the distance between humans and nature, between thought and action—work that eliminates the distance, irony, and spectatorlike quality of modern life. I am glad to know that independent, small-boat fishermen are killing fish for me to consume.*

I first want to thank all those Alaska fisherfolk whose labors allow the rest of us to enjoy a meal of wild salmon now and then, and whose lifestyles tend to buck against the homogenizing trends of modern life. The contemporary era has seen a dramatic loss of biodiversity: industrial agriculture has transformed complex natural ecosystems into highly simplified cash-crop monocultures. But what about the loss of human diversity, as distinctive occupations are pulverized in the churning gears of globaliza-

* A short note on terminology: I would never call an Alaska fisherman a "fisher" to his or her face. I would be told, rather vehemently, that "fishers" are four-legged animals with thick brown fur. However, in an attempt to avoid excessive repetition, I have used "fishermen" and "fishers" synonymously throughout this book. I have also used "fisherman" or "fishermen" when referring to female fishers, both for the sake of simplicity and because all the female fishermen I have encountered in Alaska refer to themselves as fishermen.

tion? Here's to the hope that both fishermen and fish continue their annual migrations long into the future.

This book would not have been possible without fishermen and fish. It would also not have been possible without the support of Columbia Basin College and the CBC Foundation, which provided me a summer research grant in 2005. College president Lee Thornton granted me a two-quarter sabbatical to work on this book. Vice president Richard Cummins and Deborah Meadows, dean of the Social Science Division, encouraged my researching and writing as a legitimate form of "professional development." All three had the vision to recognize that even at a community college history teachers sometimes need to be historians.

This book owes its existence to an extended community of friends, scholars, and public servants that stretches from Los Angeles to Naknek, Alaska. Norris Hundley, my graduate school mentor and the first person to read the entire manuscript, probably did not realize that he would still be advising me nearly ten years after graduate school. There is no historian whom I trust and admire more. Other historians from the UCLA community offered encouragement, suggestions, and, most important, friendship, including Philip Minehan, Chris Friday, Mark Spence, Edward Hashima, Tom Mertes, and Lissa Wadewitz. I thank you all for your continuing intellectual and emotional support.

I owe a special thanks to Julidta Tarver at the University of Washington Press, for simply being interested, concerned, and supportive long before I had produced anything that merited her attention. It was at a conference in Bellingham, Washington, during the spring of 2003 when I told Lita, with firm resolve, that I was giving up any pretense of ever producing anything: teaching and raising a family were enough without the pressure of research and writing, which at a community college were not part of my job responsibilities anyway. For some reason her friendly e-mails did not stop, and a few years later I was able to hand her this manuscript.

It was at that same Bellingham conference in 2003 that I became reacquainted with Katie Johnson-Ringsmuth, an old friend from my cannery days in South Naknek. Remarkably, we had both gone from working in the fisheries to researching and writing about the fisheries. Since 2003, Katie has become a great friend whose interest in, and contributions to, this book have been invaluable. Also at that Bellingham conference was Steve Haycox—the avuncular dean of Alaska history—whose suggestions, scholarship, and general knowledge of Alaska history have likewise made this a better book. Since 1992, Steve's interest in my own development as a historian has been generous and unwavering.

I cannot possibly chronicle or even list all the people who have contributed in some way to this book, but some deserve special mention: Bill Cronon, whose books have inspired a generation of young historians to explore environmental history, is perhaps even more inspiring for his unpretentious professionalism and advocacy of meaningful and accessible scholarship. I feel privileged to have him write the foreword to this book. Meg Woods—a model colleague through good times and bad—read and copyedited some early chapters and exhibited real enthusiasm. Jerry Lewis and Donna Starr offered technical assistance at critical junctures. Nancy Ratner, Andy McGregor, and Mike Turek of the Alaska Department of Fish and Game promptly returned all my e-mail queries and provided me with great information and leads.

Librarians and archivists at the Alaska State Library in Juneau and the National Archives in Anchorage, notably Gladi Kulp and Bruce Parham, were indefatigably helpful. Gunnar Knapp generously provided some of his own photographs, drawn from his excellent work on the rise of global salmon farming. Peter Cahan granted me the rights to use his grandfather's beautiful painting on the book's cover. For the rest—friends, family, colleagues, and scholars—I offer my sincere thanks: Mike Dunning, Robert Hill, Monty Buell, Robert Chisholm, Mark Taff, Jerry Delich, Kay-Lynn Beard, Brad Sealy, Barb Sandness, Cathy Hampton, Raelene Cuillier, Theresa Thonney, Dave Abbott, Ron Nebert, Mike Orth, Trish Caron, Del Hayes, Jim Creevey, Mom, Dad, Grandma, and Aunt Rosemary.

I owe my greatest debt and deepest affections to my wife, Arienne, and our two children, Samuel and Grace, to whom this book is dedicated. There is little I could say about you that doesn't sound cliché, but here's one futile attempt: without your love a project such as this would be meaningless. I cannot thank you enough.

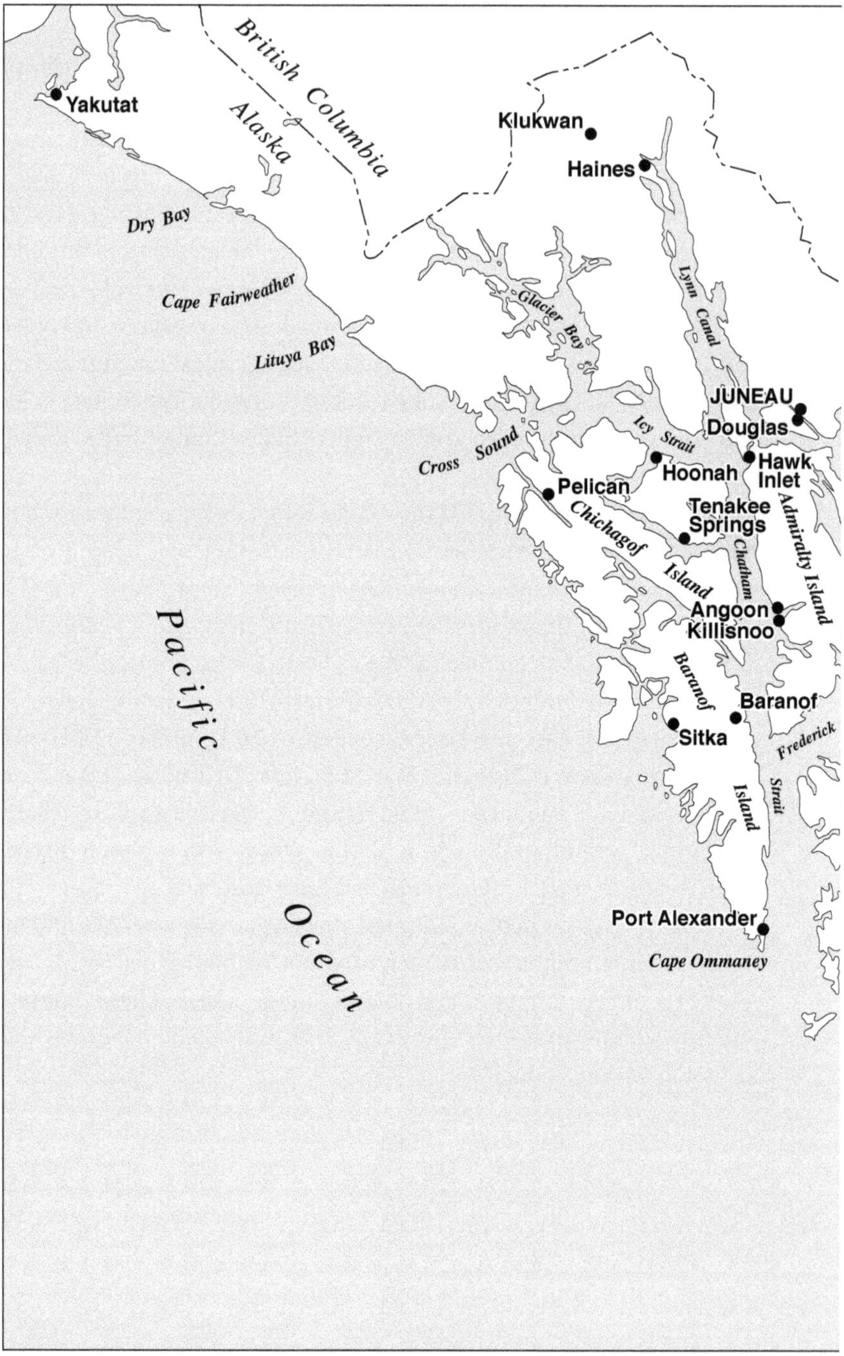

British Columbia
Alaska
Yakutat
Klukwan
Haines
Dry Bay
Cape Fairweather
Lituya Bay
Glacier Bay
Lynn Canal
JUNEAU
Douglas
Icy Strait
Cross Sound
Hoonah
Hawk Inlet
Pelican
Chichagof Island
Tenakee Springs
Chatham
Admiralty Island
Angoon
Killisnoo
Baranof
Baranof
Sitka
Frederick Strait
Island
Pacific Ocean
Port Alexander
Cape Ommaney

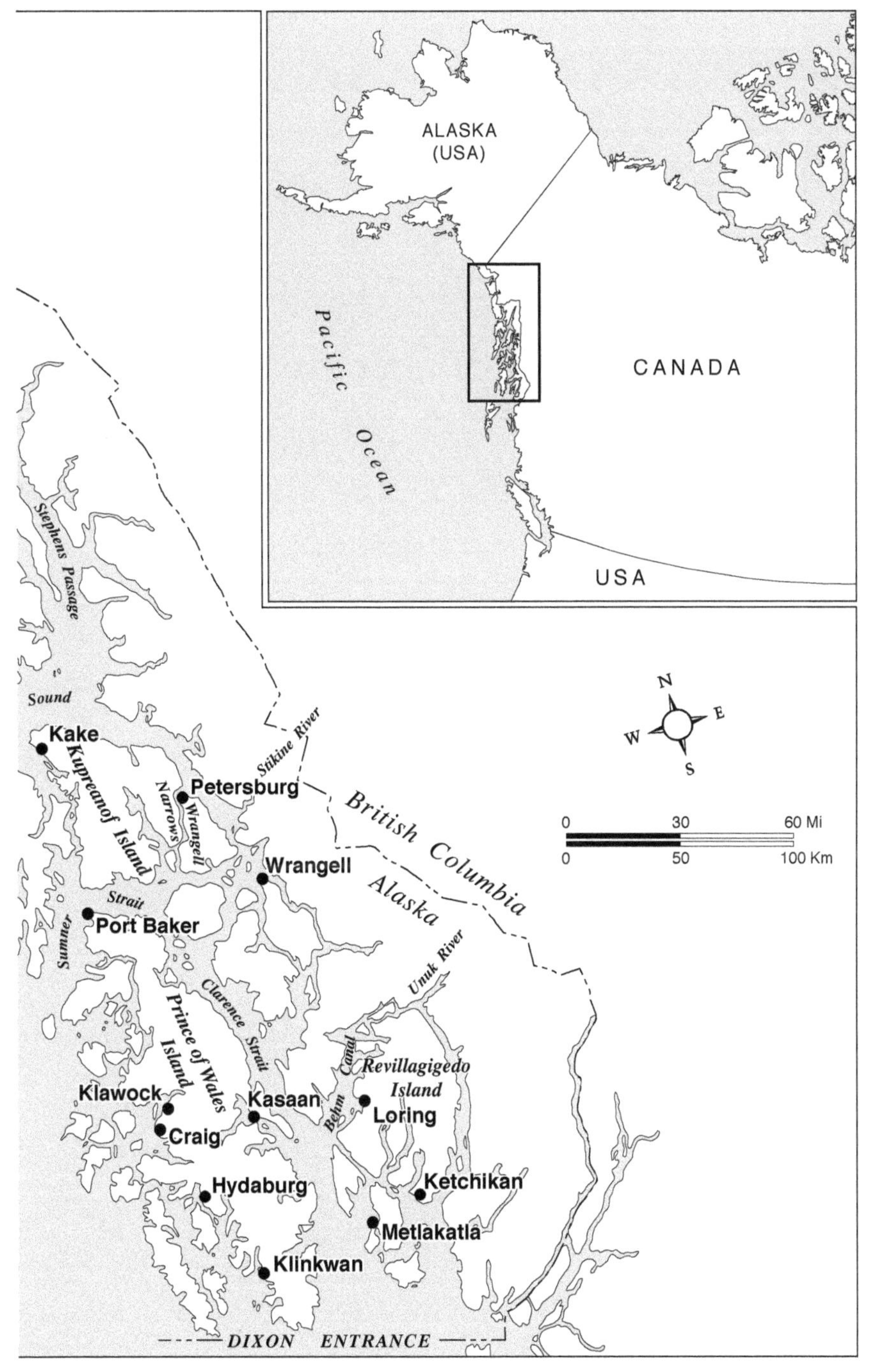

ALASKA
(USA)
Pacific
Ocean
CANADA
USA
Stephens Passage
Sound
Kake
Kupreanof Island
Wrangell Narrows
Petersburg
Stikine River
British Columbia
Alaska
Wrangell
Strait
Sumner
Port Baker
Clarence Strait
Prince of Wales Island
Unuk River
Behm Canal
Revillagigedo Island
Klawock
Kasaan
Loring
Craig
Hydaburg
Ketchikan
Metlakatla
Klinkwan
DIXON ENTRANCE
N
E
W
S
0
30
60 Mi
0
50
100 Km

THE FISHERMEN'S FRONTIER

Introduction

THE FISHERMEN'S FRONTIER IN SOUTHEAST ALASKA

Where are your monuments, your battles, martyrs?
Where is your tribal memory? Sirs,
in that grey vault. The sea. The sea
has locked them up. The sea is history.
—DEREK WALCOTT, "The Sea Is History"

The idea of nature contains, though often unnoticed, an extraordinary amount of human history.—RAYMOND WILLIAMS, *Problems in Materialism and Culture*

Surveying the literature on the Pacific salmon fisheries, one notices a distinct trend. It is primarily about decline. It echoes a larger narrative about the destruction of the natural environment under the forces of colonization, capitalism, and industrialization. It is a story of the mythic natural abundance that existed in North America before the arrival of Europeans—"of flights of passenger pigeons so numerous they darkened the sky, of herds of bison that shook the earth as they passed, of forests so dense that a squirrel could walk from the Atlantic Ocean to the Mississippi River without touching the ground"—and of the propensity of humans to transform those natural resources into individual wealth.[1] It is about the myopic inability of Americans to see any limits to their own exploitation of the natural world until, inevitably, the resource is destroyed. It is a story about fourteen species of Pacific salmon that are extinct or reside on the endangered species list, with more teetering on the edge of the same fate. The storyline is suggested in the titles of studies that speak of "abundance to extinction," "salmon without rivers," "the Northwest fisheries crisis," the "decline of the Alaska salmon," and "the fisherman's problem."[2]

This is also a story about the Pacific salmon fisheries, but it is not a tale of environmental decline. In Southeast Alaska* there is still an ecologically healthy—if not economically sound—salmon fishery. No variety of wild Alaska salmon is considered officially "endangered" by the Environmental Protection Agency. In the 1990s, while salmon fisheries on the Columbia River and throughout the Puget Sound dwindled to all-time lows, commercial harvests in Alaska reached all-time highs. The year 1995 saw the largest recorded salmon catch in Alaska's history; ten years later, in 2005, the commercial harvest was the third biggest on record.[3] In other words this book is not a postmortem. The salmon fishery in Alaska is still alive, entangling salmon, fishermen, industrialists, scientists, and consumers in a living web of biological and human activity that has continued for thousands of years.

While this study is not a jeremiad on the fate of salmon in Alaska, neither is it an uncritical celebration of the progress of an industry under scientific resource management, for the story of salmon fishing in southeastern Alaska has its share of winners and losers. Animals, humans, and the inanimate natural world alike have all shared roles as heroes and villains in a drama that has seen the fortunes of fish and fishermen rise and fall. As in the declining fisheries further south, southeastern Alaska has seen the impact of colonization, capitalism, industrialization, scientific management, and globalization. Unlike those southern fisheries, however, the salmon fishery in southeastern Alaska is not *currently* in a state of ecological crisis. The fishery—although its stability is threatened by many factors, including long-term climate shifts and the rise of global salmon farming—is still *alive*. Salmon fishermen, although their livelihoods are seriously imperiled by market forces, can still scrape a living from the sea.

My objective with this book was to write a history of a living salmon fishery—and salmon fishermen—from precontact to the present. For landlubbers unfamiliar with the term "fishery," it refers simply to the act of catching and processing fish. A fishery, however, is also composed of laws, economic and social relationships, cultural attitudes, and even religious systems. I use the term to refer to a wide-ranging set of social and environmental relationships among the environment, humans, and fish that emerged in Alaska when humans began to catch salmon and use it for their

*Native Alaskans use "Southeast Alaska" whereas writers and scholars from outside the state tend to use "southeastern Alaska." I use the terms interchangeably throughout the book.

own purposes. In this book the environment is Southeast Alaska—a long, narrow strip of coastal range and archipelago that extends northward along the Northwest Coast from Dixon Entrance to Yakutat Bay, otherwise known as the Alaskan Panhandle. The human players are primarily Native American and Euro-American fishers but also industrialists, scientists, salmon managers, politicians, and bureaucrats. The fish are the five species of Pacific salmon: the red or sockeye, the king or chinook, the silver or coho, the chum or dog, and the pink or humpy.

As the northernmost reach of the Northwest Coast, Southeast Alaska has an environmental unity—characterized by dense rainforest, glaciers, and salmon-rich waterways—and a cultural unity, embodied by its aboriginal inhabitants, the Tlingit and Haida Indians, who shared a dependence on the five species of Pacific salmon. In the late eighteenth and early nineteenth centuries Southeast Alaska became the capital of Russian America as well as an important destination for maritime fur traders, spawning the first extensive contacts between European and Native peoples in the region. Later it was Southeast Alaska—rather than the more remote northern and western parts of the territory—where Americans first settled, where they located their center of government and industry, and where they built their first salmon cannery in 1878, an enterprise that became the economic engine of the territory and made Alaska the world's leading salmon producer by the turn of the twentieth century.

It was also in the more heavily settled Alaskan panhandle where salmon canners came to rely on industrial fish traps—touching off a longstanding feud between resident small-boat fishermen and canning corporations—and where the greatest conflicts occurred between local fishers and conservation officials over who controlled the so-called commons. Southeast Alaska, with its large resident fishing communities, played a central role in the push for local control over the salmon fisheries, which was finally achieved in 1960, one year after statehood. In the mid-twentieth century the region was also home to a vibrant maritime union movement and a Native rights movement that sought to protect the aboriginal fishing rights of Tlingit and Haida peoples. In the contemporary period Southeast Alaska is at the center of the struggle over the future of the wild salmon fisheries, as local fishing communities try to survive amid an economic landscape that has been redefined by the rise of farm-raised salmon. These conflicts and controversies constitute the core of this work.

This book has five thematic chapters. The first examines aboriginal salmon management through the lens of "conservation." Were Native fishermen "ecological" Indians? How did they manage their fisheries? The second chapter chronicles the impact of the fur trade, Russian settlement, and American industrialization on the Indian salmon fisheries. While laissez-faire capitalism transformed the fishery, Native fishers selectively adapted to the commercial economy while preserving their subsistence fishing economy. Chapter 3 discusses federal management of the Alaskan salmon fisheries, showing how conservation became a social struggle that pitted local fishermen against federal salmon managers. It also focuses on the rise of fish traps—industrial fish-catching devices used by large canneries—which became emblematic, from the perspective of local fishers, of "outside" control, ruthless efficiency, greedy corporate colonialism, and federal indifference. Chapter 4 places salmon fishing within the context of work and nature, revealing how Native American and Euro-American fishers viewed nature differently, built unique work cultures, and socially constructed the fishery by creating fishermen's unions and intertribal associations. Chapter 5 highlights three contemporary topics—limited-entry policy, Native subsistence fishing, and global salmon farming—all of which suggest the extent to which fishing cultures in Southeast Alaska are today threatened by forces beyond their control.

It should be clear by now that this book is more about humans than salmon. This is not to slight the importance of the fish—without them entire cultures and economies would not exist. The existence of Pacific salmon gives life to fishermen and fishing communities and of course to this book. Fish inhabit a world that is shaped by many factors, such as fluctuating ocean temperatures, which are not controlled by human manipulations. Nature, as environmental historians insist, has its own agency. It makes its own history. However, nature is also undeniably shaped by human actions and culture. It is not hard to see how human actions shape salmon. By damming rivers, logging forests, making cities, and catching salmon, humans have directly affected the life cycle of salmon stocks. Human cultures also shape salmon by constructing identities, occupations, recreations, religions, rituals, mythologies, social hierarchies, and systems of reciprocity and exchange that are fundamentally derived from the act of catching a salmon.

This human story of social construction, whereby the act of fishing itself is woven into webs of cultural meaning and social significance, is central to the book. The role of nature—salmon, waterways, tides, forests, and animals—will not be overlooked. The sea needs to be studied as nature, wildlife, and biology, but as the chapter-opening epigraph from Derek Walcott's poem suggests, the sea also needs to be recognized as a terrain of *social* interaction—a place of work, labor, commerce, class, race, gender, and conflict. The primary focus of this book is to examine the economic, social, cultural, and political context in which salmon have been harvested. As the title conveys, this work is a social history before it is an environmental history, although I contend that in a salmon fishery, and indeed in any economy, the two cannot be separated.

The complicated history of a simple salmon-catching device, the fish trap, serves to illustrate how the salmon fishery—in one sense a "natural" phenomenon—is also profoundly the product of human culture. In all its forms—aboriginal or industrial, floating or fixed, in rivers or in bays, made of log pilings or cedar sticks—the fish trap (which is described more fully and also pictured later in the book) has always performed the same basic task: entrapping migrating salmon as they made their way to their spawning grounds. There is a fundamental continuity between aboriginal and industrial varieties. Both successfully harnessed natural forces—tidal swings and fish migration patterns. Yet although the essential function and form of fish traps has changed very little over time, human communities imbued the devices with dramatically different meanings. To Northwest Coast Natives, for example, fish traps were the most efficient means of capturing enough calories to support village populations throughout the year. The traps also provided a surplus that could be used in both trade and ritualized giveaways. Fish traps, for Native societies, supported the accumulation of collective and individual wealth within a social economy. To later industrialists, fish traps were the most effective method of catching millions of salmon for a global market. Industrial traps transformed common property into individual wealth within a market economy; they also transferred the labor of fishing from small-boat fishermen to cannery employees. To federal conservation managers, fish traps exemplified rationality: they were not only the most efficient way of catching salmon, but, because they were "fixed" in one place, they were also the most easily regulated type of fishing gear.

To naturalists, fish traps epitomized industrial waste and laissez-faire exploitation of the natural world. To small-boat commercial fishermen, both Indian and white, fish traps were like William Blake's "dark satanic mills," despised industrial contraptions intended to reduce them to wage slavery. To Alaska residents generally, and proponents of state sovereignty in particular, fish traps represented corporate colonialism and other nefarious forms of outside control—a view that many Alaskans still hold. To some contemporary economists and innovative modern fishermen, fish traps (which were made illegal after Alaskan statehood) are now seen as a possible solution to the economic decline of the wild salmon fisheries and a means of competing with global fish farming. Salmon still return to the rivers and streams of southeastern Alaska, as they have for thousands of years, but the simple act of catching a salmon with a stationary trap is not so simple when human culture is added to the story.

This book takes its cue from historian Lance Van Sittert's recent call for scholars to "get their feet wet" as well as from the pioneering work of environmental historians Arthur McEvoy and Joseph E. Taylor III, whose studies of West Coast fisheries have moved Pacific history well beyond the shore.[4] In my own venture offshore, however, I am more like those historians who in Taylor's words "are more interested in the next landfall than the intervening sea," since this book focuses primarily on humans and only secondarily on fish and oceans.[5] In that sense I am influenced by recent histories, such as historian Richard White's *Organic Machine*, that bring race, class, and labor—*humans*—into the purview of environmental history.[6] White has suggested that "we cannot understand human history without natural history and we cannot understand natural history without human history." The relationship between humans and nature, he argues, is expressed primarily through "energy and work." He acknowledges that "human work and the work of nature" are different, but "it is our work that ultimately links us, for better or worse, to nature."[7]

It is certainly no great revelation to suggest that humans have historically come to know nature through their labors. Yet environmental history and labor history tend to remain separated from each other, largely because of their competing sympathies. Labor history is sympathetic to workers, whose lives became dominated and controlled by industrialization. Its perspective has been humanistic. Environmental history is sympathetic to the vulnerable landscapes that have similarly been abused and exploited by industrialization. Its perspective has been "eco-centric." In labor histories loggers and fishermen command our empathy and respect. In many environmental histories, however, loggers and fishermen are the enemy—the storm troopers of ecological devastation. This separation suggests the sympathies of authors with differing agendas, but it does not adequately reveal the deep interconnections that exist in reality between humans and the natural world, an intimacy that is fostered largely through work.

Preservationists have no desire to romanticize the ecological intimacy that springs from environmentally destructive labors. Environmentalists, in White's words, "call for human connections with nature while disparaging all those who claim to have known and appreciated nature through work and labor."[8] Workers—especially those who labor in close proximity to nature—also bear some responsibility for this false separation, as they have disparaged "tree huggers" and viewed efforts toward responsible environmental stewardship as threats to their livelihoods. Politicians have furthered this divide by falsely stressing the zero-sum relationship between jobs and the environment: more of one means less of the other. The work of fishing—an occupation whose practitioners come to know nature deeply through their labors, but which has also been transformed by industrialization, technology, and government regulation—offers a window into these interwoven relationships among humans, nature, and labor.

This is a book about Native and Euro-American fishers, local fishing communities, and the way that various groups—fishermen, industrialists, resource managers—have shaped the salmon fishery, arranging it to conform to understandable patterns of social organization and endowing it with cultural meaning. I have tried to resist both romanticizing and demonizing. I do not romanticize Native peoples when I explain how they created sustainable fishing economies in the precontact period, adapted to market economies in the late nineteenth and early twentieth centuries, or struggle to maintain their rights to subsistence fishing today. I do not demonize them when I suggest that they have now become invested in logging enterprises that are destroying salmon habitat. I do not romanticize Euro-American fishermen when I depict them as countercultural refugees escaping mass industrial society. I do not demonize them when I describe them as agents of laissez-faire capitalism, partly responsible for the commodification of nature and the decline of salmon runs.

If I have done any romanticizing, it is simply by asking if there is anything intrinsically valuable in the continued existence of local, small-boat fishing cultures. It is a persistent tension to balance the romantic with the realistic, myth with history, and tradition with change. To suggest that modern societies will have lost something if the small-boat fisheries and local fishing communities go extinct is simply a statement of fact. But what will they have lost? And will those losses be greater than new opportunities that will inevitably arise? These are questions that cannot be answered objectively, but they are important questions for consideration, especially because they challenge us to struggle with our own biases concerning the value of "local communities," "honest work," "nature," "subsistence living," "progress," "modernization," and "globalization."

Balancing myth and history is a cottage industry for historians of the American West. By evoking the "frontier" in the title of this book, I have taken the small risk of alienating those academics who believe the so-called "F" word should be relegated to the dustbin of history. To many, the word invokes an antiquated and uncritical narrative of American westward expansion that romanticizes the conquest and exploitation of both Native Americans and the natural world. The so-called New Western history has, since the late 1970s, debunked the frontier mythology of earlier historians, most notably that of Frederick Jackson Turner.[9] If Turner's West was a place of democracy, freedom, and social mobility, it is now seen to share with the East a complex past that included class struggle, racial oppression, and gender subordination. If Turner's American West was a sparsely populated frontier of self-reliant rugged individualists, it is now depicted—quite correctly—as having been largely urban and mostly dependent on large corporations and big government. Corporate investment and federal subsidies—in the service of industrial capitalism—were the primary agents of western "progress" (and the New Western historians would not likely call it progress, since it came at a great cost to Native peoples and the environment).

Opportunity, equality, independence, individualism, self-reliance—those vaunted characteristics of the frontier—were really part of a nationalist self-delusion, still perpetuated today in places like Alaska, the self-proclaimed "last frontier," where 70 percent of the population lives in cities rather than rural communities, where everyone receives a "dividend" check from corporate oil revenues, and where 60 percent of the land is still owned by the federal government. "The people [in Alaska] work for wages and salaries," historian Stephen Haycox has written, "like nearly everyone else in America they are dependent for their economic livelihood on decisions made by corporate managers and banking officers in places far from their homes and by people over whom they have little influence. Yet like many people across America they tend either not to know or to ignore these facts. They are more likely to be convinced that they are independent and self-reliant, adopting easily the mythology of the frontier West that is held so tenaciously by residents of the region from Omaha to Redding."[10]

I agree with Haycox: frontier "mythology" was, and still is, often more a social construction than an objective reality. As a student myself of the New Western history, I also take to heart historian Patricia Nelson Limerick's many critiques of Turner's "frontier thesis," including the essential fact that the notion of a frontier simply does not apply to Native Americans, who never inhabited the "frontier" but rather lived at the center of their own worlds. But no idea is as evocative or descriptive of the American West, and particularly Alaska, as the "frontier." In this book the concept of frontier works on a number of different levels. First, for nineteenth-century Americans the existence of a frontier implied abundant raw materials ready for unrestricted human exploitation. Indeed, when natural resources became overexploited in one area, the frontier always promised another horizon of opportunity. Salmon industrialists held this philosophy in the late nineteenth century. After exhausting the Sacramento and Columbia rivers, they moved northward to Alaska, believing, once again, that infinite natural wealth awaited them. Their belief in "the frontier" as a place of natural abundance drove the rapid and unregulated exploitation of Alaska's salmon resources in the late nineteenth and early twentieth centuries.

Second, as Haycox suggests, the *idea* of the frontier as a place of independence and freedom compelled emigrants to the Far West, shaped their self-identities, and colored their relationships with Native peoples and the natural world. This was certainly the case with non-Indian fishermen, many of whom sought to escape the confines of modern society and carve out for themselves a sphere of autonomy and self-sufficiency well into the twentieth century. Many of these people were successful in relative terms even if they found themselves ultimately dependent on new forces over which they had little control—fluctuating salmon runs, federal and state fisheries managers, and the vicissitudes of the world market for salmon. Whether fishermen were *really* independent and free is less important than understanding that their identities and lifestyles reflected their determination to obtain independence, freedom, and self-sufficiency. Alaska pioneers may have sometimes deluded themselves, but their delusions are an important part of the story.

Third, in the case of Alaska—the self-proclaimed "last frontier"—frontier ideologies have not disappeared, and they are continually reinforced by the state's bold landscape. The so-called last frontier state was recently described in the *New York Times* by journalist Timothy Egan as "flamboyant . . . in the scale of its scenic extremes, in the pure size and wonder of its fish and wildlife." Alaska, notes Egan, "is, after all, more than two times the size of Texas, with a shoreline, more than 33,000 miles, that exceeds that of all other states combined."[11] Such expanses still tempt Alaskans—fishermen included—into believing they inhabit the final American frontier. And who can argue with them?

Fourth, frontiers are not just imaginary places or edges of known territory; they are also meeting grounds for peoples and cultures. For Tlingit and Haida peoples southeastern Alaska has never been a remote frontier. But even for Indian peoples the region has always been a place of fluid cultural interaction, as indigenous peoples encountered other villages, other tribes, other cultures, other economies, which in turn reshaped their own lives. In this sense southeastern Alaska has been a kind of frontier for Native peoples as well, where they have continually built "new worlds" for themselves.[12]

Finally, a frontier in its purest sense conjures up new horizons where humans have not explored. In the twenty-first century what remains is the sea. This is a history that connects land and sea by looking at the cultures and economies that have sprung up around a fish—salmon—whose life cycle itself connects land and sea. It is a history that looks to the margins of American life—the waters of Alaska—and asks fundamental questions about social and environmental relationships.

1 First Fishermen

THE ABORIGINAL SALMON FISHERY

Aboriginal people lived with the fish for centuries, respectfully catching what they needed and taking care of the streams that produced a harvest essential to their way of life. —EDWARD C. WOLF AND SETH ZUCKERMAN, *Salmon Nation: People, Fish, and Our Common Home*

Our culture teaches us to take what you need, and never to waste. —HORACE MARKS, Tlingit fisherman

[Tlingits] inhabit the country only to extirpate everything that lives and moves upon it. At war with every animal, they . . . are precisely on the earth what the vulture is in the air, or the wolf and tiger in the forest. —JEAN FRANÇOIS COMTE DE LA PÉROUSE, *A Voyage round the World*

In pleading with industrialists to conserve the dwindling stocks of Alaska salmon, Charles D. Garfield, a member of Alaska's Territorial Fish Commission, described Native Americans wantonly slaughtering spawning salmon with little concern for the future. In his visit to the Chilkat and Chilkoot rivers during the summer of 1919, Garfield apparently witnessed Indian fishermen "dragging every salmon they could possibly get out of the lake and stream." The Indians he spoke with did not seem the least bit concerned that by "going up into the spawning streams and taking those fish out," they were "preventing the spawning for the reproduction of the species." He asked one Chilkat Tlingit fisherman, "What do you suppose is going to become of your birthright, your heritage?" The Indian replied: "Maybe I dead then when they all gone." Garfield lamented that he found

Native fishers throughout the region that told him "practically the same thing": "They didn't care anything about their children, they didn't care anything about the future of the industry, all they cared was about themselves."[1]

In stereotyping Indian fishermen as wasteful, opportunistic, and myopic, Garfield was engaging in a long-standing Euro-American tradition of depicting Native Americans in self-serving ways. Since the time of European contact, Native American history and identity have been bound up with caricatures—the "idle savage," the "barbarian savage," the "noble savage." Each stereotype expressed more about Euro-Americans than it did about Native Americans. The "idle savage" portrayed Indian peoples as lazy and undeserving of the vast "wild" territories that surrounded their villages. To a people like the English, who believed that land ownership carried with it the legal and moral responsibility of "improvement" (indeed, God had admonished humankind to "subdue" the earth), "idle" Indians therefore had no legitimate claim to the land. The ruthless and heathen character of the "barbarian savage" justified the military dispossession of his lands. Even the more romantic notion of the "noble savage," which associated primitiveness with virtue, was used by Euro-Americans for their own purposes to critique modern society and, in the twentieth century, to promote conservation and environmental concerns.[2]

Garfield drew on a variant of the "idle savage" stereotype—that of the Indian as lazy, improvident, childlike, and helpless without the guiding hand of civilized whites. His use of Indians to convey the *opposite* of conservation is ironic, given that Indians were already being used as emblems of an emerging conservation ethic. By the turn of the twentieth century, a generation of Boy Scouts was learning to live like the "ideal Indian," who "condemned accumulation, waste, wanton slaughter" and "held land, animals, and all property in common."[3] The icon of the "ecological Indian," as historian Shepard Krech III has labeled this stereotype, gained ground in the post–World War II period as the environmental movement used images of nature-loving Native Americans to critique the greedy, materialistic, and wasteful character of modern American life. Increasingly, popular culture conveyed "the Indian in nature who understands the systemic consequences of his actions, feels deep sympathy with all living forms, and takes steps to conserve so that earth's harmonies are never imbalanced and resources never in doubt."[4]

The nature of Indian ecology became a lively academic debate after the 1967 publication of anthropologist Paul Martin's "overkill hypothesis." Martin argued that Paleo-Indians "exterminated far more large animals than has modern man with modern weapons and advanced technology," causing the Pleistocene extinctions of numerous "megafauna."[5] The questions that form the heart of this ongoing discussion cut to the very essence of Native American cultures: Were they careful stewards of their natural resources? Were their societies sophisticated enough to overexploit their resources? Did they engage in wasteful and wanton destruction of the natural world? Were they "rational" economic actors who maximized productivity and material gain? Did their religions prevent them from destroying the natural world?

In his book *The Ecological Indian: Myth and History*, Krech contends that Native peoples could and sometimes did overexploit their environments; they did not always act in ecologically sound ways; and they had religious systems that posited an intimate relationship between humans and nature, but those beliefs did not always foster ecologically sound practices. If measured by modern definitions of "environmentalist," "ecologist," and "conservationist," indigenous peoples in North America, even in the period before European contact, Krech suggests, were not the nature-loving Indians of popular mythology. Indians are humans, endowed with the same myopic capacity to destroy the landscape as other populations. The ecological Indian stereotype, he contends, is "ultimately dehumanizing" to Native Americans because it denies "both variation within human groups and commonalities between them."[6]

This chapter examines the question of Native American resource conservation with regard to the salmon fisheries. The intention is not simply to use the ecological Indian stereotype as a straw man, but to use the concept as an invitation to ask serious questions about the nature of Indian environmental stewardship on the Northwest Coast. Did Native salmon fishermen have the technological capacity or the cultural inclination to overexploit salmon populations? Did they manage their fisheries with an eye toward the sustainability of the resource? Did they ever waste or overexploit salmon populations? What was the source of aboriginal salmon management—was it driven primarily by spiritual or ecological knowledge, or other factors?[7]

The Native peoples of Southeast Alaska—the Tlingit and Haida—believe that their ancestors were conservationists and ecologists. Indian fishers, in their view, did not waste salmon, as whites did when they arrived. Native fishers had an intimate relationship with salmon, in both the modern sense of ecological knowledge and the traditional sense of spiritual affinity, which has continued to the present. Sam G. Davis, a Haida Indian who was born in 1865 and had witnessed "traditional" salmon fishing as a child, testified that his ancestors "didn't try to clean those creeks out . . . the same as they do today." He continued: "They simply dried [salmon] until they thought that they had enough, and then they just opened it . . . so that the fish could go on their way up to the lakes."[8]

In 1944 proceedings on whether to establish reservations that would protect traditional Indian fishing sites in southeastern Alaska from further commercial intrusion, Davis and other Indian witnesses painted a picture of Native salmon fishers who understood the biological necessity of allowing a certain amount of fish to ascend to the spawning grounds. Like Krech's ecological Indians, Natives "used [salmon] as it came, as nature brought it to us," and refused to "hoard," "grab," or "pile up the fish, the same as they do in America."[9] Sha-Ta, a Tlingit fisherman who likewise witnessed the preindustrial aboriginal fishery and the twentieth-century commercial one, explained that Natives "never made a practice of taking all the fish, or whatever it was from a certain area, because it was the custom always to leave some behind for seeding."[10] Tlingit elder George Dalton, interviewed in 1979 as part of a U.S. Forest Service study to record the "subsistence lifeways" of Indian peoples in Southeast Alaska, claimed that Indian fishermen only caught what each family required. "They were conservationists," he recalled, "that's why there were so many fish in those days."[11]

Another Tlingit elder, Nelson Frank of Sitka, was interviewed by former Canadian Supreme Court Justice Thomas Berger in the early 1980s to document the importance of legally protecting Alaska Native subsistence rights in the wake of the Alaska Native Claims Settlement Act of 1971, which had extinguished the aboriginal rights of Native peoples throughout the state. Frank described to Berger how "the relationship between the Native population and the resources of the land and the sea is so close that an entire culture is reflected." He continued: "The Traditional law . . . was passed from generation to generation, intact, through the repetition of legends and observance of ceremonials which were largely concerned with the use of land, water, and the resources contained therein. Subsistence living was not only a way of life, but also a life-enriching process. Conservation and perpetuation of subsistence resources was a part of that way of life, and was mandated by traditional law and custom."[12]

Certainly these Native voices convey the unmistakable message of conservation and deliberate resource management. However, oral testimonies, like all primary historical sources, need to be placed within their proper context. Many of them are drawn from twentieth-century land and fishing rights hearings meant to legitimate aboriginal land claims, or from interviews intended to highlight the distinctive relationship between Native peoples and their lands. The land claims hearings are especially problematic, as non-Native judges were in the business of defining what constituted "authentic" Native American land use. The moral legitimacy of these claims often rested on Indian people's ability to highlight "traditional" relationships with the natural world, which in the twentieth century came to mean—quite unfairly—that Native Americans were only authentic when they acted as so-called ecological Indians. For Native peoples, appropriating the image of the ecological Indian could yield tangible results. This does not mean that their oral testimonies do not convey essential truths about Native American relationships to nature. But it does make uncritical acceptance of such sources problematic.

Is it true, as Native writer Nora Marks Dauenhauer has claimed of her ancestors, that "Tlingit people historically practiced subsistence hunting, fishing, and logging without dominating or destroying the natural resource"?[13] Or did salmon peoples in Alaska have the technological capacity and cultural inclination to sometimes overtax their resources? Did they ever waste salmon? Did aboriginal salmon fishers practice a conservation ethic? Before addressing the question of Native resource management, however, we must first examine the nature of salmon populations and then the characteristics of the human populations that exploited them. Then we will find out if Native peoples in southeastern Alaska had the population density, technology, and motivation—in other words the *potential*—to overexploit their supply of salmon.

THE NATURE OF SALMON

How large were salmon populations on the Northwest Coast before the arrival of Europeans—or even before the arrival of humans altogether? One answer is certain: however large, salmon runs in the North Pacific fluctuated dramatically as they adapted to a multitude of geologic and climatic transformations. A quick history of the development of the Pacific salmon species is a case study in natural flux, and an admonition to anyone who would think of nature unaltered by humans as stable and balanced.

It is not known when the earliest ancestors of the salmon branched off from the larger family of ray-finned fishes, but the earliest salmonidae fossil found on the Northwest Coast dates back to around forty million years ago.[14] Between forty and twenty million years ago ancestral salmon, who most likely lived their entire lives in freshwater systems, experienced a global warming trend that saw their food supplies decrease in terrestrial water bodies—streams, rivers, and lakes—while productivity increased in the cooler Pacific ocean. Unable to survive and prosper solely in their freshwater environment, early salmon responded by developing their distinctive anadromous life cycle: birth and early development in freshwater, migration to more fertile oceanic feeding grounds (where they gain more than 90 percent of their body mass), and return to their natal streams to spawn and die.[15]

Between twenty and six million years ago Pacific salmon adapted to the dramatic reformulation of the western American landscape, as geologic cataclysms created the coastal mountains that run from northern California to Alaska. These upheavals created a new waterscape of rivers, streams, and lakes, inducing the Pacific salmon to branch into five distinctive species, each equipped to take advantage of a unique ecological niche. Pink salmon (*Oncorhynchus gorbuscha*), the most abundant species in southeastern Alaska, spawned in the lower reaches of short coastal streams; silver salmon, or coho (*O. kisutch*), preferred shallow tributaries or narrow side channels; red salmon, or sockeye (*O. nerka*), returned to the gravel shoals of lakes; king salmon, or chinook (*O. tshawytscha*), spawned in the main channels of large streams and mainland rivers; and the spawning habitat of chum salmon (*O. keta*), the second most abundant species in the region, ranged from the tidal flats of short coastal streams to springs in headwaters of large river systems.[16] As geologist David R. Montgomery has explained, "The salmon and the topography of western North America appear to have evolved together in response to tectonic forces that drove mountain building along the West Coast."[17] If the emergence of mountain ranges was not enough, Pacific salmon also weathered at least ten glacial advances in the period between two million and ten thousand years ago, before experiencing another five thousand years of instability, as sea levels rose and coastal areas flooded in the wake of the last ice age.

Not all species of Pacific salmon made it through these cataclysms. At least one became extinct: the gigantic "sabertooth salmon," for example, which grew up to ten feet long and 350 pounds, did not survive the ice.[18]

The five species that persevered had to deal with still further hardships: volcanic eruptions that smothered salmon habitats; earthquakes that collapsed entire mountainsides into streams and rivers, causing obstructions as great as modern dams; forest fires that decimated vegetation alongside stream beds, leading to warmer water temperatures and triggering erosion that dramatically altered spawning grounds; droughts that diminished water flows and stranded young salmon in isolated pools. If salmon made it through such biblical-scale disasters, they still had to deal with more quotidian dangers, like natural predation from eagles, bears, and marine mammals, and cyclical swings in ocean temperatures, which altered feeding areas and introduced warm water competitors into northern waters. For salmon the "stabilization" of the North Pacific coastline around five thousand years ago did not mean "stability." There never was a golden age of ecological "climax," where salmon populations maintained a state of balance and abundance. The numbers of salmon rose and fell. They faced temporary extinctions due to catastrophe in certain streams, only to recolonize those streams when conditions improved. A dynamic nature ensured the variability of salmon populations.

Since Pacific salmon, in the words of biologist Jim Lichatowich, "had to survive millions of years of cataclysmic habitat disruption," they developed amazing survival mechanisms that allowed them to adapt to such adversity.[19] First, their breeding patterns are profligate. Spawning salmon produce thousands of eggs. Even though most of them never make it out of the spawning grounds to begin their journey to the ocean, and very few of them make it through their entire life cycle and return to their birth streams, salmon still produce enough offspring to ensure that salmon populations will grow until they push up against the limitations of their environment. Second, the anadromous habits of salmon ensured that even when terrestrial ecosystems failed due to natural disaster, salmon populations at sea were saved from catastrophe. Finally, the small percentage of salmon who "strayed" from their birth streams served as pioneers in the colonization or recolonization of new waterways.[20] Salmon were "pioneers" or "ecological imperialists" (depending on one's perspective) long before humans arrived on the scene.

So what does this "prehistory" of Pacific salmon tell us about the size of salmon populations before human occupation of the far Northwest Coast? One conclusion is that prehistoric salmon runs were so variable that they are impossible to predict. Another interpretation might be that the salmon's extreme adaptability, resilience, and fecundity ensured that, even though erratic, prehistoric salmon stocks must have been great indeed, perhaps exceeding the greatest recorded runs of the late nineteenth century, when observers spoke of waters "boiling" and "black" with fish. Such a view of pristine abundance needs to be tempered with the knowledge that salmon, without a certain amount of predation to thin the runs, will destroy their own spawning beds. But given that coastal bears (who derive the majority of their biomass from marine nutrients, primarily salmon) and other predators (such as eagles, seals, otters, walrus, and whales) also helped to limit the size of salmon populations before the arrival of humans, it would be fairly conservative to speculate that during "good" years, prehistoric salmon populations (after the stabilization of the coastline five thousand years ago) must have at least equaled, if not exceeded, the largest known historic salmon runs: as many as a hundred million salmon, composed of all five species, might return to southeastern Alaska on the largest years, and as few as five million on the smallest years.[21]

Another far less speculative conclusion we can draw from the prehistory of salmon is that humans, when they finally colonized the Northwest Coast, would not be the sole determining factor in the rise and fall of salmon populations. They simply added one more dynamic variable into an ecosystem that was already extremely volatile.[22]

FIRST PEOPLES

Scholars have long pondered when Northwest Coast peoples entered the region. They postulate that it must have been at the end of the Pleistocene, between fifteen thousand and ten thousand years ago, but at what point were coastlines habitable? And how did these peoples come to the Northwest Coast? Conventional theories have suggested that early peoples migrated across Beringia and southward through an interior "ice-free corridor" before populating the Northwest coastline from the south as glacial retreat permitted. Other scholars have proposed the possibility of early pioneers coming by sea.[23] Tlingit clan histories suggest migrations from the south but also include stories of westward migrations down river drainages as well as over glaciers. The Tlingit Kaaḵáakw clan recall their ancestors migrating down the Stikine River from the interior (passing under a retreating glacier) and then going northward along the coast to their current home in Basket Bay on the east side of Chatham Strait. The Teqwedi clan also describe their forebears as moving from south to north along a coastal route, from near present-day Ketchikan to Sitka, and then to their present village at Yakutat. Other Yakutat clans, however, claim to have moved southeastward from the Copper River, and still others westward from the interior. The Kwackquan clan apparently walked over receding glaciers into Yakutat.[24]

Who were these early peoples? Were they big-game hunters, who participated in the Pleistocene extermination of nearly 75 percent of North America's megafauna before turning their attention to coastal resources? Were they maritime peoples, already equipped with boats, hooks, and nets, ready to exploit the abundant coastal ecosystems? Or were they a hybrid of northern fishers and southern hunters? Much of the debate, as is the case with nearly all prehistorical speculations, revolves around the midden heap, which, depending on the midden heap you happen to dig up, might point to any of the above possibilities.[25] What is clear, however, is that salmon did not begin to play a primary role in the diets of these settlers until sometime between four thousand and six thousand years ago. From that point on, marine-rich middens suggest that Northwest Coast peoples began to build their societies around the availability of salmon, which comprise more than 80 percent of the animal remains at certain archeological sites in British Columbia.[26] As early as three thousand years ago, Native peoples were already building highly efficient wooden salmon weirs throughout southeastern Alaska.[27]

The stabilization of coastal ecosystems thus coincided with the rise of salmon cultures. Early settlements emerged where salmon were most easily exploited. Anthropologist Steve Langdon's study of prehistorical migrations on Prince of Wales Island shows that the availability of sockeye salmon was the primary factor in determining the location of early villages, which emerged first in upriver locations where shallow streams made salmon most accessible to humans. Settlement was also influenced by the specific ecological characteristics of the different species of Pacific salmon. On Prince of Wales Island pink and chum salmon were far more abundant and therefore more accessible. But sockeye runs were longer and more predictable, and their flesh had greater oil content than either chums or pinks.[28] Villages clustered first around sockeye streams and then near river systems that contained the greatest variety of species and therefore the most stable and productive runs. As a tribal historian of Glacier Bay succinctly explained, "Salmon of all kinds ran there. That's why the people lived there; they made it a village."[29]

Their predictability and nutritional value made salmon the staple of

Northwest Coast peoples, but other food sources also played an important role in the Native diet. Indeed, the coastal environment was a breadbasket of rich food sources. Coastal peoples exploited the eulachon (or candlefish), which they rendered for oil, as well as herring, sturgeon, halibut, and such sea mammals as seals, otters, and sometimes whales. On land they hunted deer, mountain sheep and goats, bears, river otters, martens, minks, beavers, porcupines, muskrats, and raccoons. They also gathered shellfish as well as an incredible variety of wild and cultivated plants, roots, and berries, including kelp, eel grass, yarrow, fiddlehead ferns, wild peas, nettles, dandelions, black laver, beach asparagus, sea ribbon, currants, wild rhubarb, crab apples, licorice fern, salmonberries, strawberries, gooseberries, huckleberries, thimbleberries, raspberries, blueberries, cranberries, cloudberries, wild sweet potatoes, and wild rice.[30]

Such an amazing grocery list conveys the profound natural abundance found on the Northwest Coast, but it is misleading and helps to foster the mythology of "idle savages" living in an Edenic landscape of plenty. Nothing could be further from the truth. The North Pacific Coast offered a plenitude of resources for human exploitation, but as anthropologist Wayne Suttles has noted, "abundance there consisted only of certain things at certain places at certain times and always with some possibility of failure."[31] The coastal environment was patchy. Salmon were plentiful, but streams were miles apart and runs were inconsistent and always subject to natural catastrophe. Foods had to be exploited at particular seasons and often for concentrated periods of time, especially on the far northern coast, where growing seasons and salmon runs were compressed into a few short months. Nature provided but on its own terms.

Because foods were not "simply there for the taking," Native peoples developed efficient systems for capturing nature's bounty.[32] This was especially true of salmon runs, which provided a lucrative treasure of calories, but one that could disappear upriver before fishers could catch them. Pink salmon, the most abundant species in southeastern Alaska, have migration patterns that can be alarmingly condensed. A ten-year record of pink salmon runs in Sashin Creek during the twentieth century shows that 80 percent of the fish passed upstream in fourteen to twenty-six days, while in two specific years 40 percent of the entire run migrated in fewer than three days.[33] With opportunities for harvest limited, Northwest Coast peoples developed intensive and efficient methods for catching and storing salmon. Especially for northern peoples, like the Tlingit and the Haida, who experienced the most concentrated runs, this entailed mobilizing labor on a scale that demanded a tremendous amount of leadership, social organization, and technical proficiency. Anthropologist Randall Schalk believes that short salmon runs spurred the development of highly efficient and specialized productive units, centralized authority, and greater social stratification among northern salmon peoples.[34]

Most scholars, in fact, directly attribute the rise of "complex hunter-gatherer" societies on the Northwest Coast to the ability of coastal peoples to efficiently exploit their natural resources, especially salmon, whose surpluses could be stored to sustain populations throughout the year. Storing salmon allowed Northwest Coast Indians to defy conventional stereotypes of "hunter-gatherer" people, who are generally portrayed as small-scale, nomadic, egalitarian, with no surplus wealth, no concept of property, and no elaborate culture and art. Indian peoples in southeastern Alaska, and all along the northern coast, exhibited characteristics that anthropologists usually apply to sedentary agricultural populations: they produced surpluses that sustained large populations, allowing some to be liberated from productive work and "specialize" in other tasks, such as art, religion, or governing; they had social hierarchies, with permanent nobility and slaves; and they had an elaborate material culture, characterized by totem poles and cedar canoes that even today are emblematic of Northwest Coast cultures.[35] The creation of such complex, hierarchical, and populous societies on the Northwest Coast, it should be stressed, was not predetermined by the environment—not even by the existence of salmon. Rather, it was the product of both environment and culture. The stabilization of the coastal environment and the growth of salmon runs allowed human populations to thrive, but only as long as they were able to take advantage of nature's unpredictability.

THE NUMBERS GAME

As Northwest Coast cultures mastered the ability to store the salmon's energy, they were able to sustain larger populations, but just how large were Native populations? The answer is part of an ongoing scholarly debate over the size and sophistication of Indian societies and the subsequent impact of European disease. There are high counters and low counters, each arriving at their conclusions by using different historical methodology and relying on dramatically different assumptions about Native cultures and the impact of European colonization. A higher number suggests that Native peoples were technologically advanced enough to support large populations, while also dramatizing the epic scale of their subsequent losses. A lower number implies the opposite—that Indians were more primitive and that the population collapse initiated by European colonization was not as severe. The lower estimates moreover lend support to the belief that Indian peoples treaded only lightly on the land, which really might have been the "virgin wilderness" that early European explorers described.

The most reliable and well-documented estimates for the Northwest Coast come from anthropologist Robert Boyd, who strikes a middle ground between high and low counters. By utilizing historical epidemiology, ethnography, and Native oral histories to corroborate instances of epidemic disease, Boyd concludes that more than 180,000 Native peoples inhabited the entire Northwest Coast culture area at the time of intensive European contact in the late 1700s. For southeastern Alaska, in particular, Boyd projects a precontact population of approximately 12,000 Tlingits and Haidas, a number that was not exceeded by white settlement until the 1920s.[36] Boyd's numbers are as conservative as precontact population estimates come, but they still paint a picture of a region that had a population density greater than any other in North America inhabited solely by hunter-gatherers, and even greater than agricultural societies in the precontact American Southwest, Midwest, and Northeast.[37]

But were these dense populations large enough to overexploit their natural resources? Anthropologist Gordon Hewes estimated salmon consumption for the Tlingit at five hundred pounds per capita per year, based on indigenous food requirements and available resources. If his calculations are correct, Indians in southeastern Alaska would have consumed approximately six million pounds of salmon a year. Using a fairly conservative estimate of four pounds per fish (the most abundant species in southeastern Alaska, pinks, generally weigh less than four pounds, while sockeyes and chums average between four and six pounds), this means that Tlingits and Haidas would have consumed 1.5 million fish. When compared with historic salmon harvests in southeastern Alaska, which range between 1 million fish in the 1890s and over 100 million fish in the 1990s, it appears that the aboriginal fishery would have barely dented salmon populations (see figure 1.1).

Using these figures, one might conclude that conventional wisdom is correct: precontact harvests were moderated primarily by the small size of the Indian population and had little to do with aboriginal management.[38] If we

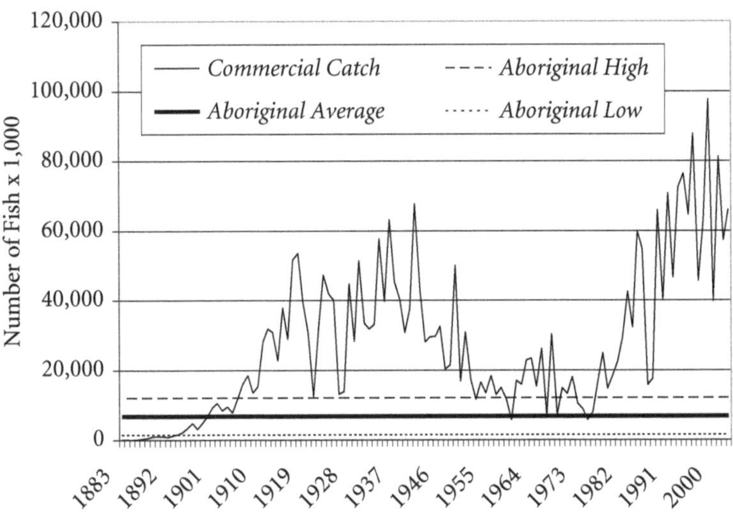

FIG. 1.1 *Estimated aboriginal harvest compared with commercial harvests, 1883–2003. The low estimate for aboriginal harvests, taken from Gordon Winant Hewes, shows that the precontact fishery was much smaller than the twentieth-century commercial fishery, while the high estimate suggests that Native fishers could harvest at levels approaching later commercial fishers.* SOURCES: *Hewes 1947: 223–24; Petroff 1884: 69–71; and Alaska Department of Fish and Game, "Historical Salmon Harvest and Value Charts, 1878–2003," Zephyr database.*

use the much larger consumption estimate of between three thousand and four thousand pounds of fresh fish per year per capita made by census agent Ivan Petroff in 1880, the picture looks much different, especially if we compare his estimates to the commercial salmon fishery in the nineteenth century (see figure 1.2).[39] It would be a dubious proposition to uncritically accept Petroff's figures for southeastern Alaska, but for the sake of debate Petroff's numbers place aboriginal consumption between thirty-six and forty-eight million pounds, or between nine and twelve million fish. If we use his high number, the aboriginal fishery still does not approach the largest catches of the twentieth century, but it exceeds even the largest commercial harvests in the nineteenth century and the smallest commercial catches for both centuries. If we accept the proposition known as "Liebig's law of the minimum"—that environmental carrying capacity is determined by years of shortage not of abundance—then clearly aboriginal catches of this magnitude might have

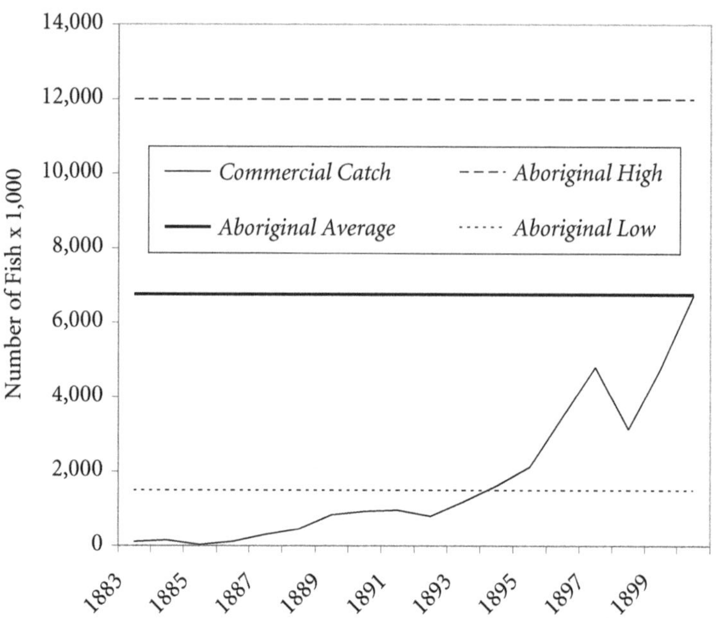

FIG. 1.2 *Estimated aboriginal harvest compared with late nineteenth-century commercial harvests, 1883–1900. Even the lowest estimates for precontact consumption exceeded the industrial fishery until 1894.* SOURCES: *Hewes 1947: 223–24; Petroff 1884: 69–71; and Alaska Department of Fish and Game, "Historical Salmon Harvest and Value Charts, 1878–2003," Zephyr database.*

overtaxed salmon runs during years of scarcity. Aboriginal salmon fishers in southeastern Alaska, it would appear, had the *potential* to put pressure on salmon resources.

However, calculating aboriginal fish consumption in a "scientific" manner using quantitative data is much like estimating precontact populations—it is an extremely uncertain venture with many variables. It is no surprise that, like debates over Native population levels, there are high counters and low counters. At best, these numbers provide food for thought. At worst, they are outright misleading. First, we should remember that Northwest Coast populations, like coastal resources, were patchy—fishers were concentrated around the most productive ecological zones and had nowhere near the reach of the historic or modern commercial fishery. Modern powerboats, for instance, exploit offshore fishing grounds, whereas Native fishers restricted themselves to nearshore waters. Numerous river systems that later became centers of commercial production, such as the Unuk, Stikine, and

Taku rivers, were not exploited effectively in their lower reaches by Native fishers during the precontact period.[40]

The expansiveness of the commercial salmon fishery contributed to harvest levels that certainly exceeded the precontact fishery, but that does not mean that Native peoples—even with a smaller overall harvest—did not overexploit the local salmon streams around which they settled. As mentioned earlier, generalized consumption and catch data do not speak to the natural fluctuations of salmon populations, which varied dramatically from year to year, from stream to stream. Proficient fishers might not have overtaxed resources in years of abundance, but what about years of scarcity? Finally, population levels and consumption figures provide insight into the *possibility* of overexploitation, but they cannot tell us if Native peoples ever caught more fish than they consumed or processed. During the height of the runs, did Native fishers ever harvest more salmon than they could use, much as early Plains hunters seem to have done with buffalo?[41] In short, neither population nor consumption levels matter if they cannot tell us if rotting salmon carcasses littered the banks of Northwest Coast fishing sites in late summer. Since they obviously cannot, we must rely on qualitative sources that provide insight into the fishing systems and social systems of southeastern Alaska. Did Tlingit and Haida fishers have the *technology* as well as the *motivation* to potentially overexploit salmon populations? Did they have the *potential* to damage salmon runs?

ABORIGINAL FISHING SYSTEMS

Tlingit and Haida fishing technologies in the precontact period ranged from simple spears with barbed points used in shallow upriver waters to trawl or "reef" nets made with cedar bark, wooden floats, and stone sinkers, which were fastened between two canoes and used in nearshore waters and estuaries.[42] In between those technological extremes, Indian fishers used every tool in their kit to harvest salmon: gaff hooks, toggle barbed harpoons, simple lines with hooks, spears with seal-bladder floats, wooden weirs, stone tidal traps, conical basket traps, and fence-work "box" traps.[43]

Each method reflected an adaptation to different ecosystems—shallow streams, larger rivers, intertidal zones, offshore waters—and to the habits of the various species of salmon at different junctures of their migratory cycles. Fence-work weirs and traps installed far upstream during the height of a particular run allowed Indian fishermen to easily harvest large volumes of salmon in shallow, slow-moving streams, where salmon were most accessible. Although their construction required a great deal of cooperative effort, their operation was fairly simplistic—salmon were diverted into wooden baskets, where they were netted, speared, and clubbed. When the run was at its height, Native fishers sometimes did not need the help of a trap to take large numbers of fish in the upriver shallows. As tribal elder Matilda Gamble recalled, "They used gaff hooks—a real long flexible pole and they made their own hooks. You could stand in the river and as the fish are going up or maybe coming down you could just gaff them and get 30–40 in about a half hour."[44]

As one moves downstream toward the open ocean, salmon became harder to catch, requiring the use of more complex devices like "tidal weirs," trawl nets, and sophisticated individualized methods.[45] For example, king salmon, which did not spawn in most southeastern Alaska creeks but did feed in nearshore waters, were caught either by trolling or with a combination of canoes, toggling spears, lines, and seal bladder buoys, as described by Klawock Tlingit Charles Webster Demmert, who remembered how Indian men would "spear them, with a line fastened to the spear and a little buoy, and as soon as they would spear them, the spear would get loose from the stick, and it goes out in the water, and they go out there with a canoe, and drag it in."[46]

A single king salmon taken in this way required far more effort than hundreds taken in upriver traps. The reward was that fish taken downriver and offshore, especially the king and sockeye salmon, were prized for their fat content and superior taste, while migrating salmon captured close to their spawning grounds had the least nutritional value. Pink and chum salmon were superior for drying and smoking, because their flesh carried less oil and dried without spoiling. Indians harvested large numbers of these fish in traps during late summer and early fall as they prepared their winter stores. Fishing technology therefore reflected the importance of timing and location—and the intimacy with which Native fishermen understood the seasonal migrations and characteristics of various species of fish. Leaving out the question of whether Indians fished with regard to the biological sustainability of salmon populations, it is clear that they exhibited what we might call an "ecological" understanding of the natural world.

Fishing gear varied throughout the Alexander Archipelago. Nets and gaff hooks, for instance, worked in the murky glacial waters of the mainland but not in the clear streams and rivers of the islands. Mainland Yakutat people apparently never trolled for king salmon with lines and hooks, instead catching them as they ascended the rivers to spawn, while Tlingit and Haida fishers on Prince of Wales Island trolled for kings in offshore and nearshore waters.[47] Stone traps—which were erected in tidal flats to trap fish at low tide as well as to prevent milling fish from migrating upriver (and thereby lengthen the harvesting season)—were used solely by coastal peoples and never by interior fishers. Fence-work weirs and traps, the most efficient and productive technology, seemed to have been widespread throughout southeastern Alaska.

Wooden weirs were the most efficient, productive, and potentially destructive of all Indian fishing technologies. Traps targeted salmon on the upper reaches of river systems near salmon spawning grounds, where fish were most vulnerable to overexploitation. In shallow waters streams could be completely blocked off and migrating salmon could be taken with the least amount of physical effort. French explorer Jean-François Galaup comte de la Pérouse witnessed such an operation among the Yakutat Tlingit in 1786: "The salmon, coming up the river, are stopped by the stakes: unable to leap over them, they turn back towards the sea; in the angles of the dike are placed very narrow wicker baskets, closed at one end, into which they enter, and being unable to turn in them, they are thus caught."[48]

According to anthropologist Frederica de Laguna, who described a large basket trap used among the Yakutat peoples, "one trapful was said to have been enough to supply all the people of a small village for the entire winter."[49] In 1899, Jefferson Moser, captain of the U.S. Fish Commission steamer the *Albatross*, heard the Indian owner of a fish trap at Klawock boasting that "not a fish could get up that stream; that he caught them all."[50] In 1902, Moser examined an Indian trap on the Chilkoot River that "looked as if few fish could pass without being trapped."[51] The capacity of such traps to potentially annihilate salmon runs is why historians have labeled the use of similar aboriginal methods further south as "frighteningly efficient," "as effective as modern methods," and "comparable to those of the pioneer industrial fishery."[52] La Pérouse concluded that traps allowed Indian peoples to "live in the summer in the greatest abundance, as they can catch more fish in an hour than is sufficient for their family." Nature's wealth, in his view, allowed Natives to "remain idle" for the rest of the day, "spending it in gaming," while they were "exposed to perish with hunger in the winter, when the chase cannot be very productive."[53]

Apparently La Pérouse did not witness Yakutat peoples curing fish for winter consumption, an integral component of the aboriginal fishery. Indeed, fishing technology was not the only factor in determining the effectiveness of the aboriginal salmon fishery. Equally important were salmon storage techniques and trading patterns that allowed Native peoples to extend salmon consumption throughout the entire year. Without the ability to preserve salmon, in fact, efficient fishing methods would not have been required. With effective storage techniques the only limits on salmon production were those imposed by the amount of household labor that could be mobilized, for surplus harvests could always be traded for luxury goods or used to enhance the status of clan leaders through ritualized giveaways. This is why storing salmon engaged entire households for periods of heightened intensity in late summer and early fall. Men provided the primary labor of fishing, but women, aided by household slaves, filleted and stripped the salmon while shamans and house leaders presided over the process of smoking and drying.

Processing salmon for winter consumption was perhaps the most critically important step in the entire fishing complex, for failure could lead to impoverishment or starvation. Henry Katasse, an elder Tlingit and "cultural specialist," explained that the "Tlingit had discovered generations ago that certain streams produce better salmon than others for drying purposes."[54] Chum salmon was the preferred drying fish, as it contained the least fat of the five species. Native fishers had to know the proper place and time for catching them to ensure successful preservation. According to Tlingit Ruby Jackson, "You never smoke and dry the first run in the rivers and creeks, it is better to wait until they have spawned. If salmon is smoked when it is oily, it turns rancid before winter and spring when it is needed."[55]

Dried salmon was fundamentally important for household use, but it was also important for the purposes of trade, redistribution, and ritual gift-giving. Because a dried fish became a source of "wealth"—not just subsistence—Native fishers had even more motivation to increase the intensity of their harvesting and storage tasks. Although salmon has often been discussed in the anthropological literature within the context of a subsistence economy, fishing on the Northwest Coast was about far more than living from hand to mouth. It was also about wealth, status, prestige, and reciprocity in a culture that valued accumulation and gift-giving as a form of leadership and social responsibility.

The social hierarchy of Tlingit and Haida societies revolved around the accumulation and the ritual redistribution of wealth, primarily through the potlatch ceremony. Potlatches were initiated for a number of reasons, including funerals, marriages, building lodges, and recognizing a new leader. They consisted of dancing, speech-making, theatrical performance, singing, and gift-giving. Although some scholars have viewed the potlatch as a kind of primitive welfare system, where wealthy chiefs provided for impoverished clan members, its primary function was to raise the prestige of the host through ritualized generosity—a core value of Tlingit and Haida leadership. Another function was to engender future reciprocities and mutual obligations with people of an "opposite" clan, who were thereafter obligated to return the favor.

Status in potlatch cultures was driven not by the accumulation of wealth, but by giving that wealth away. Dried salmon, fish oil, and other subsistence goods were given away as part of the potlatch feast, but, more important, abundant stores of salmon provided surplus for trade in more exotic goods and also enabled leaders of the richest clans to employ artists and craftsmen to carve totem poles or canoes, thus enhancing the status of clan leaders and their entire kin group.[56] Abundant salmon was at the foundation of this interplay between material accumulation, prestige, gift-giving, and mutual reciprocities. Tlingit and Haida fishing was not only driven by technical expertise, it was driven by social and cultural desire and it was supported by a tightly organized system of labor that included slaves.

The issue of slave labor is a controversial subject in Northwest Coast ethnography. Most scholars have contended that slaves contributed little benefit to the subsistence economy of coastal Indians. Their main importance was not to produce wealth through their labors, as in a slave-based economy, but rather to serve as an item of prestige and display for their owners, whose status was raised through the ownership, exchange, and ritual sacrifice of slaves. This view holds, in anthropologist Philip Drucker's words, that "slaves' economic utility was negligible" and, because they needed to be clothed and fed, slaves actually constituted a drain on tribal resources.[57]

Anthropologist Leland Donald has challenged this prevailing scholarly interpretation of Northwest Coast slavery, arguing that slaves were integral to the native subsistence economy even while they served as "prestige objects" for their owners. Their labor, he argues, liberated Indian aristocrats from "common labor" and helped to generate the wealth that supported social stratification and cultural complexity among Northwest Coast societies.[58] While Donald perhaps goes too far in stressing the economic primacy of slavery among coastal Indian peoples, the ethnographic literature seems to bear out his assertion that slaves provided important labor within the subsistence economy. It would be erroneous to suggest that the native subsistence economy was primarily a "slave economy," whose entire organization rested on an edifice of servile labor, but it cannot be disputed that the hierarchical and complex cultures that developed along the Northwest Coast resulted from the interactions of human—including slave—labors with the salmon-rich marine environment. This is only to reiterate the uncontroversial assumption that those peoples with access to abundant natural resources, and with the means to effectively transform those resources into calories or items of trade, had "more disposable wealth and energy to devote to cultural pursuits than did others."[59]

SOURCES OF SALMON MANAGEMENT

Considering the technological proficiency of Native fishing systems, the organization and productivity of Native labor systems, and the sociocultural motivation of Tlingit and Haida fishers, it is likely that they had the *ability* to overtax the salmon runs.[60] If we conclude that Native fishing technologies and social systems were complex enough to harm the salmon runs, we might also conclude that Native peoples—while not necessarily "ecological Indians"—developed strategies that prevented them from wreaking havoc on their natural resources. What were the sources of these management strategies? Were they deliberate or unintentional? Were they based on a biological knowledge of salmon migration patterns or social, cultural, and religious prescriptions?

For the Northwest Coast, the management and use of fish traps was especially critical. Because traps had the ability to block an entire run of salmon from reaching the spawning grounds, it is clear that Native fishers voluntarily removed them from streams so as to allow fish passage upriver. Did their actions always convey an unmistakable concern for the sustainability of salmon resources? Did their actions suggest an aboriginal conservation ethic?

An example from southeastern Alaska suggests that, in one instance at least, trap sites were not overexploited, but for reasons unrelated to aboriginal management. Ironically, on Prince of Wales Island, population growth and the expansion of new fishing technologies—developments that might have led Native fishers to deplete salmon resources—help to explain why sockeye and pink salmon runs were *not* overfished at upriver sites where they were most vulnerable. Anthropologist Steve Langdon's work has shown that the early Klawock village emerged first on the upper river, where settlers had ready access to salmon. However, as the prehistoric Klawock's population grew, residents overexploited "local non-salmon resources" and began to migrate toward the coast, where they could use a wider variety of marine resources, including "bright" (and more nutritious) salmon in nearshore waters where they were available for longer durations.

This migration occurred, according to Langdon, as Tlingit peoples at Klawock developed more sophisticated technologies for taking salmon in estuary and offshore environments, including tidal weirs, bag nets, and, importantly, large canoes that could be used to transport salmon from harvesting sites to villages. Fish still might be taken more efficiently at upriver trap sites, but such harvests could not be easily transported by canoe from rocky upriver shallows to newer village locations nearer the coast. The emphasis on fishing accordingly shifted downriver to the mouths of streams, estuaries, and offshore waters rather than upriver tributaries and lakes where the sockeye went to spawn.[61]

This is a compelling example of how human actions unwittingly fostered conservation. There are other examples of Native fishers reducing fishing intensity at trap sites for reasons that apparently had little to do with sustaining salmon runs. In California and British Columbia, for example, trap owners removed their gear from streams so that fish could pass upriver to inland peoples.[62] In these cases removing fish traps reflected a concern for upriver human populations, with whom the Native fishers had made such agreements, rather than for salmon populations. Their actions do suggest, however, that Native fishers understood that the supply of salmon was finite and their own catches limited fishing for peoples further inland. But the fact that downriver populations either unknowingly (as in the case of Klawock village) or deliberately moderated their harvests does not explain why upriver peoples likewise removed their traps from salmon streams. Langdon, after conducting extensive fieldwork among Tlingit salmon fishers on Prince of Wales Island in southeastern Alaska, concluded that Native "salmon management included the concept of escapement—that is, allowing enough fish to reach the spawning grounds to maintain the strength of the run."[63] But what informed this aboriginal concept of "escapement"—ecological knowledge, spiritual concern for the "salmon people," or other social prescriptions?

Anthropologists Michael Kew and Julian Griggs have suggested that when Native fishers on the Fraser River in British Columbia removed fish traps, they were motivated less by conservation than by their spiritual relationship with salmon. "The removal of the [fish] dam," they argue, "is an act called for by the protocol of proper relationships with the fish who are gift-bearing visitors."[64] Indeed, Native American resource management is often depicted largely as a function of religious rituals and taboos that required humans to treat animals with respect or risk starvation. Tlingit and Haida peoples, like other tribes all along the Northwest Coast, believed that salmon belonged to a powerful tribe, divided into five clans representing the five species of Pacific salmon. Each year, the "salmon people" donned their silver clothing and traveled in invisible canoes to give up their flesh to grateful fishers.[65]

In the social economy of the Northwest Coast, gifts always demanded reciprocity. In return for the great gift of salmon, Native peoples needed to treat salmon—and all animals—with proper respect and be attentive to the many ritual requirements surrounding the hunt. For Tlingit fishermen those rituals included rising early, bathing in the sea, fasting, abstaining from sexual relations, and refraining from anger or violence of any kind.[66] After salmon were caught, further rituals were observed. Salmon bones were placed in the river after the flesh was used so that the spirit of each fish would return to its underground home, regain its human form, and visit again the next year. If the bones were thrown away on land, the spirit of the salmon person could not return; if some bones did not make it back to the water, the salmon person, when resurrected, might be missing a leg or an arm, and in his anger would not return to the stream where he had suffered mistreatment.[67] Menstruating women stayed away from fresh salmon. Women butchered the salmon on cutting surfaces with the fish pointing upstream while they themselves faced downstream. They similarly hung salmon on the drying racks with heads pointed upstream. Northwest Indians, in historian Richard White's words, "took the biological necessity of obtaining the caloric energy needed to live and elaborated it into a web of social meaning and power that took on consequences of its own."[68]

But what were the consequences of these rituals with regard to conservation? Certainly they reaffirmed a deeply intimate relationship between humans and animals, but did they actually serve to minimize fishing intensity, as they apparently did further south on the Columbia River and in California? Historian Joseph Taylor has shown how on the Columbia religious rituals and taboos unintentionally placed limitations on Native fishing, but in southeastern Alaska there is no evidence to suggest that there was ever any causal relationship between such ritual observances and fishing intensity. Furthermore, if we are to assume that Native peoples took their mythology literally (which was probably not always the case), religious rituals might have worked against conservation insomuch as it redirected human understandings of environmental scarcity toward supernatural explanations: that is, salmon runs failed because of human failure to observe certain rituals rather than overfishing or environmental conditions.

At bottom, religious rituals relating to salmon fishing were not about sustaining salmon runs by limiting or regulating fishing intensity, but about encouraging even larger returns of the "salmon people" through ritual propitiation. Anthropologist Frederica de Laguna, who worked closely with the Yakutat Tlingit, observed that "since dead animals were thought to become reincarnated in new bodies," Native fishers showed little concern that overharvesting might contribute to declining salmon stocks.[69] In this sense Northwest Coast salmon fishers were little different from buffalo hunters on the Plains, who believed that buffalo emerged from an underground country and could never be exterminated by human actions as long as ritual relationships were maintained.[70] By suggesting that the abundance of animal populations was affected primarily by human attention to ritual procedures, Native religion had the power to deflect attention from the ecological impact of human fishing and hunting activities.

Religion may not have effectively moderated salmon harvests in southeastern Alaska, but it did express a powerful social code of respect for animals that may have discouraged humans from wasting—not because overharvesting threatened animal populations, but because it was disrespectful and might cause animals to take revenge on humans. There are numerous stories in Tlingit and Haida oral tradition that convey a message of "wise use" when it came to killing animals. One tells of a village that enjoyed years of abundant salmon runs until four boys went fishing and, caught up in the process of pulling fish from the river, caught too many and even laughed at one salmon as he squirmed on the hot rocks. In retaliation, the boys died and the village was saved only when the people vowed to never treat animals with disrespect again.[71]

In another Tlingit legend an eagle father admonishes his newly winged son to "try and keep greed out of [hunting]. Don't overkill. Kill only one at a time."[72] As a grown man, the boy ignores his father's advice and kills two whales in one hunting trip and dies himself upon reaching shore. Both stories related a valuable lesson: Native peoples carried the responsibility of taking only what they needed and, more important, of treating animals with respect. Tlingit Lydia George described her ancestors' seriousness about the issue: "Since fish was our main food, we were very careful; the fish were treated well. If a man broke any of our laws, his fishing equipment was taken from him; sometimes his spear was broken up."[73]

If "breaking laws" meant wasting salmon, perhaps Tlingit and Haida ethics concerning the proper treatment of animals did discourage overharvesting and thereby limit fishing intensity. However, it is possible that such stories never entirely prohibited waste but, like all codes that prescribe proper social behavior, merely expressed an ideal expectation of human conduct—albeit one that was not always obeyed. Arguing that such stories prevented waste would be little different than arguing that seventeenth-century laws against miscegenation prevented interracial sex in Virginia. Although Native religion or belief systems suggest a deeply intimate and respectful relationship between animals and humans, there is no evidence that they fostered conservation in practice.

If not supernatural beliefs, then what constituted the basis of aboriginal management systems, which successfully sustained salmon runs for generations? Surprisingly, the most *effective* source of resource management in the Tlingit and Haida salmon was property rights. While hunter-gatherer peoples generally did not have strict notions of property, Northwest Coast peoples, especially the Tlingit and Haida, had an acute sense of territoriality. Property was owned by clans and stewarded by clan leaders, who claimed the right to regulate hunting, gathering, and fishing by preventing outsiders from infringing on clan territory. Salmon streams, because of the wealth they bestowed to clans, were "jealously guarded."[74] Origin stories, repeated at the potlatch, delineated the geography of clan and house ownership and preserved this information in human memory. Carved poles and markers literally asserted property rights through symbolic imagery. An old grave post in the Tlingit village of Tuxekan, for instance, depicted a "basket trap full of fish," three sockeye salmon entering a stream, a brown bear pawing a salmon, and the clan leader holding a wolf by its tail. These images recorded ownership of a particular salmon stream by the Sockeye Salmon House of the Brown Bear Clan of the Wolf Moiety.[75]

Violation of clan ownership could lead to serious conflict. This is evident in an oral account of a nineteenth-century fight over fishing grounds: "The Hmyedi [house] were pretty strict with that humpy stream. Some of our boys went to that stream to get some salmon. The Hmyedi caught them and got hold of them and broke up their spears."[76] In one sense Tlingit and Haida peoples had a much more highly defined sense of property than did Europeans, since Tlingit and Haida property rights covered such resources—water, game, fish, wild plants—that Europeans considered "common property."

By defending their rights to territory, Tlingits and Haidas effectively limited fishing intensity. Their goals were not "ecological" in nature, but rather social and cultural: abundant resources, as discussed earlier, guaranteed the prosperity of the clan and the prestige of the clan leader. Clan leaders therefore oversaw the construction, use, and disassembly of fish traps, and they likewise monitored other types of fishing gear. They determined who would fish and for how long. After ensuring that their own people had caught enough, they might open the fishery to outsiders, but such generosity was contingent upon the success of the harvest. Restricting access in years of scarcity moderated harvests, while opening access in years of abundance intensified harvests, preventing too many fish from ascending to the spawning grounds. The intention of such management may not have been biological conservation, but such prohibitions on use implied that Native peoples clearly understood the relationship between human use and the size of fish populations. Even anthropologist Gordon Hewes, who believed that "primitive peoples" had no sense of conservation in the modern sense, admitted that "the restriction of hunting or gathering in a particular territory to the members of one's own group (or family) is apparently motivated by the realization . . . that unlimited participation by outsiders would diminish the supply available to one's own group."[77] Property rights, far more than religious ritual, served as the basis for Tlingit and Haida resource management—an ironic conclusion, given popular stereotypes of Native peoples as communal and motivated to steward natural resources primarily out of their supernatural relationship with wild animals.

ECOLOGICAL FISHERS?

Native peoples had the population density, the fishing technologies, and the social and cultural motivation to overexploit local salmon resources—and they probably did from time to time. Writing in the 1930s, ethnographer C. Daryll Forde noted that Nootka Indians in British Columbia "practiced a unique device to ensure their salmon supplies." "If the run on a particular stream began to fail," aboriginal salmon managers "actually restocked it, obtaining spawn from another river at the breeding season and carrying it back in moss-lined boxes to start a new generation in the depleted stream."[78] This example from Northwest Coast peoples further south—if it is accurate—suggests that Native fishers had both the capacity to destroy salmon runs and the ecological knowledge to save them.

Northwest Coast fishers developed strategies over time that allowed them to sustain salmon resources, but the nature of aboriginal resource management is a source of continuing debate. Writing on the Native peoples of Alaska's northern interior, anthropologist Richard K. Nelson has argued that empirical as well as supernatural knowledge of the natural world combined to create a "well-developed conservation ethic" in Koyukon culture, fostering "the use of sustained yield principles to govern [the] harvest of resource species."[79] Native fishers in southeastern Alaska shared with Koyukon peoples both an intimate ecological knowledge of their environment and a supernatural relationship with animals, but whether those sources constituted a well-defined "conservation ethic" is highly questionable.

Native Americans, like all humans, effectively exploited their natural resources and in some instances had the capacity to overexploit them. This is an important corrective to those who would idealize Native Americans to the point of stereotyping them—like the first English settlers did—as lazy Indians who "lived in the midst of a landscape endowed so astonishingly with abundance" but did little to transform or "improve" their environment. Despite the fact that Native peoples supported large populations and effectively utilized their natural resources for thousands of years, those first Europeans chose to believe that Indians had been blessed with the bounty of nature, but chose instead to live, as one settler put it, "like to our Beggers in England."[80]

Clearly, Native peoples had the technology and the motivation to transform their natural world. This entailed constructive change—like the use of fire to enhance the productivity of the landscape—and sometimes destructive change, as when early Aleut hunters on Amchitcka Island decimated sea otter populations, allowing the number of sea urchins to increase, and ultimately causing "nearshore fish populations to collapse."[81] It is naïve to assume that Native Americans were somehow immune from acting in ways that were myopic, short term, wasteful, environmentally destructive, and ultimately human. It is also deeply biased to assume that they didn't have the technologies to affect their environments—constructively or destructively.

It is equally naïve to assume, however, that all humans and all cultures have shared likeminded values with regard to nature. Native fishers on the Northwest Coast may not have always understood the environmental consequences of their actions, nor did their actions always reflect a concern for the biological sustainability of their resources. They were not conservationists, ecologists, or environmentalists in the *modern* sense of those terms. But they undoubtedly had a deep ecological understanding of their world, as reflected by their ability to successfully exploit a vast range of flora and fauna, including the five species of Pacific salmon. Furthermore, they constructed cultures that placed a high value on the nonhuman world and posited a deep intimacy among humans, animals, and nature. Such intimacy fostered relationships of reciprocity and respect between humans and animals that may have deterred (but not always prevented) overharvesting and waste.

But those two sources of knowledge—ecological and supernatural—did not constitute the most effective form of salmon management. Native management and regulation of salmon resources emerged primarily as a function of territoriality: houses and clans fiercely guarded their rights to salmon streams. Northwest Coast societies built social and cultural hierarchies on the wealth derived from salmon, and those hierarchies limited use of the resource by imposing an intricate pattern of user rights throughout southeastern Alaska. Native American management of the salmon fisheries might not prove that "when people live in harmony with the cosmos, the salmon return in abundance and the land provides."[82] But it certainly proves that Northwest Coast Indians successfully managed their marine environment for thousands of years "at sustained levels of harvest that might well incite the envy of twentieth-century fishers and lawmakers."[83]

Nineteenth-century Euro-Americans would impose on the salmon fisheries a very different pattern of resource use based on their own conceptions of law, economy, class, race, religion, and nature. The great irony of this transition, which is the subject of the next chapter, is that while tribal peoples—usually considered egalitarian and communal in nature—managed their fisheries with a strict notion of property rights, Euro-Americans—so vested in the notion of property and ownership—would promote the legal concept of an "open-access" fishery. The consequence would be a system that opened the fishery to laissez-faire industrial exploitation and transformed "common property" into individual wealth.

2 The Industrial Transformation of the Indian Salmon Fishery, 1780s–1910s

By and by they began to build canneries and take the creeks away from us . . . and when we told them these creeks belonged to us, they would not pay any attention to us and said all this country belonged to President, the big chief at Washington. . . . We make this complaint because we are very poor now. The time will come when we will not have anything left. . . . We also ask [the chief at Washington] to return our creeks and the hunting grounds that white people have taken away from us.
—KAH-DU-SHAN, Tlingit chief

The Indians of the Territory are not dependent upon Uncle Sam as are those of the States. They do not live upon reservations. The government provides native schools, and helps in every way possible to the natives' best development, but the Indians are self-supporting. They have quickly adapted themselves to the changes which the opening of the Territory has brought. They have their cooperative stores, their canneries and sawmills, their power launches, their neat, pretty homes.
—AGNES RUSH BURR, *Alaska: Our Beautiful Northland of Opportunity*

In Alaska contact and colonization occurred in three overlapping phases: the maritime fur trade (1785–1825), Russian colonization (1795–1867), and American settlement and industrialization after 1867. For Native peoples these developments paralleled those experienced by American Indians further south. Newcomers arrived in their midst, armed with deadly microbes and charged with the desire to transform natural resources into quick profits. Tlingit and Haida fishermen maintained their control over the salmon fishery during the fur trade but were supremely challenged by the rise of salmon canning in the late 1870s. The industry commodified an animal whose value, in the view of Native fishers, was more than purely economic. Taken together, the processes of contact, colonization, commerce, and industrialization transformed the social and environmental landscape of southeast Alaska forever.

From the perspective of Native peoples, these developments heralded change but not cultural annihilation. In California and Oregon the vectors of disease and civilization were far more catastrophic, sweeping Native peoples to the margins and leaving behind a landscape almost unrecognizable as a result of mining, farming, and the growth of cities. Alaska's remote location and northern climate meant that farming did *not* take hold on a large-scale basis, population growth did *not* occur rapidly, and the related processes of white settlement—damming, deforestation, urbanization—were not conducted with the same swift and destructive force experienced further south. Moreover, the cultural characteristics of Tlingit and Haida peoples allowed them to creatively adapt to changes, maintaining their cultural footing on uncertain ground.

For the Pacific salmon, the story was more destructive, but it did not culminate in the kind of crisis and collapse that occurred on the Sacramento and Columbia rivers. The much sought-after sockeye, with its eminently marketable rich red flesh, was aggressively pursued by an ever-growing and increasingly mechanized fleet of commercial fishermen. The abundant pink salmon was largely neglected until the 1910s, when declining sockeye harvests and increasing demand for canned salmon fueled by World War I led to the proliferation of canneries throughout the region. The life cycle of wild salmon—already challenged by the natural dangers of environmental instability—was now threatened by overfishing. The result was that the livelihoods of certain salmon runs and the humans that depended on them—especially Native Americans—were increasingly jeopardized, although not altogether ruined. Indian peoples actively responded to such developments. Salmon, however, had little room to maneuver. Although not technically passive objects of human exploitation, the salmon increasingly depended on human actions for their survival.

THE MARITIME FUR TRADE AND RUSSIAN SETTLEMENT: BALANCING TRADE AND SUBSISTENCE

Contemporary historians have often searched for ways to acknowledge that at certain times and certain places, Native peoples wielded power over their

European invaders. They argue that indigenous peoples were not just "passive victims" of imperialism and colonization but active agents of their own destinies. Given the extent to which Native populations in North America were devastated by disease and forced from their lands and lifestyles by Euro-Americans, this view of Native American empowerment can be greatly overstated. It is not overstated, however, with regards to the maritime fur trade that developed between Tlingit and Haida peoples and Euro-American traders.

The fur trade was one of the few instances in the history of Indian-European relations where both sides essentially got what they wanted and where neither side was entirely dominated or destroyed. Although it introduced capitalism to the Northwest Coast and thereby began the process by which humans assigned cash values to the wild animals of southeastern Alaska, the coastal trade did not destroy the subsistence economies of Native peoples. In the fur trade economy animals were saved or destroyed according to how readily their bodies could be converted into quick profits. Fur-bearing animals, such as the sea otter, lost out, while salmon, because their flesh could not be easily converted into wealth until the development of canning technologies later in the century, remained a secondary item of trade.

The maritime trade on the North Pacific began during Captain James Cook's third voyage (1776–1779), when his crew traded for sea-otter pelts in Nootka Sound and sold them in Canton for "fabulous" prices. The publication of Cook's journals in 1784 spurred a rush of vessels—English, French, and American—to the Northwest Coast to participate in the lucrative and risky "otter trade," inaugurating the first extensive contacts between Europeans and Indians in Alaska.[1] Europeans encountered savvy Native traders who controlled the dynamics of the exchange from start to finish. Coastal peoples demanded that Europeans accept Indian rituals with regard to trade. Gift-giving, speech-making, and hostage exchanges were all dictated by Indians while European traffickers, like Captain George Dixon, who visited Port Mulgrave in May 1787, "patiently submitted to the tantalizing method of these people in hope that something better might possibly be brought [to] us."[2]

Indian demand determined the items of exchange, from iron goods to blue cloth, coats, blankets, beads, knives, guns, rum, tobacco, and molasses.[3] Native traders manipulated prices and deftly played European traders against each other. "The Indians are sufficiently cunning to derive all possible advantage from competition," noted Captain Richard Cleveland in 1799, after he witnessed them going "from one vessel to another, and back again, with assertions of offers made to them, which have no foundation in truth; and showing themselves to be as well versed in the tricks of trade as the greatest adepts."[4] In short, Indian traders in southeastern Alaska, as French explorer Jean François de la Pérouse described them in 1786, "appeared well accustomed to traffic, and bargained with as much skill as any tradesman of Europe."[5]

A classic interpretation of this trade has ruthless Europeans preying on unwitting Indian dupes in a relationship that was "at best . . . unequal" and for the most part "predatory."[6] Indeed, Europeans did obtain valuable pelts in exchange for items they perceived as worthless. In 1820, Russian official K. T. Khlebnikov noted that "in Sitkha [*sic*], the [Tlingit] pay one sea otter skin for a shell with a blue tint." He observed: "They remove the best part of the shell and use it as an earring."[7] For Khlebnikov, who counseled Russian American Company (RAC) employees that they "should not feel that it is beneath our dignity to make use of any blessing of nature" in securing a trading advantage, Native demand for such items was an invitation to reap easy profits.[8] His approach, like that of other traders, may have been "predatory," but such a judgment does not consider the fact that Native traders *wanted* shells, beads, blue cloth, blankets, and other relatively inexpensive European goods for reasons that went beyond purely economic motivations. Such items fueled the social and ceremonial demands of the Native prestige economy and could be more valuable in the potlatch, and therefore in enhancing one's social status, than more practical merchandise.

This does not mean that Indians were not "rational" actors. There is little doubt that Indian peoples bargained "rationally" to maximize profits, but Indian participation in the maritime trade is best understood when grounded in an Indian, rather than a European, worldview. The potlatch complex allowed Tlingit and Haida peoples to direct the profits of the otter trade into preexisting structures of status, prestige, reciprocity, and social responsibility. This meant that participation in European commerce had the potential to enhance, rather than destroy, Indian culture. It did not make Native peoples into capitalists—rather, it pushed them more rapidly in the direction they were already headed. The proliferation of totem poles, ornate carved canoes, potlatches, and slaves in the first part of the nineteenth century indicates that the maritime trade may have "enriched" rather than weakened Native society, as new wealth was channeled into traditional patterns of reciprocity and exchange.[9] Native peoples participated in the trade, and indeed controlled the trade, for *their own* purposes.

Native ability to control the trade and maintain cultural stability was not solely a function of their own cultural attributes, but it was also contingent upon a number of other factors, including the Indians' population advantage over European traders, the noninvasive nature of the sea-borne trade, and most important the fact that salmon and other essential foodstuffs were not central commodities in the trade. Unlike the land-based trade in deer or buffalo hides, which destroyed Native self-sufficiency and forced Indian peoples into economic dependency on the Great Plains and in the American Southeast, the otter business allowed Native peoples market participation without market dependency. European motivations—to trade and be on their way rather than to settle and exploit local resources—also contributed greatly to Native cultural stability.

Salmon was an important item of trade because European traders were starved for fresh food, but it was not a *primary* commodity, and its production and distribution were controlled by Native houses and clans. Immediately after arriving in Lituya Bay in 1786, La Pérouse encountered Indians seeking to trade fish, furs, and clothing for "hatchets, adzes, and bar iron." La Pérouse marveled at the shrewd bargaining sensibility of the Yakutat Tlingit people. "At first they gave us salmon in exchange for pieces of old hoops," he wrote, "but they soon became more difficult, and would not part with this fish unless for nails, or small implements of iron."[10]

Europeans were eager to obtain salmon and other foods either through trading or fishing themselves. In 1797, Captain Nathaniel Portlock described his crew hauling the seine and catching a "good supply of excellent salmon."[11] In 1799, Cleveland's crew obtained "abundant" supplies of salmon and halibut by "both catching them ourselves, and procuring them from the natives."[12] While European crews were deployed to catch salmon, especially during the peak of the summer runs, non-Indian traders often realized that acquiring adequate supplies of fish was better left to Native fishers. "Our whale-boat was one day sent with seven hands . . . on a fishing party," noted Dixon in 1797, "but their success was greatly inferior to that of *two* Indians . . . Thus we were fairly beat at our own weapons, and [with] the natives constantly bringing us plenty of fish, our boat was never sent on this business afterwards."[13]

Despite its economic and spiritual significance, Indian traders clearly had no reservations about trading salmon and other fish with Europeans. Native fishermen eagerly sold their summer salmon surpluses for beads, cloth, or pieces of iron. In doing so, they strictly controlled the amount of fish that entered the commercial market. However, dried fish, cured for winter consumption, remained outside the realm of European exchange. Dixon observed that "large quantities of salmon [were] frequently hung up on shore to dry" but that the Indians "were not very willing to sell." Their unwillingness to barter their subsistence goods, as Dixon concluded, showed "that fish is a principal and favourite article of food here."[14] It also demonstrated that Tlingit and Haida peoples could engage in new economic relationships while still controlling their subsistence economy.

Russian incursions into Southeast Alaska, beginning in the 1790s, constituted a far greater threat to Indian subsistence patterns and cultural autonomy than did the maritime trade. By the 1780s Russian fur-trading companies had already established themselves in western and central Alaska.[15] Their primary method of operation was not to trade with Native peoples but to rely on the forced labors of Aleut and Eskimo slaves in procuring pelts. Alexander Baranov, general manager of the Shelikov-Golikov Company, dispatched the first of these hunting expeditions to southeastern Alaska in 1794. The party of five hundred Aleut, Koniag, and Chugach slaves captured two thousand otters in Yakutat Bay before returning to the Russian headquarters on Kodiak Island. Throughout the late 1790s teams of Aleut hunters raided the waterways of southeastern Alaska, from Yakutat to Sitka, harvesting otters for their Russian masters. These invasions invited attacks by Tlingits. Archibald Menzies, who sailed with George Vancouver on the *Discovery*, witnessed the first of these confrontations at Yakutat Bay in 1794. The Yakutat people, observed Menzies, viewed the Russians and Aleuts "as intruders in their territories, draining their shores & coasts of Seals Otter & Fish on which their subsistence chiefly Depends, & that too without making the least return for their depredations."[16]

Russian settlement, first at Yakutat in 1795 and then near present-day Sitka in 1799, led to more intensive strains on Native resources and engendered increased resistance from Indian peoples. In June 1802, Tlingits destroyed the first Russian fort at Sitka only two years after its establishment, killing twenty Russians and a hundred and thirty Aleuts, taking three thousand otter pelts, and burning the entire camp.[17] In 1804, after a bitter fight with Indians at Sitka, the Russians reestablished their settlement, renaming it New Archangel. Sitka Tlingits—"armed by the Bostonians with the best guns and pistols," according to RAC investor Nicolai Rezanov, who visited New Archangel from 1804 to 1806—continued to threaten the fledgling colony.[18] Aleut hunting parties remained under "constant harassment on the part of the Kolosh."[19] In September 1805, Tlingit warriors destroyed the northern settlement of Yakutat.[20]

Indian resistance prevented hunting parties from leaving New Archangel during the summer of 1806, and further attacks in 1809 and 1813 kept Russian inhabitants "in a constant state of terror."[21] For decades Aleut hunters found coastal tribes, in the words of RAC official Khlebnikov, "ready to attack on the slightest provocation."[22] When George Simpson, the head of the Hudson Bay's Company, visited Sitka in 1841, he noted that "the Company's hunters, who are chiefly Aleutians, are peaceful even to cowardice, being in great dread of the Indians of the coast, who are numerous, treacherous, and fierce."[23] Indian attacks threatened non-Indian settlements and hunting parties throughout the region as long as the Russians remained in southeastern Alaska. Only factionalism among Tlingit clans allowed the Russians to continue their operations. In 1823 a Russian official in New Archangel warned RAC directors in St. Petersburg that "the koloshes [Tlingits] are still fighting among themselves but when they make peace, it will be impossible to send our men after beavers."[24] Twelve years later the Russian governor informed British naval captain Edward Belcher of the potential threat of Indian solidarity: "Although seven hundred only were now in our neighborhood, seven thousand might arrive in a few hours."[25] As late as 1860, Russian official P. N. Golovin expressed the same fear: "If they were to unite under the leadership of a brave chief, the Kolosh would easily conquer our settlements and kill all the Russians."[26]

Although Native resistance and Russian incompetence prevented the colony from ever truly extending its control over the peoples of southeastern Alaska, the Russian American Company put far more pressure on salmon streams and spawning grounds than the maritime traders ever did. The biggest problem for the Russians in America, as geographer James R. Gibson has documented so thoroughly, was supplying their colony with the bare necessities of survival.[27] Their attempts at making Russian America self-sufficient involved the establishment of farming operations at Kodiak and in northern California, but neither settlement provided adequate provisions for southeastern Alaska. In Sitka, Russians traded for goods with Europeans and Americans if they could, but ultimately Russian colonists would be sustained primarily by fish—fresh, salted, and dried. Khlebnikov, who was in Sitka from 1817 to 1832, explained that "aside from bread, fish represents the chief food" for company laborers.[28] Russian dried salmon, or *yukola*, was such a staple that it was referred to in Sitka as "Kamchatka bread."[29]

At Sitka, Russians caught salmon primarily in upriver permanent stone traps, called *zapors*. These traps "greatly inhibited, if not totally precluded, the movement of salmon up the streams to their spawning grounds" because, unlike Native traps and weirs, zapors were not removed from streams after the harvest had been obtained.[30] The Russians established fish processing facilities, for salting and drying, both at Sitka and at an inland lake camp called the Ozersk Redoubt. At the redoubt salmon traps were also set directly in the lake, where hundreds of thousands of salmon returned to spawn. According to Khlebnikov, during the early part of the salmon season, "as long as the run of fish is small," Russian laborers transported "the fresh fish by baidarka [canoe] to the port for consumption." As the summer progressed, Russian employees salted and dried salmon for their winter consumption, packing salted fish at the lake camp between June and September and at New Archangel during the fall runs of chum and silver salmon. These late runs were "taken with nets" using a "special boat with nine men."[31] Such fishing operations, explained Captain Golovin, allowed the Russian company to provide its workers with "fresh fish from the Company without cost . . . [when] the fish are running," while "the rest of the year salt fish is also given out free, and is used as food in the communal kitchen."[32]

Estimating Russian salmon catches is nearly as tenuous as predicting aboriginal harvests. Khlebnikov, observing fishing operations from 1817 to 1832, estimated that the Russians at New Archangel and Ozersk Redoubt salted an average of 20,000 salmon every year. He also observed that "the Aleuts dry about 10,000 fish for iukola [dried fish]" and "go along rivers where fish come in and take all they need for themselves" during the summer months. If the Russians and the Aleuts consumed two times more salmon than they prepared for winter consumption, this would put their total consumption at 90,000 salmon a year.[33]

In 1841, Simpson noted that "within a mile of the fort [at Sitka], salmon are so plentiful at the proper season, that, when ascending the river, they have been known literally to embarrass the movements of a canoe." He estimated that "about a hundred thousand of the last-mentioned fish . . . are annually salted for use of the establishment . . . [but] they are not adapted for exportation."[34] In 1862, however, Golovin recorded a much larger Russian catch of 558,000 salmon: 114,000 "salt fish," 64,000 "fresh fish," and 380,000 "iukola."[35] By then, the Russians were also exporting anywhere between 100 and 1,000 barrels of salt fish per year (each barrel containing an average of 150 fish), with a high of 1,070 barrels produced and sold in 1858.[36]

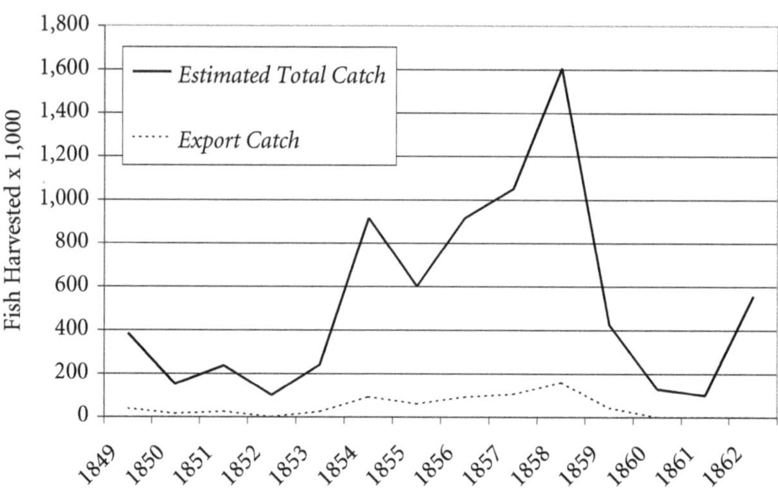

FIG. 2.1 Estimated Russian harvests, 1849–1862. Russian harvests fluctuated dramatically, as suggested by these harvest estimates drawn from P. N. Golovin, who recorded the export catch and the 1862 total catch. The other numbers were calculated by estimating the export catch as 10 percent of the total catch, since Russian sources all indicate that salmon was used primarily for subsistence, with exports comprising only a small percentage of the total harvest. SOURCE: *Golovin 1979: 82–83 and appendix 9.*

Considering that all accounts of Russian salmon production agree that, in Golovin's words, salmon were "prepared in the colonies for the most part as food for the inhabitants" and that "only a small amount" was prepared for sale, and given the fact that the Russian colonists were continually teetering on the brink of starvation, we might safely estimate that Russian exports represented at most 10 percent of the total Russian salmon harvest per year.[37] If that were the case, Russian harvests averaged between 150,000 and 1,605,000 fish in the years between 1849 and 1860 (see figure 2.1). It is not clear whether the Russians overexploited the salmon runs at Sitka, but their fishing methods—taking fish directly from the spawning grounds at permanent trap sites—clearly would have given them that potential.

In 1899, Jefferson Moser, an agent for the U.S. Fish Commission, contended that "the injury caused to the fisheries" by Russian traps "is acknowledged by everyone who has any knowledge of the subject."[38] Anthropologist Steve Langdon has concluded that "in conservation terms, the Russians apparently did not have a concept of escapement."[39] But how much did Russian fishing, even if carried out with little sense of long-term sustainability,

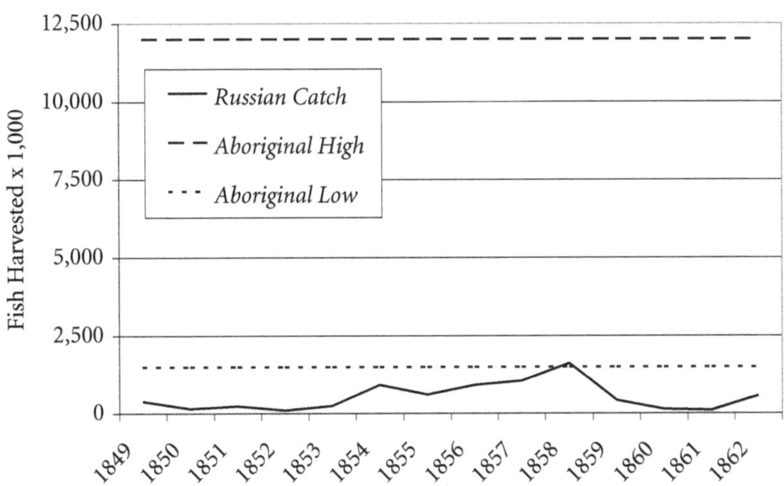

FIG. 2.2 Estimated Russian harvests, 1849–1862, compared with aboriginal high and low estimates. Russian harvest estimates barely approach even the low estimate for aboriginal harvests, but that does not mean that the Russian fishery did not have a significant impact on salmon populations and Native culture in and around Sitka. SOURCES: *Golovin 1979: 82–83 and appendix 9; Hewes 1947: 223–24; Petroff 1884: 69–71.*

affect salmon resources? If we use Khlebnikov's figures, Russian production and consumption of salmon was comparatively small when compared with aboriginal harvest estimates. Golovin's numbers indicate that the Russian catch was much more significant, with the largest Russian harvests rivaling the lowest precontact estimates (see figure 2.2). However, both high and low figures take on new meaning when we remember that the Russian harvest figures are derived from a concentrated area around Sitka and Ozersk Redoubt on Baranof Island. Although the Russians did not even begin to tap into the vast salmon populations that migrated throughout the entire Alexander Archipelago, their catches most likely made a significant impact on salmon runs near Sitka itself.

By intruding on aboriginal salmon streams, using fish traps, and unleashing Aleuts on the region's marine resources, Russians placed pressure not only on the environment, but also on the finely tuned balance of aboriginal management systems and property rights. Clearly, such unwelcome intrusions were the cause of much enmity between coastal Indians and Russians. Yakutat tribal histories, for instance, cite encroachments on traditional fishing sites as among the primary reasons leading to the 1805 attack on the

Russian settlement at Yakutat. According to these oral accounts, Russian fishers "put a gate up across the creek" that prevented the salmon from reaching the spawning grounds. Furthermore, "the only time the Russians opened the gate was when the chief came by. [Clan leader] Tanux said they would all starve together because the fish couldn't go up past the gate."[40]

As this narrative suggests, Russian fishing not only deprived the Yakutat Indian population of their most reliable food source, but it challenged Native property rights and ultimately the power of Indian clan leaders to steward and regulate clan house subsistence resources. Lack of traditional fisheries management signaled more than starvation—it represented loss of traditional authority, since clan leaders profited from subsistence wealth in goods procured and ultimately in status obtained. As American fur trader John D'Wolf recognized in 1805, "Success in fishing and in the chase constitutes the source of their wealth, and consequently their influence."[41] Russian fishing operations therefore impinged on both Native wealth and influence.

However, Russians did not have the power to expropriate Native resources at will, any more than they had the capacity to conquer Native peoples. Their small numbers, which never exceeded five hundred in southeastern Alaska, and their lack of adequate provisions and trading goods made them precariously dependent on the goodwill of Native peoples, whom they courted with decorum, ritual, and respect.[42] Unlike American and English traders, who were "rude and undiplomatic," the Russians for the most part "behaved properly—showing an understanding of and respect for the hierarchical nature of Tlingit society and the fundamental principle of balanced exchange."[43] With regard to the user rights that Native peoples attributed to salmon fishing sites, this meant that the Russians generally acknowledged Indian property rights, requested the right to use tribal resources, and offered proper payment for such use. According to interviews conducted in the 1940s, Native informants have suggested that the Russians "recognized the ownership" of the salmon stream near Sitka, which supplied Ozersk Redoubt with its abundance of salmon, by paying the Sitka clan leader who "owned" the stream and treating him "like a prince of the Russians."[44] In 1932, Tlingit elder Sam G. Davis similarly depicted the Russian presence as noninvasive: "The Russians never came and took our streams and trapping grounds from us; they never told us how we might catch salmon; and when we might stop."[45]

Indeed, it would be hard to imagine the Russians unilaterally forcing any demands on Indian peoples by the 1830s. By then, the otter trade had played itself out, and the Russians in Sitka had become almost entirely dependent on Tlingit hunters for basic foodstuffs. In 1830 the Russian governor Baron F. P. von Wrangell remarked with impatience that "we buy much of our food every year on the Kolosh [Tlingit] market, in spite of the ever-increasing prices, which are now extremely high."[46] In 1831 alone the Russian company exchanged 29,100 rubles worth of trade goods for Indian furs and subsistence goods—mainly "mountain sheep, halibut, salmon, birds' eggs, grouse, ducks, geese, and berries."[47] In 1860, Golovin explained that Tlingits brought such large quantities of wild sheep to market because they were "the only ones who can hunt the chamois in the high mountains which are covered by impenetrable forests."[48]

The same was true of salmon. Russian supplies of salted salmon fluctuated dramatically for various reasons beyond natural instability, including improper preservation techniques, damp weather that prevented the drying process, and lack of salt. When English captain Richard Collinson visited Sitka in 1850, he "learned with regret, that the salmon fishing having failed this year, we could not expect a supply of what I had hoped to obtain in abundance."[49] During the 1850s Russian salting operations failed twice, while Tlingit fishermen supplied the inhabitants of New Archangel with more than 50,000 pounds of halibut and salmon each year from 1846 to 1866.[50] "Whenever the Kolosh are in any way unhappy with the Russians," complained Golovin, "or when they are quarreling among themselves, or when they celebrate their holidays, they stop bringing in supplies to the market, and New Archangel suffers accordingly."[51] Another Russian observer admitted candidly that "Tlingits in no way may be considered dependent on the Company. It may even be stated that the settlements of the Company on the American shores are *dependent upon them*; as soon as, the local saying goes, they 'make noise,' the New Archangel Post with all its population is deprived of fresh food and the possibility of stepping some score of paces outside the fortress."[52]

In Russian America it would appear that the standard story of the fur trade—that of Native Americans becoming increasingly dependent on European goods—was inverted. The very environment—salmon rich and remote—that supported the growth of complex cultures during the pre-contact period, and later helped Native peoples to maintain a degree of autonomy uncommon for indigenous peoples in the continental United States, doomed Russian America to failure for the same reasons that it helped preserve Native culture: its distance from Western markets and its unsuitability to agriculture. From their first contact with Europeans until the 1860s, Tlingit and Haida peoples still controlled their culture and the marine environment on which their lives depended. Salmon had yet to become a commodity in the Euro-American marketplace.

This is not to suggest that Indian peoples in southeastern Alaska did not suffer negative consequences during the fur-trading era. Interaction with Europeans may have in some instances tipped the balance of Native society away from social responsibility, cooperation, and mutual obligations, and toward individualism, competition, and acquisitiveness. Anthropologist Leland Donald, for example, has contended that the coast trade fueled the expansion of aboriginal slavery as well as prostitution.[53] Anthropologist Kalervo Oberg has argued that communal subsistence activities, such as fishing and gathering, "diminished in importance with the increase in individual wealth and purchasing power."[54]

While the velocity of social change may have increased, the characteristics associated with the trade—rivalry, ambition, individualistic competition, slavery, feuding, and war—had existed in Tlingit and Haida society long before Europeans arrived. The most destructive, and least malleable, consequence of the trade came from European disease. Major smallpox epidemics in 1836 and 1862 reduced Indian peoples in southeastern Alaska from a precontact population of over ten thousand to approximately seventy-five hundred by 1867.[55] Although destabilizing, this tragic loss of population was less severe for the Tlingit and Haida peoples because it was not accompanied by the destruction of Native subsistence resources or the devastating influx of large settler populations, as was the case in the lower American West. By the 1820s sea otter populations had been depleted, but otherwise, Native peoples in southeastern Alaska were still in control of their resources. With the transfer of the region to the United States in 1867, however, that was about to change.

LAISSEZ-FAIRE INDUSTRIAL CAPITALISM AND THE SALMON FISHERIES

European fur traders and Russian settlers did not have the manpower, the technology, the military might, or the motivation to fully exploit southeastern Alaska's salmon resources for commercial gain. Americans did. American corporations provided the manpower and technology, transporting both immigrant laborers and new fish-canning technologies to Alaska in the late

1870s. The U.S. Army and Navy provided the military force necessary to subdue Indian resistance. Motivation would be supplied by the doctrine of laissez-faire capitalism: the belief in unrestrained free markets where individuals could pursue profits without interference from government regulation or control.

One of the core assumptions of nineteenth-century laissez-faire thinking was that natural resources were inexhaustible. Especially in the extractive industries of the American West—fishing, logging, mining—American industrialists proceeded with the expectation that new frontiers of raw materials always awaited them when present resources were depleted. They viewed Alaska as an untapped storehouse of natural wealth. From 1867 on, visions of Alaska's natural abundance were sown into the national consciousness. While some Americans decried Seward's "folly," supporters of the Alaskan purchase, such as Senator Charles Sumner, touted the region's seemingly limitless fisheries as one of the primary virtues of the acquisition. "Nothing is clearer than that fish in great abundance are taken everywhere on the [Northwest] coast," observed Sumner, an avid booster of New England fishing interests. "Here is the best that the sea affords for the poor or the rich," he continued. "Here also is a sure support . . . to the inhabitants of the coast."[56] Congressman Nathaniel Banks concurred, boasting that the Alaska fisheries (which in his mind had "never been fished so far as we know") "will give occupation to at least one-hundred and twenty thousand men in the cod and halibut fisheries alone."[57] In a letter to Secretary of State Henry Seward, a Coast Guard officer pronounced that "the fisheries alone are worth more to us than the whole cost of the country."[58]

In the late nineteenth and early twentieth centuries Alaska boosters described the region's fisheries—especially its supply of salmon—in the most hyperbolic terms. The amount of salmon in Alaska was "unsurpassed," "beyond all calculation," "extravagant," "inexhaustible," "a wonder," "unprecedented and beyond belief."[59] One claimed that the "prolific waters of Alaska" would "supply the nations of the world for centuries to come."[60] Another—territorial governor A. P. Swineford—speculated that it was impossible "to either definitely estimate or fix a limit to the value of Alaska's undeveloped resources," among them "fisheries from which the world's millions might be fed."[61] Another of Alaska's governors believed that it was "an utter impossibility to so fish the streams as to denude them of salmon life."[62] Frontier attitudes about unlimited natural resources encouraged the unlimited and unrestrained exploitation of the salmon fisheries. Indeed, like the booster literature that compelled so many profit-seekers westward, such hyperbole was intended to induce industrialists and entrepreneurs to Alaska. When they arrived, they were already conditioned by visions of infinite natural bounty.

Another core assumption of laissez-faire capitalism was an instrumentalist approach toward nature: natural resources were useful only when put in service of human progress. Since "progress" in the nineteenth century did not entail the use of nature for recreational or aesthetic purposes, this meant that the value of natural resources was realized only through their commercial exploitation. Nature was thus viewed primarily as a passive "object" for human exploitation rather than as a life force of its own, containing animate and spiritual properties. Such an approach sharply differentiated Euro-American from Native American views of nature. Euro-American attitudes were guided not only by capitalism but also by the Judeo-Christian admonition to "multiply; abound on the earth and *subdue* it"—that is, the belief that God created nature expressly for human exploitation and humans alone were endowed with spiritual capacities.[63]

Native attitudes, however, were shaped by a belief in the spiritual qualities of nature, especially animals. These convictions did not prohibit Native exploitation and use of the natural world, but they did impose certain limitations and restrictions on how it was used. Native culture moreover prohibited a sense of "ownership" over animals. Northwest Coast Indians "owned" or maintained the "rights" to use certain locations for fishing, hunting, or gathering. Individuals, though, could not own the animals they caught in those places—not only because those animals were spiritual beings who existed beyond the limits of human control, but because houses and clans used such resources collectively. Euro-Americans, in contrast, had for centuries asserted individual ownership and domination over animals, especially through the process of domestication. In their view animals—both wild and tame—could be owned and commodified, just as nature itself could be objectified and converted directly into riches.

The laissez-faire doctrine was nowhere more evident than in American property law regarding the fisheries, which encouraged individual initiative and unregulated competition. In the Anglo-American tradition the fisheries, like other forms of wildlife, were considered "common property" resources, meaning that no one actually "owned" them, but rather everyone had the right to exploit them. Although property ownership did not extend to the fishing grounds, when fish were caught, they became the property of the fisher. Fisheries law reflected the Anglo belief—best reflected in the writings of the philosopher John Locke—that in a "state of nature" property was secured through the exertion of individual physical labor, like plucking an apple from a tree or scooping a salmon from the stream.[64] God provided apples and salmon for the use and enjoyment of all humans, but apples or salmon became the property of those individuals who labored to obtain them. Such a doctrine—that property "in wild animals can be acquired only by possession"[65]— contrasted starkly with Northwest Coast Native legal doctrines, which limited use by demarcating property boundaries and discouraging open competition for finite resources. One American fisheries agent tried, with some degree of futility, to impress upon Native fishers in southeastern Alaska in the 1890s that "their occupancy of a home on the bank does not, as they claim, extend their property rights over the waters, which must be maintained free for all, under the restrictions of the law."[66]

The Anglo-American doctrine promised "open access" to all who were willing to expend effort; it also promised the overexploitation of the fisheries, since profit-seeking individuals had little incentive to limit their harvest of common resources. This dilemma—labeled the "tragedy of the commons" by ecologist Garrett Hardin and the "fisherman's problem" by historian Arthur McEvoy—was not the inevitable result of common property, but rather the inevitable result of common-property resources *within a laissez-faire economic system.*[67] The result, in the late nineteenth century, was that commercial fishers waged an all-out assault on the salmon resources of Alaska, engaging in the kind of cutthroat competition described by a Bureau of Fisheries agent in 1894: "Rather than allow A to make a good haul of fish, B will dam the stream and prevent the ascent of the salmon, or C will destroy the fish already on the spawning grounds and thus destroy the crop which would otherwise appear off the mouth of the stream four years hence."[68] Another government report described competition so fierce "that at times one cannery will catch and destroy tens of thousands of fish which they are unable to can rather than allow the rival cannery's fishermen to catch them."[69]

Such attitudes—along with the destruction of salmon habitat by mining, agriculture, logging, and urbanization—had by the 1860s already depleted the nascent salmon-canning industry on the Sacramento River in California. The Hume brothers, New England transplants who pioneered salmon-canning technology and the use of Chinese labor on the Sacramento, took their ingenuity and their low-paid Chinese cannery workers north to the Columbia River in 1866, where they sparked the rise of the Pacific Northwest's first great industry.[70] Like other western enterprises in the nineteenth century, especially mining and logging, the salmon-canning boom at first offered tremendous opportunity for a relatively small investment to both fishers and canners. As competition increased and salmon runs were depleted, however, securing one's "pack" of salmon and competing on an international market required increasing capital investment, both on the fishing grounds and inside the canneries themselves, where labor-saving machinery such as can-making machines, filling machines, and fish-butchering machines (like the "iron-chink," named for the Asian workers it replaced) were introduced in the late-nineteenth and early-twentieth centuries.[71] Like western mining, which progressed from the individualistic "placer" phase to the corporate and capital-intensive "hard rock" phase, the fisherman's frontier, in historian Vernon Carstensen's words, became "characterized by relatively large scale organization and absentee ownership; it was seasonal, it depended on transient labor, and it sought a world market."[72]

Statistics, albeit abstract, provide a sense of the industry's frenetic growth, unbounded competition, and insatiable appetite for salmon. In 1873 there were eight canneries on the Columbia, and within a decade the number had grown to thirty-nine.[73] From 1866 to 1883 production increased from 4,000 cases (a case consisting of forty-eight one-pound cans) to nearly 630,000 cases, most of which were exported to England, Australia, and Central America.[74] A visitor to the region in the 1880s observed the prodigious pace of extraction and processing that characterized the bustling seasonal industry: "There are twenty-six canneries [in Astoria], and some of them are running nights to keep even with the catch, and you count as many more of these manufactories from here to the Cascades. The boats engaged in this traffic dot the river for ninety miles and the nets are so thickly scattered over the lower part of the Columbia, that vessels with difficulty pick their way among them. . . . [B]y a law of the State these nets cannot be set on Sunday, so these luckless fish can ascend the streams unmolested for twenty-four hours."[75]

Along with this fleet of gillnetters the canneries employed fish wheels in the harvesting process. Thirty or forty feet in diameter and fixed to the shore or tied to a scow and placed in channels with swift-moving currents, these devices rotated on an axle powered by the river current and scooped up migrating salmon in wire nets. Brutally efficient, fish wheels "literally pumped fish out of the river" day and night, catching an average of twenty thousand pounds of salmon a day during peak season.[76] Overfishing—along with the destruction of salmon habitat—contributed to the decline of the great Columbia River salmon runs by the 1880s. It was then that salmon fishers and industrialists began to look northward to Alaska for the next great frontier of natural abundance.

In the remoteness of Alaska, few obstacles stood in the way of the industry's growth. Government regulators did not begin visiting the region until the early 1890s, and even then they could scarcely cover the region's vast fishing grounds. Nor did settlement and development impinge upon salmon-spawning grounds, as they had on the Sacramento and Columbia rivers. Alaska's only drawback was the absence of a large resident workforce, but this was overcome by importing Asian and Euro-American laborers from San Francisco or Seattle and, in southeastern Alaska, by hiring Native American fishermen and cannery workers. The industry catapulted from two canneries in 1878 to thirty-seven by 1889, packing nearly 720,000 cases in that year alone, significantly more than produced on the Columbia. By 1899, Alaska's industry was producing over a million cases per summer, and by 1901 its output had surpassed two million.[77] By then, the Pacific Coast salmon industry, propelled by Alaska's bumper yields, was exporting over twenty-seven million pounds of salmon (worth more than $2.5 million) to Africa, Asia, Europe, and South America.[78] Alaska's remote fishing frontier was now part of the global market economy.

As in other industries throughout the U.S. economy, fierce competition in the Alaska salmon-canning industry led to industrial consolidation during the 1890s. In 1892 eighteen industrialists entered their twenty-eight canneries and packing companies into a cooperative arrangement known as the Alaska Packing Association.[79] Within a year they created another, more permanent organization that merged twenty-nine canneries into the Alaska Packers Association (APA).[80] By 1894 the corporation had purchased sixteen steam launches and nineteen steamers in its march to control every aspect of the industry.[81] At its peak from 1893 to 1903, APA production comprised 68 percent of the Alaskan salmon-canning industry's total output, contributing 80 percent of that productivity from 1894 to 1899.[82]

By the turn of the twentieth century the APA and a few other corporations completely dominated Alaska's canned-salmon market. Like other western industries salmon canning in Alaska became colonial in nature—"outside" capital exploited local resources, including salmon and labor, and exported their profits at the end of each season while leaving precious little behind. As one fisheries agent put it, "The canning factories in Alaska are owned by three or four corporations in San Francisco, who have mil-

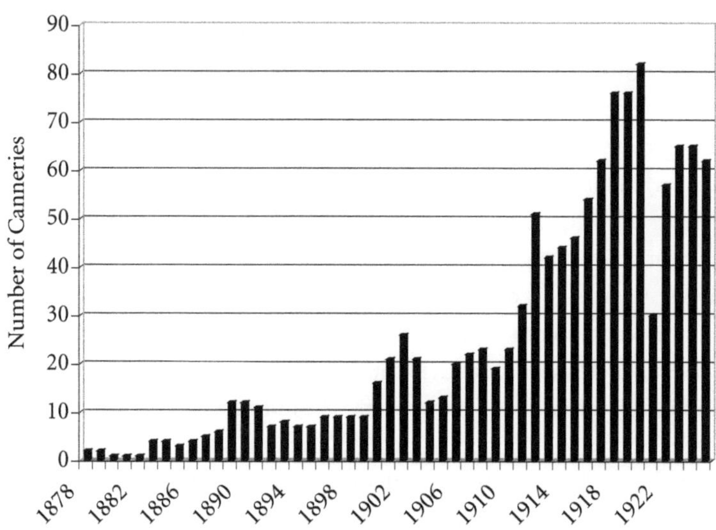

FIG. 2.3 Canneries in Southeast Alaska, 1878–1925. After a period of consolidation during the 1890s, the number of salmon canneries grew dramatically in the era immediately before and during World War I. SOURCE: *Cobb 1930: 572–73.*

lions invested in the salmon-canning industry, but who have no interest in the development of Alaska, and who, as a matter of fact, do not add one dollar to the wealth of the young Territory from which they take millions of dollars annually."[83] Salmon industrialists often perceived themselves as swashbuckling frontiersmen—and indeed they were pioneers, bringing a new industry to the Alaskan "wilderness." But like pioneers before them, they succeeded less in creating something altogether "new" than in transplanting the technologies, labor systems, and attitudes of nineteenth-century laissez-faire capitalism to Alaska. The result would be an industry that favored large corporations over small entrepreneurs, that reduced even "independent" fishermen to wage workers, and that transformed nature into quick profits for absentee owners and investors. This belief in unlimited resources and the consequences of unregulated competition also led to overexploitation of salmon resources in Alaska.

In Southeast Alaska the trajectory of the industry was not as dramatic as in central or western Alaska, primarily because red, or sockeye, salmon was the species most desired by canners, but it was the least abundant kind in the region. There were never more than six canneries until 1889, when the number doubled to twelve (see figure 2.3). For three years about a dozen

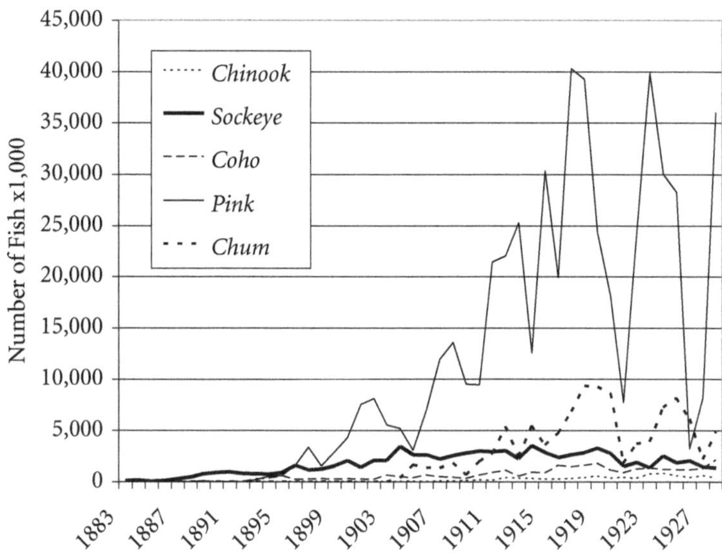

FIG. 2.4 Southeast Alaska salmon harvest by species, 1883–1928. Pink salmon harvests surpassed sockeye in 1896 and continued to grow in the years approaching World War I. Sockeye remained the most prized species, however, and was still pursued with great intensity. SOURCE: *Alaska Department of Fish and Game, "Historical Salmon Harvest and Value Charts, 1878–2003," Zephyr database.*

canning operations produced around 150,000 cases of sockeye salmon per year.[84] The number of canneries declined in the early 1890s as mergers consolidated the industry, but after 1896 cannery production steadily increased as canners began to pack more pink salmon, especially in the years approaching World War I (see figure 2.4). By 1902 twenty-six canneries produced nearly 1 million cases of salmon; by 1912 fifty-one canneries produced over 2 million cases; by 1918 seventy-six canning operations packed nearly 3.5 million cases, each case containing forty-eight pounds of processed salmon.

On the surface such production numbers indicate a healthy fishery—or at least a fishery that was not in decline before 1920. But such a large increase in salmon production did not necessarily indicate that salmon populations were steadily abundant, but rather that the fishing industry had expanded its effort and intensity. This was especially true for the treasured sockeye, which canneries purchased from fishermen for seven cents per fish, while they paid only one cent—or less—for pinks.[85] Furthermore, most of the increase reflected the fact that canners were packing more pink salmon as sockeye were less easily obtained. "Canneries have multiplied, new waters have been explored, and men and gear enormously increased, [but] individual instances . . . of total extinction or immense depreciation of fisheries are unhappily plentiful," observed one government agent in 1899. "In southeastern Alaska," he noted, "the [sockeye] pack does not hold its own and many establishments have closed."[86] The naturalist George Bird Grinnell, who visited southeastern Alaska in the same year, similarly explained that "if one inquires of an individual connected with the salmon industry in Alaska something about their numbers, he is at once told of the millions found there, and informed that the supply is inexhaustible." However, if one continued his inquiries, according to Bird, he would find that "it now takes far longer to secure a given number of fish than it used to, and that the fishermen are obliged to travel much farther from the cannery than formerly to secure their catch."[87]

This expansion of fishing intensity proceeded with little government regulation. Congress implemented rudimentary laws for the Alaska fisheries in 1889, 1896, and 1906. The Bureau of Fisheries—located in the Treasury Department until 1903, the Department of Commerce and Labor from 1903 to 1913, and then the Commerce Department from 1913 to 1939—sent two to three inspectors to Alaska yearly from 1892 through the 1910s, but they were charged with the impossible task of patrolling more than four thousand miles of shoreline on cannery steamers, mail boats, and the occasional Indian canoe. This total lack of oversight encouraged a laissez-faire environment where even the most basic fishery regulations, such as the weekly "closed" day or the prohibition of "dams and barricades" in streams, were routinely ignored by fishermen and industrialists. "It must be admitted that the laws and regulations pertaining to Alaska salmon fisheries are very generally disregarded, and that they do not prevent the illegal capture of fish," lamented U.S. Fish Commission inspector Jefferson Moser in 1899.[88]

The fisheries agents who surveyed the territory in those years recorded numerous fishing violations, from nets and traps planted directly in salmon spawning beds, to dams, fences, and barricades blocking salmon streams, like the one erected by the Alaska Packers Association cannery in Loring that stretched "clear across from bank to bank." "That fence had been there for years," noted fisheries agent Joseph Murray in 1895, "and the salmon running up against it in their efforts to enter the stream every year for purposes of reproduction, were caught and canned until the regular supply was exhausted."[89] Federal regulators lacked the resources, and the often the will, to punish violators, who for their part usually had ample time to pull barricades or nets from the fishing grounds by the time conservation officials arrived anyway. Furthermore, until the 1920s fisheries laws were so permissive that even legal operations could do certain damage to fish stocks. In 1899 special agent William Ballard observed that even without illegal barricades, APA fishermen at Loring had "stretched their nets across the stream, so that not only were others prevented from catching fish, but the salmon were even cut off from their spawning grounds in the lake."[90] Industrial fish traps, the most destructive—and productive—fishing devices, were also quite legal.

Commercial fishers imported three primary types of commercial gear to Southeast Alaska in the late nineteenth century: gillnets, purse-seines, and fish traps. The first two devices were so-called movable gear, operated by "cannery fishermen" or local "independents," Native American and white. Industrial fish traps—fixed pilings and netting placed in the path of migrating salmon—were owned almost exclusively by large canning companies and operated by company wage workers. Traps became the most efficient and controversial method of catching salmon. The controversy over traps sprung primarily from the fact that they were anchored, or "fixed," in place. In the ocean commons, where fish were supposedly free for the taking and property rights were granted to no one, fixed gear—according to gillnetters and purse-seiners—monopolized choice fishing locations and mocked the Anglo tradition of an open fishery. Yet stationary devices had long been used in fisheries on both the Atlantic and Pacific coasts.

On the Columbia River gillnetters battled fixed-gear operators throughout the late nineteenth and early twentieth centuries. Those debates, pitting independent "producers" against "capitalists," foreshadowed later battles over fish traps in Alaska. Gillnetters and purse-seiners despised industrial traps because of their ruthless efficiency and their labor-saving qualities. Traps, unlike fishermen, could fish around the clock without complaint or collective action. By relying primarily on fish traps, corporations like the Alaska Packers Association liberated themselves from inefficient and independent small-boat fishermen and extended near complete control over the labor of fishing (see figure 2.5). For these reasons fishermen in Alaska joined their counterparts on the Columbia in labeling fish-trap operators "capitalists" who "perverted work by using machines to plunder nature and displace human labor."[91]

The image of demonic industrial contrivances destroying nature and reducing the producing classes to dependency is ironic, given that industrial fish traps as a technology were little changed from those operated by

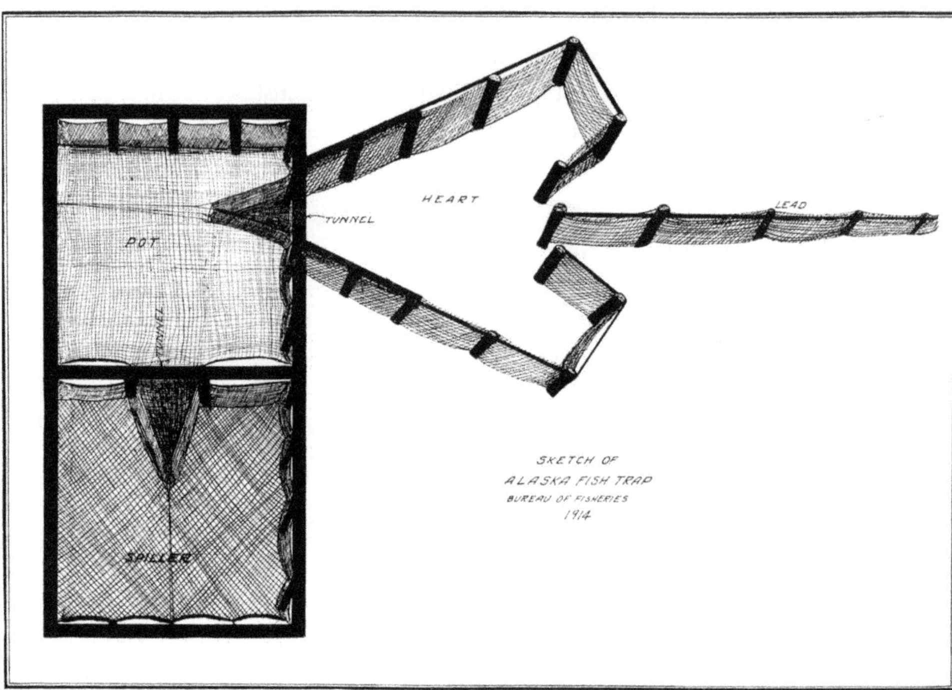

FIG. 2.5 Fish traps were stationary devices that took advantage of two powerful natural forces: the force of tides and the homing instincts of migrating salmon. SOURCE: *Jones 1915: 12.*

aboriginal fishermen for hundreds of years. Both aboriginal and industrial fish traps consisted of woodwork scaffolding that harnessed the energy of tides and the natural spawning impulses of salmon. The major difference between aboriginal and industrial forms was their placement: Native fish traps were always constructed in rivers, streams, or tidal zones, whereas industrial fish traps, although sometimes constructed near river mouths, were forced by government regulation further out into bays and channels, where, in the words of an Indian fishermen, "every shore line that's a natural route for fish to travel to the streams where they go to spawn [became] lined with fish traps."[92] Considering that salmon took the same route home to their birth streams every year, the fixed salmon trap—whether erected in rivers or bays—made sense. Industrial fishers understood this, as did Native fishermen before them.

Although despised by small-boat fishermen, commercial fish traps were not the perennial machine in the garden, alienating man from nature. They were an industrial apparatus, but fish traps at work were also a consummate meshing of man and nature, industry and elements. They were free from churning gears and belching smoke. They were quiet, motionless devices that simply channeled nature's bounty into their enclosures (see figure 2.6). For the company watchman, stationed in his tiny shack on the edge of a trap and surrounded only by the sounds of wind and sea, life ebbed and flowed with the cycles of tide and the patterns of fish migration. Only when the cannery steamer arrived to transfer salmon from the trap's "spiller" to a wooden scow did the fish trap become a machine of industrial productivity. Then, surrounded by men, boats, and the smoke and holler of marine engines, the sea became a roar of men, machines, and flailing fish. At those times wood, mesh, tides, and human labor were transformed into what one Indian fisherman called the "great big machinery that catches fish."[93]

Industrial traps yielded tremendous volumes of fish. In 1906, for example, the Anan Creek commercial salmon trap near Ketchikan caught more than a million fish, while approximately fifteen seining crews in the same area netted less than one hundred thousand salmon.[94] Stationary traps, however, required large capital investments and also had to be rebuilt yearly, as winter storms and ice floes took their toll. Such costs made trap-fishing prohibitive for most canneries, until 1907, when J. R. Heckman invented the "floating salmon trap." Heckman's traps were not only cheaper to construct and purchase, but they could also be beached during the winter to avoid damage and could be towed to different locales to maximize their catch. The first floating trap, installed at Port Higgins, ten miles from Loring in what was considered poor fishing waters, took 20,000 fish on its initial day of operation and "yielded in 24 days no less than 500,000 salmon, of various kinds."[95] The remarkable success of this trial induced the Alaska Packers Association to order five traps for the 1908 season.[96]

Denied the use of their upriver traps, Indian fishers became outspoken opponents of commercial traps. Indeed, the impact of fish traps on the Indian salmon fishery was dramatic. Traps forced Indian fishers—as well as white "independent" fishermen—to fish in less productive fishing areas "beyond the trap locations where the salmon had not yet begun to congregate into definite schools and runs."[97] The result, as Tlingit fisherman Powell Charles recalled, was that fish traps forced them from "inside fishing [near streams and river mouths] to outside fishing [in open ocean waters]." Such a

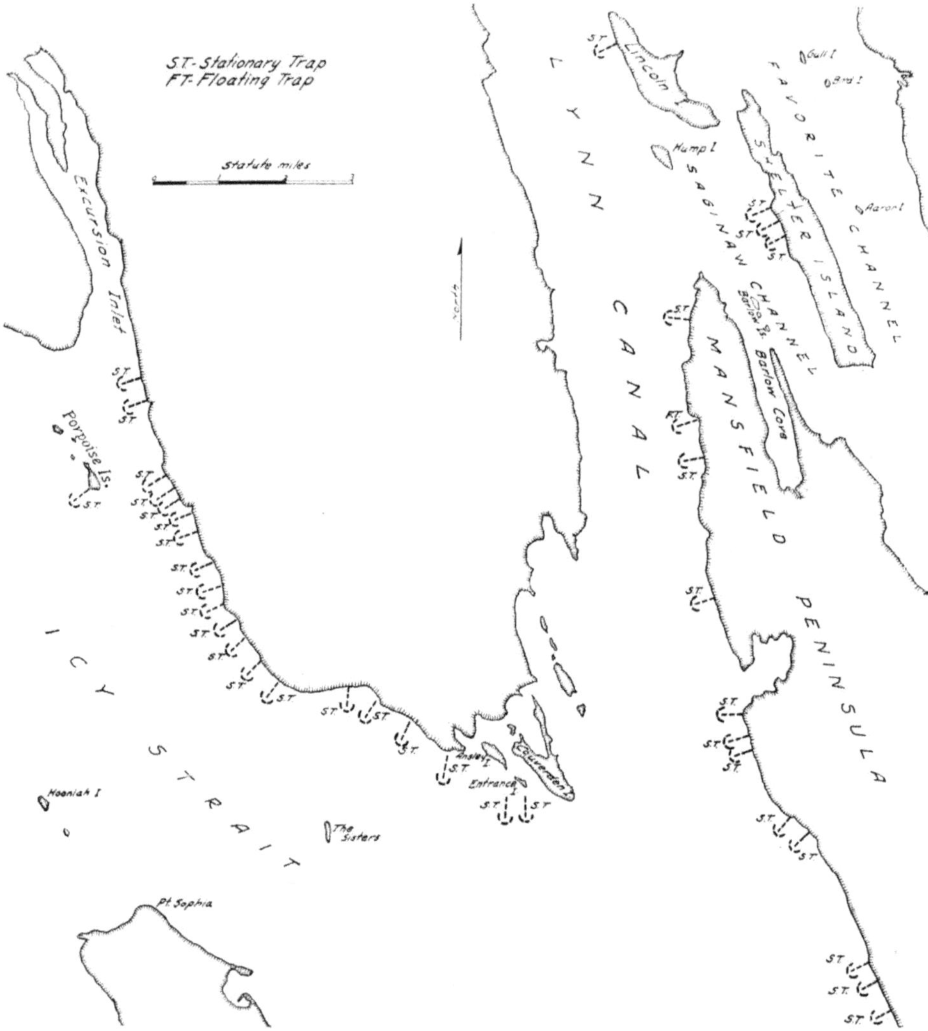

Part of Icy Strait region, showing 37 fish traps operated in 1914.

FIG. 2.6 Fish traps operating in the Icy Strait region, 1914. Stationed along the shores in prime fishing locations, these fish traps in Icy Strait and Lynn Canal pushed small-boat fishermen from their accustomed fishing spots. SOURCE: *Jones 1915: 14.*

transition made it hard on all Indian fishermen, but it especially affected those who could not afford to buy motor-powered fishing boats. "Those of us that could go out with power boats found places out there [in the outside waters]," he remembered, "but those that had weak boats—poor boats—could not make those places."[98]

A 1908 article in the *Tlingit*, an Indian newspaper published at the Sitka Training School, called fish traps "simply another means of taking all the wealth of Alaska's salmon away from the people and placing it in the hands of [a] few men." If canneries continued to use them, the author warned, "it is only a matter of a few years until the salmon of Alaska will be a thing of the past."[99] Indeed, by the 1920s most Indians believed that "the [sockeye] salmon is a thing of the past in the rivers where [the Tlingit] once caught them for his children to eat. The salmon are now caught in large traps before they go up the river to spawn. So the Indian must go hungry because the traps get the fish first."[100]

The commercial fishery, with its large canneries and industrial traps, was not only characterized by incredible productivity, but also by incredible waste. Because pink salmon were the least desirable species for canners, but the most abundant one in southeastern Alaska, "tens of thousands" of pinks, in the words of Jefferson Moser, "were hauled on the banks and left to decay."[101] George Dalton, a Tlingit who worked for the Superior cannery in Tenakee from 1914 to 1916, remembered that "often they would throw away everything but the Reds. . . . [T]he whole bay Tenakee Inlet was just full of sour fish. . . . That's the beginning of the dying off of the salmon . . . They just threw [them] away."[102] George Bird Grinnell likened the "particularly wasteful" practices of the industry, especially the practice of salting salmon bellies but wasting the remainder of the fish, to "the old time method of killing buffalo for their tongues alone, and the more recent one of killing elk and deer for their hides or heads or hams."[103]

While boosters continued to insist that the volume of salmon in Alaska's waters was infinite, from the 1890s on others warned that the industry's "methods are such as, if continued, will very soon destroy them."[104] Speaking of southeastern Alaska in particular, fisheries agent George Tingle concluded in 1896 that "many streams in this portion of Alaska are being fished to excess, and many already show unmistakable signs of depletion or exhaustion. Without a doubt, if the present practice of catching every fish possible is carried on for a few years longer, the canning industry will be seriously crippled."[105]

While Tlingit and Haida fishers had maintained control of the salmon fishery during the period of the maritime fur trade and Russian settlement, the commercial fishing industry was destroying the system of clan house–based fisheries management that had been developed over thousands of years. Swept away in the flood of canneries, machines, fish traps, and immigrant laborers who inundated the salmon fishery was the sense of moderation and intimacy that had characterized Native fishing. The new industrial regime began to deplete sockeye streams, which for so long had been coveted and controlled by Indian clan leaders. In doing so, the industry threatened not only a primary food source, but also the ability of Indian peoples to control salmon resources for commercial and social uses. The threat posed was ecological, but it was also cultural. "These streams, under their own administration, for centuries have belonged to certain families or clans settled in the vicinity, and their rights in these streams have never been infringed upon until the advent of the whites," noted Moser in 1898. He then summarized Native concerns regarding the commercial fishery: "They claim the white man is crowding them from their homes, robbing them of their ancestral rights, taking away their fish by shiploads; that their streams must soon become exhausted; that the Indian will have no supply to maintain himself and family, and that starvation must follow."[106]

Federal fisheries agents heard many such complaints from Native peoples throughout the late nineteenth and early twentieth centuries. Some agents, like Moser, were sympathetic. Others, like Howard Kutchin, simply recited the seemingly egalitarian doctrine of the open-access fishery. Although Indians were "wrong about the possession of privileges superior to those of the white men," Kutchin explained to Tlingit fishers on the Chilkoot River in 1901, "they could fish under the law wherever the white men fished" and "in all respects their rights were absolutely equal" to non-Indian fishers.[107] The principle of "equal rights" to the salmon fishery was little consolation to a people whose previous system of regulating the fisheries was based on the delineation of strict property rights to fishing sites. It was as if hunter-gatherers colonized Kansas and determined that the landscape of privately owned farms would become an open-access hunting grounds in which the farmers could compete equally with their invaders for game. It is no surprise that Tlingit and Haida fishers rejected the open-access doctrine.

Indian resistance to the common-property doctrine imposed by American fishers began immediately after the establishment of the first canneries near Sitka and Klawock in the late 1870s. At Klawock in 1881, Tlingit fishers apparently "drove off the cannery seiners who were taking fish too near their summer village."[108] In 1882 a naval commander in Alaska warned his superiors about escalating tensions between Indian and white fishermen, describing how Indian fishers "threatened to cut the seines if any fishing is done except by themselves."[109] Sometimes conflict was averted when non-Indian commercial fishers recognized Indian rights to salmon streams by paying clan leaders for fishing privileges, as had long been the custom in Native society. Charles Webster Demmert remembered that in the 1890s, the cannery superintendent at Klawock "used to pay Chief Tekite . . . so that [the cannery fishermen] could fish near that creek."[110]

Indian stream "owners" sometimes intimidated white fishermen into paying for the rights to fish tribal waters. Tlingit fisherman Shoutshon Stuteen described how in 1903 his grandfather confronted an intruding fisherman with two alternatives: either hand over a hundred dollars or "if you put your seine out, I will cut it with a knife."[111] When such threats were not heeded, Indians often did resort to violence in defense of traditional fishing areas. In 1890, for example, Indians from Klukwan and Haines objected to an industrial fish trap erected by the APA cannery at Pyramid Harbor because it blocked traditional fishing sites in Lynn Canal. When the cannery refused to remove the trap, Tlingit fishermen, armed with guns, destroyed it.[112]

Sometimes white fishers respected Indian claims to tribal fishing sites, but Americans in general were less interested in bending to Native American customs than in forcing their own laws over Native fishers. Industrialists and non-Indian fishermen often simply ignored Native protests or, if they felt threatened, called on the American military to protect what they believed was their inalienable right to participate in an open-access fishery. The American military presence was much lighter in Alaska than in the lower West, but it was not averse to intimidation or the use of force against peoples it generally regarded as "both warlike and treacherous."[113] In 1869 the U.S. Army shelled the Tlingit village of Kake—destroying about thirty houses and several canoes—when Indians killed two white merchants to avenge the death of two tribesmen at the hands of army sentries in Sitka.[114] In 1882 the U.S. Navy bombed and destroyed the Tlingit village of Angoon after Indians had seized property belonging to the Northwest Trading Company and demanded payment for the death of a Native shaman killed in a whaling accident.[115]

In 1890 the military came to the aid of white commercial fishermen seeking to exercise their right to the open-access commercial fishery in Sitkoh Bay, a traditional Tlingit fishing site where two clans claimed aboriginal ownership. The clans, who had previously fought over control of the bay, launched a "common [defense] against the Americans," claiming for themselves an "exclusive right to fish" in waters that whites considered "open and navigable."[116] When white fishermen, working for the Baranoff Packing Company, began fishing the bay, they encountered over a hundred Indians armed with guns. Responding to the company's appeal for help, the navy dispatched Ensign Robert E. Coontz with orders to "protect the lives and property of the whites with the full force under your command."[117]

Coontz, accompanied by Marines and an interpreter, found the white fishermen "with their seines and everything ready to haul, and a band of one hundred and twenty-five Indians . . . armed with shotguns, rifles, and other implements of war."[118] Indian fishermen refused to allow the outsiders to cast their nets until each white fisher had paid them twenty-five cents a day. Coontz succeeded in arresting and taking twenty Tlingit "leaders" to Sitka for trial. Before leaving, Coontz "ordered the white men to start fishing" and "on the first haul of the seine they took in more than a thousand salmon."[119] With the power of the U.S. military protecting their right to an open fishery, white fishers were free to exploit tribal fishing grounds with impunity. Indians might protest, but they were unable to stop the process by which clan-owned territories were usurped by the capitalist open-access regime. By the late 1890s, according to Jefferson Moser, there were no longer any "legal rights or title to any fishing-grounds in Alaska except what force or strategy furnish."[120]

When resistance failed to protect their property rights, some Indians appealed to the federal government for protections, even calling for reservations to be extended to Alaska. One of the earliest appeals came in 1890 when a number of Tlingit clan leaders, complaining of "the White man's usurpation of Indian fishing grounds as well as other grievances," drafted a letter to President Benjamin Harrison asking for self-government and the protection of their land and fishing rights, or at least payment "for their relinquishment."[121] In 1898, Indian leaders met with territorial governor James G. Brady and implored the U.S. government to protect their rights to "places where we can hunt and prepare fish." Chief Kah-du-shan explained how whites "began to build canneries and take the creeks away from us," even though "we told them these creeks belonged to us." He concluded by asking the government to "return our creeks and hunting grounds that white people have taken away from us." Another elder suggested that the American government give Tlingits reservations "where we could live by ourselves and have our property and homes where the white people could not bother us."[122]

Such pleas for isolation and a return to traditional living may conform with popular stereotypes of noble Indians retreating from the advance of modern civilization and defending their heritage, but they do not fully capture the extent to which Tlingit and Haida peoples willingly and successfully adapted to the market economy in general and the commercialization of the fisheries in particular. The story is not a simple one of powerful colonizers and victimized Indians. While their options may have been limited, Indian responses to the commercialization of the fisheries reflected the resilient power of Native culture. From the inception of the canning industry, Indians seized upon economic opportunities as both fishermen and cannery workers, often revealing a business sense that rivaled that of whites.

In 1878, Tlingits in Sitka refused to let Chinese workers disembark from a ship owned by the Cutting Packing Company, when they learned that the cannery—the first in all of Alaska—intended to employ Asian rather than Native workers. The standoff ended only when an agent from the U.S. Treasury Department convinced the cannery boss to "buy all his fish from the Indians" and to use Chinese labor only in the production of tin cans. If the Indians learned how to make tin cans, the company promised to hire only Native workers.[123] Sheldon Jackson, a Presbyterian missionary who would later administer federal education programs for Alaska Natives (and who would also found the Sitka Industrial Training School for Indians), observed the same Sitka cannery in 1879. He described how "all the operations, from the catching of salmon to the boxing of the cans ready for market, were carried on by Indians under the supervision of white men." He marveled: "It was a new sight to see over a hundred Indian men working as steadily and intelligently as the workmen in an Eastern factory." Jackson saw such labor as "a partial solution of the problem [of] how to elevate and civilize the Indians."[124]

The second cannery constructed in Alaska, at Klawock on Prince of Wales Island, also became known for its reliance on Native labor. "The fish are caught almost entirely by the natives," observed a census agent in 1890: "They constitute the principal help employed on the launches, and, aside from a dozen white men employed, native men, women, and children do the entire work."[125] Although their "ancient rights have now been taken from the natives by force," wrote George Bird Grinnell, "they are still anxious to get what they can from the fishing."[126]

Without a large resident workforce, canneries relied on Native labor as a central feature of the workforce in southeastern Alaska. In a gendered division of labor that resembled the precontact Indian fishery, men fished while women and children processed the salmon in the canneries. Indian fishermen, who constituted the majority of the region's commercial fishers through 1910, fished with traditional methods or rented modern commercial gear from canneries. It was not uncommon, in the early years of the commercial fishery, for Native fishers to take salmon with canoes, bark lines, wooden hooks, gaffs, dipnets, or aboriginal fish weirs and then transport their catch great distances to the canneries. Census agent Miner Bruce observed Tlingit fishermen routinely making the sixty-mile trip from Boca de Quadra Inlet to the APA cannery at Loring "in a little over a day with their canoes laden with salmon."[127] Although acquiring sufficient capital was harder for Native fishers than whites, they too began to mechanize their fishing operations in the twentieth century. By 1913, Indian fishermen in southeastern Alaska owned approximately 225 gas-powered fishing boats worth an estimated $150,000.[128]

During the 1890s such participation earned Native workers anywhere from one to four dollars a day inside the plants to ten dollars a day fishing during the peak season. "The work is not steady," observed Moser in 1898, "but for the season the native women make from $80 to $100, and the better class of men $200."[129] Such wages, in his view, left the Indian "better situated now than he was before the canneries were established." Although Moser admitted that pressures on the fishery made it harder for Natives to put up their yearly supply of dried fish, he was convinced that "if he [the Native] is at all industrious he can earn sufficient during a canning season to support himself and his family during the winter."[130] Fisheries agent George Tingle likewise believed that the commercial fishery afforded Native peoples "with the means to enjoy life better than formerly." Despite the fact that "bitter complaint may be heard from the native regarding the taking away of his food supply," Tingle concluded that "industrious" Natives were more than compensated for their losses by the prospect of earning "$100 per month by supplying the canners with fish or working in the cannery, thereby enabling him to clothe himself comfortably and provide his family with what are regarded in civilized communities as the necessaries of life."[131]

Indian industriousness appealed to the ethnocentrism of white observers, who depicted Indians in southeastern Alaska, in contrast to Native peoples in the lower West, as shining examples of the transformative power of both capitalism and Christianity (see figure 2.7). White Americans praised Alaskan Indians as "intelligent, honest and good workers; an accumulative, thrifty people, quick and anxious to improve their condition." The Sitka *Alaskan* applauded them for having "established themselves as an independent, self-supporting population . . . wholly through their own exertions and industry, [and] without any material assistance from the general government."[132] The famous naturalist John Muir, who visited southeastern Alaska in 1879, remarked: "It was easy to see that [Alaska Indians] differed greatly from the typical American Indian of the interior of this continent." Especially, he noted, "in [their] being willing to work."[133] "Unlike the Indian tribes of our Western States, most of which have treaties with the government by which they are supported," wrote Grinnell, "these dwellers along the Alaska coast depend for their subsistence wholly on their own exertions and draw their food largely from the sea."[134] Indian reformer Vincent Colyer, who surveyed conditions among Alaska Natives in 1869, described them as "more intelligent, more adaptable, and more industrious than other North American natives."[135]

While such glowing depictions undoubtedly reflected the extent to which Indians were successfully navigating the market economy, talk of self-supporting Indians also served as a ready argument against extending the federal reservation system to Alaska, which, many non-Indians feared, would quarantine the region's natural resources and stymie industrial enterprise. The Sitka *Alaskan* reflected this popular view, praising Alaskan Indians for their industriousness and warning against "anything looking towards land indemnity or money payment or tribal reservation."[136] Most Alaskans believed that the creation of Indian reservations would threaten white property claims, prohibit the unlimited exploitation of Alaska's natural resources, and make Alaska's thrifty Indians idle and dependent. In the 1890s the missionary William Duncan called on the U.S. government to "proclaim all salmon streams Indian reservations" and "only allow fishing in them to proper persons and under proper regulations."[137] But other missionaries, like Sheldon Jackson and James G. Brady, saw the reservation system as a hopelessly corrupt breeding ground of laziness and heathenish tribalism, which threatened to halt the material and moral advancement of Native peoples who already were "self-supporting and of keen commercial instincts."[138]

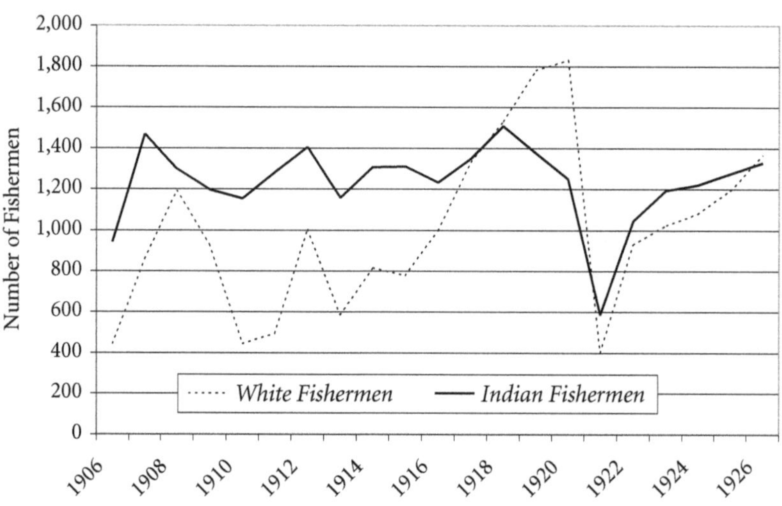

FIG. 2.7 *Indian and white fishermen in the canned-salmon industry, 1906–1926. Indian fishermen were integral to the salmon-canning industry in southeastern Alaska, generally outnumbering white fishers in the late nineteenth and early twentieth centuries.* SOURCE: *Bower, Alaska Fishery and Fur-Seal Industries, 1906–1926 (titles and authors of these Bureau of Fisheries documents vary).*

What white Alaskans often failed to comprehend was that Indian acquisitiveness and adaptation reflected as much cultural persistence as it did cultural change. From potlatches to subsistence strategies, Indian tradition marched on. In fact, it was often the very activities lauded by reformers that contained the seeds of cultural continuity. Indians praised for being industrious and materialistic, for example, were often collecting silver dollars, bags of flour, or blankets for potlatch festivals, which continued well into the twentieth century. The same values that fueled Indian traders in the nineteenth-century fur trade—acquisitiveness and individualism balanced by reciprocity and social responsibility—were likewise driving Indian participation in the market economy. For Native peoples, taking part in commercial activities was not a zero-sum proposition. Aboriginal ethics guided their adaptations to the marketplace.

Nowhere was this intermingling of tradition and innovation more prevalent than in salmon fishing, where Natives continued to visit ancestral fishing sites and "put up" traditional foods for winter consumption, while at the same time they fished commercially and worked in canneries. Indian efforts to protect their traditional fishing grounds were motivated as much from a desire to maximize commercial fishing opportunities as to protect their subsistence food supply from overexploitation. This was the case on the Chilkoot and Chilkat rivers, where Native fishers continued to gaff salmon from canoes or platforms, little different than they had done for thousands of years, in order to sell them to the canneries, while at the same time they tried to prevent white commercial fishers from intruding on their fishing sites. One fisheries agent believed that "the Indians wish the whites stopped from fishing that the canneries might be forced, in all cases, to buy fish from them at an arbitrary price."[139] If true, it only underscored their longstanding desire to control tribal fishing grounds for purposes of both commerce and consumption.

The same observers who praised Indians for their eagerness to assimilate also described the persistence of Native subsistence economies. In the mid-1880s traveler Horace Briggs described how permanent Indians villages were vacated during the summer months, "for the males are away at work in mills and canneries, or *catching and drying fish for their food supply*."[140] A decade later, Moser made a similar observation: "The permanent Indian villages during the spring and summer months are practically deserted except by a few old people, the young men and women being away, living in camps and *curing their winter supply* during the spring, and when the canneries open, fishing for them or doing work about them."[141] Clearly, Tlingit and Haida peoples were able to balance subsistence strategies with commercial participation.

Native fishers were developing a strategy that twentieth-century anthropologists would label a "mixed subsistence-market economy."[142] Balancing production for household consumption with market relations made Native peoples in southeastern Alaska more resilient and adaptive. It also allowed them maximum freedom and mobility within the constraints of a colonized world. Unlike the immigrant laborers who were transported north by the canneries, Indians could move fluidly between wage work and subsistence lifestyles. "Their frequent boast," wrote Moser, "is that white men and Chinese must work to get something to eat, while the waters and the forests furnish the Indians with all they want." After making "sufficient wages to supply their personal wants and getting a few dollars ahead," Moser observed, the Indian "desire for hunting or fishing seizes them and they are apt to leave when they are most wanted."[143] This made Indian fishers more autonomous, but from the perspective of salmon canners it also made them more unreliable, insubordinate, and less easily controlled. Even at Klawock, where Indian labor dominated both the fishing and the cannery work, their unpredictability and insubordination made them a problematic labor force. This belief resulted in the cannery hiring more Chinese workers, "chiefly upon the ground of economy, but also because Chinese labor is more certain and more easily controlled."[144]

To "not be controlled" was unique for Native peoples in the American West by the turn of the century. Certainly Tlingit and Haida fishers no longer completely controlled their destinies. Their options were limited. But neither were they destroyed by American colonization. Like hunter-gatherers throughout the world, they resisted colonial processes when they could or, when outright resistance failed, creatively adapted to new circumstances, mixing older traditions with newfound ways. The persistence of a salmon fishing economy allowed Tlingits and Haidas the ability to make such choices. But increasingly those choices would be constrained by forces over which they had little control.

CULTURAL CHANGE AND ADAPTATION

The transformation that occurred in Southeast Alaska was not as dramatic as what had occurred in California, where Native populations collapsed, aboriginal landscapes were dramatically transformed, and the Native fishery was obliterated with "apocalyptic ferocity."[145] In Alaska's remote northern environment the salmon fishery survived into the twentieth century, and Native fishers did as well. But everything had changed. In a few short years the salmon fishery had passed from Indian to American control, and with that transition the social, cultural, and natural landscape of southeastern Alaska was permanently transformed. The local salmon fishery had become a global fishery, shaped by an international market. The new commercial fishery—because of the participation of Native fishers—still contained the cultural legacy of a deep past, but it was increasingly characterized by new technologies, new systems of labor, and new value systems—especially that of laissez-faire industrial capitalism. Shortly, it would be transformed by a new management regime implemented in the early twentieth century by federal resource managers. Chapter 3 examines the transition from laissez faire to government stewardship in the first half of the twentieth century as federal conservation officials tried to impose their own vision of order on Alaska's salmon fishery.

3 Federal Conservation, Fish Traps, and the Struggle to Control the Fishery, 1889–1959

Any practical fisherman knows more about fish than a whole army of book-learned-fish-commissioners. —*Petersburg Progressive*, 1914

Whatever his name may be . . . he is predestined when he accepts the position of Commissioner of Fisheries, to be a hated man. We are Americans, a free people in a free land, yet we are ruled by a dictator as surely as if we were controlled by the Nazi Government. Fishing is our life. When the salmon come in the spring, they bring with them the promise of food and clothing for the winter. . . . They are our life, yet they are controlled by an outsider who, when he takes his position, knows nothing about them and must learn from the ground up. . . . His power is absolute. His every whim is law. He can control our progress; make or break our prosperity with a word.—GEORGE B. CASE, Alaska Salmon Purse Seiners Union

In January 1904, President Theodore Roosevelt directed the U.S. Fish Commission to "make a thorough investigation of the salmon fisheries of Alaska" for the purpose of determining "the extent and causes of decline, if any; the effects of regulations, and the extent to which the laws are violated." The commission was also asked to assess the "necessity or desirability of salmon-hatching operations on the part of the General Government."[1] Roosevelt's interest in Alaska's salmon fisheries coincided with a sense of crisis among America's governing elite concerning the nation's store of natural resources, which, according to the president, were "in danger of exhaustion if we permit the old wasteful methods of exploiting them longer to continue."[2] Roosevelt became the icon of a movement that rejected laissez-faire development and increasingly turned toward federal stewardship of natural resources in the interest of both efficiency and sustainability.

By the late nineteenth century the extractive economies of the Far West—fishing, logging, and ranching—all suffered from rampant competition, falling prices, and resource depletion. Previously, the federal government had left western industries alone, confident that if laissez-faire capitalism did not always ensure rational growth, at least the frontier would provide an infinite cushion of natural resources for the expanding nation. By the 1890s, however, the nation had consumed its frontier, and industrial society exhibited an appetite beyond the wildest imaginations of preindustrial policy makers. It was in this context that Roosevelt and other Progressives began to call on the federal government to regulate and rationalize the extractive economies of the West in the name of "national efficiency." They believed that "unrestricted individualism" and the quest for "temporary and immediate profit" should yield to government-regulated "wise use."[3] The movement toward conservation reflected the optimistic spirit of the times and an almost mystical faith in the powers of science to solve human problems. By stewarding natural resources on the basis of rational management and scientific expertise, federal technocrats hoped to stabilize industries, ensure economic growth, and protect the long-term sustainability of natural resources.

Roosevelt and other conservationists believed that, in regulating and controlling public lands, they were acting for the *public good*. Federal resources managers, such as forester Gifford Pinchot, defined the public good in utilitarian terms, as "the greatest good for the greatest number for the longest time."[4] But in Alaska's salmon-canning industry, as in other western extractive economies, federal conservation raised questions about how the public interest would be defined and translated into policy. *Which* public would best be served by federal management? In Alaska would large "outside" corporations be the prime beneficiaries, or would the interests of local fishermen, Indian and white, also be served as the industry moved toward a new era of rationalism and efficiency? Would utilitarian standards that sought "the greatest good" for society be defined solely in terms of economic productivity, privileging efficient industrial fish traps over independent fishermen operating less efficient "movable gear"? Would federally enforced conservation marginalize or empower Indian fishers? Would federal prerogatives trump local concerns, as conservation managers increasingly defined the *public* as the *nonlocal* public? Would concerns for social equality guide conservation policies as much as desires for rationality and efficiency?

In Alaska these questions would be negotiated in a struggle among fishers (Indian and white), conservation officials, and industrialists that highlighted the social consequences of conservation policies and revealed the numerous cleavages that existed within the salmon fishery: local control versus federal authority; independent fishermen versus large "outside" corporations; movable gear (mostly purse-seines) versus "fixed gear" (fish traps); fishermen versus federal managers; and proponents of a conservation ethic rooted in social equality versus proponents of a conservation policy that emphasized rationality and efficiency.[5]

Conservation of the Alaska salmon fisheries, in other words, was not simply a heroic and disinterested movement of public-spirited and scientific-minded resource managers battling against the unrestrained and selfish exploitation of the natural world. It carried significant consequences for local populations and salmon populations. Moreover, conservation officials did not simply impose their wills unilaterally upon either people or nature. Fisheries managers tried—through artificial propagation and other methods—to simplify and rationalize the complex life cycles of salmon, but nature refused to be guided toward bureaucratic goals of efficiency and productivity. Fishers were even less easily managed. They resisted regulations, protested management policies, and clung to their unwieldy and inefficient traditions. Neither fish nor humans were easily controlled, and the behaviors of both were shaped by forces—instinct, climate, culture, tradition—beyond the reach of conservation managers. Fishery conservation in Alaska therefore became a contested terrain, as federal policies tried unsuccessfully to impose order and rationality upon fish populations and fishers. Fish responded in mysterious ways, waging what might be described, from the perspective of beguiled wildlife managers, as an unintended campaign of passive, nonviolent civil disobedience. Fishermen, both Indian and white, responded by challenging the right of regulators to control the commons and redefine the open-access fishery according to the dictates of federal conservation policy.

PLEASING CORPORATIONS AND IMPROVING UPON NATURE: THE SPIRIT OF FEDERAL REGULATION

In the late nineteenth century many voices began calling for government protection of Alaska's salmon fisheries. Emerging from an era of totally unrestrained competition, there was a growing sense that something needed to be done before the salmon disappeared and, worse, before "the capital put into the canneries must cease to yield any return."[6] Although many still insisted that it was "an utter impossibility to so fish the streams as to denude them of salmon life," others began speaking in apocalyptic tones.[7] The conservationist George Bird Grinnell, who visited Southeast Alaska in 1899, castigated salmon industrialists for their "grasping," "wasteful," and "thoughtlessly selfish" practices, warning that salmon, like the wild pigeons and buffalo before them, "were being destroyed at so wholesale a rate that before long the canning industry must cease to be profitable."[8] Jefferson Moser, commander of the U.S. Fish Commission (USFC) steamer the *Albatross*, which conducted scientific investigations of Alaska's salmon fisheries in the 1880s and 1890s, believed that if fisheries laws were not "amended and *enforced*, the time will come in the not very distant future when the canneries must suffer through their own actions."[9] William Duncan, a Presbyterian minister and founder of the Tsimshian village of Metlakatla at the southern edge of southeastern Alaska, lamented that the territory was "in danger of losing one of its greatest food supplies through cannery operations."[10]

The perceptions of Grinnell, Moser, and Duncan were reflective of an emerging Progressive worldview that was concerned with corporate accountability and increasingly looked to the federal government for solutions. All three men saw Alaska's fisheries crisis in similar terms: greedy and wasteful corporations were to blame, and federal conservation was the answer. Duncan proposed that "salmon streams be declared government property, and the fishing in them be absolutely controlled under Government regulations and by government agents." He advocated a comprehensive program of scientific conservation, encompassing a permit system based on "the capacity of the stream," and industrial quotas that limited cannery production and allowed for the natural reproduction of the species.[11]

No such comprehensive system of scientific management ever emerged during the period of federal control. Instead, early federal conservation efforts were piecemeal, haphazard, and underfunded. In fact, the primary characteristic of early regulation in the Alaskan salmon fisheries was that it was nearly nonexistent. There were no laws to regulate the fisheries until 1889, when Congress passed a bill to prevent "the erection of dams, barricades, or other obstructions in any of the rivers of Alaska."[12] Even then, no fisheries managers arrived to enforce the law until 1892, when Max Pracht, designated as the "Special Agent for the Protection of the Salmon Fisheries of Alaska," landed in Sitka after most of the salmon had already passed upstream or landed in tin cans. "Now that the salmon canneries along the

Alaska coast have secured their pack," quipped Sitka's *Alaskan*, "a special agent of the Treasury has arrived . . . to guard against infringements of the salmon fishing regulations."[13]

Pracht's arrival had been delayed by Congress, whose belated appropriation of funds forced him to wait in San Francisco until September, when he caught a steamer for southeastern Alaska. Upon arriving in Sitka, Pracht was entirely dependent on cannery operators for transportation. They shuttled him on company boats from cannery to cannery, where he met with industry owners and superintendents in prearranged meetings. If there were any fishery violators, Pracht certainly did not catch them off guard. Despite "damming" reports, he never caught anyone actually barricading the streams, but "evidences of such [obstructions] having been removed previous to my visit were found by me at a number of points."[14] Pracht's story encapsulated the failure of early federal efforts at fisheries regulation, which were hindered by three primary factors: the utter lack of resources to carry out effective management; the limitations of the fisheries laws themselves; and an overwhelming concern by conservation officials for economic productivity rather than the ecological health of the fishery.

From 1889 until 1939 federal regulation of the fisheries in the territory of Alaska was conducted by agents within the Treasury Department, the Department of Commerce and Labor, and the Department of Commerce, whereupon management responsibilities were transferred to the newly created Fish and Wildlife Service within the Department of the Interior. For its first fifty years, in other words, federal fisheries management in Alaska was directed by agencies whose primary responsibility was to promote and foster economic growth and development, not to restrict it, and whose primary clients were businessmen, not salmon or fishermen.[15] Even when early fisheries managers recommended restricting access to salmon resources, they always did so in a manner that was, in the words of one Alaska agent, "consistent with the best interests of all who have investments made, and business established in the territory."[16] This did not make them opposed to conservation. Rational use and long-term economic productivity stood at the core of the conservation ethic. But sustaining resources—not just industrial output—required a concern for the ecological condition of the resource never exhibited by Treasury Department agents, who consistently measured the health of the fishery solely in terms of canning productivity.

The prospects for an ecological approach to resource management increased after 1903, when the Bureau of Fisheries was created and Treasury Department agents were gradually replaced by a new breed of scientific regulators, epitomized by Barton Evermann, who became chief scientist of the Bureau of Fisheries in 1911. Although previous fisheries management was predicated primarily upon delivering to canners the largest volume of fish with a minimum of expense or government interference, Evermann began to call for more "intelligent regulations" that were based less on political expediency and more on a thorough scientific understanding of fish populations. He admitted that "the fundamental propositions on which legislation is based are hypothetical, deduced from the general knowledge and beliefs as to the various species of salmon and their relatives rather than inductions from known facts."[17]

In seeking to base fisheries regulations on good science rather than speculations or economic and political concerns, Evermann's efforts reflected the Progressive-era obsession with using science to create effective, rational government policy. Although they were often unsuccessful, bureaucrats and policy makers, like Evermann, challenged explicitly corrupt or inefficient "rule of thumb" practices and sought to reorganize the activities of both government and industry on the basis of efficiency and rationality. In the extractive economies of the American West this meant shaping public policy according to the scientific and utilitarian doctrine of maximum sustainable yield (MSY). The Forest Service, founded in 1907, spearheaded this strategy of resource management, which held simply that well-regulated harvests balanced by replanting could provide a yearly yield of timber forever. The same doctrine was applied to the salmon fisheries, which were also considered a renewable resource that, like trees or crops, could be controlled and managed on a sustainable basis.

According to the theory of MSY, the size of salmon populations was determined by two primary factors: fishing intensity and the reproductive capabilities of salmon stocks. To compensate for losses due to predation—and the human fishery was considered "simply another predator"—salmon produced an overabundance of offspring.[18] If fisheries managers could regulate harvests so as to take just the amount of salmon that were "surplus," leaving behind only the optimal number to maintain future runs at sustainable levels, they could create a stable fishery that would last forever. All they had to do was to calculate the maximum sustainable yield of each salmon run and limit fishing to that point, thereby allowing a certain amount of upriver "escapement," the term salmon managers used for the number of fish who reached the spawning grounds.

The theory was fine, but as a practical device for measuring salmon populations, MSY was nearly impossible for early fisheries managers to calculate. Before the use of more accurate (but by no means failsafe) modern methods—such as hydroacoustics, aerial surveying, floating fish weirs, and mark-recapture studies—fisheries managers could only guess at the size of salmon runs. Often they simply relied on hearsay reports from the field, such as in 1925, the first year the Fisheries Bureau was officially charged with calculating the numbers of fish that reached the spawning grounds. In that year fisheries agent Ward T. Bower reported that "persons in various localities in southeastern Alaska, including hunters, sports fishermen, and others, indicated that the escapements of spawning salmon were the best they had witnessed in years and reminded them of old times."[19]

Rudimentary salmon-counting weirs were not used until 1928, when Bureau of Fisheries employees built four salmon-counting stations in southeastern Alaska, a district that had over a thousand salmon streams.[20] These early picket devices allowed conservation officials to make predictions regarding the size of particular salmon runs, but they were highly inaccurate. Because they were useless during extremely high tides (often when the largest volumes of fish were migrating upstream), the weirs were "not operated throughout the duration of the run" and they allowed smaller fish to pass through the pickets uncounted. All of these problems, according to fisheries biologist Andy McGregor, meant that counting weirs in southeastern Alaska commonly missed "substantial portions of the escapement."[21] In the 1930s and beyond the Bureau of Fisheries still relied largely on the unscientific and unverifiable observations of stream watchmen like Herman J. West, who reported from Prince of Wales Island in the summer of 1932 that "I am unable to give an estimate of the total escapement but feel that the spawning areas are well stocked."[22]

On a philosophical level the MSY model of fisheries management represented a dramatic improvement over the laissez-faire doctrine that posited infinite resources and endless frontiers, but as fisheries historians Arthur McEvoy and Joseph Taylor have shown, regulators often failed to take into consideration the many factors beyond overfishing that affected the size of salmon runs, including the impact of logging, dams, and urban settlement, not to mention nonhuman variables such as cyclical shifts in ocean temperatures.[23] Without a complex understanding of either salmon life cycles or marine ecosystems, fisheries agents in Alaska simply credited fishery management on years of abundance and blamed overfishing during years of scarcity.[24] This allowed them an effective method of casting blame, but it did not make for rational fisheries policy.

Even if the early Alaska agents had been nuanced analysts of the salmon runs, even if they had been motivated as much by concern for salmon as for industrial output, and even if they had desired more than anything to create and enforce fishery regulations that were effective and unbiased, fisheries managers would still have been constrained by the lack of resources available to them in carrying out their duties. Congress was generous in appropriating money for artificial propagation but seemingly could not spare monies for basic resource protection and regulation. This left fisheries managers in tough situations, such as when Assistant Agent William S. Ballard "secured the services of an Indian and his canoe" and rowed dozens of miles to conduct his inspections of remote canneries in southeastern Alaska.[25]

Ballard's experience was the norm for regulators in the late nineteenth and early twentieth centuries. Fisheries agents struggled to maintain their dignity as they jumped from rowboat to cannery steamer to fishing boat to Native canoe. The situation would have been laughable, except that it made their duties embarrassing, futile, and dangerous. The lack of transportation facilities apparently contributed to the death of Assistant Agent J. C. Boatman, who spent much of his summer ferrying to isolated canneries with the help of a "whaler's tugboat or with Indian canoes," before he was found dead on the beach in Sitka. "He complained of the hardships of service, resulting in the utter lack of transportation facilities, except such as could be got from Indian canoes and chance trips on the vessels of the fishing companies," explained lead agent Kutchin in a letter to the secretary of the Treasury reporting Boatman's death. "In the latter cases," Kutchin went on, "he felt that his efforts were largely nullified for obvious reasons, and that his position was rendered embarrassing and the results inadequate and unsatisfactory."[26]

Kutchin undoubtedly dramatized Boatman's death to make a plea for more resources, but he did not exaggerate the extent to which the lack of appropriations made it impossible for only *three* inspectors to patrol the nearly four thousand miles of coastline and over one thousand salmon streams in southeastern Alaska, not to mention the rest of the territory. Regulators relied on cannery operators—the very people they were supposed to be policing—not only for transportation, but also for information about their fishing operations (see figure 3.1). The situation made rigorous enforcement impossible. Fishery managers complained yearly, but appropriations

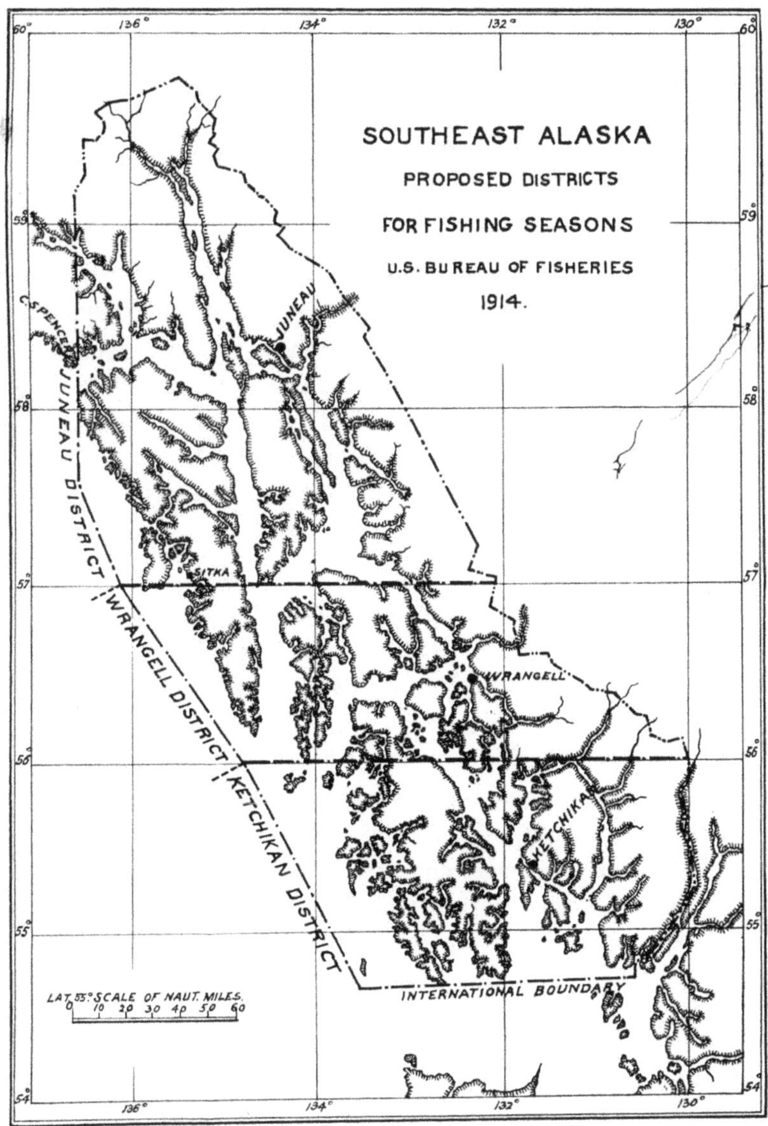

FIG. 3.1 Proposed districts for fishing seasons in Southeastern Alaska, 1914. The U.S. Bureau of Fisheries managed the Alaska fisheries until 1960, but the task was daunting. Southeastern Alaska, stretching nearly five hundred miles along the North Pacific, contained over a thousand salmon streams and more than four thousand miles of coastline. SOURCE: *Jones 1915: 25.*

did not improve appreciably until the 1920s. Laissez faire continued in practice, if not in principle, during the first thirty years of federal control.

Even if Congress had provided them an entire fleet of steamers, launches, and speedboats as well as an army of motivated and competent regulators, the Bureau of Fisheries still would have been limited by the fisheries laws themselves, which between the 1890s and the 1950s were vetted, defanged, and sometimes even written by the politically powerful salmon-canning lobby.[27] The most telling characteristic of the early fishery laws was the extent to which they encouraged the artificial propagation of salmon rather than the restriction of commercial fishing. The 1896 law actually exempted companies that maintained "fish hatcheries of significant magnitude" from all fishery regulations.[28] The 1906 act provided a generous tax rebate for those companies that operated private salmon hatcheries.[29] Canners, Congress, and fisheries bureaucrats refused to enforce significant prohibitions on fishing intensity, but they needed little encouragement in promoting the artificial propagation of salmon, a phenomenon Taylor has called "making salmon."

Indeed, by the late nineteenth century, making salmon rather than protecting the natural fish stocks and habitat already in existence became the favored form of fisheries management for both federal and local fisheries managers. Its appeal was irresistible for two powerful reasons. First, it tempted industrialists and government bureaucrats into believing that declining fish stocks could be resuscitated without protecting habitat or reducing fishing intensity—both of which were politically unpopular, if not impossible, in the late nineteenth and early twentieth centuries. Second, it played into the growing belief that humans could fashion narrow technocratic solutions to complex problems; in Taylor's words it played into the "burgeoning notion that science would enable civilization to compensate for the destruction it caused."[30]

The first of these reasons—the belief that hatcheries would increase fish stocks and eliminate the need for regulation—supplied the most powerful momentum to the hatchery movement in Alaska. Focusing on artificial propagation, as Taylor shows, allowed the federal government to assist regional fisheries without impinging on the right of states to regulate—or not regulate—fishing as they saw fit. The situation was somewhat different in the territory of Alaska, where the federal government retained full control over the fisheries until one year after Alaska became a state in 1959. Even after Alaska gained a legislature in 1912, Congress, in an unprecedented move supported by the salmon-canning lobby, prevented the territory from regulating its own fisheries.[31] This meant that federal fisheries managers, at least in theory, could regulate and prohibit fishing without local resistance. However, federal managers still had to contend with the powerful salmon-canning industry—the "fish trust" as they were known to residents of the territory—who fiercely resisted every attempt to increase regulation. Even in Alaska, manufacturing salmon represented a more favorable and less confrontational strategy than addressing the reasons for their decline. "Should artificial propagation . . . prove practicable, all problematic devices of protection would be eliminated and the work [of conservation officials] immensely simplified," reasoned Special Agent Kutchin. "Closed seasons, prescriptions as to methods of taking, etc.," he continued, "would then become unnecessary."[32] An editorialist in *The Alaskan* believed that with hatcheries contributing to the salmon supply, fisheries management in Alaska would "interfere with the rights of no one, and need cost nothing."[33]

Such optimistic forecasts were borne of an almost religious faith in the power of science and technology to improve upon nature. "The wastefulness of nature is enormous," noted Kutchin, who estimated that less than 1 percent of salmon eggs were hatched in salmon spawning beds (see figure 3.2). Nature's "wastefulness," he believed, could be dramatically decreased by "artificial processes" whereby "fully 90 per cent of the eggs are hatched."[34] Kutchin was a regulator, not a scientist, but his belief that "nature must be assisted in the maintenance of the Alaska salmon fisheries," and that "reinforcing nature" was "well within the scope of human effort," was supported by two important federal investigations of the Alaska fisheries.[35]

In 1889, Tarleton Bean, an ichthyologist for the USFC, reported that Alaska was "a most promising field for fish-cultural operations." He believed that government hatcheries in Alaska would "insure [*sic*] a permanent and improving fishery" by "avoiding the enormous waste of eggs and young fish under their natural conditions."[36] In 1904 the Alaska Salmon Commission investigations, conducted by USFC scientist David Starr Jordan, concluded that the dangers of natural predation could be almost entirely eliminated by artificial methods: "practically every egg can be fertilized: the danger of disease can be greatly reduced; all the enemies that feed upon the eggs and fry can be eliminated, and vastly larger proportion will grow to maturity." Jordan predicted that "the key to the whole question of the future of the Alaska salmon lies in artificial propagation." Producing salmon at hatcheries would allow salmon stocks to "be repopulated when exhausted" and an industry "once crippled or destroyed . . . [to] be restored."[37]

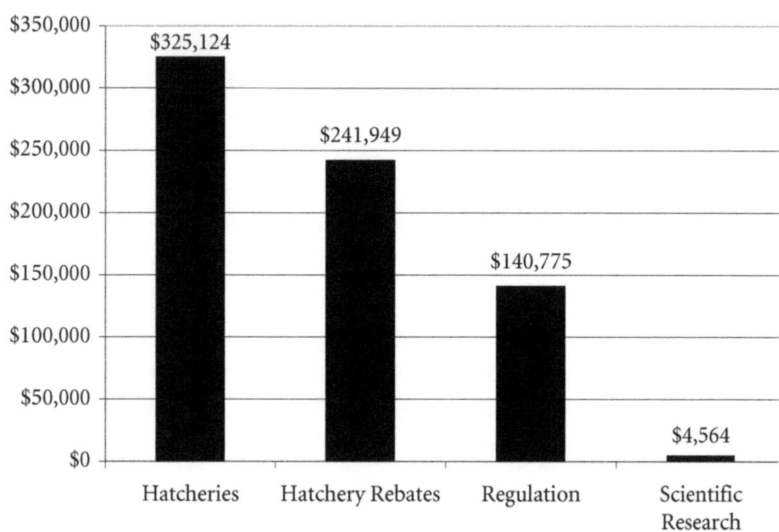

FIG. 3.2 Bureau of fisheries expenditures in Alaska, 1906–1915. In the early twentieth century the Bureau of Fisheries directed most of its resources toward manufacturing salmon rather than regulation or research. SOURCE: *Bower and Aller 1915: 19, 31.*

The realities of early hatcheries in Alaska did not match these grandiose visions. Between 1892 and 1928 canning companies and federal fisheries managers released nearly two billion salmon fingerlings into the waterways of southeastern Alaska, but the fish never returned.[38] Salmon hatcheries failed for three primary reasons. First, without adequate means of measuring the number of hatchery fish that survived—and with little attention paid to the reasons why most hatchery fish never returned—fisheries managers focused obsessively on the number of eggs hatched and fingerlings released. This was especially a problem with private operators who received government rebates for the number of young salmon they released, regardless of how many of those hatchlings successfully supplemented salmon stocks. Second, early hatchery efforts in southeastern Alaska focused on producing the valuable sockeye salmon, even though pink salmon constituted the vast majority of natural stocks in the region. Hatchery operators therefore sought to impose an unnatural order upon the fishery based on market considerations rather than the region's natural history—and the results were understandably disappointing.

Third, the primary problem with the hatcheries was that both federal and private operators suffered from a narrow focus on producing salmon rather than on preserving the habitat in which salmon, and people, lived. Modern fisheries managers have made aquaculture more effective by using it alongside strict fisheries regulations and habitat rehabilitation as a means of restoring healthy runs of wild salmon.[39] Early managers, however, saw hatcheries as a simple technological fix to a problem that required a broader ecological approach. Fisheries managers poured millions into maintaining government hatcheries and providing generous rebates to private operators, but they had little to show for their efforts. The size of the runs continued to fluctuate wildly. Salmon populations simply refused to comply with the abundant hopes of fish culturalists.

Artificial propagation was not, however, the only management program where early conservation officials tried to improve upon nature and maneuver it toward their desired goal: namely the growth of salmon runs and increased economic productivity. Beginning in the mid-1910s, fisheries managers began to focus on "improving" salmon habitat in southeastern Alaska, but they did so in a way—like artificial propagation—that overestimated the extent to which humans could effectively direct nature toward narrow economic outcomes. Instead, they focused on enlarging salmon populations without a complete understanding of salmon ecosystems, and they relied on management strategies that enhanced the supply of salmon without restricting fishing intensity, an approach that met the approval of industrialists.[40] One such program was called "stream improvement."

Stream improvement became a major focus of the Bureau of Fisheries after the 1914 investigation of Alaska's salmon industry by the deputy commissioner of fisheries, E. Lester Jones. His observations in southeastern Alaska led him to conclude that natural obstructions, such as rock dams and wind-fallen trees, prevented many salmon from ascending to their spawning grounds. Such barriers not only blocked fish passage, Jones believed, but corralled salmon into pools where they were preyed upon by seals, trout, bears, eagles, gulls, terns, and mergansers. On Prince of Wales Island, for instance, Jones traveled to Silver Salmon Falls, where he saw that "thousands of fish, unable to ascend this natural barrier, had fallen back tired and worn out, only to be cast ashore by bears."[41]

Jones believed that fisheries managers could improve the salmon runs simply by removing these natural barriers to salmon migration. His views were praised by salmon canners who maintained that the bureau should focus on fostering salmon populations rather than prohibiting fishing. One operator insisted that fisheries agents need not close fishing near his cannery on Lake Bay, because the greatest threat to the salmon was not human fishers, but rather "the existing waterfalls and rocks that barricade the rivers . . . [and] make it impossible for salmon to ascend these barriers into the natural spawning grounds and fresh water lakes." He had witnessed "thousands of dead fish lying in the deep hole just below these falls." Citing the report by Jones, this operator told conservation officials that by building a fish ladder or destroying the rock falls—not by prohibiting fishing—"the run of fish in this district would undoubtedly be increased."[42]

Acting on the recommendations of Jones, the fishery managers inaugurated a large-scale effort of stream improvement in Southeast Alaska. Their goal was that "all streams in Alaska which were once open to salmon will be cleared of debris and log jams and be restored to their former condition." A further goal was that waterways never before accessible to salmon, "because of falls and other natural obstructions," be opened up to salmon spawning. The bureau heralded the program as "most important in providing additional spawning grounds, thus materially aiding in restoring and maintaining the supply of salmon."[43]

Stream improvement was constrained in the 1910s because the bureau lacked the manpower to carry out their ambitious plans, but with increasing appropriations, the program expanded dramatically in the late 1920s and early 1930s. In 1928 the Fisheries Bureau employed 201 men in southeastern Alaska, compared with just a handful in 1915, and in the summer of 1934 the Civil Works Project furnished 198 unskilled laborers for stream reclamation projects.[44] Most of these were temporary workers, employed for as little as a few days or as much as the entire summer, but they provided much-needed fodder for the labor-intensive process of "improving" salmon streams. With hundreds of workers busy clearing debris from the creeks, the bureau could claim vast improvements made to salmon-spawning habitat.

The daily records of these workers suggest the diligence with which eager young recruits transformed the waterscape of Southeast Alaska. John Hanson, stationed in Redfish Bay during the summer of 1931, spent all of July 4 "working on a log jam at the mouth of the lake which prevents the salmon from entering the lake." He spent the next five days "removing windfalls and debris from the creek in order to allow the salmon to ascend the streams," announcing on July 9 that he had "completed clearing stream . . . and at this time the fish can ascend the stream and enter the lake." Later in the month Hanson was again at work removing "log jams" from spawning streams.[45] G. A. S. Anderson, employed in the summer of 1932 along the west coast of Prince of Wales Island, spent the period between August 5 and 25 "busily engaged in clearing barriers in the stream that prevented the ascending salmon to the spawning grounds; improving the falls to assist the salmon to ascend them; [and] cutting a trail from the salt water to the lake and around the edges of the lake."[46]

Clearing rocks, logs, and even beaver dams from salmon streams provided tangible results that bolstered the bureau's record of conservation. Unlike their efforts at artificial propagation, where the results vanished as soon as they were released from the pens, efforts at stream improvement allowed fisheries managers to chart their progress simply by counting the number of streams that they had "restored" to their free-flowing condition. In 1930 the bureau boasted that "log jams and other obstructions that hindered the ascent of salmon to the spawning grounds were removed from 74 streams in southeastern Alaska."[47] The cruel irony of these efforts, however, was that by making "perfect" spawning streams—ones cleared of all debris and thereby, they believed, friendly to fish migration—fisheries managers were destroying salmon habitat. If salmon could have spoken, they might have told conservation officials that they much preferred messy streams and creeks filled with windfalls and debris.

While E. Lester Jones feared that logjams made salmon vulnerable to predation, such natural "debris" actually creates pools—known as "microhabitats"—where juvenile salmon can rest, feed, and hide from predators.[48] The larger the logjam, the deeper the pool, the more salmon can obtain refuge. In fact, field studies of Puget Sound rivers show that the abundance of salmon correlates to the number of pools created by natural logjams. Moreover, logjams and other seemingly temporary obstructions can permanently alter the contours of riverbeds by causing sand and gravel to accumulate into islands downstream, thereby producing habitats more beneficial to migrating salmon than the clean streams produced by fisheries agents.[49]

The doctrine of stream improvement at least acknowledged that factors beyond fishing affected salmon populations, but conservation officials "restored" salmon habitats with the same myopia with which they manufactured fish—and with similar results. Their efforts were guided foremost by their own preconceptions of what constituted an ideal salmon stream—and salmon simply did not agree. Their labors were also constrained by their belief in rational solutions that addressed only one problem—in this case obstacles to fish passage—in isolation from the larger ecology of salmon habitat. Pulling a log from a stream may have indeed appeared to clear the way for migrating salmon, but it was simply one more lesson in unintended consequences. Fisheries managers unwittingly learned naturalist John Muir's observation that when you "tug on anything in nature . . . you will find it connected to everything else." With so many factors influencing salmon runs, such selective "improvements" did not enhance salmon populations.

Early conservation efforts in southeastern Alaska reflected an overwhelming concern for economic productivity and an inclination to see fluctuating fish populations in the most simplistic terms, as primarily the result of fishing intensity—a problem that could be overcome by improving upon nature. Without modern methods of determining fish returns and without an approach that considered the entire life cycle of the salmon, however, conservation managers were shooting in the dark. They were also driven primarily by economic and political imperatives rather than ecological concerns. It is no surprise, therefore, that salmon were uncooperative to the ambitious designs of salmon managers. It is also unsurprising that conservation policies—driven as they were by economic and political concerns—affected fishers far more than they did fish.

FEDERAL CONSERVATION, FISH TRAPS, AND THE STRUGGLE FOR CONTROL, 1912–1940

If fisheries managers could not direct nature toward their rational goals of efficiency, stability, and economic productivity, they had a much harder time managing humans. Humans—especially fishermen—were a particularly nonmalleable and irrational variety of nature. They had their own wills, traditions, dreams, and lifeways, which did not always conform to the wishes of federal fisheries agents. Alaskan politicians were even worse, from the perspective of federal managers. They played upon the populist sentiments of the "fishing classes" to build local opposition to federal control over the fisheries. Bureau of Fisheries agents may have simply wanted to control the fishery through "rational" policy, but at every turn their policies became subject to an often vicious debate over who should control the fisheries. Should the federal government continue to manage the resource, or should Alaska, like every territory before it, have the responsibility of regulation? Should large corporations using fish traps dominate the extractive side of the industry, or should small, independent fishermen have priority? These debates over home rule and federal control, democracy and monopoly, labor and capital, pulled fisheries managers unwittingly into the realms of social policy. Fisheries policy in Alaska came to have social implications that were far more profound than their biological impact. The social struggle over federal conservation began to take shape in the early 1910s, as three important events defined the emergent struggle to control the fisheries.

First, a second Organic Act in 1912 gave Alaska a territorial legislature. After nearly a half century as a customs district and then a territory, the region finally had an elected body that could represent a homegrown Alaskan viewpoint. Many Alaskans hoped that self-government would entail local control over the fisheries, as had been the custom with previous territories. Territorial politicians such as James Wickersham, who became Alaska's delegate to the U.S. Congress in 1908, believed that the fisheries would be "very much better controlled and conserved, very much better preserved and protected if the Territorial Legislature of Alaska had the duty of looking after them."[50] He resented the distant and corporate-friendly oversight of Congress and the Bureau of Fisheries, which had in his view allowed large "outside" canning companies from San Francisco and Seattle to run wild in the territory, importing temporary labor and exporting volumes of wealth but investing little in the long-term development of the region. The reign of the "fish trust" in Alaska, according to Wickersham, had depleted the resource and generated "huge profits for the packers, but not a penny for the people."[51]

Wickersham envisioned Alaska's salmon resources controlled by territorial officials and exploited by local companies and local fishermen. His vision was Jeffersonian in essence—salmon should not be a source of profit for greedy capitalists, but rather a "constant food supply" that would "support 50,000 resident Alaskan fishermen and their families."[52] Under local control independent yeoman fishermen would replace an economic system consisting of corporate overlords and wage slaves. But Wickersham's hopes were crushed when the 1912 Organic Act, which he authored, was amended on the floor of Congress to prevent the territorial legislature from altering or repealing "existing laws in respect to the fisheries of the Territory."[53] Indeed, his quest for local control faced powerful opposition from both the salmon-canning lobby and the Bureau of Fisheries—and the U.S. Congress also lent its consent in denying the territory of regulatory control over the fishery.

The secretary of commerce, William C. Redfield, believed that it would be irresponsible to place the sizable private investment of Alaska's salmon fisheries in the hands of a small, dispersed territorial population. "Shall the Government," he asked, "turn over to a population of 55,000 white people . . . an investment in excess of $37,000,000?" Sounding every bit the imperialist arguing against colonial independence, Redfield wondered if "Alaska has reached the point where it can take control of so enormous a problem and handle it either to its own or the public's satisfaction."[54] The deputy commissioner of the Bureau of Fisheries believed that local control of the fisheries would "prove a handicap to the greatest development of Alaska's rich fishery resources."[55] The salmon packers agreed. The attorney for the Alaska Packers Association argued that "the Federal Government should have complete and full control over the entire arrangement and method of operating the fisheries and canneries in Alaska" because the industry was "of extreme importance to the people of the United States in developing a wholesome and cheap food supply."[56] Salmon canners, the Bureau of Fisheries, and Congress proved too powerful for the proponents of local control. But the creation of Alaska's legislature in 1912—and the subsequent deracination of its regulatory powers—served as a powerful symbol of colonialism and as a rallying point for local resistance. Wickersham would be the first in a line of populist territorial politicians who would fight against "outside" control of the salmon fisheries.[57]

The second important event of 1912 was the founding of the Alaskan Native Brotherhood (ANB), which would similarly serve as a voice of local—and particularly Indian—opposition to both the Bureau of Fisheries and outside corporations. Created by twelve Christian Indians, with the encouragement of Presbyterian missionaries at the Sitka Industrial Training School, the ANB initially promoted the abolition of tribal customs and the complete assimilation of Natives into American society.[58] Under the leadership of William L. Paul Sr., a fisherman and lawyer who would become the first truly influential Tlingit politician, the ANB evolved into a powerful lobby for Indian political, social, and economic equality. Although it continued to emphasize Americanization and integration, the ANB also aspired to give Tlingit peoples "control over the circumstances and direction of Indian life," which meant, to Paul at least, protecting "small" Indian fishermen from the economic and environmental exploitation of large salmon-canning companies.[59]

By the early 1920s the loyalties of the Alaska Native Brotherhood were summed up on the masthead of its monthly newspaper, the *Alaska Fisherman*, published from 1923 to 1932 by Paul and his brother Louis F. Paul: "A Paper for the Common Folk Treating Subjects of Labor and Fishing and Taxes without Fear or Favor, Depending for its Life on the Support from the 'Little Fellow.'"[60] The *Alaska Fisherman*'s battle cry of "Alaska for Alaskans" appealed not only to Indian peoples, but also to white Alaskans who likewise perceived themselves on the losing side of a colonial relationship whereby nonresident capital and labor benefited disproportionately from the exploitation of their region's natural resources.[61]

Finally, 1912 was also a turning point in the battle over who would control the fisheries because it was the first year that industrial fish traps took nearly half of the catch. The use of fish traps had been on the rise since the invention of J. R. Heckman's floating fish trap in 1907.[62] Previously, the expense of building and maintaining stationary traps had restricted their use to a few large packing companies. The floating trap, however, was more easily operated and maintained, and by 1911 fish traps were catching one-third of the commercial harvest in southeastern Alaska. In 1912 a major fisherman's strike pushed more canneries to switch to trap operations, ensuring them a steady salmon supply without having to rely on "independent" fishermen operating movable gear. In that year industrial traps caught just over one-half of the salmon run. In 1920 cannery traps accounted for two-thirds of the catch; in 1926 the percentage of trap-caught fish had risen to nearly three-quarters of the entire harvest (see figure 3.3).[63]

With their rapid expansion fish traps became the focus of a wide-ranging debate over fisheries management, economic efficiency, social justice, local control, "moral economy," and the very nature of the "common property" fishery. The issue of fish traps, in fact, would consume congressional hearings on the Alaskan fisheries from the 1910s through the 1950s. Their primary importance highlighted the extent to which fisheries conservation carried social and economic implications far beyond its impact on salmon populations. Fishermen voiced their discontent against fish traps from the very first, even before their use was widespread. In 1901, Special Agent Kutchin reported that the general antipathy against the devices "was so pronounced that a movement was being contemplated . . . among the fishermen themselves, to petition to the Department to prohibit their use."[64] While investigating the salmon fisheries in 1904, USFC scientists Jordan and Evermann observed similar resentments. "The fact that traps work automatically without the help of laborers," they noted, "is the cause of much of the feeling against them, strong among fishermen."[65] Such grumblings escalated in 1912, when "independent" fishermen in southeastern Alaska—who were primarily purse-seiners—faced the prospect that corporate traps manned by company wage laborers could force them from their livelihoods.

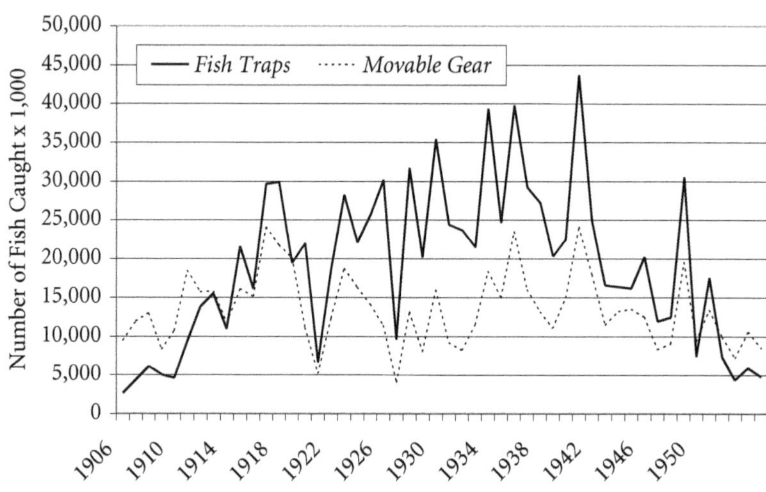

FIG. 3.3 Commercial harvests by fish traps and movable gear, 1906–1954. The percentage of trap-caught salmon in southeastern Alaska escalated dramatically during the 1910s. Traps became the dominant form of gear until the 1950s, challenging "independent" fishermen with an efficient fish-catching device that reorganized the labor of fishing along industrial lines. SOURCE: *Bower, Alaska Fishery and Fur-Seal Industries, 1906–1954.*

The concerns of fishermen were taken up by territorial politicians such as Wickersham, and later Dan A. Sutherland and Anthony J. Dimond, who believed that cultivating a population of "independent" fishermen (meaning those who operated their own boats and gear) was central to Alaska's social and economic development. Only by building the resident population could the territory obtain statehood and in their view become liberated from the shackles of federal control and corporate colonialism. Fish traps thus became the subject of impassioned debate during the Alaska Territorial Legislature's first session in 1912, as two bills were introduced to abolish the devices. Neither bill passed, but "a heated discussion was precipitated, which soon resolved itself into a controversy between trap fishermen and purse-seine fishermen."[66] This controversy would remain central for the entire territorial period, pitting independent fishermen against large corporations and government conservation officials, territorial officials against federal bureaucrats, and advocates of economic justice against proponents of economic rationality and efficiency.

Fishermen—and the territorial politicians who represented them—posed their criticisms of fish traps in terms that played well among Alaskan residents. The devices, after all, had a lot going for them. Corporate fish traps were efficient salmon-catching machines that operated without the need of small-boat fishermen. They also produced a fresher product because fish remained alive inside the pot of the fish trap until they were "brailed" into cannery scows that transported them directly to processing plants. In an age that heralded economic innovation, rationality, and scientific management, opponents of traps could not critique them on the basis of market rationality. As fisheries chief Evermann understood, "an employer's right to use labor-saving devices can not, for itself alone, be successfully assailed."[67] Trap opponents could, however, attack corporate fish traps on moral grounds: they were operated by large, parasitic corporations who plundered Alaska's salmon and reduced its producers to dependency.

They could also draw on other resonant Progressive Era concerns: conservation and economic monopoly. They argued that fish traps—because of their efficiency—were the primary cause of resource depletion in Alaska's fisheries. "More fish are destroyed in one trap, in one season," contended Wickersham, "than all the bears, seals, and gulls in Alaska will kill." Not only were the devices destructive, but they were wasteful—another enemy of conservation. Wickersham continued: "As the tide recedes, the mass of fish settles in the trap; the air is exhausted, thousands die, and if not brailed out promptly, a trap full [of salmon] may be destroyed."[68] Fishermen commonly referred to traps as ruthless "machines" and pointed out that, while fishermen needed to sleep and refuel (giving fish a chance to migrate upstream), traps kept fishing around the clock. "We in Alaska know that intensive fishing means fishing with traps," explained Native leader William Paul, who believed that "traps must be abolished if the salmon industry is to remain with us."[69] Trap antagonists also believed that fish traps, because they permanently monopolized fishing sites, constituted, in Wickersham's words, an "exclusive right and an exclusive privilege to fish" from which "the rest of the world is barred." He feared, as did independent fishermen, that trap owners would obtain legal title to trap sites, thereby violating common-property doctrines and making "a complete monopoly of these fisheries."[70] Concerns for conservation, economic monopoly, and protecting independent producers would form, with only minor alterations, the primary arguments against traps for the next five decades.

The salmon-canning industry and the Bureau of Fisheries defended fish traps on the basis of conservation, food quality, and economic rationality, which were also Progressive Era concerns. "That traps are destructive to the fish and the fish industry is decidedly an erroneous and narrow view," asserted an article in the *Pacific Fisherman*, the industry's trade journal. Fish traps could be opened, closed, and easily regulated, the author explained, so as "not [to] destroy any more fish than desired." Moreover, the devices held fish alive until they were needed, ensuring a fresher product to consumers and preventing waste, whereas a "fish once caught in a seine or net is doomed."[71] The Bureau of Fisheries defended and elaborated the industry argument. In 1912, in the midst of the escalating debate over fish traps, Evermann, now head scientist with the bureau, argued that traps were superior to movable gear for two reasons. First, they held salmon "living till the cannery is ready to use them," and second, trap sites allowed for "convenient and comparatively inexpensive inspection and regulation." Movable gear, however, was nearly impossible to regulate because it was "carried on in numerous remote and difficultly accessible places contemporaneously."[72]

Evermann did not go as far as fisheries manager Ward T. Bower, who contended that "purse seines and gill nets threaten the future supply of salmon in Alaska more than any other form of fishing gear," but he clearly preferred fish traps from a conservation standpoint as well as from the perspective of consumer cost and quality.[73] Evermann moreover defended fish traps against the charge of monopoly, arguing that any "individual stands an equal chance with the largest company" of acquiring a fish trap. He saw the trap controversy largely as a self-interested dispute over fishing gear. Fishermen wished to abolish traps, he believed, not because they were conservationists or defenders of free markets, but simply because they were in "direct competition" with the devices—a narrow concern that did not foster the "public good."[74]

Conservation officials sought to transcend such narrow "gear conflicts" and make their decisions based on objective science and a concern for the *public good*, but in doing so, they tended to privilege economic productivity and rationality over other values, including community, tradition, culture, economic equality, and the welfare of small producers. While some fisheries managers viewed questions of economic efficiency as subordinate to the primary issue of conservation, others were more explicit in advocating traps simply because they saved "time and labor," a perspective that squared with their position as Commerce Department employees.[75] Deputy commissioner of the fisheries E. Lester Jones, for example, believed fish traps to be superior because "fewer men are required to operate a trap than are needed to operate a haul or a purse seine." He advocated the use of traps primarily "for the sake of economy in labor."[76] "It is absolutely understood in business," Jones reasoned, "that if anyone can devise a simpler and more economical method . . . , any up-to-date business house will encourage it and discourage the old business method."[77]

Pitting economic rationality, efficiency, and innovation against backward "rule of thumb" methods and inefficiency, the fish trap controversy resonated with larger historical conflicts between "progress" and "tradition." Would the fisheries industry rely on the labor-saving fish trap and unskilled wage laborers or on independent artisan fishermen? The question harked back to the fight over mechanization in Britain's weaving industry, the conflict between small farmers and mill dams in early-nineteenth-century New England, or to numerous global struggles over the transition from artisan manufacturing to industrial wage work—transformations that dislocated and deskilled craftsmen, created a class of urban proletariats, and shifted societies in an urban and industrial direction.

From the perspective of industrialists and conservation managers the fish trap represented progress and rationality—it was more efficient and produced a more satisfactory product. For fishermen, however, fish traps threatened their livelihood, their heritage, and the tradition of fishing as an independent occupation. Fisheries managers believed themselves unbiased arbiters of the public good, prioritizing conservation over issues of labor and economic organization, but indeed their decisions were freighted with social implications. Their faith in rationality and efficiency blinded them to questions of social equality. They sided consistently with large canning corporations rather than independent fishermen. Although Progressive conservation has often been depicted as a movement that challenged "the interests" in the name of "the people," fisheries conservation had a limited view of the "public interest" that favored rationality, science, and central planning over the concerns of social equality or local control.[78]

The fight over fish traps involved not only a struggle over the meaning of conservation, but also a contest over the fundamental rights of fishers in an "open access" fishery. Curiously, both proponents and opponents of traps drew on the Anglo-American common-law tradition that "air, water [and] fish belong to everyone; they are common property."[79] They cited the same legal precedents to defend their positions, but they had dramatically different interpretations of what "common property" and "open access" actually meant in practice. Independent fishermen—and their advocates—believed that fish traps violated the core premise of a common-property fishery: that no one "owned" the seas and that all fishers should have an open and equal opportunity to capture fish. A fish trap, once placed on the fishing grounds, permanently prevented other fishermen from taking fish from that location. And although trap owners technically could not claim legal title to their trap locations (although they lobbied for such a privilege throughout the 1910s and 1920s), the Fisheries Bureau officially recognized and licensed trap sites, which could be traded, sold, or leased to other users, just like fee-simple property.[80]

Moreover, it was a common practice for trap owners to surround their prime trap locations with "dummy" traps that created a buffer zone around productive traps, preventing fishing boats from locating their movable gear anywhere near the mouth of an operating fish trap. Such methods, from the perspective of trap opponents, constituted an "exclusive right" to catch fish in a given location, thereby violating the principle that the "right to take fish" is "common to all persons."[81] "You can not have common right of fisheries if you have traps," explained one fisherman, "because that is the same kind of land tenure, the same kind of tenure of the soil underneath the water that has existed throughout all periods of time . . . [and] if that is done, of course, it won't take long before the fishing grounds become property in fee simple."[82]

Trap operators similarly defended their rights on the basis of the common right of the fishery, also drawing on a populist rhetoric that opposed exclusive rights and special privileges. "Congress ought not to include any legislation granting the right to fish for salmon to one class of fishermen to the exclusion of another," warned an industry representative. Abolishing traps, in the minds of salmon canners, would "grant special privileges to seine fishing and . . . discriminate against trap fishing."[83] Canners went beyond the open-access argument, however, to assert special "possessory rights" to trap sites. E. S. McCord, an attorney for the salmon-canning industry, argued that trap operators, similar to mining prospectors, acquired trap locations on the public domain "by discovery" and "in expenditures of money and development." Such investments, he argued, should be honored with a property right allowing trap owners to retain their claim to certain locations even if fishing was temporarily prohibited. McCord continued: "Whenever fishing is again permitted in the waters where these locations are situated they should be permitted to resume their possessory rights."[84] Such rights—moving toward permanent title—were precisely what trap opponents feared.

Both defenders and opponents of fish traps pointed toward the 1902 decision in *Heckman v. Sutter* as validating their position. Sutter had acquired a homestead along the Tongass narrows near the mouth of Ketchikan Creek, where he had cleared the tide flats of "stones, trees, stumps, and other debris" at the beginning of each fishing season. After having "prepared the said flats for fishing purposes," he erected a cannery "and other improvements" and set about catching salmon with a long seine that was connected at one end to his wharf. In July 1900, Sutter was prevented from fishing by employees of the Alaska Packers Association, who invaded his tidal flats with larger seines and hauled their catches on his beachfront. Sutter enjoined the APA seining crews from interfering with his own fishing operations, and his argument was upheld by the Alaska District Court and the Ninth Circuit Court of Appeals. The appeals court ruled that although "the right to take fish in the waters of the sea, and even along the tide flats, is one common to all citizens," Sutter had acquired a certain possessory right over the tidelands by "cleaning away the debris and . . . making it a clear and proper road-way from the deep water to the upland over which he may pass and repass with his nets in the act of fishing, unobstructed and uninterrupted by the nets or other appliances of those who have a common right to take fish in the waters of the seas and rivers of Alaska."[85]

The ruling was a mix of property law and fisheries law—asserting the common right of fishery, while also recognizing the privileges of possession that flowed from both *inhabiting* and *improving* the land. Alaska territorial delegate Dan A. Sutherland, a former fisherman and miner who took up James Wickersham's battle against fish traps in the 1920s, drew on the portions of the decision that protected the rights of individuals to fish without being "interfered with or hindered by the other fishermen." In his view the case revolved around "establishing and reaffirming the common right of fishery."[86] Trap advocates believed the case validated the existence of "possessory rights"—a term used in the judgment—within the domain of the common fishery.[87]

The debates over fish traps, conservation, and the open-access fishery converged in the early 1920s, when President Warren Harding signed an executive order allowing the secretary of commerce—then Herbert Hoover—to create fishery reservations throughout Alaska as a means of limiting access, reducing fishing intensity, and restricting new operators from entering the fishery. The policy—which allowed "no individual or concern" to "engage in the business of catching, canning, or preparing salmon . . . without first securing a permit from the Secretary of Commerce"—was meant to foster conservation and economic rationality in an industry that had rapidly expanded during World War I and was suffering from overcapitalization, falling prices, and resource depletion in the postwar period.[88]

The reserves in practice insulated large canners from competition without reducing overall fishing intensity. They also allowed packers operating within them to obtain and reserve the rights to fish-trap locations. The fish reservations infuriated small operators, independent fishermen, and territorial officials who believed they violated the principle of the common fishery and granted special privileges to large outside corporations. Sutherland attacked the policy for creating a "private monopoly in the Alaskan salmon-packing industry" for a "few individuals or corporations" from Chicago, San Francisco, and Seattle, who were "not in any sense residents of the territory."[89] A representative of the Alaska Fishermen's Union believed that the reservation policy along with fish traps would "in due time pave the road to absolute monopoly by a few large corporations of all these vast natural resources."[90]

The Commerce Department never extended fishery reserves to Southeast Alaska, where the voice of independent fishermen was the loudest.[91] The possibility that it might, however, provoked considerable opposition among locals, particularly Native fishers. In defending the fishery reservations, Harding had not only invoked the "public welfare" but also the nation's "obligation to the native Alaskan Indian."[92] Ironically, Tlingits and Haidas—through the Alaska Native Brotherhood—were some of the harshest critics of the policy, which they believed was "framed up" by the large packers and carried out by the Bureau of Fisheries, who were "mere tools of the fish trust."[93] Since fishery reservations called for reducing the overall pack without prohibiting fish traps, Native fishermen feared that canneries would fill their quotas with trap-caught fish, leaving independent Indian seiners without a market.[94] With the creation of reserves, fish traps would proliferate, but, queried the *Alaska Fisherman*, "what becomes of our fishing population?"[95]

Fish reservations, in the view of the ANB, created a façade of conservation while impoverishing Indian fishermen and allowing large canneries and fish traps to consolidate complete control over the fishing grounds. "The fish trap has taken our food from our children and wives and we do not want a reserve made here for the cannery men," declared a resolution from Indians in Kake. "We have more right to a reserve than the Seattle cannery men, but all we ask for is a chance to make a living; that is why we are against the fish trap." The ANB in Hoonah called the reserves a distraction from "the real cause of fish depletion," which were "the enormous traps maintained and operated by these same large interests." A letter from the Native community in Yakutat protested that a fish reserve there would leave Libby, McNeil & Company "in absolute control of the fishing and life of our village."[96]

The highly publicized charges of monopoly and special privilege ultimately doomed the Alaska fishery reservations, much to the disappointment of both conservation managers and industrialists, who believed them to be a rational solution to resource depletion and economic competition.[97] The reservations were repealed immediately after the enactment of the White Act in June 1924, a law that dramatically expanded the powers of the secretary of commerce to limit and prohibit fishing throughout Alaska and extended police-power to fisheries agents.[98] The law did not abolish fish traps. In fact, the number of fish traps expanded rapidly in the years immediately after 1924, increasing from 442 in 1923 to a high of 799 in 1927, 575 of which were located in southeastern Alaska.[99]

From the perspective of independent fishermen and territorial interests the law simply increased the power that corporations and distant bureaucrats wielded over their lives. In that sense the White Act, as Joseph Taylor has argued, consolidated the victory of efficiency and rational exploitation over social equity as the defining parameter of federal conservation in the 1920s. Taylor shows how concerns for social equality became subordinated to the ethos of efficiency during the battle over the White Act, as Herbert Hoover's brand of conservation, rooted in corporate efficiency and rationality, prevailed over the kind advocated by Dan Sutherland, whose vision reflected a concern for small fishermen and a hatred of corporate monopolies. The debate itself, in Taylor's words, "narrowed the definition of conservation by severing efficiency and equity." Resource management would follow the pro-corporate, scientific management emphasis of Hoover's "associational state" rather than the more democratic approach that had inspired earlier Progressive Era reforms.[100]

However, the victory of rationality over social equality, as reflected in the White Act, was neither complete nor final. In many ways the 1924 law was a compromise between the desires of the federal government, large canners, and independent fishermen, even if it continued to ignore territorial desires for local control. Industrial traps remained, but the controversial fish reserves were gone, and a provision denying any "exclusive or several right of fishery" put to rest the question of whether fish trap owners might claim fee-simple title to trap locations.[101] A total victory of efficiency and rationality might have eliminated movable gear altogether, giving traps a true monopoly over the fishery, but cultural and political resistance made such a move unthinkable. In fact, other forms of gear—including seines, gill nets, and lines—increased at a rate similar to fish traps in the years after 1924. So the White Act accomplished neither conservation nor economic rationality in the industry.

As testament to the compromise nature of the law, both small fishers and large packers had complaints. The Alaska Native Brotherhood denounced the law as discriminatory against purse-seine and gill-net fishermen. The ANB insisted that increased restrictions on movable gear without the abolition of traps would bring economic collapse to Indian communities as well as environmental destruction to salmon runs.[102] The salmon packers, however, found new regulations on fish traps during the weekly closed period too stringent and fisheries regulators too eager to enforce them. More than thirty canners supported a lawsuit against the Bureau of Fisheries "to restrain the officers of the government directly concerned in the enforcement" of the White Act.[103] The 1924 law, in other words, was not a beginning or an ending in the contest between traps and fishermen, federal authority and local control, or the efficiency and equity branches of conservation, but simply a continuation in the long struggle between these forces that began in the 1910s and continued through the 1950s. Independent fishermen, the Alaska Native Brotherhood, and territorial politicians continued to wage their war—in congressional hearings and on the fishing grounds—against fish traps, outside corporations, and federal regulators, as they had for over twenty years. Furthermore, in the 1930s the Fisheries Bureau itself began to show signs of straying from its ideological attachment to the efficiency brand of conservation in favor of a policy based on social equality.

Just as rationality and efficiency dominated the conservation ethos in the 1920s, other social concerns, forged in the context of the Great Depression and the New Deal, came to shape fisheries policy in the 1930s. Frank T. Bell, the new fisheries commissioner appointed by President Roosevelt in 1933, immediately moved to bring Alaska fishery management "in line with the President's policy of spreading employment."[104] This meant that Bell would pursue a voluntary program of reducing fish traps in order to "increase employment for the fishing population of Alaska" and establish "a proper relation between catches of salmon by the various kinds of fishing gear."[105]

He sent letters to the major salmon-packing companies explaining his intention to eliminate dummy sites and reduce "more productive sites" so as to equalize opportunity for all gear types, especially in southeastern Alaska, "where the catch is now overwhelmingly in favor of traps as against seines and other smaller forms of gear."[106] The new strategy was applauded by resident fishermen. Here was a policy that squared the concerns of conservation with those of independent fisherman and factored social equality into fishery management. But Bell's effort was extremely short-lived, as the salmon-canning interests waged a full-fledged war against the implementation of his policy, claiming, among other things, that the commissioner did not have the authority to "curtail fishing except for the purposes of conservation."[107] Faced with powerful political opposition and lacking adequate resources, Bell retreated. Fish traps were not reduced at all in southeastern Alaska, although the number of purse-seines was somewhat increased.

Commissioner Bell's vision of an "equitable" fishery remained unfulfilled, but the struggle between fishermen and fish traps waged on with increasing bitterness during the 1930s. In 1936 territorial delegate Anthony J. Dimond, following in the footsteps of his predecessors Wickersham and Sutherland, introduced a bill in the House of Representatives to gradually abolish fish traps, and in 1939 he initiated a congressional investigation into the management of the Alaska fisheries. The stormy hearings in 1936 and 1939 were largely a reiteration of previous arguments, but they were also reshaped by depression-era concerns. Fishermen still framed their criticisms against traps on the basis of fisheries conservation and economic monopoly, but they also argued their case more forcefully on the grounds of social and economic justice.

In the context of economic crisis it now became acceptable to attack fish traps on the basis of their labor-saving efficiency. There was now more traction to the argument that eliminating traps would increase the incomes of small fishermen, allow them to feed their families, earn a decent living, and keep them from the breadlines and relief offices. "If you wipe out these fish traps," reasoned one longtime Alaskan resident, "you will conserve salmon" and "give hundreds and thousands work during the fishing season." Resident purse-seiners from southeastern Alaska claimed that eliminating traps would make it so that "a poor man, with only a rowboat and a trolling outfit or a gill net, will be able to make a decent living." The fishermen reminded the congressional committee that they were not asking for government handouts. Their plan, they explained, would revive Alaska's economy without any cost to the federal government, enabling "the fishing population, which is now almost destitute and depending largely on federal relief," to become a "prosperous, contented, and happy class of people instead of dragging out a miserable hand-to-mouth existence."[108]

People in the industry defended fish traps, as they had for decades, on the basis of conservation, free competition in an open fishery, and the cost and quality of food for consumers, but their arguments were also conditioned by the Great Depression. They emphasized the fundamental role that fish traps played in promoting regional economic growth, developing resources, and providing employment. One industrialist insisted that if fishing were left to independent fishermen, salmon would once again "choke the streams" and the industry would collapse. Native fishermen, who comprised a majority of the resident fishers in southeastern Alaska, were "wholly inadequate in numbers and unable to even supply a small percentage of the fish now required for a normal pack." He believed that "the present agitation for the abolition of fish traps has been fostered largely by agitators with a purpose of destroying the industry that has been supplying Alaska almost solely with its wages and taxes."[109] W. C. Arnold, an attorney for the canned-salmon industry, explained how fish traps had transformed the southeastern Alaskan town of Ketchikan—previously "of no consequence as a fishing center"—into the "salmon capital of the world." He argued that "fish traps are the backbone of this town," and their elimination would bring economic ruin to the town and the entire territory. Another packer predicted simply that the "abolition of traps would spell the death of the industry."[110]

Despite Commissioner Bell's abbreviated attempt to reduce the number of fish traps, during the 1930s the Bureau of Fisheries continued to hew to the pro–fish trap party line: fish traps were more efficient, easier to regulate, and produced a fresher product. Fisheries scientist Frederick Davidson, like the salmon packers, believed that eliminating them would "handicap the salmon industry" because "the supply of fish furnished by the purse seines is rather erratic." Fishermen pleaded with the Fisheries Bureau to "consider the welfare of human beings as well as the conservation of the fish" in establishing "just and equitable rules and regulations." Even some congressmen began to wonder if "the power ought to be in the Bureau of Fisheries to also take into consideration . . . the social problem" of fisheries management, rather than simply resource conservation.[111] But fisheries managers held fast to their belief that true conservation transcended the self-interest of fishers and followed the dictates of science and the public welfare, which in their view decidedly favored the efficient, rational, productive, and easily regulated corporate fish traps over the inefficient, individualized, movable gear of independent fishers.

Despite continuing protests by fishermen and territorial officials, fish traps remained the dominate form of gear in southeastern Alaska throughout the remainder of the territorial period. The hearings in the 1930s—much like those in the 1920s surrounding the White Act—suggested the continuing dominance of rationality over equity in resource management, but they also highlighted the extent to which fisheries management was not resolved: it remained a source of continuous social conflict among fishers, corporations, and federal conservation officials.

LOCAL RESISTANCE AND THE "MORAL ECOLOGY" OF THE SALMON FISHERY, 1910s–1950s

Corporations influenced management policy, legislators created laws, and fisheries bureaucrats issued dictates, but their actions, initiated from Seattle or Washington, D.C., did not unilaterally decide the course of conservation policies, which became subject to opposition and conflict on the fishing grounds themselves. Conservation was a social struggle—not simply a set of policy decisions or laws—that was not only waged in congressional hearings, legislative chambers, bureaucratic offices, and corporate boardrooms, but on the water itself, as different interests competed to control the commons. The struggle was not simply about ideas but about power—the power to forge a livelihood from the sea, the power to regulate and prohibit fishing, the power to label certain fishers as "violators" and punish them with state power. It was a battle that pitted fisheries managers and bureaucrats, armed with scientific expertise and legal authority, against common fishermen, armed only with their practical and traditional knowledge of their trade. Fishermen—whites and Indians alike—refused to be passive victims of federal bureaucrats or outside corporations. They challenged the right of fisheries managers to control the seas—and they did so with acts of resistance, large and small.

In 1915 fisheries agent Ward T. Bower, in an effort to justify his department's increasingly stringent enforcement of fisheries laws—and the growing protests against those efforts by fishermen—explained that the fishery regulations were intended neither to "stifle legitimate enterprise nor to cause oppressive hardship," but rather to "benefit directly and indiscriminately" everyone who had a concern in the fishery.[112] But fishermen, from the 1910s on, came to feel particularly victimized by punishments that they felt were disproportionately harsh for small, independent operators like themselves and unusually lenient for large corporations and fish traps—an inequity that William Paul believed was yet another example of "one law for the seiner and another for the big trap owner."[113]

The intensity of fisheries surveillance and enforcement increased dramatically after the enactment of the White Act in 1924, which for the first time gave fisheries agents the police power authority to arrest violators and seize fishing gear, a provision that fell especially hard on independent fishermen. In 1930 the Fisheries Bureau decided to give fishermen "the alternative of pleading guilty to a fishery violation and paying a fine rather than have their gear condemned." In September of that year conservation agents arrested a troller for illegal fishing. The U.S. attorney, working under the new guidelines, "ordered the operator released, but the boat held, with instructions that if the operator plead guilty to illegal fishing, the boat and gear would be returned to him, providing he paid the fine assessed which, in this case, was $400."[114] Fishermen were likely to acquiesce to such extortion and plead guilty, even for violations they believed unwarranted, unfair, or simply false, rather than risk losing their boat for the remainder of the fishing season. They sometimes appealed for leniency, insisting that tidal conditions, inclement weather, or a poorly marked stream helped to cause the violation.

When conservation officials arrested two seine boats for illegal fishing near Ketchikan in early August 1930, one captain claimed that "the outgoing tide forms an eddy there which pulled their seines within the markers," while the other maintained that "they were unable to see the stream markers against the rocks in the light of the early dawn."[115] After he was cited for fishing too close to the seiner *Pansy*, Carl Haug, skipper of the *Clermont*, wrote an extensively detailed letter to the Bureau of Fisheries explaining that the violation was "caused by the strong flow of the tide against the wide expanse of seine," setting them toward the *Pansy*, which "was at this time not subject to such great drift as she had gone into her set some time before us . . . and has less web in the water."[116] Such appeals, however, were not often successful, and most fishermen simply admitted their guilt and accepted their punishment, such as Indian fisher Samuel Johnson, who was fined $250 for trolling "450 yards off the mouth of Eagle Creek," only fifty yards within the legal limit—a charge that without modern loran coordinates or adequately marked streams was at best nit-picky and at worst outright hostile.[117]

The resentments that fishermen harbored against conservation officials, and their belief that they were being treated unfairly, was supported by the statistics: between 1930 and 1942 fisheries agents arrested 1,207 violators, of which only 46 were trap operators, compared with 746 purse-seiners and 220 gillnetters.[118] Such inequity, according to William Paul, was "the foundation of all the discontent that you will find among the fishermen of Alaska."[119] While the responsibilities of the Fish and Wildlife Service were supposedly "limited to the conservation of fish," Paul and other resident fishermen believed it had become instead a "custodian of trap interests."[120]

The perception that they were victimized might not have been so acute had fisheries regulations accomplished their intended goal of increasing and stabilizing fish populations. Fisheries managers believed that since 1924, "the pink salmon resources of southeastern Alaska were not only restored to the original state of abundance but increased beyond this point through the controlled management of the Bureau of Fisheries."[121] But fishermen were not so sure. They experienced seasonal fluctuations and saw firsthand the impact of depletion on local streams. They often questioned the rationality of regulations that seemingly did not improve runs, but apparently worked in the opposite direction. A case in point was an ongoing debate over a general regulation that opened salmon fishing early in the spring but closed it early in the fall—a policy that in the view of many fishermen "did not jibe with the run of fish" and was responsible for depleting the "early" run and building the "late" run to the point of overabundance.

They called for a more nuanced policy that kept "close account of the run of the different streams" and managed "opening and closing dates accordingly."[122] Native fishers believed that the prohibition of late-season fishing not only deprived "fishermen and their families of an opportunity to earn a sufficient amount of money," but caused "over-escapement . . . resulting in destruction of spawn."[123] Conservation officials justified the policy scientifically as a means of protecting smaller salmon that they believed were sexually immature and not ready to spawn. Fisheries scientists believed that larger, fully developed salmon migrated early in the season while late runs consisted of small fish who had not yet attained their full maturity and had therefore "stay[ed] out there attempting to attain it."[124] This logic held that early fishing harvested bigger salmon that were ready to return to their natal streams, while late fishing preyed on small fish still trying to mature. In this case, however, the fishermen, not the conservation managers, were right: early and late fish were part of genetically distinctive runs, and early fishing simply depleted early runs and preserved late runs. Scientists prevailed, though, as their data carried more credibility with legislators and policy makers than the experience of fishers. Fishermen lost the war that pitted local knowledge against bureaucratic expertise, but they could fight in other ways.

One form of resistance to the regime of conservation was simply to defy fisheries laws—an act that was commonplace among fishermen of all gear types. Independent fishermen could justify such behavior because of what they perceived as the inherent injustice of fisheries management. Believing that federal fisheries agents and large corporations colluded to force them from their livelihoods, fishermen often supposed they had no other alternative than to take fish by any means necessary. Because fisheries managers enforced unfair prohibitions against movable gear while letting fish traps harvest the majority of the salmon, one fisherman explained that independents were "bound" to break the law or else "go hungry." He admitted: "All the seiners broke the regulations this year. . . . The Bureau of Fisheries makes a bunch of thieves out of us."[125]

In deliberately violating conservation laws, fishers were acting out of self-interest, but they also were constructing what environmental historian Karl Jacoby has described as a "moral ecology." Drawing on historian E. P. Thompson's idea of a "moral economy," where economic relationships are regulated informally by local communities on the basis of tradition, community standards, and fairness, moral ecologies are landscapes, or commons, managed informally by local communities rather than private holders, corporations, or distant bureaucracies.[126] Just as proponents of moral economies resisted market values—such as grain prices determined by supply and demand rather than fairness—moral ecologists resisted formal conservation strategies that favored nonlocal elites. For resident fishers in Alaska illegal fishing was a means of resisting fisheries management policies that appeared to enrich large corporations at the expense of local communities.

The most forceful example of local resistance was the act of "fish piracy" or "trap robbing," which became widespread in southeastern Alaska during the 1910s and 1920s. Fish pirates were common fishermen—almost always purse-seiners—who simply helped themselves to the salmon already captured in the pot of a fish trap. Sometimes trap robbers used violent intimidation to achieve their ends, but more often they raided traps when watchmen were absent, or trap employees cooperated with the raiders and received a share of the profits. One old-timer recalled how fish pirates paid off trap watchmen and then sold their plunder back to the cannery that owned the trap: "They know the trap watchmen, and they pay 'em off you know. . . . They'd get a couple quarts of whiskey, flip 'em a hundred dollars, and they'd just brail the goddamn old seine boat full . . . and take 'em in and pedal 'em to the same guy they stole them from."[127]

Fish piracy escalated in 1919, as the number of traps and canneries increased during the wartime salmon boom, and the trap harvest neared 60 percent. Bower described a fishery gripped by "a lawless element" who "raided and robbed," in one instance stealing more than sixty thousand salmon from one company. In that year vessels and men from the Navy, Coast Guard, Forest Service, and the Bureau of Fisheries were mobilized "to take summary action in dealing with the evil," and "piracy was brought to an end chiefly by an organized patrol under Federal and Territorial authorization and the cooperation of several packing companies."[128] But the scourge continued into the 1920s and in 1924, according to the industry journal the *Pacific Fisherman*, "the situation was aggravated . . . by the boldness and apparently desperate character of the fish pirates, who did not hesitate to use firearms, and on one occasion at least fired into the pilot house of an approaching cannery tender with evident intent to kill."[129] The next year piracy was "reduced to a minimum" through the efforts of a patrol "organized by the largest canners and operated under the supervision of deputy United States Marshals."[130] But trap raiding persisted, as independent fishermen continued to deal with the trap problem through direct and extralegal methods. As late as the 1930s, one cannery superintendent lamented that "neither the government boats nor the armed patrols maintained by the packers can stop the practice."[131]

Were trap pirates "moral ecologists," "social bandits," or simply a "lawless element"? Were they reckless outlaws motivated by base self-interest or class-conscious rebels justifiably seeking redress from large corporate fish traps? Were they shady outlaws or upright citizens, "common fishermen" who simply desired to participate in an open-access fishery that they believed was being destroyed by corporate fish traps and federal bureaucrats?

The Hollywood version of Alaskan fish pirates, as could be expected, is—literally and figuratively—black and white: a tale of moral simplicity with clear heroes and villains. In Henry Hathaway's *Spawn of the North* (1938), cannerymen and trap owners (often referred to simply as "fishermen") are upstanding citizens bringing civilization to "virgin territory," while fish pirates are pariahs who threatened the honest enterprise and social cohesion of the community. Except for the salmon-spawning scenes, the pet seal, and the fact that the posses jump on boats rather than horses, *Spawn* simply transposes the Hollywood Western to Alaska, with degenerate cattle rustlers now cast as fish pirates and law-abiding ranchers playing trap owners who own herds of salmon rather than steer. The story is a familiar tale of frontier justice: in the absence of established law, earnest vigilantes vanquish the outlaws and restore order and stability to the fledgling community, ultimately making way for the advance of civilization itself. Just as good men before them had "forced a respect for law upon the desperadoes of the Old West," the prologue to the film tells us, fish-trap owners, such as Jim Kimmerlee (played by Henry Fonda), would bring to heel "the fish pirates of the Alaskan frontier."[132]

Contrary to the Hollywood version, however, fish pirates—although clearly outlaws—were also respected members of their local communities, while powerful nonresident cannerymen (who imported nonresident workers and operated large fish traps instead of buying salmon from independent small-boat fishermen) were often despised by local residents. In her study of fish rustlers on the U.S.-Canada border, historian Lissa Wadewitz persuasively argues that trap pirates sometimes operated on loftier principles than sheer greed. In her view they were engaging in a form of "just" thievery that carried a larger social message: that "rustling fish from traps owned by the largest corporations was a way to contest how class privileges increasingly aligned with access to the region's natural resources."[133]

It may be overly romantic to assign such lofty and well-articulated motives to those who were simply lining their pockets with profits from other men's labor. Yet in Southeast Alaska, as already discussed, resident fishermen and local boosters drew from a deep well of resentment against corporate fish traps: trap operators were denigrating the value of honest labor, stifling the growth of a local resident fishing population, plundering local salmon populations, and taking their profits south. Coming from the mouths of trap pirates, these arguments could be dismissed as sour grapes or outright rationalizations for criminality. Independent fishermen were clearly losing fish (and money) to the traps and were seeking ways to eliminate their fiercest competitors, or at least share the wealth. Conservation managers saw the conflict in these terms. To them it was a fish fight, pure and simple, a battle between competing gear types, neither of which owned the moral high

Fish trap in Tamgas Stream, Annette Island, Alaska, July 26, 1910. Native fish traps operated in upstream locations, allowing Northwest Coast fishers to harvest large volumes of salmon during the peak of the annual salmon runs. Despite their efficiency and their proximity to salmon spawning grounds, aboriginal fish traps did not decimate salmon populations. When the United States acquired control over the salmon fisheries in Alaska, the first conservation law, passed by Congress in 1889, placed very few restrictions on commercial fishers, but it did outlaw aboriginal fish traps, even while allowing industrial traps free rein. SOURCE: John N. Cobb Photograph Collection, University of Washington (UW) Special Collections, neg. no. Cobb 3111.

Tlingit fish-drying station, Killisnoo, Alaska, June 20, 1907. Perhaps more important than fishing techniques was the development of storage methods, which allowed Native peoples to extend salmon consumption throughout the year. Native peoples dried salmon at fish camps like this one well into the twentieth century. SOURCE: John N. Cobb Photograph Collection, UW Special Collections, neg. no. NA2729.

(*Facing page, top*) Salmon trap, Ketchikan, Alaska, circa 1912. Industrial fish traps became the most efficient and controversial method of catching salmon in Alaska. Pile-driven traps, like the one pictured here, initiated a half century of conflict between "movable-gear" fishers and "fixed-gear" operators. SOURCE: John E. Thwaites Photograph Collection, UW Special Collections, neg. no. Thwaites 247.731.

In the late 1800s large canning enterprises transplanted the technologies, labor systems, and attitudes of nineteenth-century laissez-faire capitalism to Southeast Alaska. This picture shows a cannery steamer preparing to transport the season's "pack" of canned salmon from the Alaska hinterland to a world market. SOURCE: Early Prints of Alaska Photograph Collection, Alaska State Library, ASL-P297–129.

Brailing a salmon trap, Ketchikan, Alaska, circa 1912. When the cannery steamer arrived to transfer salmon from the trap's "spiller" to a wooden scow, wood, net, tides, and human labor were transformed into a machine of industrial productivity. SOURCE: John E. Thwaites Photograph Collection, UW Special Collections, neg. no. Thwaites 247.723.

(*Facing page, top*) Fishing boats in harbor, Kasaan, Alaska, circa 1912. Non-Native fishers invaded tribal fishing sites at Kasaan and numerous other traditional villages throughout Southeast Alaska, sparking conflict between Natives and whites. SOURCE: John E. Thwaites Photograph Collection, UW Special Collections, neg. no. Thwaites 247.641.

(*Facing page, bottom*) Indian dwellings at the Yakutat salmon cannery. In the late nineteenth and early twentieth centuries, Native peoples relocated from traditional villages to cannery towns, where they could participate in the market economy. SOURCE: General Photograph File. Alaska Museum of History and Art, AMRC-b80–28–6.

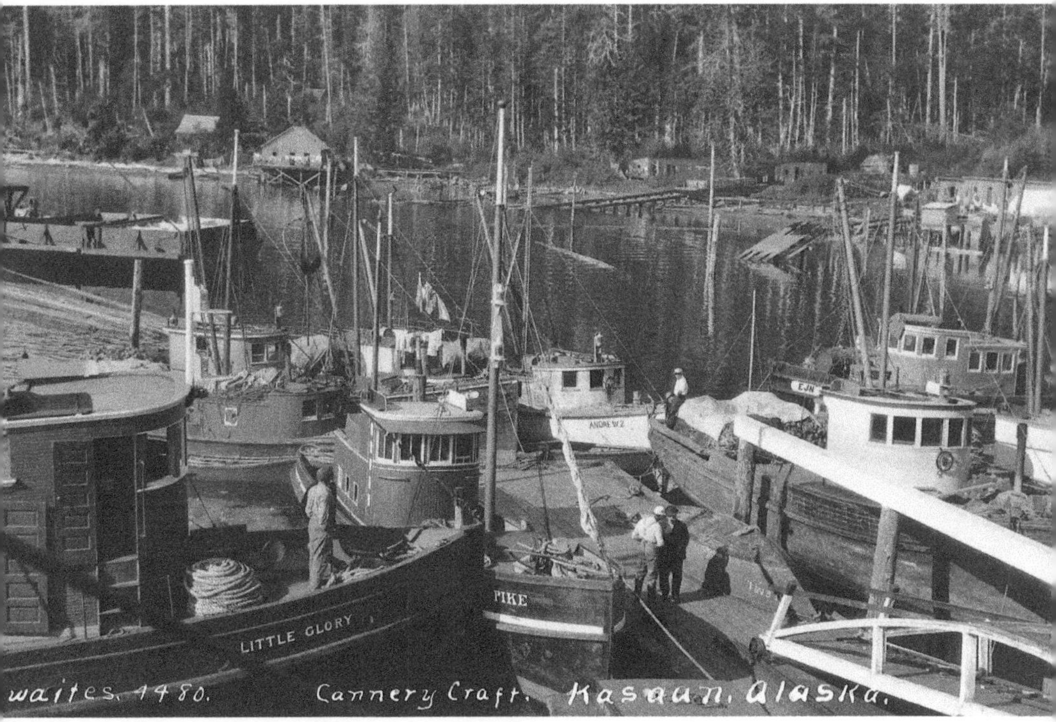

waites. 1480.
Cannery Craft.
Kasaan, Alaska.
LITTLE GLORY
PIKE

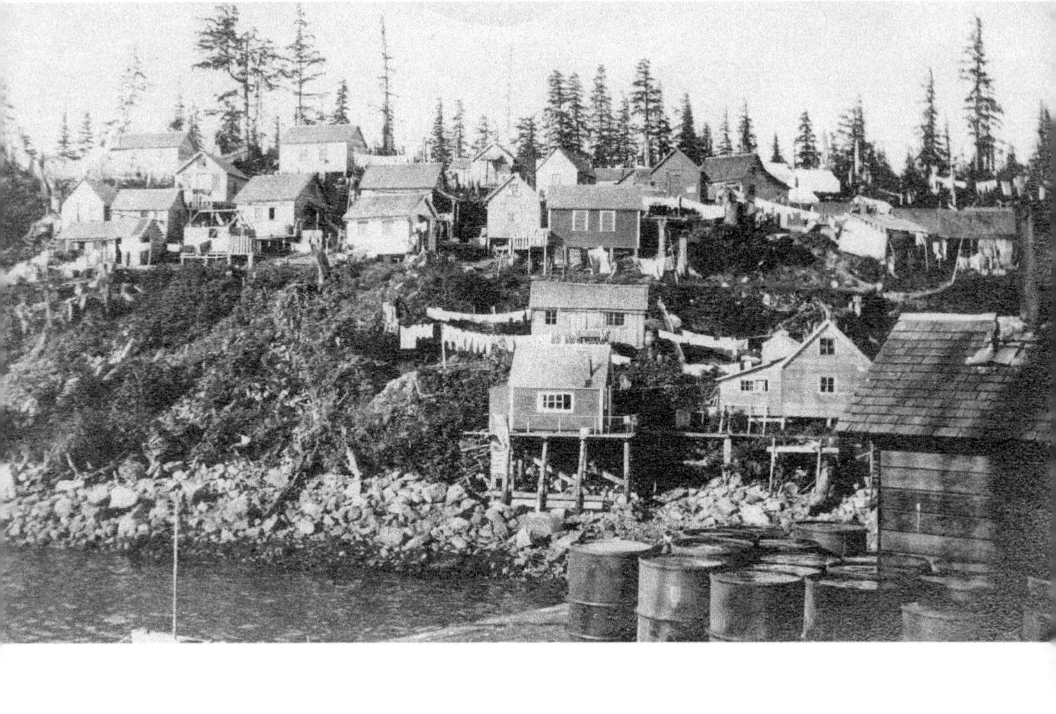

"Cannery workers, unidentified cannery interior," no date. Salmon canneries depended primarily on Asian American and Native American workers. In a pattern that resembled the traditional fishery, Indian women and children processed salmon in canneries while Indian men fished. SOURCE: John N. Cobb Photograph Collection, UW Special Collections, neg. no. UW21386.

Guests from Angoon, Alaska, at a 1904 Sitka potlatch. From potlatches to traditional subsistence strategies, Indian tradition marched on. While whites praised Indian industriousness as a sign of cultural assimilation, Indian workers used their wages to acquire silver dollars, bags of flour, and blankets for potlatch festivals, which continued well into the twentieth century. SOURCE: Elbridge W. Merrill Photograph Collection, Alaska State Library, ASL-P57–028.

(Facing page, top) "Shore-seining five miles from cannery site in canoe," probably late nineteenth century. These Indian fishers near Sitka combined traditional technologies—such as cedar canoes and traditional paddles—with modern gear, such as this purse-seine. They also combined commercial fishing with subsistence fishing, allowing them to adapt to the market economy while still engaging in traditional economic activities. SOURCE: Core File-Place Photograph Collection, Alaska State Library, ASL-Sitka-Indians-31.

"Securing salmon eggs at unidentified hatchery, Alaska," likely an APA hatchery around 1910. Early fisheries managers saw hatcheries as a simple technological fix to a problem that required a broader ecological approach. Cloaked in their oilskins, these hatchery employees sought to improve upon nature, but their methods were clumsy and the results were disappointing. SOURCE: John N. Cobb Photograph Collection, UW Special Collections, neg. no. UW15528.

(*Facing page, top*) Alaska Packers Association Fortmann Hatchery, Loring, Alaska, probably 1910s. Salmon packers and federal conservation officials put far more resources into "making salmon" than they did protecting salmon ecology or limiting fishing intensity. Corporations like the APA operated their own hatcheries to increase fish stocks and obviate the need for regulation; they also received generous rebates from the federal government, regardless of the fact that their efforts were a complete failure. SOURCE: John N. Cobb Photograph Collection, UW Special Collections, neg. no. UW21387.

(*Facing page, bottom*) Fishing fleet and Deer Mountain, Ketchikan, Alaska. This photo from the 1920s reveals the sublime natural beauty of the fishermen's frontier; it also shows the fishing fleet at rest, literally bound together in a calm solidarity. The social reality of the fishing community was far more complex and far less serene. SOURCE: John Urban Collection, Anchorage Museum of History & Art, AMRC-b64–1–642.

06 Fishing Fleet and Deer Mt. Ketchikan, Alaska

Schallerer ©

Gillnetters at Taku Harbor with their day's catch, 1910. In the fragmented fishery, craft solidarity divided gillnetters from purse-seiners from trollers. SOURCE: Roberta Johnson Photograph Collection, Alaska State Library, PCA 330–22.

Salmon trollers, Southeast Alaska, from the 1920s or 1930s. Trolling epitomized the freedom, independence, and natural setting that many salmon fishermen sought in commercial fishing. SOURCE: Early Prints of Alaska Photograph Collection, Alaska State Library, photo no. 01–2326.

Tlingit Indians fishing, Boca de Quadra, Alaska, August 2, 1904. With less access to capital many Indian fishermen in Southeast Alaska—like this six-man crew of Tlingit fishers—purse-seined with cannery gear. SOURCE: John N. Cobb Photograph Collection, UW Special Collections, neg. no. 418.

"Purse seiners and crew at dock, Alaska." For the 1910s these gas-powered purse-seine boats were state of the art. They required a great deal of capital investment, but they also caught massive volumes of salmon. Vessels like these, most often from the Puget Sound, generated almost as much resentment among resident Alaskan fishers, especially Natives, as did fish traps. SOURCE: John N. Cobb Photograph Collection, UW Special Collections, neg. no. UW15531.

WELCOME VISITORS
ALASKA
SALMON

A fisherman at a Norwegian fish farm overseeing the operations of a giant fish pump as it vacuums salmon from net pens. Photo: Gunnar Knapp, "Implications of Aquaculture for Wild Fisheries: The Case of Alaska Wild Salmon," paper presented at the International Institute of Fisheries Economics and Trade Conference, August 22, 2002, Wellington, New Zealand.

(Facing page, top) Chinese workers in the "Fish House," Southeast Alaska, late nineteenth century. The identity of Euro-American fishermen was constructed partly in opposition to Asian cannery workers, whom they perceived as weak and dependent wage slaves. Fishermen, in contrast, believed themselves liberated from the drudgery and oppression of the industrial workplace. SOURCE: Early Prints of Alaska Photograph Collection, Alaska State Library, photo no. 01–2775.

(Facing page, bottom) Ketchikan's main street. The arch read: "More canned salmon packed in Ketchikan than any other city in the world." By 1930s, however, many residents wondered if the salmon boom was finally over: global demand for canned salmon was falling, salmon harvests were down, fishermen and trap operators attacked each other in congressional hearings, and shortly the issue of aboriginal fishing rights would offer one more challenge to the ailing industry. SOURCE: Ickes Collection, Anchorage Museum of History and Art, AMRC-b75–175–598.

The post-fishermen's frontier: a sea devoid of small boats. Chilean net pens containing Atlantic salmon create an orderly, efficient, and tightly controlled environment for salmon production. Much like the way that industrialization de-skilled artisans, salmon farms threaten to render obsolete the craft knowledge of fishing. SOURCE: Gunnar Knapp, personal collection.

ground. Bureau of Fisheries' support for traps was based on what conservation officials believed to be disinterested rationality—traps were economically efficient and more easily regulated. By taking such a view, however, fisheries agents turned a deaf ear to the social considerations and moral outrage that lay at the heart of the conflict. It would be folly to accept uncritically the rhetoric and rationalizations of criminals, but the determination of whether one is a common thief or an outlaw crusader for social justice comes from communities, not the criminals themselves, and the case against traps carried a popular appeal in southeastern Alaska that extended well beyond fishermen.

Perhaps the most powerful and resonant argument that trap pirates used to justify their banditry was that fish-trap operators did not own either the ocean or the fish, both of which were common property. Fish pirates believed, according to one trap owner, that as long as "salmon in traps are alive and actually still in the sea, they are anybody's property."[134] As Red Skain, the Russian villain in *Spawn of the North*, put it: "These trap owners . . . they don't own the ocean. . . . Nobody owns the fish . . . they got their own law. They come and go when they want to. They don't belong to Alaska."[135] Skain's words could easily be confused with those of a real fish pirate, Bert Jones, known as Fish Pirate Jones, who robbed salmon traps in Puget Sound in the early twentieth century because "the fish were made for everybody" and fishermen simply "wanted their share."[136]

Convicted trap pirates took such arguments into the courtrooms, contending that "trap operators had no legal rights to fish alive in the traps until they were actually removed from the water."[137] This view—a simplification of the common law belief that wild animals could not become individual property until they were actually possessed by an individual—may have been popular on the streets of Sitka, but it was not supported by case law, which regarded traps as an effective and legitimate form of "possession," defined as the act of confining or entrapping an animal to the point where "they cannot escape and resume their natural liberty."[138] Legally, the issue was settled by the Ninth Circuit Court of Appeals, which upheld the larceny conviction of an Alaskan fish pirate in the 1927 case *Klemm v. United States*. Klemm argued, much like Hollywood's Red Skain, that "no person has any property in fish in the ocean." The appeals court agreed that fish in the ocean could not be owned, but it upheld previous rulings that recognized trap-caught fish as having already been "reduced to possession."[139]

Although it was a loser in court, Klemm's argument resonated among fishers and local residents—lawless and upstanding—who believed that traps indeed violated the fundamental rights of independent fishermen in an open fishery. It might be a stretch to call fish pirates latter-day Alaskan Robin Hoods—stealing salmon from the corrupted and greedy corporations and redistributing wealth among the fishing classes—or to label them twentieth-century crusaders for social justice. Perhaps a comparison with Luddites has some value, since they both struck out at the machines that threatened their livelihood. But fish pirates did not destroy the traps, they simply pilfered from them. What they share with Luddites, as well as Jacoby's moral ecologists, is a sense of righteous outrage and a desire to defend their local communities against forces that they perceived as immoral, hostile, nonlocal, greedy, and destructive. Like other populist outlaws, they also shared a bond with law-abiding but sympathetic members of the local community. Juries in Southeast Alaska were hesitant to convict trap robbers, "even when the evidence seemed quite conclusive to impartial observers."[140]

J. R. Heckman, the inventor of the floating fish trap, lamented that "the feeling is so strong against fish traps, it seems impossible to get a conviction against fish trap pirates." Heckman was told by an attorney in 1934 that "the grand jury did not indict alleged fish pirates this year . . . [because] they could not get a conviction, and it meant a large useless expense."[141] Lauren Casaday, after interviewing Alaskan fishermen for his doctoral dissertation in the mid-1930s, concluded that "rare indeed is the Alaska jury that will convict on the charge of pirating a company trap."[142] This fact alone seems enough to overturn the Hollywood myth—also held by cannerymen and fish-trap operators of the day—that the story of fish piracy was as simple as good guys versus bad guys, upstanding trap owners versus common outlaws. Instead, it was a story of local resistance to both corporate power and federal control.

Another source of local resistance came from Native Americans. If it is a stretch to suggest that non-Indian fish pirates, many of whom were recent arrivals to Alaska, were motivated by moral imperatives and guided by a desire to defend longstanding community practices, Native fishers, who had managed the salmon fishery of southeastern Alaska long before the arrival of salmon canneries and U.S. fisheries managers, could legitimately claim the moral and historical high ground. Native fishers were not content to simply assert their equal rights to the open-access fishery, as was the case with the white fishermen, but rather to defend Northwest Coast traditions of clan and household ownership over particular fishing grounds. The salmon fisheries in southeastern Alaska had never been an "open access" commons, but rather a landscape of strictly delineated tribal fishing sites stewarded and regulated by local clan leaders in the interest of the local tribal community.

Such property rights had been overrun in the nineteenth century by salmon canneries and non-Indian fishers operating under the legal doctrine of a free and open fishery and the economic principle of laissez faire. Native property rights to the salmon fisheries were further diminished in the twentieth century by federal resource managers who restricted Indian fishing in the name of conservation and the public welfare. Native Americans had resisted these incursions in multiple ways, but not until 1942 did they directly confront the right of fisheries managers to restrict them from fishing in tribal territory. On July 30 of that year Louis F. Paul and his seine crew, all members of the Tee-Hit-Ton tribe of Tlingit Indians, were arrested by Bureau of Fisheries agent Clarence Olson for taking fish in Salmon Bay, an area that had been closed to commercial fishing since the White Act of 1924. The Indian fishers who, according to Olson, "did not follow instructions upon apprehension" claimed to "possess the exclusive right of fishery" in Salmon Bay, which they had occupied from "time immemorial."[143]

Louis Paul—represented by his nephew William L. Paul Jr. and encouraged by his brother William L. Paul Sr., the longtime ANB activist—challenged his arrest by filing a legal complaint against the U.S. Fish and Wildlife Service on the grounds that the Tee-Hit-Ton tribe was entitled to "an exclusive right of fishery" in Salmon Bay.[144] The tribe contended that their fishing rights had never been legally extinguished but had been rendered "ineffectual, unprofitable, and impossible" to maintain because of "unreasonable, capricious, and arbitrary" fisheries regulations enacted since the White Act of 1924, which had closed down Salmon Bay to purse-seining. Paul Jr. argued that Indians used "to take great numbers of red salmon for personal and commercial purposes," but that regulations closing the area "were so designed and contrived" to prohibit Native fishers from "making any use and occupation of their said rights of fishery," while at the same time enabling canneries to operate their fish traps "in the best possible location" and "at full 100% capacity."[145]

The lawsuit drew on a deep well of resistance and discontent among Native fishers, whose tribal fishery had been expropriated by industrialists and conservation officials. In the late nineteenth century Indian fishers, even while participating in the emerging commercial fishery, had resisted the open-access regime by physically denying non-Indian fishers access to tribal sites or by insisting that they pay for the rights to fish. Although this strategy was sometimes successful, the growing non-Indian population backed by the power of the U.S. military had smothered Indian resistance by the end of the nineteenth century.[146] Indian protest in the early twentieth century largely took the form of petitioning fisheries regulators and legislators. With the emergence of the Alaska Native Brotherhood, Indian complaints no longer focused on protecting aboriginal property rights. Instead, they criticized corporate fish traps and unfair fisheries regulations and even defended the open-access fisheries regime, asserting their common grievances with white commercial fishers. But Native critiques of federal conservation policy escalated dramatically after the White Act, which in the view of most Indian fishers privileged corporations and fish traps while subjecting their tribal fishing grounds to increased regulation, if not closure, as was the case in Salmon Bay and a number of other traditional fishing sites. The White Act, in the opinion of the Tlingit newspaper the *Alaska Fisherman*, had forced the "small Indian fisherman" to "bear the whole burden of conservation."[147] In 1925 the newspaper called not only for the abolition of fish traps but also for the abolition of the Bureau of Fisheries.[148]

It was not until the 1930s, however, that Indian fishers began to explore the possibility of resisting fisheries regulations—or securing exclusive rights to fishing sites—on the basis of their aboriginal rights. At congressional hearings in 1939, William Paul Sr. expressed his belief that Tlingits and Haidas were "still the owners of the fish that swim from spawning areas of Alaska." Indian peoples had not abandoned their ownership of the salmon fishery, he argued, but had been forced from it by the "rules promulgated by the Bureau of Fisheries." "The right to catch fish, our fish," he declared, "has been taken from us by the United States Government."[149]

Paul's appeal to aboriginal rights reflected changes that were taking place within the Department of Interior in the 1930s. The Bureau of Indian Affairs, under Commissioner John Collier, began encouraging tribal economic development with the extension of the Indian Reorganization Act to Alaska in 1936. The secretary of the interior, Harold Ickes, was looking for ways to support both fisheries conservation and aboriginal rights in the territory.[150] With the encouragement of Collier, Ickes asked solicitor Nathan Margold to provide an opinion on "whether Indians of Alaska have any fishing rights which are violated by control of particular trap sites by non-Indians," and whether such violations might justify the Interior Department in the "closing down of certain trap sites" or even allocating fish traps to Indian peoples.

Margold's opinion, approved in February 1942, held that Native peoples in Alaska clearly had preexisting aboriginal fishing rights—which he described as "exclusive rights, under which the right to exclude others from a given area is an integral part"—that were being violated, with the aid of fisheries regulations, by non-Indian trap operators.[151]

In elaborating his opinion a month later, Margold argued that the interior secretary not only had the right to regulate the fisheries for purposes of conservation, but also for social purposes, such as to effect "a more equitable or less equitable distribution of fishing rights."[152] It was Margold's opinion that prompted Ickes—with little support from fisheries managers—to include a provision in the 1942 Alaskan fisheries regulations which provided that "no trap shall be established in any site in which any Alaskan native or natives has or have any rights of fishery."[153] It was also Margold's opinion that encouraged William Paul Sr. to tell fisheries managers in June 1942 that he intended "to fish for private and/or commercial use in Salmon Bay . . . notwithstanding your regulations prohibiting it."[154]

The Tee-Hit-Ton tribe's 1942 challenge to conservation officials did not succeed. Paul and his fishing crew were convicted of fisheries violations in court, while a new Interior Department solicitor, Warner W. Gardner, took the opinion that Indian resistance to fisheries regulations could not be justified on the basis of aboriginal fishing rights. Even though the Interior Department was partly responsible for encouraging the insubordination of the Tee-Hit-Ton tribe, Gardner held that fishery laws were "applicable to all natives and that the appellants were properly convicted." While acknowledging the existence of Indian fishing rights, Gardner believed that even "aboriginal rights are subject to conservation regulation" and that Native fishing sites could even "be closed down altogether as a conservation measure."[155] The civil case brought by the tribe against the Fish and Wildlife Service was dismissed. Interior Department lawyers argued that the United States, not the Tee-Hit-Ton tribe, owned the fishery, and was charged "with the obligation of perpetuating the supply for the benefit of all the people." The tribe's desire to "take salmon in great numbers from their very spawning grounds" violated this basic premise of conservation policy.[156] The judge agreed. The Ninth Circuit Court of Appeals upheld the dismissal, encouraging the tribe instead to pursue compensation through the newly created Indian Claims Commission.[157]

The setback did not discourage Native fishers from challenging the right of federal managers to control the waterways of southeastern Alaska. The early 1950s saw a new wave of defiance, beginning in 1952, when a Native purse-seine crew deliberately cast their nets in illegal waters directly in front of a U.S. Fish and Wildlife vessel that had just issued them a warning. The five Indian men, who were fined $1,200 and placed in jail because they refused to post bail, argued that the stream was not properly marked, its closure was not listed in the federal register, and the secretary of interior could not delegate the authority to close fishing grounds to his subordinates.[158] Two other cases involving Indian seining crews were identical—in each case Native fishermen purposefully set their gear in closed areas, received heavy fines, and argued that the interior secretary had no statutory right to entrust his power to "some seasonal stream guard of deficient mentality."[159] The government prevailed in each case, but the incidents revealed the underlying struggle between fisheries managers and Native fishers, who had long believed that the "burden of conservation under the FWLS [Fish and Wildlife Service] closed area policy has fallen almost exclusively upon Indian fishermen."[160]

A more revealing case—and one that cut to the heart of Indian notions of moral ecology—involved the right of Native communities to harvest fish for subsistence purposes. The White Act—still the basis of federal fisheries law in Alaska in the 1950s—had allowed that fishery regulations did not "prevent the taking of fish for local food requirements."[161] In 1952 fisheries managers tried to close this "loophole," which they believed was being "seized upon and abused" by Indian fishermen, by declaring that "all fishing for personal use with gill net, seine, or trap shall be subject to the laws and regulations governing commercial fishing" and that "bona fide personal use fishing" could only occur more than twenty-five miles from "waters legally open to commercial fishing."[162] It was on the basis of this new regulation that fisheries agents arrested Steven Hotch, an Indian fishermen from Klukwan, for gillnetting in Taku Inlet during a weekly closed period. Hotch had caught only "two king salmon for food for his family." His lawyer, William L. Paul Jr., contended that Hotch was simply "pursuing the custom of his people" when he was arrested by conservation officials. He "had cut up the salmon and was smoke-drying them" for household consumption. Paul argued that the new 1952 regulation limiting subsistence fishing would "vitally affect not only the defendant, his wife and eight children, but also many hundreds of others, especially among the Natives of Alaska who put up so much of their winter food supply during the summer."[163]

The government argued that the secretary of the interior had the "authority to regulate the means of taking personal use fish" so as to ensure "a continual source of fish for present and future generations."[164] From the perspective of the government and federal fisheries agents the case pitted local self-interest against the public good; from the perspective of Native fishers, however, the case hinged on the right of local communities to manage and use fish for their own purposes. Once again, federal control prevailed over the local moral ecology, but local communities—both Native and white—continued to resist federal authority. An editorial in the Alaska Native *Voice of Brotherhood*, in November 1956, called again for the Fish and Wildlife Service to be relieved of its "responsibility in regards to fisheries," since the agency had "proved incapable of coping with existing deplorable conditions" in the southeastern Alaska salmon fishery.[165]

AN IRRATIONAL FISHERY

The Steven Hotch case revealed, yet again, the underlying tensions of the salmon fishery—and the extent to which conservation policy was the subject of continuous debate and opposition. Fisheries managers once again won the battle—but they were losing the war against both fish and fishers, where victory was the creation of a sustainable, rational, and scientifically managed fishery. In fact, by the 1950s the fishery was in the midst of a dramatic downswing that would reach its nadir in 1960, just as the power to regulate the fisheries was transferred from the federal government to the territory. Salmon hatcheries, stream improvement, rigorous regulations, and increasing enforcement had failed to bring order, stability, and economic productivity to the salmon fishery.

The rise of federal regulation completed the transformation from aboriginal fishery to industrial fishery. No longer did Native peoples regulate or manage the fishery. Even when fishing for their own consumption, their actions were constricted by resource managers. The federal government now managed the fishery according to scientific management in the interests of economic development, sustainability, and ultimately the *public good*. But federal management was only *good* for a portion of the public. The beneficiaries were primarily large canning corporations based in Chicago, San Francisco, and Seattle, while the losers were local fishers and local communities—both Native and white.

The degree to which federal managers actually took "control" of the fishery, however, can be overexaggerated (see figure 3.4). Rationality and efficiency may have guided conservation policies and prevailed over other values,

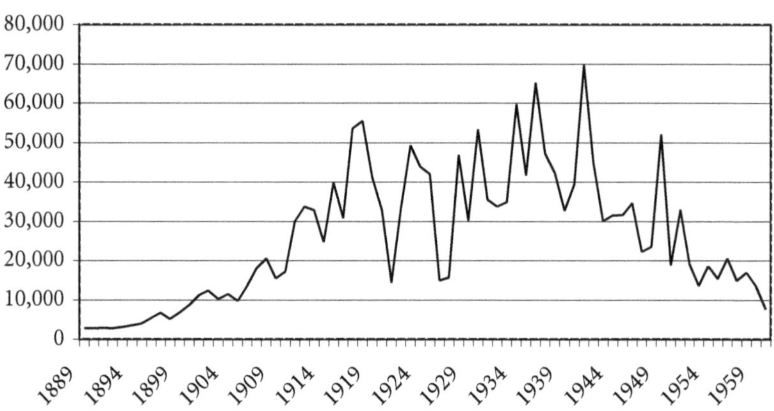

FIG. 3.4 *The fluctuating fishery: Salmon Harvests in Southeastern Alaska, 1889–1960. Despite the best efforts of fisheries managers, salmon runs fluctuated dramatically throughout the period of federal control. Artificial propagation, "stream improvement," and increased surveillance could not "stabilize" salmon populations, whose life cycles were influenced by many factors beyond the reach of conservation officials.* SOURCE: *Alaska Department of Fish and Game, "Historical Salmon Harvest and Value Charts, 1878–2003," Zephyr Database.*

such as social equality, but conservation managers failed to make the fishery more rational. They tried to rationalize and simplify an unwieldy, complex ecological system. They tried to manufacture salmon by the billions. They "improved" salmon streams by weeding out the messy nature and making streamlined, open avenues for spawning salmon. They killed thousands of predatory fish and birds and tried to minimize salmon mortality. Their simplified ecosystem, however, was less productive than complex, chaotic nature. Salmon moreover acted in unpredictable ways, their runs fluctuating dramatically from year to year as they were influenced by a multitude of factors, both terrestrial and oceanic, that were beyond the scope or understanding of fisheries managers. Changes in ocean temperatures often had much more to do with the fluctuations of salmon runs than resource management, but conservation officials interpreted the size of salmon runs almost exclusively as the product of management policies and fishing intensity—convenient variables that they assumed they could control.[166]

The human part of nature was even less easily controlled, and just as "irrational," as nature itself. Fisheries managers tried to rationalize the fishery by giving priority to fish traps—but they could not control markets, population migrations (which dramatically increased the number of individual fishers between the 1930s and 1950s), territorial politics, or the values, attitudes, traditions, and cultures of the fishers they sought to control. Neither could they stifle continued resistance to their own authority, waged by independent fishers, both Indian and white. Humans, like fish, could not be easily streamlined into a rational scheme of management.

If the story of federal fisheries management in Alaska tells us anything, it is that government conservation efforts are never unilateral. They always take place on contested ground (or contested waters), as central governments and local communities struggle to control resources and direct them toward their desired goals. For governments this often means, in theory, stewarding resources in the interests of the public good, while in practice privileging nonlocal and corporate elites. For local communities this means, in theory, managing resources in the best interests of custom and community, while in practice exploiting resources without oversight or constraint.

One irony in the debate over traps and movable gear is that neither industrialists nor fishermen were right in their apocalyptic or utopian predictions. The elimination of fish traps, which occurred shortly after Alaskan statehood, did not "spell the death of the industry," as one industrialist had predicted in 1939. But neither did it resurrect the salmon runs to a mythic level of preindustrial abundance, as many fishermen believed it would. Salmon populations continued to waver and decline throughout the 1960s and 1970s until a number of factors helped to resurrect the wild runs in southeastern Alaska: better ocean conditions; a new management strategy of "limited entry" (which, ironically, eliminated once and for all the cherished American institution of the open-access fishery); the restriction of foreign fishing vessels; a less arrogant and more effective hatchery system; increased knowledge of salmon ecosystems; and declining markets for wild salmon as the result of global salmon farming.

Another irony: limited entry protected independent fishermen, while reducing competition and limiting the catch, meaning that in fishing, unlike in agriculture or industry, the independent owner-operator was protected, at least temporarily. In one sense economic irrationality and the tradition of independent fishing won out over rationality and labor-saving efficiency in the Alaskan fisheries. Fishermen continued to work independently in the open sea as they had for generations. The evolving traditions of fishing—born of the fundamental relationship between men and nature—is the subject of the next chapter.

4 Work, Nature, Race, and Culture on the Fishermen's Frontier, 1900s–1950s

To watch gillnetters at work was to witness an elaborately choreographed dance of fish, river, and men. The habits of fish, the hydraulics of the river, and the organized labor of men all intersected. Labor and nature merged. —RICHARD WHITE, *The Organic Machine*

"You know, Ott, we got to do something soon," Henry continued. "Something. Else we'll end up like the purse-seine fishermen with the sardines. When's the last time you saw a sardine in a salmon's belly? They caught 'em all. Wiped out because fishermen couldn't get together for a price and the canneries knew it. The boats fished nonstop, from sundown to sunup, for years, just to break even. In the end, the fish were all gone." —MICHAEL KÖEPF, *The Fisherman's Son*

There should exist the condition in which laboring men of one craft would not cut the throats of the laboring men of another. —"THE FISHERMAN'S UNION," *Alaska Fisherman*, 1926

The salmon fishery in Southeast Alaska was nothing if not a landscape of work: salmon labored upstream, fishermen labored to catch them, cannery workers to process them, and fisheries managers to conserve them. The process began with the salmon—but was quickly elaborated by humans into systems of economic organization and webs of social and cultural meaning. From the Native American fishery to the modern commercial fishery, fishermen pulled salmon from rivers and bays and, in doing so, they created economies, cultures, traditions, communities, and identities. The salmon and waterways were natural, but the fishery was a human construction.

This is not to say that fishing was not natural—humans catching fish was as natural as the tides—or that nature was fully contained within human constructions. Indeed, much of what affected fishermen—the fluctuations induced by climate change, the tides, and migratory habits of the fish—were beyond the scope of human control. In this sense the movements of *both* salmon and fishermen were "natural." Historian Richard White, whose book *The Organic Machine* tries to put nature back into human history by showing how humans have historically known nature through work, has suggested that nature was not only the "salmon swimming" and "the river flowing," but also "humans fishing."[1] The difference between human work and the migrations of the salmon or the shifting of the tides was that the latter occurred without the fanfare of consciousness and culture while the former was organized socially and inscribed with cultural meaning. Fishermen constructed identities as frontiersmen, rugged individualists, subsistence gatherers, and tribal traditionalists; they joined unions and tribal brotherhoods, and they subdivided the fishery by race, ethnicity, craft, geographic location, and occupation.

Fishermen shared common experiences: all were affected by world markets, government regulations, fluctuating fish stocks, and their everyday interactions with wind, tide, and weather. All of them—Indian and white—engaged in a tug of war between the forces of tradition and modernization. But fishermen came to know nature differently depending on their culture and the larger context in which they labored. Indians and whites experienced work and nature in distinctive ways, as did trollers, gillnetters, purse-seiners, subsistence fishers, and so on. This chapter examines the varied ways that fishermen took the economic necessity of fishing and elaborated it into distinctive work cultures and identities. Three themes are especially important. First, the relationship between work and nature: how did fishermen come to know nature through work, and how did they construct identities born of this relationship between work and nature? Second, the social construction of the fishery: how did the natural act of fishing become demarcated not only by the patterns of fish migrations, but also by the social geography of race, ethnicity, and culture? Third, how did fishermen's unions and Native brotherhoods reflect both the natural and social dimensions of the fishery?

The conventional storyline of modern humans and their relationship to nature is well known. With the Industrial Revolution older ways of knowing nature through work were eliminated. Workers became alienated from the natural world. Industrialization and urbanization dislocated farmers and peasants from rural living, pushing them into urban factories where modern work made them mere tools of industrial capitalism, laboring against nature rather than within it. In America this process occurred alongside the "closing" of the western frontier. Wage workers could no longer escape eastern cities (if they ever had) for the alleged independence and comparative freedom of the countryside. Americans were becoming industrial "wage slaves," permanently disconnected from the patterns of rural life and the cycles of nature. Environmental historian Virginia Scharff has observed that "most environmental historians treat the rise of capitalism as a process that rationalized, mechanized, and commodified work; alienated people from nature; transformed workers from producers to consumers; and in the process created distinct boundaries between work and leisure."[2]

Fishermen in Alaska were not isolated from these trends. In the twentieth century a series of technological advances—combustible engines, steel hulls, hydraulic winches and reels, VHF radios, electronic "fish finders," nylon nets—made fishermen less dependent on the vicissitudes of nature. Scanning the advertisements in the trade journal *The Pacific Fisherman*, twentieth-century fishers could begin to imagine how new innovations would increase their efficiency, comfort, and safety. Technology promised to extend human mastery over nature from the land to the sea.

The labor of fishing mimicked industrial trends in other ways as well. Similar to industrial wage workers, fishermen in Alaska in the late nineteenth and early twentieth centuries were often immigrants—Slavic, Italian, Scandinavian, Finnish—carried to the region by international labor migrations. In Alaska fishermen found themselves employed by large corporations that were producing for a global market. They were poorly compensated for their labors, and they worked in conditions that were as dangerous, if not more so, as eastern factories. Ed Hibler, who worked in the Alaska-Juneau Mine until its closure in 1944, at which time he became a salmon troller, noted that both fishing and mining required long hours and were hard on the body: "It's just like working in the mine," he remembered. "It's really a tough life and it's hard on a person."[3] Like miners and other industrial workers, fishermen formed unions in an effort to improve their working conditions, and, like other workers, their unions were riven with sectarian conflict. A reasonable case could be made that the working lives of fishermen were little different from those of their brethren in more urban and industrial settings.

Historian Stephen Haycox has shown that the major streams of Alaskan settlement in the twentieth century—especially after the 1940s—were primarily urban and underwritten by government investment. Alaska was not so much a "frontier" as a federal welfare state, punctuated by pockets of hyperexploitative laissez-faire capitalism. Alaska residents may have imagined themselves as rugged individualists, but their self-sufficiency was more imagined than real. Their economies were bolstered by federal stewardship and their connections to world markets and American culture made their lives more like those in the East than they believed.[4]

What they *believed*, however, was often more powerful than the realities of their lives, and they often believed they were frontiersmen settling an untrammeled wilderness. Even in the mid-twentieth century the idea of the frontier still inspired Americans with visions of promise and economic opportunity. Alaska—so vast and abundant—became a symbol of the frontier already lost in the Lower 48. In the 1930s, in the midst of economic depression, Alaska became an escape from the wreckage of industrial civilization.[5] Amid the prosperity of the postwar period Alaska's seemingly untapped resources beckoned those seeking new economic opportunities. During good times and bad, in other words, homesteaders, construction workers, loggers, miners, and fishermen all came seeking a new life in the Alaskan "wilderness," where possibilities were still fresh and the land was not already worn out and fished out. They came seeking what one Alaskan simply described as "the great American dream! To be independent. To be completely self-reliant and, if possible, self-sufficient. Not necessarily to be rich, but to be one's own boss and beholden to no one. This is what brought our forefathers to this continent in the first place. . . . This is the magnet that still draws people to Alaska."[6]

Non-native fishermen, as migrants to Alaska, constructed heroic narratives of finding independence in a wilderness landscape. In their own words they described southeastern Alaska as a frontier—a place of freedom and opportunity where they could be liberated from the drudgery of industrial life.[7] More than other migrants to Alaska, fishermen actually fit the stereotype of the self-reliant, independent, individualistic, rugged frontiersman. While industrialization in the late nineteenth and early twentieth century separated workers from nature through mechanization and the regimentation of the workday, salmon fishing in Alaska fostered a livelihood that looked almost preindustrial by comparison. Their working lives were characterized by an intimate connection with the natural world and freedom from the industrial time clock. Working in nature allowed fishermen to elaborate a sense of identity rooted in the rejection of industrialization. Fishing was thus an escape from cities, bosses, and wage dependency. Bound together with this view of fishing as escape was a perception of Alaska as virgin wilderness—the antidote to the industrialized society they were escaping—and themselves as modern-day frontiersmen, carrying out their labors in a truly grand and pristine landscape.[8]

Labor economist Lauren Wilde Casaday interviewed Alaska salmon fishermen in the mid-1930s, and he captured the white fisherman's perspective on the difference between fishing and industrial wage work: "The clean, dangerous, and comparatively free life of the fisherman predisposes him to look with contempt upon the cannery 'mucker' who must spend his days amid the din of clanking machinery and the stench of cannery offal."[9] Indeed, in the minds of fishermen the labor of fishing posed a stark contrast to factory labor. If industrial work constrained personal freedom, treated the individual like a cog in a machine, and subjected the worker's every move to the regimentation of scientific management, fishing, by contrast, liberated the individual from those constraints by nourishing individual freedom, autonomy, and self-ownership. Moreover, while the industrial system subjected workers to dehumanizing conditions and alienated them from the natural world, fishing connected individuals to the natural world and allowed them to carry out their labors amid the fresh air, wind, and tides. Like the British author Rudyard Kipling, who saw the salmon canneries on the Columbia River as the antithesis of the nature that surrounded them, salmon fishers drew a strict distinction between their labors outside and those of cannery workers inside. "For Kipling the canneries encapsulated a basic spatial division between the mechanical and the natural," writes Richard White: "Inside, crowding, humanity, death, machines, routinization; outside, solitude, nature, life, the organic, and freedom."[10]

Toivo Andersen, who was born in Nome, Alaska, in 1910 and began fishing out of Ketchikan in 1927, described Alaska then as a "virgin country" and his fishing life as one of "challenge," "adventure," and freedom from restraint. He became a fisherman because "you're strictly an individual and you're your own boss. . . . It's a free life. It's a good, healthy, free life. You don't have to have a boss, you're your own damn boss. . . . You're not obligated to anybody but yourself." Andersen believed that trolling, which yielded the fewest fish but also required the least investment, was preferable to seining or gillnetting, where the need for capital made fishermen dependent on canneries: "[If] you're gillnetting or you're seining, you are more or less obligated to . . . the canneries [which] buys their boat, helps them finance their boats, helps them finance their seines. . . . But a troller doesn't have that big of an investment to begin with when he starts off, and he can be strictly an individual. It's the freedom of the life."[11]

John Bahrt, born in Sitka in 1916, began trolling in 1930 because of the "independence." He explained: "There was nobody to demand upon us that we go out. If we wanted to go hungry, we could go hungry, it was our prerogative."[12] Ed Hibler, a miner who began trolling in the 1940s because he was "tired of working for somebody else," echoed the sentiments of both Andersen and Bahrt: "Fishing was always better than working for wages, because you got nobody looking down your shirt collar all the time, you know. You're your own boss. If you want to go fishing, you can go fishing. If you don't, you can stay home."[13]

Fishermen invariably contrasted their labors with life in the mines, the woods, and other wage-labor jobs. Lahja Puustinen, like Ed Hibler, worked in the Alaska-Juneau Mine until 1944. He contrasted mining—where "you just went to work and did what the boss told you to do"—with fishing, where you "do all the pushin' yourself instead of having someone pushing." On the water Puustinen "enjoyed a free life, where nobody is my boss except myself" and he carried out his labors in "fresh air."[14] Otto Hellen came to Alaska as a logger on government crews in 1941 before moving to Point Baker to fish, homestead, and live a "subsistence" lifestyle. The primary difference between logging and fishing, in his view, was that as a fisherman "you're working for yourself" and "you ain't got no goddamn boss looking down your goddamn neck." He explained: "You ain't got no whistles to go by. . . . You can eat when you want to, go to sleep when you want to, come home when you want to, do what you want. If you're working for a boss, you gotta be there, get up at six o'clock, you gotta eat at seven, gotta be out in the woods, and they tell you when to eat dinner, and then when you come home, they tell you to eat supper, and then when you go home, they pull out the lights and tell you when to go to bed. Who in the hell wants to live that kind of life? All you are [is] a wage slave."[15] Roman Keleske also came to southeastern Alaska in the 1940s and began fishing after working in railroads, construction, and logging. "A construction worker, his life is regulated by the clock, by the hour, by the day," but a fisherman, Keleske noted, "calls his own time." He continued: "If he wants to fish in a day, he can do it. If he doesn't, he don't have to. And he's his own boss. . . . It's a lifestyle more than anything else."[16]

For these fishermen "lifestyle" was more important than wages. The monetary rewards of fishing were secondary to the fact that fishing freed them from bosses, time clocks, and external control. "We never did expect to make a whole lot of money," remembered Arthur Petraborg, who also came to Alaska during the wartime construction boom. Petraborg and others took their pay in liberation from industrial regimentation. Fishing was a "free life" and an "interesting life" that saved one from a life in "industry" and "production," where "the jobs are so darn lackluster" that workers "just get bored to death when they go to work on some simple job."[17] "There wasn't much money to make, but I think people was just as happy," concurred Norwegian-born Oscar Otness, who started fishing out of Petersburg in 1922.[18] Peter Larson worked in shipbuilding, coal mining, and road construction before he took up fishing in 1944. He did so not for money but because of "the freedom, the freedom of fishing."[19]

No one life story symbolized the dream of finding freedom on the fishermen's frontier more than that of Al Brookman Sr., who began fishing in the late 1920s and was still fishing in the 1980s. Born in Southern California in 1906, Brookman's hardscrabble youth was a picture of working-class poverty: broken homes, poor health, fist-fights, transient labor, and a hand-to-mouth existence. A Christmas dinner, if they were lucky, consisted of "two skinny jack rabbits" shot by Brookman's father, who raised Al to be proficient with a .22 bullet and a fishing pole. Those skills allowed the boy to fend for himself in the mountains of Idaho when he was still shy of ten years old. From Idaho, to Michigan, to California, to Mississippi, Al's younger years were spent following his father from one back-breaking job to the next. Still in his teens, Brookman drove a mule team on road-building crews, worked in an iron foundry, and laid drainage tile on a cotton farm. In 1926, when he was twenty-one, they landed in Sitka, ready to try their luck trolling for salmon. Knowing "nothing about rigging salmon trolling gear," they got no help from white fishermen, who "looked upon us as competitors, and wouldn't tell us anything about fishing." The Brookmans had a better reception from Native fishermen: "It was the first Native friends we made who showed us how to rig trolling gear, and they marked our charts to show us where to try fishing, and where there were safe anchorages." Even so, their first attempt at trolling left them "broke and in debt to McGrath's general store."[20]

After deckhand jobs on a purse-seiner and a halibut schooner, Al began trolling on his own boat, the *Spark Plug*, in 1929. The fishing started slow, and he couldn't keep the thirty-foot boat watertight, but he finally hit the jackpot: "When I got abeam of Sitka Point, I saw at least a thousand sea gulls wheeling and diving and picking up herring. I sure got excited, for here was a hot fish sign. As soon as I got to where the gulls were, the lines starting jerking wildly, and in about five minutes every spoon had some kind of salmon fighting on it. . . . By four that afternoon the fishing slacked, so I caught up on my cleaning. . . . I was dead tired from my frantic struggles all day pulling fish, and half-blind from the fish flipping blood and slime into my eyes." When Brookman delivered his fish that day, the fish buyer handed him $141, "a fabulous amount then, when if a guy had a hundred dollar day trolling he bragged about it for years."[21]

Brookman was hooked. He would spend the rest of his life chasing the big load of fish, much like a placer miner searching for pay dirt, and with similar uneven luck—but always with the hope of a hitting a windfall "jag" of salmon. It was an exciting life, but not an easy one: "Sometimes, after a long day trolling in bad weather, I feel as if I have been in a long fist fight. The nervous strain is terrific. Navigating the boat, listening to the engine run, pulling fish and dodging other boats is a full-time job for about four men, but we have to do it alone because there isn't enough money in trolling to hire anyone."[22]

Trolling for salmon in the summer and hunting the rest of the year made for a life—self-sufficient and free—that few modern Americans could imagine. "We were as free as birds and enjoyed life to its fullest."[23] Sitting aboard his troller in 1978, Brookman guessed that "the average pulp-mill worker" in Sitka made far more than "the average troller." He explained: "The guy who sweeps the floor out there makes more money than the average troller . . . but it's the thrill of being your own boss and being out there."[24] Being "out there" with "all that nice, clean fresh air all around ya," as the cook on an Alaskan purse-seiner put it, allowed fishermen the chance to escape industrial conditions and work in an invigorating natural environment.[25]

Ed Hibler developed a lung condition working in the Alaska-Juneau mine, which vanished when he began working on the sea. As his wife explained: "He worked in the mine there [in Juneau], and he was getting tired of that, and he was getting to cough, and he was sick half the time. So he just quit and we moved to [Admiralty Island], and that was the next thing to do, go fishing. So he could be out in the air, and he liked the water."[26] For Hibler and other fishermen commercial fishing in Alaska also provided the opportunity to fish and hunt for their own consumption. When he came to Alaska in the 1910s, Finnish-born fishermen Henry Yryana liked the territory best for its natural abundance, which allowed a man to fish, hunt, pick berries, and do "whatever you feel like."[27] By combining commercial fishing, trapping, and prospecting with subsistence hunting, fishermen fashioned themselves as twentieth-century frontiersmen. "With a boat you could get your wild game, you could trap in the wintertime, you weren't dependent upon anybody," explained Toivo Andersen.

According to Andersen, fishermen in Alaska heard about the Great Depression only by reading about it in the newspaper. That was true only of the fishermen, he emphasized, "not the worker in the labor market, that's a different thing. I mean the fisherman."[28] Peder Liadal worked as a harp-sealer and then a seaman in the Norwegian and British merchant fleets during World War II. He remembered economic hard times in southeastern Alaska that were always tolerable because "out in the wilderness there I can always find something." He extolled the self-reliance of living off the land: "As long as I have a trap, and I'm hungry, I go set the trap and I get a deer. . . . And there's clams. As long as you've got a sack of potatoes, you can always scoop up something. . . . I [can] get a fish. That I can always get. All I have to do is throw a gillnet over[board]."[29]

The lifestyle of an independent fisherman in Alaska during the first half of the twentieth century reflected a preindustrial self-sufficiency reminiscent of nineteenth-century rural life. Mixing seasonal commercial activities with subsistence hunting freed fishermen from the regimentation of modern industrial society. The fishing lifestyle was both seasonal and diverse—periods of heightened intensity during the summer months gave way to the leisurely pace of fall and winter. For Arndt Peterson, who began fishing in Alaska in the 1920s after working in shipyards and other industrial jobs, the lifestyle not only allowed him the ability "to decide for himself his workday," but its seasonal nature let him "loaf in the wintertime."[30] John Clauson similarly appreciated the "variations" of fishing as well as the "time between seasons when you can do other things," such as hunt. Clauson, for one, preferred to hunt when the weather was right, not just because "it's the weekend or some damn fool thing."[31]

Like the gold prospectors in Kathryn Morse's environmental history of the Klondike gold rush, Alaskan fishermen believed that they could "work as free men and . . . get their rewards from nature, rather than from bosses or corporations." Beyond its monetary rewards (which were often meager), fishermen, like Morse's gold seekers, looked to fishing for "adventure, simplicity, freedom, independence, satisfaction, a connection between hard work and wealth, and an invigorating physical engagement with the natural world," virtues that were missing from industrial labor.[32] But they were not seeking an escape from work itself. Indeed, their daily lives were a catalogue of labors: baiting hooks, mending nets, building, repairing, and maintaining boats, fishing for cash, fishing for the pot, building homes, picking berries, and hunting for household consumption. These men were, more precisely, escaping from the drudgery of industrial work through what they perceived to be good, productive, healthy, and virtuous work. They were not escaping "*from* work," they were escaping "*through* work."[33] When compared with other industrial occupations in the twentieth century, fishing offered a comparatively free life. It reconnected men with nature through work that moved with the tides and the seasons. It was an individualistic and self-sufficient lifestyle, conducted in what was, by comparison to more settled regions, truly a "wilderness." In these ways the construction of Southeast Alaska as a "frontier wilderness" and fishermen as "pioneers" was justified.

In another sense, however, the frontier metaphors were deeply flawed. Fishermen considered themselves "free," but they were often obligated to canneries for loans and leases. Non-native fishers envisioned themselves as pioneers, exploring uncharted waterways in search of more productive fishing. Toivo Andersen, for instance, was one of four non-Native fishermen who "pioneered," "opened up," and "discovered" the Cape Fairweather fishing grounds to trollers after the Cape Ommaney king salmon fishery was depleted in the late 1940s.[34] But Andersen and his companions were not really discovering the unknown. Indian fishers had done that long ago. Nor were they conquering and subduing an untamed region—U.S. military power had accomplished that in the late nineteenth century. Nor were they solitary individualists—they were commercial fishers connected to canning companies and world markets, tied to fishing communities, and regulated by conservation officials. Because many non-Native fishers initially "didn't know how to rig the gear, or what gear to buy or anything," they were also reliant on Native fishermen in the early years, who, according to Al Brookman Sr., "advised us on what to get and how to rig up."[35]

Euro-American fishermen, in other words, sought refuge in the isolation and self-sufficiency of the "fisherman's frontier," but, in seeking independence, they became dependent on a myriad of forces that were beyond their control: long-term climate change and other environmental fluctuations (which caused dramatic shifts in the size of salmon populations), market fluctuations (which caused dramatic shifts in the price of salmon), Columbia River dams (which greatly diminished the number of king salmon that trollers caught off the continental shelf of southeastern Alaska), and national and international conservation policies (which determined where and when fishermen could fish), to name only a few. No history is truly local or self-contained. This is especially true in environmental history, which shows us that nature—tides, salmon, wind, weather, climate—does not recognize local or national political boundaries. In the modern era the same can be said of economic history. The connections between local and global, independence and interdependence, were strikingly apparent in the ecology of the salmon fishery—an ecology that included both humans and nature in a complex web of interrelationships.

Nowhere was the frontier ideology of non-Native fishermen more obtuse than when applied to Native peoples, who told very different stories about their own work and the environments in which they labored. Native fishermen did not see their surroundings as "virgin wilderness" and themselves as "frontiersmen"; rather, they viewed southeastern Alaska as a historical and cultural landscape and themselves as connected to that landscape, and to fishing, through their membership in families, houses, and clans. The land was what sustained their families and communities physically and culturally: it was not "wilderness"—it was the center of their world.[36]

On the one hand, white fishermen saw the waterways of southeastern Alaska as a vast, common-property resource awaiting their own explorations. Native fishermen, on the other hand, saw those same waterways as an intricate map of clan-owned fishing sites, passed down from generation to generation through specific clan lineages. White fishers saw a wide-open landscape of natural abundance; Indian fishers saw a landscape that was becoming increasingly crowded and overrun.[37] They told stories of former abundance and subsequent decline.[38] In the early years of the commercial fishery, there were numerous conflicts between clan leaders and non-Native fishermen, some of which were resolved, according to Native tradition, with the outsiders paying Native fishermen for use of their fishing grounds. At other times white fishermen simply ignored Native protests or, if they felt threatened, called on the American military to protect their "rights" to fish. When Indians themselves began to participate in the commercial fishery, they often continued to fish near their traditional fishing grounds. Tents, drying racks, and smokehouses were erected at makeshift summer fish camps, which served as a base for both commercial and subsistence fishing.

Roy Bean, who was born in Kake, Alaska, in 1900 and began seining with his tribal uncle at the age of nine, recalled how these temporary fish camps—often erected at "old" sites—allowed Native fishermen to live among their families while they fished: "They have a camp they put up there right where they going to fish all the time, you know, and they come in at night, after night work they come in and live with their family. . . . They're special camps there where the old camping ground is . . . well, there's so many places . . . around Petersburg, or Mitkof Island, and then Red Bay of course . . . where the seiners camp. . . . When the red salmon fishing is over, well, they go around and pick up the gang, the seine skiffs, and tow 'em to humpy streams and then places like that. They put up camps to live and rest in it. . . . Each person, if they're married, they'd bring their family along with them and sometimes there's five or six families in one [camp]."[39]

These fish camps, where men fished commercially and for subsistence and women and children "put up" fish for household consumption, served as gathering spots for extended kin and community networks. The size and location of the camps, the pace and orientation of work, fluctuated with the salmon runs. Spring and fall were taken up with subsistence activities that included hunting, trapping, berrying, and fishing, while the height of summer was dominated by commercial pursuits—purse-seining for men and cannery work for women. In summer hand-lines and nets gave way to commercial gear; putting up fish for family use gave way to wage work. The subsistence economy and the commercial economy became entangled at summer fish camps, as did individual, family, and community pursuits. To Tlingit and Haida people, southeastern Alaska was not a virgin wilderness, but a cultural geography of salmon streams, fish camps, Native villages, and canneries. It was not a landscape to be overtaken by individualistic conquest, but one to be stewarded by communities, protected from intrusion, and delineated by a complicated set of property and user rights.

Ironically, while salmon fishing connected Indian fishers to their families, clans, and tribal heritage, fishing was by no means a rejection of industrial society or the market economy. White fishermen may have envisioned fishing as an escape from modern society, but for Native peoples salmon fishing offered a culturally sanctioned and customary route *toward* the modern commercial/industrial economy. Fishing for cash reflected their very real desire to participate in the market economy while still maintaining their connection to their tribal heritage and traditional subsistence economy. Indeed, for Indian fishermen subsistence knowledge provided the framework for their success in commercial fishing. No one better personified this harmony between subsistence and market activities than George Dalton Sr., who was born in Hoonah in 1897 and grew up working in both tribal and commercial fisheries. Dalton learned to fish for salmon from Tlingit elders at his family's summer fish camp on the Dundas Bay River. He took those skills into the commercial fishery, where he became a highly successful hand-troller and "master seiner" in Icy Straits.

Dalton's biographers note that "traditional knowledge and his lifetime of experience combined with his use of modern equipment" to produce "a formidable fisherman, a hunter of fish." They wrote: "It was said that [Dalton] could smell the fish swimming in the sea. He made no show of his ability except always to catch fish. . . . George did not give useless advice on fishing. Nor, for all his love of what he did, did he regard it as a sport. It was what he did to get fish."[40] For Dalton and other Tlingit fishers salmon fishing for household consumption or the market was not sport *or* work, it was "what they did," a cultural lifeway that connected them to their past while helping them navigate a world that had been dramatically transformed.

Tlingits and Haidas engaged in what some scholars have described as "purposeful modernization" or "selective adaptation." Brian Hosmer, writing about the Tsimshians who lived in Metlakatla, at the southern edge of southeastern Alaska, argues that Native cultures were not invariably destroyed by their encounters with market capitalism, nor did they move ineluctably toward total economic dependency. While faced with a new world that was not of their own making—a world that undoubtedly limited their choices and autonomy—Hosmer contends that Indian peoples acted in purposeful ways that reflected their ability to negotiate new economic and cultural relationships on their own terms. Their choices, moreover, were not limited to either traditional resistance or progressive assimilation. Indians could adapt and still be Indian; they could draw on familiar cultural frameworks as a means of negotiating new realities, which combined market participation with cultural tradition.[41]

Just as modern Americans do not assume they have lost their cultural heritage because they no longer ride carriages or use wooden stoves, it is overly simplistic to suggest that Tlingits and Haidas jettisoned their cultural heritage by adapting to the market economy. If anything, their cultural heritage—as traders, potlatchers, and acquisitive individuals—taught them how to seize upon economic opportunities. Hosmer suggests that all Metlakatlans were "entrepreneurs" to a certain extent, and the same could be said for Tlingits and Haidas. Tribal divisions existed, but they centered around cultural orientations and political strategies rather than economic participation.[42] Few Indians resisted commercial participation in the salmon fisheries. Indeed, as late as 1943, Tlingit and Haida fishermen outnumbered white fishermen in the salmon-canning industry.[43]

For Natives commercial fishing was not necessarily a liberating alternative to other occupations, but often a necessary choice made by people whose options were becoming increasingly limited (see figure 4.1). Like their white counterparts, Indian fishers may have enjoyed the "freedom" of the seas, but for them the decision to fish was most often made for economic and unique cultural reasons. Unlike white fishermen, who were born elsewhere and migrated to Alaska, Tlingit boys were raised fishing the waters of southeastern Alaska, and their progression toward commercial fishing was quite natural. Ronald Bean began seining as a young man. His introduction to fishing at the age of six, in 1920, was typical of other Tlingit fishermen. "Well, my dad fished as far back as I can remember," he recalled. "As soon as I was able to . . . , why I got to go on a boat with him, and I done that all my life."[44] Thomas Jackson Sr. was born in Kake and began seining with his uncle in 1926, at the age of thirteen. He remembered his initiation into commercial fishing as fulfilling a common expectation for Native boys: "Well, when you live up here in Alaska, your livelihood is fishing. It's either seining or trolling. So as soon as I became old enough, which was 13 years old, I started fishing with my uncle."[45]

Dick Hotch, who was born in Klukwan in 1922, "learned gillnet fishing from subsistence fishing in the river." He carried those skills into the commercial fishery, gillnetting in Taku Inlet beginning in 1937, when he was fifteen, and continuing until 1977.[46] Archie Brown and Horace Marks began fishing when they were nine; Albert Davis and Daniel Paul when they were thirteen.[47] Paul, who was born in Kake, Alaska, in 1922 and began seining with his grandfather, father, and older brother in the 1930s, explained that "it was expected of the boys to go into purse seining sooner or later." Moreover, he remembered, "it was the only avenue I had for income."[48] For Tlin-

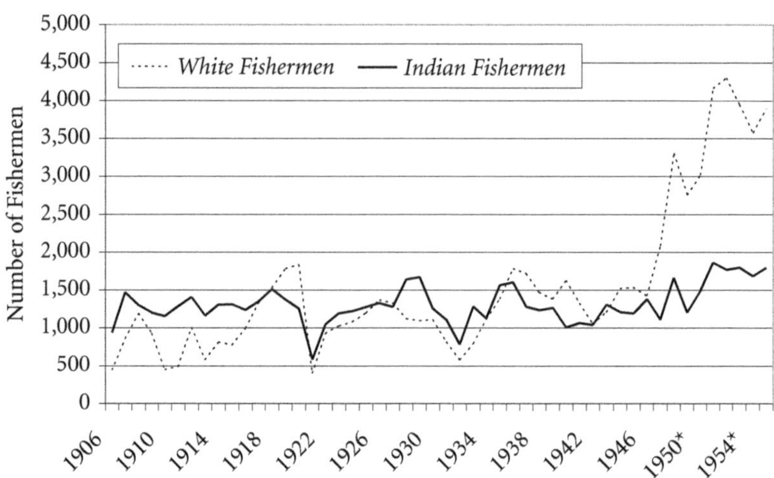

FIG. 4.1 *Indian and White fishermen in the canned-salmon industry, 1906–1955. Indians played an important role as commercial salmon fishers in the canned-salmon industry throughout the twentieth century. The numbers of Indian and white fishers were about even until the postwar period, when increasing numbers of white fishermen tipped the balance in their favor.* SOURCE: *Bower, Alaska Fishery and Fur-Seal Industries, 1912–1954.* NOTE: *The statistics for the years 1948 through 1955 include employees in the fresh, frozen, cured, and salmon byproducts industries, as well as in salmon canning.*

gits of Paul's generation commercial fishing was one of the few sources of economic opportunity.

Raised in local fishing communities and trained by their elders from a young age in the ways of fishing, Native fishermen acquired a cultural orientation, a set of skills, and a body of knowledge that was distinct from that of non-Native fishers. Part of this training involved observing the habits of fish and stewarding the resource. George Dalton remembered how, as a young man, his father taught him "how to protect the fish." Albert Davis recalled: "The first thing that was ever taught to me was to be conservative. Always conserve. Never waste it." Howard Gray told of the days before game wardens, when the salmon were abundant because the people "were raised on fish and they took care of that stream." Andrew Johnnie believed that Native fishermen "knew at that time that if they overfish a place they won't get another return of a certain amount of fish on that cycle."[49]

Such expressions (leaving aside the question examined in chapter 1 concerning aboriginal resource management) were born out of an intimate relationship with the natural world. Tlingit boys learned the story of "salmon boy," about a young fisherman who fell in the water and was rescued by the salmon people. He lived with the salmon, learned their ways, and returned to his own tribe four years later (the normal sockeye spawning pattern), where he taught his people about the ways of salmon. Indian men fished until, according to Dick Hotch, "you just about think like a fish." He continued: "You don't only have to know where to put the net, but the tides. . . . Some spots you catch a sockeye when the tide is going down. And some places you have to catch them when the tide is coming in."[50] This was the kind of ecological knowledge that white fishermen had to gain from Natives—an interlocution that bred resentment from those who felt, in the words of Andrew Johnnie Sr., that they "were being intruded upon." Despite the hard feelings, though, Johnnie and other Indian fishers were "always giving out information like that to help at any time."[51] Horace Marks, who was born in Haines in 1914 and began working on trollers and seiners with his stepfather in 1923, believed that local knowledge made Natives "very much the superior fishermen." Non-Native fishermen "look to us more or less" because "we know the areas. We know the tides. And these people that are brought up off and on, . . . they're not too familiar . . . with local weather conditions and tides and so forth."[52]

Indian and white fishermen were doing the same thing: fishing for cash during the height of the annual salmon runs and fishing and hunting for subsistence during the rest of the year. Both groups came to know nature intimately through their labors. But their cultural outlook, their identities, their motivations, their ecological knowledge, and their perceptions of work and nature were vastly different. These differences manifested themselves in telling ways. For instance, Indian fishermen were less likely to adopt advanced commercial fishing technologies, while whites readily innovated and upgraded their gear for maximum efficiency. Native fishermen were more likely to fish closer to home at their usual and accustomed places (to paraphrase treaty language that did *not* apply to Indians in Alaska), while white fishermen were more likely to go beyond the sheltered channels and bays to fish more productive "outside" waters. One might see such differences as evidence of contrasting cultural attitudes: Native fishers were more community oriented, while whites fashioned themselves as pioneers and rugged individualists; Indians fishers took only what they needed, while more ambitious non-Indian fishers pursued profits in more dangerous and distant waters. But the differing behaviors of Indians and whites, in this instance, were not just cultural or conceptual, they were material. Most Native fishermen simply could not—whether they wanted to or not—purchase the boats and equipment necessary to fish the outside waters. Aside from a small number of wealthy Indian fishermen, Native fishers could not keep up with white fishermen, who generally benefited from more modern equipment. This was not because of a cultural conservatism on the part of Native fishers. It stemmed primarily from a lack of capital in the Native community—a reality that forced them to lease substandard cannery gear.

Of course, such generalizations about communities and cultures are entirely insufficient in conveying the complexity of the salmon fishery in southeastern Alaska. Neither white fishermen nor Indian fishermen belonged to monolithic communities. Some Natives were focused on the individual acquisition of wealth, while others directed their labors toward subsistence-based communal activities. Some whites—many of them immigrants—carried to Alaska a keen commitment to class and community, while others preferred to carve out a more autonomous existence. There was always a more complicated and disjointed reality lurking beneath the categories of Indian and white, and attitudes toward work and nature only begin to hint at the many different ways that the fishery was socially and culturally fragmented.

THE FRACTURED FISHERY

Fishermen in southeastern Alaska—both Indian and white—shared much in common: their antipathy toward fish traps and corporate monopolies; their resentment of distant and bullying federal fisheries managers; and their desire for stable fish runs and high prices for salmon. "There can be no question that the economic interests of fishermen are, for the most part, in common," believed Lauren Wilde Casaday, who from his mid-1930s vantage point saw the interests of fishermen as "sharply and inevitably opposed to those of all fish buyers and packers."[53]

Fishermen also shared an allegiance born of the perils and joys of working on the water. The "nature of their work," as Casaday put it, bound them together in communion with each other: "Laboring constantly in the presence of a common danger—the sea—and compelled to live in close association both aboard ship and in isolated fishing villages, a tradition of group loyalty has become strong among them."[54] Indeed, it was their relationship to nature that differentiated them from both cannery workers and cannery bosses. Fishermen were producers, farmers of the sea. They braved the weather, bent their backs, pulled fish from the ocean, and generated wealth. Their identity was rooted in the *nature* of their labors, which were carried out independently on the open seas. This producerist ideology—similar to that of nineteenth-century artisans and farmers—allowed fishermen to claim a privileged place in the hierarchy of the fishing industry. It also allowed them, as discussed in chapter 3, to denounce fish-trap operators as capitalists who despoiled nature and reduced artisan fishermen to dependent wage slaves.[55]

However, if their relationship to nature and pride in their craft drew fishermen together, it also drove them apart. Fishermen concerned themselves primarily with the distinctive problems and interests of their own craft. Purse-seiners, gillnetters, and trollers fished in different areas at different times, caught different species of salmon, joined different unions, negotiated separate price agreements with local canneries, were subject to different fisheries regulations, and in sum interacted with nature, the market, and each other in distinctive ways. Purse-seiners, fishing in crews ranging between four and seven men, sought to encircle large schools of milling fish. Like all salmon fishermen, seiners liked to catch the higher-priced and less plentiful sockeye salmon, but they made their money on volume, netting large schools of pink salmon, the most abundant (and, along with the chum salmon, the cheapest grade) of southeastern Alaska's salmon species. Gillnetters and trollers pursued the more highly prized sockeye and king salmon. Gillnetters, working alone or in pairs, fished the tide rips nearer the shores and river mouths as the salmon made their way back to the spawning grounds, while trollers, fishing solo, used lines and baited hooks to catch "bright" salmon, especially kings, as they milled in the deeper, clearer water off the continental shelf. Given the varying ecological conditions that each group sought, as well as the migratory habits of particular salmon runs (which determined the timing of each gear type's fishing season), fishermen fostered craft loyalties born of common experience. Each gear type was not only shaped by similar market conditions and fishing restrictions, but they also experienced familiar dilemmas, such as the depletion of a particular stream or the intrusion of a certain fish trap.

Although fishermen liked to think of themselves as "producers" in their fights against canners and trap operators, craft loyalties often undercut this veneer of solidarity. Fishermen of different gear types often refused to respect each other's strikes, which invariably gave cannery operators the upper hand.[56] Even more telling: instead of simply denouncing the demonic fish traps, as was the standard practice, fishermen sometimes turned their fire on each other. In 1924 the president of the International Seamen's Union, which represented gillnetters affiliated with the Alaska Fishermen's Union, told a congressional committee that in order to conserve the salmon fisheries they would have to "abolish the purse seine and the trap."[57] In a letter to an Alaska territorial politician in 1927, the secretary of the Alaska Fishermen's Union called purse-seines "even more destructive to the salmon industry than fish traps."[58] At hearings in 1939 a Southeast Alaska troller suggested that "if gill-netting is eliminated entirely . . . we will have an increase of at least 50 percent of the king salmon in the spawning grounds."[59] Internecine attacks like these were common. Passing the blame for fish depletion was a central feature of the fishery, as was competition among different gear types for finite resources. "In the early days, I was interested in trying to get us together, but it's impossible," remembered Southeast Alaska troller William Love, because "the gillnetters, they hate the seiners. The seiners hate the trollers, [and] trollers hate everybody."[60]

Race and ethnicity fostered even more vicious tribalisms than craft affiliation. Indian and white fishers, even of the same gear type, were more competitive than cooperative, and Euro-American fishermen of different ethnic origins also kept their distance.[61] Native fishers formed racially exclusive intertribal brotherhoods and, as we shall see, Indian unions; Euro-American fishermen did the same. Italian fishermen from San Francisco Bay had formed cooperatives and protective associations since the 1860s to defend their economic interests and to provide accident and illness insurance for their members. In addition to such associations, they established "companies," organized around kinship and regional affiliations, which owned boats and gear in common and divided investment and profits into shares owned by the fishermen themselves.[62] Like their Italian counterparts, Scandinavian fishermen also had a history of cooperative activity. They had organized "snag unions" (which collectively cleared the fishing grounds of "snags") and protective societies to regulate drift rights on the Columbia since the late nineteenth century.[63]

But these cooperative traditions rarely transcended ethnic boundaries. In the 1890s, Jefferson Moser, captain of the USFC steamer *Albatross*, noted that "the cannery fishermen are nearly all foreigners, the majority being 'north countrymen,' or as they are termed, 'hardheads,' though there are some fishing gangs comprised of what are called 'dagoes,' consisting of Italians, Greeks, and the like." When northern European and southern European fishermen formed their fishing gangs, Moser observed that "the north-country crew is referred to as the 'white crew.'"[64] On his journey to Alaska on an Alaska Packers Association cannery ship in the early 1920s, reporter Max Stern of the *San Francisco Daily News* noted that fishermen—mostly "Latins" from Monterey and San Francisco bays and "Scandinavians" from the Columbia River and the Puget Sound—"do not mix any more than oil and water." Because of rivalries among the fishing crews, the "Finns, Icelanders, Russians, Norwegians, Swedes, Danes and Dutchmen" took the port side, while the "Italians, Portuguese and Sicilians" occupied the starboard section of the castle.[65] Even more virulent were the animosities between the Euro-American fishermen and the Chinese cannery workers, who made the trip to Alaska below deck in the cramped, unsanitary forward quarters, also known as the "China hold."

The segmentation of the salmon fishery into racial and ethnic categories—the social construction of the fishery—did not just happen organically. It was the product initially of agreements made between fishermen's unions and cannery operators that favored Euro-American fishermen over Indian fishermen, Asian cannery workers, and women. Since the late nineteenth century, unions in the Pacific Coast salmon industry had succeeded in keeping Asians from competing with white fishermen. In 1876 the Italian Fishermen's Union of San Francisco protested the fishing methods of the Chinese in California—"their total disregard of the size of fish they caught, and their waste of all the sturgeon they took"—in an effort to drive them from the fishing grounds.[66] On the Columbia River fishermen's unions and industrialists made sure that the Chinese were prohibited from fishing and relegated to the cannery shop floor. "A Chinaman dare not fish in the Columbia," noted George Brown Goode, "it being an understood thing that he would die for his sport." Fishing, with its relative autonomy, superior pay, craft traditions, and outdoor environment, was white man's work. Asian cannery workers, who toiled within exploitative contract labor systems, were "tolerated [only] because they will work for such low wages."[67] Fishermen were free men—skilled artisans who labored in the open air, far from the routines of industrial production—while Asian workers were dependent: "abject slaves of Oriental masters."[68]

The Alaska Fishermen's Union (AFU), the oldest and most powerful maritime union in Alaska, was founded in 1902. The union worked with large canning companies, such as the Alaska Packers Association, to ensure that the salmon fishery was inscribed with a racial hierarchy that privileged white fishermen. AFU fishermen received better pay, better quarters (aboard the cannery ships as well as at the canneries), and better provisions than cannery workers or nonunion fishermen. Reporter Stern observed cannery workers eating two servings a day of "sparse fare," while the fishermen ate three squares that included a variety of meats, fresh vegetables, fruit, and dessert.[69] The canneries themselves were spatially and racially segregated. The cannery in Kake—typical for southeastern Alaska— contained a "Japanese and Filipino Bunkhouse," a "White Man's Bunkhouse," a "White Man's Cookhouse, a "Fishermen's Wash House," a "Chinese Workers' House," and an "Oriental Bathhouse."[70] The grimmest manifestation of these racial divides occurred in the fall of 1908 when the *Star of Bengal* sank in the Wrangell Narrows as it traveled from the APA's Loring cannery in southeastern Alaska. Only fifteen whites perished, compared to ninety-six Asian cannery workers, allegedly because the white fishermen had nailed down the hatches of the Chinese hold so that "most of the [white] fishermen were able to escape in the few boats they managed to lower."[71]

AFU fishermen also protected themselves from competition by Indian fishers. In something akin to a "closed-shop" agreement, their contracts guaranteed them "one-third the price paid" by the cannery to nonunion fishermen, a provision that was despised by resident Alaskans, both Indian and white, because it penalized canneries for purchasing their fish.[72] Moreover, before the mid-1930s the union did not offer membership to Indian fishers, who the union leadership disparaged as unreliable and lazy. The AFU justified its efforts to bring non-Indian fishers to Alaska on the grounds that Alaska Natives were "not skilled fishermen and cannot compete with the average non-resident fisherman."[73]

The Alaska Fishermen's Union therefore not only perpetuated racial divisions, but it also contributed to perhaps the greatest conflict within the fishery—the animosity between resident Alaskan fishermen and nonresident, or "outside," fishers. For Indian and white residents of southeastern Alaska the AFU, by importing nonresident fishermen to the region, was contributing to the colonial pattern of exploitation where outsiders plundered the region and left locals with the ecological wreckage but none of the spoils. The Tlingit newspaper the *Alaska Fisherman* denounced "this class of fishermen . . . [who] are here to rob Alaska of her resources [and] deplete our resources." It accused the AFU of aligning with the canning interests—including tacit support for cannery fish traps—and declared that AFU fishermen were "not Alaskans in any sense of the word." The Indian newspaper could not refrain from using ethnic epithets, referring to AFU craft as "dago fishing boats."[74]

In 1939, the hatred between local and outside fishermen reached a boiling point during congressional hearings over three bills introduced by Alaska Territorial Delegate Anthony J. Dimond, all of which advanced the interests of resident fishermen and fish workers. The first protected resident fishermen—but not outsiders—from overzealous federal conservation officials who used "the threat of seizure and holding of the boat or gear or seine" in order to compel fisheries offenders to plead guilty to criminal offenses. The second established an Alaskan Fisheries Commission that would be composed, in part, "of actual bona fide resident fishermen." The third, and most controversial, bill required canning companies to hire locals "in all types of work and labor involved in the Alaska fishery." The bill included a graduated plan to eliminate all nonresident employees in the Alaska fisheries by 1946.[75]

The Dimond bills, unsurprisingly, were vehemently supported by local Alaskan fishermen's unions and associations—including the Alaska Native Brotherhood (ANB)—and denounced vehemently by "outside" unions, particularly the Alaska Fishermen's Union. J. F. Jurich of the AFU predicted dire consequences if the bills passed: the "peaceful labor relations" that had characterized the salmon industry would end; Alaska would be left without an "adequate number of qualified salmon fishermen"; and poor economic conditions in Washington, Oregon, and California would be aggravated by unemployed fishermen, whose primary source of income had previously come from the Alaskan salmon fishery. Jurich's primary criticism of the bills, however, was that restricting access to common-property resources was simply un-American: "The fish in Alaska waters are not the common property of just Alaska residents. Those fish are the common property of all citizens of the United States."[76]

Other opponents likewise appealed to the sanctity of the open-access fisheries. California congressman Albert E. Carter argued that non-Alaskans "were being deprived of the pursuit of happiness if you deprive them of the right to fish." Opponents of the bills were right: according to American legal doctrines, the prohibition of nonresidents from the fishery violated both tradition and statutory law. Dimond defended the bills with an argument that was a curious combination of both riparian rights and prior appropriation: "Those who reside on the shores of any sea have the first call, or the first claim, or a prior right, whatever it may be denominated, to the fisheries of the adjoining sea as against those who reside in the more remote places."[77]

It was ironic that Alaska resident fishermen, who argued so forcefully against fish traps because they impeded the open-access fishery and granted "special privileges" to large corporations, supported an effort to destroy the common fishery and bestow special privileges to Alaska residents alone. More ironic, however, was the suggestion that the Alaskan salmon fishery was an open-access "commons" at all. The notion of a commons—a "common property" resource—was itself a social construction, an "invention" of thinkers and lawmakers.[78] The Alaska salmon fishery was certainly not "common"—it was socially subdivided and access was limited according to the boundaries of race, ethnicity, gender, craft, occupation, location, union affiliation, and federal regulations. Asian cannery workers understood the limitations of the fishery, as did Indian subsistence fishers, nonunion resident fishermen, and women, who were not categorically denied the right to fish in either Indian or non-Indian cultures, but were nonetheless guided by custom into cannery work and domestic duties. "Common property" existed as an abstract ideal, but never in practice.

THE RISE AND FALL OF FISHERMEN'S UNIONS, 1931–1954

Given the divisions that plagued the fishery, it is little wonder that even during the high point of labor solidarity in the 1930s, fishermen's organizations were riven with internal conflict. Their inefficacy was predictable. During congressional hearings in 1924, Andrew Furuseth, president of the International Seamen's Union, was asked if fishermen would "get together in a combination and make it impossible for the canneries to continue?" His reply revealed the fractured nature of the fishery: "Well, they are made up of men who are Indians, half-breeds, full whites, from every State of the Union, probably, some of them from every country in Europe—that is the way the fishing population is made up. To get them together and to organize them to stand for one absolute price for the fish, when they can go and fish and deliver to the canneries—well, it may be that that is possible; but if it is, if that is the kind of men they are, they won't remain fishermen long. So I do not think there is any danger in that."[79]

For fishermen it seemed that cooperation itself was usually predicated upon opposition and exclusion—to fish traps or nonresident labor, for example—rather than a shared sense of collectivity among a community of fishers. The union movement that arose in southeastern Alaska was in many ways a reflection of the nature of fishing itself: men were separated like small boats on the sea. Sometimes the waters were smooth, and men joined together in solidarity, like boats tied together in a calm harbor to enjoy the camaraderie of common struggle. At other times the seas became rough, boats and men were tossed apart, and communication broke down. It is no surprise that the union movement came in waves, in storms, and in strikes—and then all was calm again. If there was a time for solidarity among fishermen, it was the 1930s. The decade combined the worst of trends: increasing catches from corporate fish traps (despite the policies of Fisheries Commissioner Frank T. Bell, who had tried unsuccessfully to diminish the number of traps and thereby increase employment); increasing competition on the fishing grounds (as many people migrated to Alaska during the Great Depression); decreasing fish prices (as global demand diminished during the economic crisis); and declining salmon runs (which in other decades would have at least meant increasing prices).

The industry itself was depressed, as reflected in the experiences of the Alaska Packers Association (APA), the former behemoth of the industry. The APA withered steadily as, in the words of its president, "demand dwindled in foreign markets largely on account of the irregularity of exchange and in the home market because of the general condition of business."[80] The conglomerate operated thirteen Alaskan canneries in 1929, eleven in 1930, ten in 1931 and 1932; and then nine for the rest of the decade. From a salmon pack of a million cases in 1934, its production dropped drastically to 212,000 in 1935 (when the federal government closed fishing in Bristol Bay for one season due to concerns over salmon depletion) and never reached beyond 772,000 for the remainder of the decade.[81] In the 1930s the APA and other salmon-canning companies would not only have to battle poor markets and declining fish stocks, but also an enlivened labor force.[82] The contract-labor system was crumbling, unions were on the rise, and even formerly "independent" fishermen, who owned their own boats and fished as owner-operators instead of company employees, were beginning to organize labor locals.

The first fishermen to organize were trollers, the fastest growing gear type in southeastern Alaska, whose numbers had increased from eight hundred in 1930 to more than thirteen hundred by 1939.[83] The rise in trollers reflected the growth of southeastern Alaska's white population, which grew five times faster during the 1930s than it had during the 1920s.[84] Many newcomers sought refuge from unemployment and poor economic conditions in the allure of Alaska's "virgin" landscape and rich natural abundance. For those migrants who were not skilled fishermen, salmon trolling was a logical first choice. It required less capital investment and less craft knowledge than did seining or gillnetting, and the famed Cape Ommaney fishing grounds (known as "the King Salmon capital of Alaska") were yielding trollers the best king salmon harvests along the North Pacific. Port Alexander, the town nearest to Cape Ommaney, saw its summer populations boom as salmon trollers from Washington and Oregon migrated northward.[85]

In June 1931 the trollers in Port Alexander organized the Alaska Trollers Association (ATA), which immediately called a strike for higher salmon prices.[86] Its members complained that with "the large fleet of trollers on the various grounds," it was impossible to earn "a fair, let alone a living wage, at less than ten cents per pound" for king salmon. Fish buyers, however, claimed that bank failures and the restricted money supply had "made it almost impossible to borrow necessary capital to operate" and stood firm on eight cents per pound. The deadlock stood through most of June, while the strike spread to Sitka and other trolling communities in southeastern Alaska. According to the *Alaska Fisherman*, Indian and white solidarity was almost "complete"—"trollers, white and Indian, were tied up almost to a man in every important fishing district."[87]

The strike ended on July 18, when buyers upped their offer from eight to ten cents a pound. The Tlingit trollers at Port Alexander were the first to leave the docks and start fishing: "without funds to continue the strike in sympathy with the demands of the Alaska Trollers' Association, [Indian fishermen] . . . decided they would go fishing." Over the protests of their union leaders, rank-and-file white trollers then withdrew their own demand of twelve cents per pound and also went fishing—the rush to the fishing grounds was precipitated by the arrival of a fleet of "outside" trollers who were willing to fish without complaint for the going price. The return to fishing ended the lengthiest fishermen's strike in the history of southeastern Alaska, demonstrating, in the rather optimistic view of the *Alaska Fisherman*, that with the help of a union "fishermen can secure a solidarity—if they make an earnest effort to do so."[88]

The Alaska Trollers Association was the largest fishermen's organization in southeastern Alaska until 1936, and it offered at least the possibility of cooperation between white and Indian fishermen. However, interethnic cooperation was fleeting. The ATA represented white trollers concerned primarily with the price of king salmon, which they sold to small salteries and "mild-cure" operations throughout the region. Although some Indian fishermen trolled, most purse-seined for pink, chum, and sockeye salmon, which they delivered to larger canning companies. Furthermore, Indian fishermen overwhelmingly opposed fish traps, an issue that did not directly affect trollers, since the king salmon they caught were feeding on the continental shelf—not returning to rivers in southeastern Alaska to spawn—and were less likely to be caught in traps, which targeted schools of salmon migrating to local river systems. Finally, cooperative organization meant sharing power, a step that neither white nor Indian organizations were willing to take.

The Alaska Native Brotherhood, which by the mid-1930s increasingly sought to represent Indian fishermen and cannery workers in labor negotiations, was "willing to work with" the ATA, according to Grand Secretary William L. Paul, but not "let them decide [matters] for us." Paul urged the ANB to "abide by [its] own decisions" and not allow "the ATA to usurp the labor field and preempt the right to call other people 'scabs.'" Tlingits would respect trollers' strikes in areas dominated by the ATA, "but where we have the power in numbers," countered Paul, "we will be controlled by our own decisions." Paul envisioned the ANB dominating regional labor organizing "when the ATA and their cooperative is busted for lack of brains."[89] As for the Alaska Trollers Association, by 1936 its power was declining due to the poor market for mild-cured salmon as well as fish depletion on the Cape Ommaney grounds. By the end of 1936 "neither cooperation nor unionism on any wide scale could be said to exist among southeastern Alaska trollers."[90] The same could also be said of purse-seiners and gillnetters.

It was Asian-American cannery workers, not fishermen, who spearheaded the first large-scale unionization efforts among salmon workers in Alaska. Beginning in 1933, two Asian-American dominated unions, one based in Seattle and the other in San Francisco, began to organize cannery hands in a labor market previously controlled by ethnic labor contractors. Both unions gravitated toward the "broad and inclusive CIO vision of labor organization, rather than the AFL's narrow, ethnically-based locals." Chinese, Japanese, and Filipino workers, according to historian Chris Friday, "recognized their common circumstances" and moved to "create a loose class solidarity among cannery hands" in an industry where labor relations were usually defined by ethnic conflict rather than cooperation.[91] In 1938 these cannery-workers unions took their inclusive vision of interethnic solidarity and broad labor unity to southeastern Alaska and engaged in a struggle with AFL (American Federation of Labor) and ANB locals to organize resident labor—Indian and white.[92]

The organizational struggles of Asian salmon cannery workers and their movement northward in the late 1930s was part of a rising tide of militant unionism on the West Coast culminating in the so-called Big Strike of 1934, when seamen and shoreworkers along the entire coast slowed seaborne commerce for eighty-three days. This renaissance of maritime militancy galvanized Pacific Coast waterfront workers and unleashed a torrent of labor activity. "The institutional embodiment of the extraordinary solidarity that the marine workers had achieved during the Big Strike," explains historian Bruce Nelson, was the Maritime Federation of the Pacific Coast (MFP), which brought maritime workers together in one organization and "constituted the realization of an impulse toward organic unity" in the maritime trades.[93]

The first sign of this sea change among fishermen was the AFU's defection from the exclusive craft-based AFL to the more inclusive Congress of Industrial Organizations (CIO) and the Maritime Federation of the Pacific Coast. The reinvigorated union, recognizing that "a strike by one group of fishermen is futile if not backed by all," opened offices in southeastern Alaska in 1936, appealing to resident fishers with a vision of creating "one big union covering all of Alaska and including the workers in allied occupations." Most resident fishermen, however, still believed that the San Francisco–based AFU and the canning companies were "collaborating to maintain a fisheries monopoly . . . to rob Alaskans of their heritage."[94] Nonetheless, the ambitious Maritime Federation expanded its reach throughout southeastern Alaska as the larger struggle between the AFL and the CIO heated to a boiling point.

By the late 1930s and early 1940s every type of worker in the Alaska canned-salmon industry—fishermen, cannery workers, longshoremen, and other tradesmen—participated in the MFP, mostly through CIO locals. Seattle and San Francisco cannery locals cooperated with the Maritime Federation as did the Alaska Fishermen's Union and smaller branches of the United Fisherman's Union of the Pacific. The MFP sponsored the "All Alaska Labor Conventions," held from 1938 through 1942, which highlighted the possibilities for unity among Alaska's interethnic fishery workers. The meetings, held annually in Juneau, brought together local and nonresident labor, cannery workers and fishermen, Asian Americans, Euro-Americans, and Native Americans for the purpose of uniting maritime labor and pushing beyond the localism and ethnic identification that had stymied Alaska's labor movement. "The stand of the C.I.O. resident fishermen and cannery workers," declared a CIO fisherman, "is that they do not want to be isolated into an organization whose program and policy will not harmonize with those of the Pacific Coast and in the United States."[95] A Tlingit fisherman from Hoonah, also representing the CIO, denounced race-baiting for "disrupting general labor movements" and urged cooperation among the "working class of people."[96]

Despite optimistic reports of interethnic and interregional organizing, the MFP conferences belied strong undercurrents of divisiveness. Resident purse-seiners organizing "under the banner of Alaska for Alaskans," warned one delegate, were seeking "to disrupt the Maritime Federation of the Pacific and its program and policy to protect all Maritime workers." "The forces of reaction are not routed," he reminded conference participants, "they are reforming their lines for new attacks."[97] At the 1941 conference MFP president A. E. Harding called the slogan of "Alaska for Alaskans," advocated by Alaska resident unions, including the Alaska Native Brotherhood, "demagogic propaganda secretly initiated by absentee packing and mining interests." He also accused local unions of "alien-baiting" and deliberately attempting to "alienate residential labor from outside labor with the ultimate end in view of smashing the entire organized labor movement in the Territory."[98]

Indeed, the dream of "one big union" quickly splintered along the lines of race, region, and craft. Solidarity in the maritime trades in fact had been crumbling since the late 1930s when West Coast seamen, led by Harry Lundeberg, rejected the broad industrial unity and labor radicalism endorsed by the CIO and embraced the trade separation and anticommunism of the AFL. In May 1938, Lundeberg's sailors' union withdrew from the Maritime Federation of the Pacific Coast and rejoined the AFL. Influenced by his unyielding hatred of communists and his personal and political conflicts with Harry Bridges—the radical leader of the West Coast longshoremen—Lundeberg and his sailors went on the offensive against the CIO. In the late 1930s and into the 1940s the issue of anticommunism grew as a wedge issue and Lundeberg's sailors became the "shock troops in the jurisdictional battles that were convulsing the West Coast and much of the nation."[99] Lundeberg saw Alaska, because of its proximity to the Soviet Union, of "vital interest to the

AFL not only from a trade union standpoint but from the standpoint of national security as well." He warned that if the CIO should win the right to represent Alaskan maritime workers, "the Communist party of America will have enough stooges placed in various parts of Alaska to sabotage this country." He saw it as part of his mission to organize Alaskan workers, boasting that the "whole territory of Alaska could be organized into the A.F.L. in a short time with the aid of the Seamen."[100]

Lundberg supported the anti-nonresident "Dimond Bills" in 1939, while the Maritime Federation of the Pacific denounced the laws—and the parochial ideology behind them—as "propaganda" intended to "disrupt labor relations so that eventually organized labor in the Territory will be destroyed and the old open-shop conditions restored in the fishing and mining industries."[101] Even territorial governor Ernest Gruening—a progressive, self-proclaimed friend of labor, and contributor to the left-leaning *Nation* magazine—believed that "Alaskans should come first" in maritime employment. Referring to Alaska as "still largely a frontier," the governor stressed the importance of increasing "home rule," which meant that "labor control should be exercised from the Territory itself and not from some distant point."[102] The divide between residents and nonresidents was too wide to bridge.

Toivo Andersen, who organized a CIO trollers local in southeastern Alaska, remembered with bitterness how fishermen "could not get together": "We never gained nothing. We had a lot of trouble, but we never gained nothing. Nothing but trouble."[103] Indeed, fratricidal competition in the fishery pitted residents against nonresidents, AFL against CIO locals, trade unionists against industrial unionists, "independent" fishermen against cannery fishermen, and so on. The labor struggles of Alaska fishermen were influenced by distant markets, distant corporations, distant labor unions, and distant federal policies. Local fishermen were not captains of their own fate. Like a sea of small boats separated by fierce winds, they were scattered by forces beyond their control. Despite their dependence on such forces—and the role that outside forces may have played in shaping the fishery—white fishermen remembered their inability to organize as largely a reflection of their own independent nature. William Love recalled that it was a "tough thing to get 'em together" because the fisherman is "an independent guy." Arthur Petraborg believed that "the trouble with the fishermen" was that they were "all independent and individual and it's pretty hard to get two men to think the same."[104] In reality, however, many fishermen did think the same. They shared similar concerns and conditions. They invariably risked their lives and sacrificed personal gain to rescue fellow fishermen from peril. But this camaraderie of the seas, for Euro-American fishermen, was circumscribed by a stubborn ideology of frontier independence and self-sufficiency.

Native fishers did not share this divisive frontier ideology; for them a cultural heritage of tribal factionalism and localism similarly prevented a broader unity. As a group, Indian fishermen shared much in common—they were local residents and purse-seiners, commercial and subsistence fishermen with deep cultural attachments to their trade and to the region. Their common heritage drew them together, but tribal factionalisms also split them apart, as was evidenced by their participation in the labor struggles of the 1930s.

In 1936, Tlingit leader Frank Peratrovich founded the Alaska Salmon Purse Seiners Union (ASPSU) under an AFL charter. The union consisted of Indian and white resident fishers who sought to challenge the power of the "outside" labor organizations, such as the Alaska Fishermen's Union. Rather than uniting Tlingits and resident whites, however, the formation of the ASPSU initiated a struggle that divided the Tlingit community into factions led by Peratrovich, on one side, and the Pauls—who wished to see Native fishermen and cannery workers organized by the Alaska Native Brotherhood—on the other. These factions did not divide along "progressive" and "traditionalist" lines, as was the case in other Native American communities. Neither faction was antagonistic to market participation; rather, they split over issues of political leadership and economic strategy. Peratrovich wanted to bring whites and Indians together in a national labor organization such as the AFL, and the Pauls, formerly advocates of cultural assimilation, wanted a racially separate and independent ANB union to represent Tlingits and their distinctive interests.

William Paul argued that a non-Indian union would never make sacrifices for its Indian members, nor would it carry out the unique social functions of the ANB. In arguing for an ANB bargaining agency, Paul appealed to Tlingit ethnic identity: "We are the only union bound together by ties of blood, tradition, history, and a real spirit of sacrifice and love for each other," he told ANB members.[105] He excoriated ASPSU supporters for listening to "white leaders whom you would never admit as full members of the BROTHERHOOD," and he urged them to embrace the ANB out of ethnic solidarity: "Indians constitute 7/9ths of the Union membership and no matter what some Indians might say, down underneath we are all related and . . .

none of us can hold out against fathers and brothers."[106] Paul's racial appeal galvanized segments of the Tlingit community and divided others; at the same time it drew Indian fishers into conflict with white fishers. Tlingit efforts, like other union drives in southeastern Alaska, only contributed to the social and cultural fragmentation of the fishery.

Unfortunately, solidarity *within* the Native and white communities emerged only when each community was drawn into battle with the other. That moment came in the fall of 1944 during hearings initiated by the secretary of the interior, Harold Ickes, to determine if Natives in southeastern Alaska had aboriginal rights that were being violated by the industrial fishery. White backlash to the hearings was tremendous, and white unity against Indian claims was total. Non-Indians feared that the federal government intended "to oust white fishermen and white operators from various fishing grounds in Alaska which they have occupied for decades" and "turn over to non-reservation Indians, for their exclusive exploitation, many of the finest fishing grounds in Alaska."[107]

The salmon packers spent months preparing their case, while white fishers, labor unions, local businesses, and city councils issued an outpouring of protest against Indian fishing rights. W. C. Arnold, an attorney for the salmon-canning industry, argued that Indian petitions had "no basis in history or in law"; that they were "unfair to the white people of Alaska" *and* the Indians, in that they would make the latter "mere wards of the government" and deny them "true equality"; that they abrogated "the long recognized American principle of the common right to fishery"; and that they would ruin the commercial fisheries by "turning over to less than one thousand natives an industry developed by white people in good faith over a period of sixty-five years."[108] Whites portrayed Indian aboriginal claims as "founded on greed," while depicting themselves as hardworking, fair-minded innocents whose fisheries, mines, forests, and farms would be ceded to "small bands of Indians." The *Pacific Fisherman* called the hearings part of a "policy for the establishment of Indian collectivist communes under the guidance of the Indian service" (see figure 4.2). The Haines Chamber of Commerce declared the Tlingit petitions "undemocratic in principle," and the Juneau Chamber of Commerce, like many other protesters, claimed that the "natives of Alaska never had such rights as they are now asserting."[109]

Objections from the maritime unions, resident and nonresident, were similarly vehement. The United Trollers of Alaska claimed that if Indian petitions were upheld, "the effect would be to practically eliminate the trolling

FIG. 4.2 *"Will Bureaucracy Destroy Great N.W. Industry?" White fishers and industrialists—usually in conflict—were drawn together in their antagonism to Indian fishing rights.* SOURCE: *Pacific Fisherman 42 (October 1944): 39.*

industry" and to "exclude [trollers] from making a living." J. F. Jurich of the AFU called the petitions "pure discrimination" that would "create race prejudice" and "close America to Americans." Even Harry Lundeberg's Seafarer's International, which had previously brought Indians and resident whites together in common cause against fish traps and nonresident labor, saw the hearings as unfair and unwarranted.[110] The white community—both labor and capital, fishermen and canners—was united in opposition to Indian aboriginal claims.

Tlingit and Haida communities were by no means uniformly supportive of the hearings. Opinions differed, especially on the proposed reservations that might result if their claims were upheld.[111] But regardless of faction, Indian fishermen testified in the hearings and asserted their historical relationship to the fishing grounds of southeastern Alaska. Tlingit and Haida participants used the hearings as a forum to air old grievances against fish traps, corporate incursions on tribal property, unfair fisheries regulations, and salmon depletion. Older Indian fishers told of violent intrusions on their lands and waters and instances where, if they protested, they were "ordered to shut up" and threatened with arrest by U.S. marshals. They contrasted the traditional fishery, with its respect and moderation, with the exploitative character of the modern industrial fishery. "A white man fishing is not like my own," noted Haida Frank Nix. "When a white man fishes by me with a trap, he gets a quantity in his trap," he continued, "whereas I only get a little bit." Charles Webster Demmert, like many of the Indian participants, lamented that fish were "getting scarcer" due to industrial fishing methods and that Indians "have got no way to make a living but by fishing." Others differentiated property "ownership" in the Indian fishery from that of the commercial fishery. One Indian fisherman explained how the Tlingit still shared subsistence resources among households and communities, and nearly every Indian witness emphasized the continuing importance of subsistence fishing to Native peoples. In sum, Indian fishers articulated their distinctive relationship with the marine environment and made a strong case for their claims to the region: "We are asking for our lands here, just the same as our fathers and our grandfathers that owned it—we are asking for it back."[112]

Judge Richard H. Hanna rejected 92 percent of Indian claims, upholding only those "rights where native occupation has been continuous and exclusive."[113] This meant Indian villages, fish camps, and smokehouses, but not "tidal waters" or "ocean waters," the rights to which Hanna believed had either not been recognized by Indian peoples or had been abandoned "by the acquiescence in the use of such waters for fishing by non-Indians."[114] Hanna's decision rested in large measure on his observation that Native peoples in southeastern Alaska had "proven themselves progressive in character" and had "largely adopted the modern life of their neighbors." Because "Indians made little, if any, objection to the construction and operation of canneries within their claimed areas," and because "the Indian accepted the situation and made the best of it . . . [by] . . . winning a substantial place in the new industry," Hanna reasoned that Tlingits and Haidas had therefore ceded their "exclusive right to fish in such waters."[115]

His conclusions, echoed by others in the white community, amounted to an ironic and convoluted logic: their aboriginal claims would have merit if only Indians had violently resisted commercialization. By successfully adapting to non-Indian society and the market economy in particular—by doing, in other words, *what whites had wanted them to do*—Tlingits and

Haidas had ceased to be "real" Indians, deserving of their full aboriginal rights. His reasoning underscored the extent to which whites misunderstood the hybrid nature of Tlingit and Haida acculturation. Natives did not cede their aboriginal heritage because they participated successfully in the commercial fishery; rather, they maintained a connection to their cultural heritage *through* fishing, both subsistence and commercial. The judge's ruling also underscored, once again, the deep cleavages that existed within the fishery and the extent to which different groups of fishers, although they may have lived similar material existences, constructed for themselves different realities and different identities. Indians and whites fished the so-called commons, but they did not fish *in common.*

Even if Indian and white fishers could have achieved common ground, their moment of solidarity would have been short-lived. By 1954 fishermen's unions were considered by the Federal Trade Commission (FTC) to be a violation of the Sherman Anti-Trust Act. The FTC issued a complaint against Alaska salmon packers and fishermen's unions in November 1953, charging them with "an agreed and concerted course of action to restrain competition in the sale and distribution of salmon." In April 1954 both fishermen's unions and canners agreed to "cease and desist" negotiations.[116] With one swift federal decision Alaska fishermen's unions were dead.

The FTC decision had its roots in a long-running debate among the government, salmon packers, and fishermen themselves, over the employment status of fishers: were they "employees," "independent businessmen," "independent contractors," "venture capitalists," "employers," or "laborers"?[117] The question was not simply technical—at issue was the very nature of "wage labor" and "work." In the hearings to create the National Recovery Association (NRA) codes for the salmon-canning industry in 1933, packers contended that fishermen should not be considered "employees" because they were paid for the fish they "sold" to the canneries rather than in wages. In the view of salmon industrialists, fishermen were independent businessmen.[118] The industry view was bolstered by the 1942 U.S. Supreme Court decision in the *Columbia River Packers Association, Inc. v. Hinton et al.*, which held that a dispute between a "fish canning association" and an "association of fishermen from whom it buys fish" was not a "labor dispute," because the fishermen's association, "although called a 'union' and affiliated with a national labor organization, is actually an association of independent entrepreneurs, who own or lease their own fishing boats and carry on their business uncontrolled by any canner."[119]

In Alaska the question was not so easily settled. What about "cannery fishermen," who contracted with a particular cannery for the entire season, lived in company bunkhouses, fished with company gear, and were paid not only for fish caught but also for working on the cannery ship to and from Alaska? The NRA codes had distinguished between these "employee fishermen" and "independent fishermen," whom they considered to be "member[s] of the industry" because they participated in the industry on their own behalf as independent entrepreneurs.[120] But were "independent fishermen" really independent? Even they depended on the canneries for equipment, supplies, and loans—and such agreements often bound them to sell all their fish to certain canneries, rather than seek the best prices for their catch as truly independent businessmen would. Even for the "independent fisherman," according to economist Rosemary Schairer, "the circumstances of fishing arrangements in Alaska tie him to an individual packer in such a way that in effect the fish price becomes a wage payment." Schairer believed that "the fishermen do not consider themselves 'independent contractors' but as working men who look to their unions for coordinated action."[121] Labor economist Lauren Casaday, after interviewing dozens of fishermen in the 1930s, concluded that "all fishermen no matter how compensated," should be considered "laborers" or "workers," because that's how they perceived themselves: "A carpenter is none the less a 'laborer' merely because he owns a kit of tools."[122] However, it did not matter to the FTC how fishermen perceived themselves. In the antilabor climate of the post–Taft-Hartley 1950s the government simply decided that fishermen were "independent" and that fishermen's unions were no longer legal. A fishery that was already fragmented by social and cultural divisions was now divided even further by federal policy.

INDEPENDENT FISHERMEN?

Richard White's quotation at the beginning of this chapter suggests the extent to which nature and humans—who really are a *part* of nature—become intertwined through the process of work. Through fishing, "labor and nature merged" on the Columbia River. Fishermen in Alaska likewise came to know nature through their labors. In the process, however, they also became divided against themselves, as they inscribed the fishery with social and cultural divisions. This fragmentation was not simply the result of social and cultural processes, but also natural ones. Nature posed certain challenges—

the varying patterns of fish migrations, the different spawning habitats of each species, long-term cyclic patterns in fish populations, and of course the daily vicissitudes of weather and tides. Humans responded by developing technologies and economies to capture salmon, process them, and distribute them. Thus the conflict began between different methods of fishing (traps versus seines; spears versus gill nets), different types of processing (drying versus canning; community versus industrial), and different systems of distribution (moral versus market; commercial versus subsistence). These divisions, moreover, became framed through the lenses of race, ethnicity, and geography. Fishing was natural, but the fishery was also a social construction.

One social construction—most fully elaborated by Euro-American fishermen—represented fishing as a life of freedom and independence in a vast wilderness. White fishermen believed they could escape history by moving north and achieving a kind of nineteenth-century self-sufficiency. But fishermen, as we have seen, were never entirely able to escape. Their quest for independence brought dependence on other things: nature, markets, outside unions, federal policies. True independence implies the ability to define oneself—and fishermen could not even do that. It is ironic that the federal government, against the wishes of union fishermen, ultimately determined that fishermen, in the legal sense at least, were actually "independent," meaning that they could no longer do what they wanted—namely, form unions to protect their interests. True independence was an illusion, but one that fishermen held to with steadfast determination. They also held onto their cultural orientations—their prides and prejudices and traditions—in ways that made the fishery a sea of social conflict. For Natives the fishery was no less a social construct; it was simply defined by different terms: community, culture, capitalism, continuity, and change.

The natural and social context of the fishery would change dramatically for both white and Native fishers in the years after Alaska statehood in 1959, as competition increased, fish stocks declined to new lows, and new management strategies and economic developments redefined the fishery once again.

5 The Closing of the Fishermen's Frontier, 1950s–2000s

Over time, everything changed. Fishermen changed, cabins bristled with electronics. The fish couldn't hide. New boats were made of steel. The new men were made of deals and debt. They went longer and farther, for less and less. Competition increased. The fish declined. The government came in, and all was lost. —MICHAEL KÖEPF, *The Fisherman's Son*

So we cling to this fishing lifestyle even now, when it isn't very productive for us. It is a love affair with a type of employment we are reluctant to part with.
—JUDSON BROWN, Tlingit elder

A transition equivalent to the Neolithic agricultural revolution on land is happening in the seas in the late twentieth and early twenty-first centuries.
—J. R. MCNEILL, *Something New under the Sun*

In the postwar period the salmon fishery was dramatically transformed. Gone were the fishermen's unions. Gone was the inflexible and distant control of the federal government—in 1960 the new state of Alaska finally took control of regulating its fisheries. Gone were the fish traps, which the state immediately abolished with great popular support. Also gone, seemingly, were the fish: salmon catches dropped to record lows in 1960. Something drastic needed to be done, and it was, in 1973, with the passage of the Alaska Limited Entry Act. The new legislation finally abolished the vaunted institution of the open fishery by restricting access to a limited number of permit-holding fishermen.

It is ironic that the common-property fishery was eliminated. Open access was the one principle to which fishermen, industrialists, and politicians all appealed, even if they could never agree on its meaning. It was a revered Anglo-American tradition that for so long had defined, in part, the rights of democratic citizenship and had also differentiated the Euro-American fishery from the Native fishery. Salmon managers now embraced a property-right system that restricted use, not unlike the way that clan user rights had prohibited and restricted entry into the precontact aboriginal fishery. Limited entry had far-reaching consequences for all the participants in the fishery. For salmon it meant—theoretically at least—less gear to navigate on their way to the spawning grounds. For conservation officials it meant more direct control over fishing intensity. For industrialists it meant a more reliable, stable, professional, and efficient fleet, but one that would be increasingly "independent" and liberated from cannery control.

The consequences were most profound for fishermen themselves. In one sense limited entry echoed a trend that was reshaping the postwar world: the separation of individuals from traditional ethnocultural units. Italian, Scandinavian, and Native American fishermen had all come from fishing cultures. In Alaska they remained bound together through systems of kinship, culture, and ethnicity, and by participation in voluntary associations, such as intertribal brotherhoods and fishermen's unions. These ethnic communities did not disappear from the fishery, but limited entry made it harder for younger men to obtain permits and carry on family fishing traditions. At the same time commercial fishing permits began to make their way into the hands of a new breed of fisherman: highly capitalized independent entrepreneurs without historical ties to the fishery. This occurred as fishermen's unions were replaced by marketing associations and the Alaska Native Brotherhood turned its attention to aboriginal rights issues beyond salmon fishing. Longtime fishers—both Native and Euro-American—were cast adrift in a fishery that was becoming increasingly individualized, businesslike, efficient, and capital-intensive.

Limited entry occurred alongside other political, economic, and ecological developments that reorganized the salmon fishery even more dramatically. The passage of the Alaska Native Claims Settlement Act (ANCSA) in 1971 raised new controversies over the rights of Indian communities to fish and hunt for their own subsistence. The rise of global competition from salmon farms in British Columbia, Chile, England, and Norway sent market prices for wild salmon plummeting and threatened to destroy wild salmon fisheries both economically and ecologically. The growth of a tourist economy in southeastern Alaska redefined the demographics and economic orientation of local fishing communities—threatening to turn canneries into boutiques and fishermen into charter boat guides. Finally, a series of El Niño events wreaked havoc on salmon runs. Fishermen in Alaska would be left to navigate this brave new world largely as individual competitors, alone in the threatening seas of the global marketplace.

NET REVENUES: STATEHOOD, LIMITED ENTRY, AND THE MAKING OF A PROFESSIONAL CLASS OF FISHERS

Control over the fisheries was central to the Alaska statehood debate. Local fishermen, and Alaska residents in general, viewed statehood as a means of liberating the territory from the stranglehold of "outside" interests—namely, the corporate "fish trust" and the U.S. Fish and Wildlife Service. Frank Peratrovich—an Indian fisherman, a senator in Alaska's territorial legislature, and president of the Alaska Native Brotherhood—spoke for many territorial residents when he accused the large canning interests, aided by the corruption and "indifference" of federal resource managers, of stripping the region of valuable resources and impoverishing its residents: "They thus have taken our own fishing grounds, closed us off from them, and then controlled our legislature to deny us even relief assistance and unemployment compensation after taking away our livelihood." Peratrovich hoped that "statehood would give Alaskans control over this great resource, so it could be rebuilt and stabilized."[1]

In the view of most Alaskans the goal was not simply to eliminate the canning industry, which provided jobs and tax revenues, but to level the playing field and, in the words of one fisherman, force the salmon industry to "compete equally with the rest of us."[2] By eliminating the fish traps and the federal managers who allowed them to dominate the fishery, resident fishermen believed that Alaska would not only increase its fish populations but also its fisher populations. Statehood would bring a more egalitarian social structure with "a greater division of the fish by individual businesses."[3] For fishers and residents alike statehood was seen as a panacea that would bring ecological, economic, and social benefits.

Representatives of the salmon-canning industry challenged Alaskan statehood with arguments ranging from incendiary (Alaska statehood would set a "dangerous precedent" that could lead to statehood for Hawaii, Puerto

Rico, the Virgin Islands, and Guam, and would moreover unleash extensive Indian claims to the state's public lands) to the arcane (a concern for federal "highway withdrawals").[4] Their primary concern, however, was the impact that state control would have on fisheries management. Regulation of the Alaskan fisheries—"an exceedingly valuable and substantial food product, which is important not merely to the people of Alaska but to all the people of the United States"—should remain in the hands of the federal government, they argued, which would continue to control the waters beyond state boundaries in any case. "If you are going to have proper, adequate regulation of those fisheries, which are both inside and outside the Territorial waters," argued one lawyer on behalf of the salmon canners, "you pretty nearly have to have somebody that has jurisdiction of both."[5] The packers' concern for "conservation" was dismissed by residents such as Peratrovich, who contended that industrialists simply wanted "the Federal Government to keep control . . . so as to protect their traps from Alaskans, and thus to maintain the monopoly in price and production it has given them."[6]

When statehood finally did come, Alaska's constitution reflected the territory's long struggle against fish traps and outside control. Fishery resources were to be used by "the people for common use," and the state was prohibited from granting any "exclusive right or special privilege of fishery" in Alaskan waters.[7] Ordinance 3 of the document, adopted by popular vote at the state's constitutional convention, abolished fish traps in order "to relieve economic distress among individual fishermen," to "conserve the rapidly dwindling supply of salmon," and to "insure [*sic*] fair competition among those engaged in commercial fishing."[8] As an indication of just how important the fisheries—and all natural resources—were to Alaska's fortunes, the state constitution also contained a clause providing that fish and other renewable resources would be managed according to "the sustained yield principle."[9]

The federal government gave Alaska authority over the resource on January 1, 1960, one year after statehood. The salmon fisheries were now under state control—but they were also in a state of disaster. The summer of 1960 saw the worst salmon returns of the entire century, and the decline was not just the product of a one-year drop—runs had been on a downward slope since the early 1940s. In 1963 resource conservationist Richard Cooley published *Politics and Conservation: The Decline of the Alaska Salmon*, which he called a "history of the ruinous exploitation of one of the nation's important renewable resources."[10] The fishery was demoralized. Fishers, industrialists, regulators, and politicians were overwhelmed with a sense of crisis and an urgent desire to resurrect the industry.

There was plenty of blame to go around. Fishermen in Alaska could point to the impacts of logging, dams, foreign fishing fleets, the destruction of herring populations, increasing numbers of fishers in the postwar period, more efficient technologies, and of course illegal fishing. For fisherman Toivo Andersen the culprits were "the rise of corporate timber," overfishing by seines and traps, as well as "more participation, better gear, better electronic equipment, [and] dams in the rivers." Roman Keleske blamed "greedy canneries and greedy trap operators." For N. E. Nelson the problem was caused by distant federal managers who had enforced "rigid controls and restrictions" from "thousands of miles away from the operation point."[11] As always, fishermen saw responsibility residing somewhere else: residents blamed nonresidents, trollers blamed purse-seiners and gillnetters, and they all blamed federal conservation officials and corporate fish traps.

Alaskans hoped that the problems associated with the distant, inflexible, and procorporate policies of federal salmon managers would be eliminated with local control. The newly created Alaska Department of Fish and Game (ADFG) was designed to be more responsive to the voices of local communities through advisory committees "composed of persons well informed on the fish or game resources of the locality."[12] Although ADFG management techniques differed little from federal practices—they both relied on the biological analysis of salmon runs, maximum sustained yield, and limiting fishing by regulating gear and fishing periods—the new state agency adopted a much more flexible strategy, allowing it to micromanage particular runs by opening and closing districts according to the strength and timing of salmon migrations. State salmon managers now had the power "to summarily open or close seasons or areas or to change weekly closed periods on fish or game by means of emergency orders."[13] By using emergency orders and managing each stream for its optimum escapement, ADFG regulators rejected the rigid one-size-fits-all formula of 50 percent escapement that had dictated federal management since 1924. Local fishermen had high hopes. "With local control . . . and no traps," John Enge believed that state conservation officials could "watch the fish come into individual areas, individual bays, and they can close and open and build up the runs that have been depleted, and maintain the runs."[14]

The remedy for fish traps was even more straightforward: with statehood and the adoption of the new constitution, they were abolished. Problem solved. However, abolishing traps was not a panacea—it came with unforeseen consequences. For one, eliminating traps increased rather than decreased the power of large canneries. Before statehood smaller operations had relied on fleets of independent small-boat fishers, while large companies had relied more on fish traps. With the elimination of traps larger canneries began to compete with small outfits for fishermen and, with their ability to offer fishers supplies, equipment, loans, and subsidies, they won out, forcing small, local canneries to consolidate or merge with larger operators. By 1978 only two local, small-scale canneries remained in southeastern Alaska.[15]

The abolition of traps, it seemed, would not make Alaska's social and economic structure more egalitarian. Nor would it contribute to diminished fishing intensity, as the process of industrial consolidation occurred alongside the overall rise in numbers of fishermen. Between 1960 and 1972 canneries rapidly expanded their fleets, bringing even more competition into the fishery and increasing the amount of gear in the salmon fisheries by 74 percent.[16] As this enlarged fleet adopted new technologies—such as fathometers, "fish-finders," radars, radios, sonar, and even airborne "spotter" pilots—they raised the fishery to new heights of efficiency. A mobile fleet with more technology proved every bit as destructive as fish traps—even more so, because they could move to where the fish were, and they increasingly had the equipment to do so. Fishers found themselves trapped in a vicious cycle: increased competition and advanced technology demanded that all fishers upgrade or be squeezed out, but upgrading simply increased productivity and competition even more.[17]

The answer to rising fishing intensity was limiting entry to the fisheries—a radical proposition, given that Alaskans, and Americans generally, revered the common right of the fishery. However, there was an increasing call for drastic measures, and the tide was turning away from the notion of an open fishery, and not just in Alaska. Beginning in the 1950s, a number of North American scholars increasingly came to see the depletion of fish stocks as an economic rather than a biological problem, and one that required economic remedies. The problem—and the solution—became immortalized in Garrett Hardin's 1968 article on the "tragedy of the commons." The tragedy of the commons was, according to Hardin, the inevitability of resource depletion when resources were governed as "common property." He argued that commons would always be overexploited as long as individuals used them without externally imposed restrictions. Left alone to freely exploit the commons, individuals would always seek to maximize their economic gains and minimize their losses. On a common pasture, for instance, an individual herdsman would personally benefit by adding one animal to his herd, while the costs of his decision—overgrazing—would be shared by all the herdsmen on the commons. All rational herdsmen therefore would add to their herds until the commons was ruined, and "therein is the tragedy." According to Hardin, "Each man is locked into a system that compels him to increase his herd without limit—in a world that is limited."[18]

Hardin's theory rested on the highly contentious assumption that humans always behaved as rational, profit-maximizing beings—species *homo economicus*—and that common property would inevitably be destroyed under the vagaries of individualistic competition. His theory proved meaningless when applied to tribal societies, which had successfully managed common resources for millennia. All humans, it seems, did not behave selfishly, and the commons could thrive under certain communal regimes. But his theory proved extremely relevant when applied to cultures and societies that maximized personal freedoms and encouraged individualistic competition. Hardin's critique was not simply directed at the commons per se but at the laissez-faire administration of the commons. He referred to the "tragedy of freedom in a commons," arguing that that "freedom in a commons brings ruin to all."[19] His solution was strict regulation, or "mutual coercion mutually agreed upon," which limited the actions of the profit-maximizing individuals, forcing them to behave in ways that benefited the common good.[20] Although Hardin did not discuss the fisheries in detail, his message was clear: "the shibboleth of the 'freedom of the seas'" had brought "species after species of fish and whales closer to extinction."[21] The common fishery would inevitably bring environmental despoliation.

Hardin—much like Frederick Jackson Turner, whose "frontier thesis" put into elegant prose the nation's anxiety about the "closing" of the western frontier—was not the first to imagine the problem, but he was the first to lay the problem out in such compelling terms for popular consumption. Long before Hardin's article, H. Scott Gordon, Anthony Scott, James Crutchfield, and other economists were already arguing that fisheries managers were overemphasizing the biological health of fish stocks while ignoring the economic considerations that created fish depletion in the first place. In 1954 Gordon, presaging Hardin's later synthesis, argued that because the fisheries were not private property—"the individual fisherman has no legal title to a section of ocean bottom"—the resulting pattern of competition culminated in "the extensive margin of resource exploitation in the fisheries." The problem of the fisheries, in Gordon's view, was that "natural resources are owned in common and exploited under conditions of individualistic competition." The solution was thus to transform the commons into private property through state action: "By and large, the only fisherman who becomes rich is one who makes a lucky catch or one who participates in a fishery that is put under a form of social control that turns the open resource into property rights."[22]

Gordon's pathbreaking article was followed by other studies—all of which pointed in the same direction: managing the fisheries was as much an economic as a biological proposition, and simply focusing on maximum sustainable yield did not create a rational, sustainable fishery.[23] Fisheries conservation, these studies emphasized, needed to be carried out with more of a concern for maximizing the economic efficiency of fish stocks—more attention needed to be paid, in other words, to fishers rather than fish. "There is no purpose managing the resource except that it has value to man," concluded Cooley in his 1963 *Politics and Conservation.* His ideas were influenced by an unpublished paper given at the Alaska Science Conference in 1959 by a young economist, James Crutchfield, who argued that "it is simply impossible to make sense of conservation except in economic terms."[24]

Crutchfield's 1969 book, *The Pacific Salmon Fisheries: A Study of Irrational Conservation* (written with Guilio Pontecorvo), was an attempt to apply economic principles to fishery conservation. The problem, as described by fisheries economist Francis T. Christy in the book's introduction, was that "where resources are unowned or the common property of a community, there are no controls over access; no means for allocating or restricting inputs of capital and labor; and no way of preventing declining yields and the disappearance of net revenues to the industry." The solution, as outlined by Crutchfield, was to freeze the units of gear in the fisheries, issue highly valued licenses to certain fishers, create a voluntary buyback program to allow the state to purchase individual licenses and thereby reduce the number of fishers, and make licenses transferable "to ensure flexibility and to provide some pressure to keep the most efficient fishermen in the industry."[25] Crutchfield's vision was increasingly endorsed by scholars and policy makers looking for solutions to the salmon crisis in Alaska in particular and the Northwest Coast in general.[26]

By the early 1970s the intellectual foundations for limited entry were laid, but the political landscape was far less stable. Throughout the Northwest Coast—in Oregon, Washington, and British Columbia—governments were moving toward restricting access to the salmon fisheries.[27] In Alaska an early effort at limiting entry in the Bristol Bay fishery in 1968 was met with legal opposition from five nonresident fishermen who were excluded access. Their argument that limited entry created a "monopoly" for a "closed class of fishermen" was upheld in Federal District Court. A panel of federal judges moreover concluded that the "scheme" violated the U.S. Constitution as well as the Alaska State Constitution, which guaranteed that fishery resources were "reserved to the people for common use" and that "no exclusive right or special privilege of fishery shall be created" in state waters.[28] Those clauses, enacted with overwhelming support by the Alaskan public in the 1950s as a means of restricting fish traps and protecting Alaskan resident fishermen, were now being used by nonresident fishermen as means of protecting their own rights to the fishery.

Legal objections to limited entry were finally overcome in 1972, when Alaska's constitution was amended to allow the state to restrict access into the state's fisheries "for purposes of resource conservation" and "to prevent economic distress among fishermen."[29] The move cleared the way for a general plan to limit entry into "Alaska's overcrowded salmon fisheries."[30] Governor William Eagan commissioned a task force to study the problem, and its report appeared in February 1973, a month after the governor's limited-entry bill was introduced into Alaska's legislature. The study group believed that limited entry would create "a stable fishery that permits more effective sustained yield management and allows commercial fishermen the opportunity to make an adequate livelihood from fishing."[31] These two goals—biological and economic sustainability—formed the primary objectives of the bill passed later that spring.[32]

The final law created the Commercial Fisheries Entry Commission (CFEC), which was charged with determining how many permits would be available for each fishery—a decision that would ideally balance the demands of conserving the resource with economic productivity.[33] The entry commission would also determine which fishermen received those permits, a process that would take into consideration two primary factors: their "degree of economic dependence upon the fishery" and their "extent of past participation in the fishery."[34] It would take time for the commission to determine the total number of entry permits to be issued and to process fishermen's applications, but by the summer of 1975 the commercial salmon fisheries in Alaska—with the exception of hand-trolling, which would not become subject to limited entry until 1980—were no longer a "common property" resource.

The law generated opposition among fishermen and cannery operators alike. Fishermen agreed that the fisheries suffered from too much gear, but they had long battled against "special privileges" and fought to protect the open fishery. Roman Keleske, for instance, was not alone in believing that limited entry was essentially no different from fish traps: both were "highly discriminatory" and both gave certain fishers the right to fish while at the same time "depriving another American citizen of something that's rightfully his."[35] Even though he received an entry permit, William Love believed that it was "unconstitutional to say that I have a right to fish and you don't." Others lamented the growing influence of government restrictions and the decline of "wide open competition" that formerly characterized the open-access fishery. "The fish out in the ocean belongs to everybody," argued Arndt Peterson: "You shouldn't have to buy a license."[36] One of Peterson's friends, a young Norwegian fisherman, had moved to Alaska, worked in a pulp mill, and purchased a fishing boat on the eve of the 1973 limited-entry law, only to be denied an entry permit. Peterson had personally benefited from the open fishery. After immigrating to the United States from Norway in 1910, he worked in the shipyards and various industrial jobs before moving to Alaska in the late 1920s, where he fished, homesteaded, and prospected. The very avenue of opportunity that had pulled him northward was now closed to new migrants. For Peterson the fishermen's frontier was closed.[37]

Cannery operators had different concerns. Without fish traps they feared having enough harvesting capacity to handle big runs, and they were also concerned that limited entry would give fishermen "a monopolistic position from which to drive fish prices upward to unrealistic levels."[38] Opposition from industrialists and some fishermen, however, was swept away in the broad popular support for a law that most Alaskans—including the United Fishermen of Alaska, formerly a fishermen's union that by 1973 had become a fishermen's advocacy group—perceived as a necessary step in preserving the commercial fisheries and perpetuating the livelihoods of commercial fishermen. In the fall of 1976, 63 percent of Alaskans voted against an initiative to eliminate limited entry.[39]

Limited entry never fully achieved its stated goal of creating "an economically healthy fishery," but the law accomplished one of its unstated goals—to create a more professional class of fishermen.[40] By vesting permit-holders in a limited-entry fishery—by giving them a privileged stake in the resource and guaranteeing them permanent access to that resource—while at the same time protecting them from excessive competition, limited entry encouraged the rise of a more ambitious class of fishermen who invested in more efficient boats and technologies. Less ambitious fishermen continued in the fishery, but many sold out as permit values rose dramatically for both gill-net and purse-seine fisheries by 1980.[41] Those who acquired these high-priced permits were modern, acquisitive fishermen who had access to investment capital that they were willing to spend not only on entry permits but also on modern boats and gear.

In this sense the fishery became more efficient, modern, and professional after limited entry. Access to the purse-seine fishery—the most lucrative and highly capitalized in southeastern Alaska—required an investment of between $200,000 and $500,000 by the 1980s, depending on the quality of the boat and gear that one fished.[42] Fishing was becoming more a business and less a lifestyle. It was increasingly dominated by what troller William Love described as a "new breed of fishermen" who were simply "in it for the dollar."[43]

Salmon managers now wielded even more control over the fishing fleet—an outcome that seemingly fostered the goals of effective resource management. But limited entry also helped to create a fleet that, in the words of Carl Rosier, ADFG deputy commissioner at the time, could "simply harvest everything that's available, even on a strong run, in less time." Rosier remembered how fishermen used to fish relatively close to home, near their communities in Ketchikan, Petersburg, or Wrangell; now they were ready on a moment's notice to fish any district throughout the entire region.[44] Technology enabled such mobility, while growing capital investments in the fishery made such aggressive harvesting an economic necessity.

Investing more in the fishery, however, led some fishermen to overextend themselves—an unintended outcome of a program designed to increase the economic efficiency and stability of the fleet. The capital investment necessary to gain entry into the fishery—permits for those buying in, and modern boats and gear to make their investment worthwhile—meant that fishermen now had to make even more money to break even. There were fewer fishermen (although this was disputed by old-timers, who claimed that the fleets increased after limited entry), but they had to catch more to make reasonable returns on their investments. Everyone was forced to compete or see the fish mopped up by the new fleet of aggressive fishers. The result was that individual fishers became more efficient, but the salmon fishery, in aggregate economic terms, became overcapitalized: the fleet was more effective at catching fish but at a cost that was unsustainable.[45]

Ironically, Hardin's theory of the commons was still at work, except that the fishery was now an artificial "commons" closed to nonpermit holders. Cutthroat competition remained and investments increased. The equation worked for ambitious fishers in the late 1970s and 1980s, when improving runs and strong prices made the fishery profitable, but poor runs and falling prices now had the potential to ruin fishermen in a more thorough and devastating manner, without decreasing fishing intensity. In 1972 policy makers had predicted that "the increasing professionalization of the fisheries" would "enhance diversification and efficiency within the fishing fleets" and provide "economic stability for the fisherman."[46] If anything, limited entry pulled fishers further into debt, leaving them even more vulnerable to ecological and economic downturns.

The greatest irony—and the most profound social consequence—of limited entry was that by trying to "protect" independent fishermen from the vagaries of economic and ecological cycles, the program threatened to destroy the cultures of traditional Euro-American and Native American fisherfolk, whose lifeways had historically defined the Southeast Alaska salmon fishery. In a world where the fishery would increasingly be composed of fishermen who could afford, in the words of Oscar Ottness, "fifteen or twenty thousand for a license," and much, much more by the 1980s, fishing simply for the lifestyle was increasingly untenable. Permit prices for the low volume Southeast gill-net fishery had climbed to more than $40,000 by 1980, and to over $125,000 by 1989. Purse-seine entry permits saw a similar trajectory, and even power-troll licenses were valued at nearly $35,000 by 1980.[47] How realistic was it now—with the stakes so high—to flee modern society and re-create oneself on the fishermen's frontier? Was it still possible to mix commercial and subsistence fishing in traditional ways, where community values and needs took precedence over money making? How feasible was it to skip a commercial fishing period to go hunting instead?

"It's always been a business, but the amounts of money involved since Limited Entry has gotten kind of scary," observed troller Jamie Chevalier, who bought into the fishery in 1976 and sought to carve out an alternative lifestyle based on subsistence living. "When you've got a capital investment of, say, $60,000, that you're trying to pay off real quick," she explained, "you can no longer just smoke up part of your catch or take a day off or get real drunk and not go fishing the next day or something like that." Roman Keleske, who began commercial trolling in the early 1950s, believed that limited entry had transformed "an absolute way of life" into a "money-making scheme."[48] Fishing had become, as one fisher described it, part of the "rat race," more reflective of society's pressures and expectations than an escape from them.

There were still opportunities for "lifestyle" fishers in hand-trolling and power-trolling, the least capital-intensive and least lucrative of the commercial fisheries. A new wave of young lifestyle fishermen migrated north in the 1960s and 1970s, seeking to reconnect with nature and create alternative communities. They were countercultural fishers, refugees from the conformity, specialization, and tedium of postwar middle-class America. Like the neo-frontiersmen of John McPhee's *Coming into the Country*, new migrants to Alaska's fishing frontier were fleeing taxes, government restraint, social restrictions, urbanization, and technology.[49] Like Euro-American fishermen from previous eras they were seeking freshness, independence, individualism, and a "wild" natural setting. But they were often middle class instead of working class, and they were not escaping industrial wage labor like earlier migrants; rather, like Jamie Chevalier—a former school teacher from San Jose who began hand-trolling in 1976 when she was twenty-five years old—they were rejecting an urban, postindustrial society that abstracted the relationship between humans and nature. Fishing, in their view, reconstituted the elemental, authentic connection between humans and nature. Subsistence living—taking just what you needed—rejected the ubiquitous materialism of modern American life.

In the late 1960s and early 1970s countercultural fishing communities sprung up in places like Point Baker and Point Protection on the north end of Prince of Wales Island, populated by fishers who wanted to "make a subsistence living on the land," escape "an increasingly dull and bitter reality," and come to know nature through good, honest work.[50] Like earlier migrants to the fishery, Kathy Pfundt, who began power-trolling in the early 1970s before she was excluded by limited entry, spoke of "being on the water and being my own boss." To Pfundt, Chevalier, and other "lifestyle" fishers, trolling combined "independence" with "healthy" work in a natural setting: "just being out on the ocean" was preferable to "just punching a clock somewhere."[51]

Hand-trollers Tom Jacobson, Howard Pendell, and John Hancock were all twenty-something refugees from urban America—southern California,

Chicago, and New York—when they arrived in southeastern Alaska in the early 1970s ready to work in nature and escape the conformity of modern life. Like Pfundt and Chevalier they were committed to moderation and self-sufficiency, and they rejected the rising capital investments and business-oriented approach associated with the limited-entry fishery. "I could have gotten a license and gone into it [trolling] bigtime," explained Pendell, "but I wanted to keep my life kind of simple and I don't want to go into heavy debts or anything like that." Hand-trolling, he explained, was "just kind of a suitable way to have a modest kind of a living." He complained that limited entry was destroying the idea of fishing on a "small scale." "They won't allow you to stay small," Pendell recalled. "You've got to invest twenty grand in a boat and twenty grand in a permit or you've got to get out." Hand-trollers, however, "have the idea that enough is enough," he continued, "which is not a prevalent idea in our society, but there's a lot of people that just want a modest living and that's all."[52] Chevalier likewise criticized highly capitalized fishers, whom she depicted as "city people" who measured their catch in terms of "production," without acknowledging salmon as "fellow creatures they killed." Lifestyle fishers posed themselves as different from the modern breed of commercial-minded fishermen, throwbacks to an earlier era when subsistence, self-sufficiency, and freedom prevailed over making money. Their vision, however, was becoming marginalized in a fishery that was increasingly dominated by a new breed of ambitious "profit-seekers."

In one sense modern "lifestyle" fishermen were no different from the more business-oriented modern migrants to the Alaska fisheries—the so-called profit-seekers. Both were recent arrivals on the scene and both were variations on frontier types from previous eras. The profit-seekers—much like earlier gold-seekers—invested their capital in fishing operations intended to make them wealthy and independent. In the 1970s and 1980s these included teachers, construction workers, and small businessmen who purchased limited-entry permits, bought modern boats, and fished in a businesslike way. They brought ambition, capital, technology, and efficiency to the business of fishing. Like their predecessors—and their contemporary antagonists, the "lifestyle fishers"—they were imbued with the ideals of freedom and independence. In this battle of frontier ideologies profit-seekers—not lifestyle fishers—were the short-term winners who benefited from limited-entry policy, at least until prices for both fish and permits dropped precipitously in the 1990s.

Lifestyle fishermen were not victims, but their plight underscored the extent to which the fishery was becoming less open to alternative visions, nonconformity, self-sufficiency, small-scale investment, and lifestyle choices beyond purely material pursuits. Because of limited entry, permits were passing out of the hands of rural Alaskans—both Native and white—and into the hands of a new fleet of non-resident fishermen who had access to capital and a desire for profit. By 1980, just five years after limited entry began, nearly 30 percent of the purse-seine permits issued to rural fishermen in southeastern Alaska were now owned by outsiders. According to a study conducted by anthropologist Steve Langdon for Alaska's legislature, permit transfers indicated that nonresidents were making the largest gains in high-value fisheries, while the bleeding of permits from rural fishing communities was disrupting the cultural continuity of the fishery.[53] The most dramatic consequences, moreover, were seen in the Native community.

NATIVE CULTURE, SUBSISTENCE, AND SOVEREIGNTY

The period following statehood was not kind to Native fishermen. Increasing competition and rising technology on the fishing grounds had eliminated the advantages of local knowledge. Intensive state management further limited Native participation in the commercial fishery. Short fishing periods in districts far from home required fast modern boats and money for fuel and supplies—things that Indian fishers often lacked.

Even though Native fishermen, largely through the advocacy of the Alaska Native Brotherhood, had been forceful advocates of statehood and local control over the fisheries, after 1960 they found ADFG management just as onerous as federal management had been—and in some ways more so. Oral interviews conducted in the late 1970s show a significant degree of mistrust and resentment by Native fishers toward ADFG salmon managers, who, no less than federal conservation officials before them, were depicted as distant, ignorant of conditions on the ground, and indifferent to the perspectives of Native fishers.[54] A familiar refrain by Indian fishers, conveyed by Andrew Johnnie, was that state regulators "should listen more to the older people who have a lot of understanding about the fishing and hunting and wildlife." But, according to William Johnson, ADFG conservation officials simply did not "listen to Natives" until "after the fish was gone." Even then, according to Johnson, they were more inclined to "blame the Native people" for fish depletion, while protecting "the white people that's living around here taking all the fish." Dick Hotch was invited to sit on an ADFG local advisory panel, but came away convinced that state conservation officials were not truly interested in the recommendations that came from the local community. "So what the hell's the use in having an advisory board locally," he wondered, "if they're not going to listen." Hotch, like other Native fishermen, believed that salmon managers should be "local men" rather than outsiders who made their decisions from an "office in Juneau." From the perspective of Native fishermen state regulators, similar to their federal predecessors, controlled Native lives from a distant vantage. True local control remained an elusive dream.

The move to limited entry was an especially bitter pill for Native communities, given their historical involvement in the commercial fisheries. Now, their primary means of market participation was restricted. The immediate impact—such as the depressed value of Indian seine boats, which were useless without an entry permit—was less significant than the long-term consequences of making the right to fish a commodity that could now be alienated from Native fishers.[55] The lack of capital in Native communities had two important consequences: first, those who received entry permits initially were more likely to sell their permits to outsiders who could put up large sums of cash; and second, Natives who did not receive permits, including children who wanted to enter commercial fishing, had less access to high-volume commercial fisheries, such as purse-seining, which required a large capital investment.

The result of limited entry, according to Archie Brown, was that Indian "old-timers" were "selling their permits for the biggest amount of money that they can get [to outsiders] from Washington, Oregon, and California," while "our young people [who] are very capable of becoming skippers cannot become skippers because of lack of experience and lack of money."[56] Horace Marks complained that the "original intent of Limited Entry"—that of reducing fishing intensity—had been distorted by "expensive permits . . . being resold" to highly capitalized outside fishers who, despite entry limitations, had overfished the resource, leaving local communities in economic despair. "Our greatest source of income has always been the fishery," he lamented. "Now the bulk of us has to turn elsewhere." Instead of stabilizing the fishing economy, limited entry, he believed, had placed an "economic hardship" on Native communities.[57] Howard Gray worried primarily about the fact that children, without entry permits, were now excluded from taking up commercial fishing. He asked simply, "How would you feel if you had six or seven children and they want to go out fishing?"[58] A 1983 study conducted by the Alaska Commercial Fisheries Entry Commission showed that in the eight years after the implementation of limited entry, the number of permits in the Native community had already declined by 25 percent (see figure 5.1).[59]

For Native communities limited entry did not just constitute an economic loss, but a cultural one. Commercial fishing had always provided a link to family, community, and culture. Families and friends fished together on purse-seiners, gillnetters, and trollers; women and children joined together with men at fish camps, where commercial and subsistence activities merged. Declining participation in commercial fishing led to declining participation in subsistence fishing. A 1992 ADFG study of two Native communities showed that Indian fishers in Angoon and Kake mixed "traditional subsistence practices" with commercial participation in low-volume, low-capital fisheries. Incomes from commercial fishing were lower than average in these rural communities, but they were supplemented by subsistence harvesting. In a pattern that highlighted the important link between commercial fishing and subsistence fishing, commercial fishing families in both villages harvested hundreds of pounds of salmon for personal use (290 pounds a year in Angoon and 216 pounds in Kake), while noncommercial fishing households harvested *no* salmon for personal consumption. Commercial fishing, in other words, provided a gateway to subsistence activities. Subsistence did not exist within a vacuum: it operated within "mixed economies," where harvesting for family and community consumption worked alongside commercial participation. Indeed, according the study's authors, commercial fishing "supported subsistence systems in Kake and Angoon" in significant ways.[60]

Subsistence fishing in many ways was more essential to Native cultural identity in rural southeastern Alaska than was commercial fishing, although, as noted earlier, the two usually worked together. A 1987 ADFG study of rural Native communities in Alaska revealed that subsistence harvesting was still "a prominent part of the economy and social welfare in most rural Alaska regions." Moreover, subsistence practices—although integrated into mixed economies—were significant in ways that transcended pure economics.[61] To most Native peoples, subsistence was not simply an evolutionary step between traditional economies and modern market participation; rather, it was a significant and meaningful part of what it meant to be an Alaskan Native. According to the Alaska Natives Commission, subsistence was "much more than the consolation prize that village people are left with in

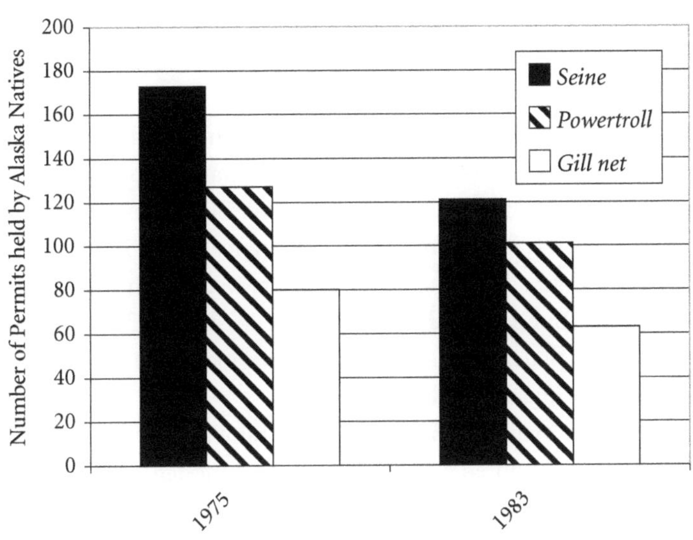

FIG. 5.1 Impact of limited entry on Alaska Natives in Southeastern Alaska, 1975–1983. In eight short years nearly 25 percent of the limited-entry salmon permits (excluding hand-trolling) initially allocated to Alaskan Natives had been transferred to non-Native fishermen, most particularly in the highly capitalized purse-seine fishery, where Native permit-holders declined from 173 to 121. This statistic that does not adequately reveal the total economic effect on Native crew members, families, and communities. SOURCE: *Kamali 1984: 18.*

the absence of jobs. It is its own economic sector, highly prized by its practitioners and fully co-existing with cash-market activities."[62]

Beyond the implications of limited entry, subsistence fishing and hunting—for so long a central component of Native lives—was challenged by other political developments after 1971. In that year the Alaska Native Claims Settlement Act (ANSCA) gave Alaska Natives $962.5 million in cash and title to forty-four million acres of land, to be stewarded by twelve regional Native corporations and numerous village corporations. ANSCA was the largest Native claims settlement in American history, but it also reduced the potential for broad tribal sovereignty in Alaska Native communities, privatized Native lands and resources under the control of for-profit corporations, and, perhaps most significantly, extinguished all aboriginal hunting and fishing rights.[63]

The legal eradication of Native fishing and hunting rights had come with the understanding on the part of Congress that the state would still continue to protect Native subsistence practices.[64] In 1978, Alaska's legislature—partly in response to pressures from the federal government that they were not living up to that obligation—enacted the Alaska State Subsistence Preference Law, which gave subsistence fishing and hunting (defined as "customary and traditional uses" of "wild, renewable resources for direct personal or family consumption") priority over other uses.[65] The law did not, however, give Native communities preference in subsistence harvesting, nor did it define "who" subsistence users were. With the passage of Alaska National Interest Lands Conservation Act (ANILCA) in 1980, the federal government defined subsistence users as "local rural residents," who in Alaska were primarily Alaska Natives.[66]

After ANILCA, village peoples could now hunt and fish for subsistence on more than two hundred million acres of newly designated federal lands in Alaska. The law was historic for creating the largest expansion of federal parklands in U.S. history as well as for respecting rural subsistence practices on federal lands, including National Parks—a dramatic reversal of long-standing Park Service policy that had historically excluded Native peoples and other subsistence users from "pristine" parklands, which were intended to be devoid of human occupation. Dispossessing Natives from the "wilderness" gave way, with ANILCA, to the construction of an "inhabited wilderness."[67] The law acknowledged that "the continuation of the opportunity for subsistence uses by rural residents of Alaska, including both Natives and non-Natives, on the public lands is essential to Native physical, economic, traditional, and cultural existence and to non-Native physical, economic, traditional, and social existence."[68]

However, Native subsistence rights were far from guaranteed by the passage of ANILCA. In fact, the fight over subsistence was only just beginning, as Native peoples became swept up in a larger battle over states rights and federal power. At issue was *who* would regulate subsistence activities in Alaska, state or federal managers, and *which* users would be given priority—rural Alaskans, meaning primarily Native peoples (which was the desire of the federal government), or *all* Alaskans (which is what the state wanted), meaning that urban, non-Native Alaskans, who were not as economically or culturally dependent on subsistence harvesting as Native villagers, would have equal rights to subsistence resources. The federal government, for its part, actually supported state regulation of subsistence activities, even on federal lands, so long as the state implemented ANILCA's mandate that rural Alaskans receive priority over nonrural users.[69]

The state, however, refused to acknowledge a "rural preference" in subsistence uses until 1986, when it revised the state subsistence law to limit subsistence fishing and hunting to residents "domiciled in rural areas of the state."[70] But this law, which finally brought the state into compliance with ANILCA, was found by the Alaska Supreme Court to be a violation of Alaska's constitution, which guaranteed all citizens equal rights to fish and game. In the 1989 case of *McDowell v. the State of Alaska*, rural preference was struck down, and the state was once again at odds with ANILCA, which demanded that the state give priority to rural subsistence users not just on federal lands but also on state lands (including navigable waterways) adjacent to federal lands, both of which were used by fish and animals who showed a careless disregard for state and federal boundaries.[71] After *McDowell* the Alaska state legislature continued to resist adopting a rural-preference subsistence law (which would now require an amendment to the Alaska State Constitution). Not only were most state legislators against privileging rural communities on subsistence issues; they also believed that complying with federal mandates, such as those prescribed by ANILCA, threatened Alaska's sovereignty. The ironic result was that their inaction forced the federal government to assume management over subsistence hunting on federal lands within the state in 1990.[72]

At first, federal control over subsistence activities did not include the fisheries, which had been managed by the state of Alaska since one year after statehood. Federal subsistence regulations issued in 1992 did not include navigable waterways, which were considered beyond federal jurisdiction generally and outside the scope of what was intended by ANILCA when it spoke of "public lands." That was soon to change due to the momentous events springing from the desire of Katie John and other Ahtna tribal members to reclaim a traditional fish camp on the Copper River. The fishing site had been closed down for conservation purposes by the Alaska Board of Fisheries and Game in 1964. Subsequently, the area became part of the Wrangell–St. Elias National Park, but state fish and game managers continued to prohibit Native fishing at customary upriver locations. Not to be denied, John and Ahtna elders pressed their case, first with the state and then with the federal government. John's goal was the unrestricted use of her people's traditional fishing sites: "We're Indian people and I don't like park rangers or game wardens coming in here telling us what to do like they own everything. That makes me mad. . . . I like to do my fishing on my own land right here."[73]

Katie John's activism spawned a series of legal battles that ended (at least for the time being) in a favorable outcome for her and Native peoples throughout Alaska. In the 1994 case of *Katie John v. United States*, U.S. District Court judge H. Russel Holland concluded that the federal government was entitled to regulate all fishing and hunting on federal lands (given that Alaska had failed to enact a rural preference subsistence law). More significant, he declared that "public lands" in ANILCA included "all navigable waterways in Alaska."[74] A decision the next year by the Ninth Circuit Court of Appeals scaled back Holland's definition of "public lands" somewhat to those waters that at the very least ran through federal lands. The result was the same: Native subsistence fishers like Katie John would now be granted preference over urban dwellers under federal management guidelines.

The prospects for Native subsistence fishing seemed secure, but the outcome was not unambiguously good for Alaska Natives. In 1998 Alaska challenged federal control over subsistence within the state. The effort failed, but the state's defiance sent a clear message to Native peoples: Alaska was more interested in resisting federal power than protecting the hunting and fishing rights of its Native citizens.[75] By 2005, despite the protestations of Alaska Natives, the state still had not passed a subsistence law that gave priority to rural users. Today the debate over subsistence remains unresolved, with Native peoples trapped in the middle of a tangled debate over federalism.[76]

In the 1980s and 1990s the conflict over subsistence joined a debate over Native sovereignty—an issue that, like subsistence, begged the question of how much control Native peoples in Alaska really had over their lands and their lives. The seeds of the sovereignty debate were planted with the passage of ANSCA. The claims settlement gave Natives in Alaska land and resources that would be controlled—and hopefully stewarded—by for-profit corporations in the best interests of their Native shareholders. By the 1980s, however, there was a growing concern within Alaska Native communities that their lands and resources—*indeed their entire cultural heritage*—could be estranged from them forever. "The land that ANSCA conveyed does not belong to Alaska Natives," wrote Thomas Berger, head of the Alaska Native Review Commission, in 1985. "It belongs to these corporations," and it could be lost by "corporate failure, corporate takeovers, and taxation."[77]

As head of the commission, Berger traveled throughout rural Alaska in the early 1980s cataloguing the fears and concerns of Native villagers in the wake of ANSCA. His book, *Village Journey*, conveyed in eloquent terms the conflict between the "profit structure" imposed on "Native lands and resources" by ANSCA and the subsistence ethics of rural villagers, who were simply interested in "continuing to pursue their own way of life," which, according to Berger, entailed living from the land by their "ancient values."[78] The alarms were raised: By privatizing Native lands, did Native peoples still hold special rights and privileges to the land? Could their land and resources—including subsistence resources—be protected from state confiscation and control? Could their lands, and consequently their subsistence base, be taken from them permanently? After 1971 did "Indian country"—with its promises of sovereignty and self-determination—still exist anywhere in village Alaska?

The state of Alaska held that tribal governments, unlike those in the Lower 48, did not have the power to tax or regulate land use. Native communities, however, believed they held sovereign rights over their lands—especially in the wake of President Bill Clinton's 1993 decision to extend federal recognition to Alaska Natives. The debate over sovereignty came to a head with the 1998 case of *Alaska v. Native Village of Venetie*. The case centered on the rights of a tribal government on the former Venetie reservation (which was extinguished by ANSCA) to tax a state contractor building a village school. The U.S. Supreme Court sided with the state, ruling that ANSCA had extinguished "Indian country" in Alaska—Native peoples in Alaska did not wield sovereign powers over their lands.[79] In a letter to the Alaska Federation of Natives the attorney for the village of Venetie called the verdict "a tremendous judicial loss in the battle to protect tribal integrity over tribal lands. . . . [W]ithout the Indian country designation tribes will be limited in their ability to regulate their land."[80]

The *Venetie* decision, along with the failure of the state to give preference to rural subsistence users, left the question of Native control over their resources unsettled. Native communities still continued to hunt and fish for their own subsistence, and salmon fishing for subsistence continued to play a major role in rural villages throughout southeastern Alaska. But what were the boundaries of Indian rights to fishery resources? How much control did they have in protecting their cultural heritage? Such questions remained unanswered.

Moreover, the debates over subsistence, land use, and the meaning of Native life in contemporary Alaska were not simply waged between Natives and whites, but were also contested *within* Native communities. Some Native peoples wanted to see their lands used in "traditional" ways—meaning that subsistence would continue to be a central part of Native life. Others wanted to see their lands developed to their fullest potential—which meant pulling Indian peoples further from salmon economies, both subsistence and commercial. Debates over the direction of tribal economic development emerged between village and regional corporations, between rural and urban peoples, and within those communities. ANSCA had exacerbated such conflicts by making Alaska Natives corporate shareholders. The desires of profit-minded corporations—even those owned and managed by Native peoples—did not always harmonize with the maintenance of Native cultural heritage, especially with regard to subsistence practices.

Such tribal conflicts were nowhere more apparent than in the development of Native logging industries in the wake of ANSCA. In pursuit of profits for their shareholders, Native corporations throughout southeastern Alaska cut timber at breakneck speed during the 1980s and 1990s. According to environmental journalist Kathie Durbin, Native logging enterprises differed little from those of non-Native corporations: they "held themselves to almost no environmental standards. Their logging roads triggered horrific landslides. Their loggers left few trees to buffer streams. Their clearcuts went on for miles."[81] In 1989 alone, Native corporations harvested 613 million board feet of timber in southeastern Alaska, a pace that was unsustainable. According to a 1992 Forest Service report by Alaskan economist Gunnar Knapp: "No village corporation has attempted to follow a sustained yield approach in its timber harvesting. Most village corporations will have harvested all their merchantable timber within twenty years from when they began harvest, about one-eighth the time needed to produce marketable volumes of timber on second-growth stands in southeast Alaska."[82] Not only were timber harvests by Native corporations unsustainable, they also jeopardized salmon streams and hunting grounds used by Native peoples for subsistence harvesting. Such was the case in the Klawock Lake watershed on Prince of Wales Island, where Native corporations clearcut fifteen thousand acres, "including shade trees along feeder streams that helped to keep the water cool" for migrating salmon.[83]

The transition from fishing to logging as the primary extractive economy for Native communities was driven most forcefully by Sealaska, the regional Native corporation created by ANSCA. By the 1980s Sealaska had become the largest private landowner in the region, and its logging enterprises were transforming the landscape of Southeast Alaska. In the early 1980s a biologist for ADFG witnessed a Sealaska contractor fell trees along the banks of a salmon stream near Craig, on Prince of Wales Island: "The stream was under piles of logs and they were yarding timber across it while salmon were spawning." In the 1990s Sealaska logging in Port Frederick, near the Native village of Hoonah, left behind a clearcut so vast that, according to one Native resident, "all the eagles are out on the breakwater because there are so few trees left on the hill." Another Hoonah villager worried about the long-term impacts on salmon fishing: "You can see through the buffer strips. There are little streams that are totally wiped out."[84] Logging like this provided short-term income to Native shareholders, but its ecological impact posed a serious threat to Indian salmon fishing.

Sealaska Corporation nonetheless claimed to promote the "careful and responsible stewardship of [Native] natural resources." On its Web site the Native corporation vowed to "protect the land and natural resources our people depend on for subsistence, and responsibly invest the profits from natural resources development in viable business opportunities."[85] In 2002, Rosita Worl, president of Sealaska, testified before Congress on the necessity of protecting Native rights to subsistence fishing and hunting. Subsistence in her view was a "way of life" to which Native peoples remained "very dependent and culturally attached." Beyond its economic importance, she believed that subsistence played a powerful spiritual role in Native lives, arguing that Native peoples "differ from the larger society and the rest of Alaskan society in that Alaska Native people believe they have a spiritual relationship to the animals and to the wildlife. This relationship requires native people to adhere to certain codes of conduct and to treat animals in prescriptive ways to ensure success in future hunts."[86] Worl's was a powerful testimony on the continuing importance of "customary and traditional" subsistence patterns to Native communities—and to Native culture. Yet Native peoples were also now invested in the life of a corporation—Sealaska—whose prime interest and obligation to shareholders was not custom or culture but profit. By 2006 the corporation's investments—forest products, financial markets, plastics manufacturing, prototyping, construction aggregates, environmental services, bio-life sciences, and international trade support—bore little relationship to customary Native lifeways in southeastern Alaska.[87]

It would be misguided to assume that Tlingit and Haida peoples, by operating profit-oriented corporations that were disconnected from—even adversarial to—traditional land uses, were violating their cultural heritage or ceasing to be "Indian." In fact, their culture had never been bound by a fixed set of "traditions," but rather had always been characterized by selective adaptations—or the creation of "new traditions," as one Tlingit leader referred to the annual Native "Celebration" in southeastern Alaska—that allowed Native peoples to negotiate change and still remain Native.[88] In this sense Sealaska was operating within Tlingit and Haida tradition, even if tribal economic development threatened other traditions, such as Indian salmon fishing.[89]

The period since 1971 has been fraught with ironies and contradictions for Native peoples. Limited entry has reduced the role of commercial fishing in the life of Native communities. ANSCA has increased the political and economic power of Native peoples, but it also threatens to alienate Native peoples from their lands and subsistence lifeways. At the same time Native corporations have been the driving force in a Native cultural revival, and salmon as a cultural symbol—and continuing source of subsistence for many rural Natives—continues to play a large role in Native life, even if many Native peoples are increasingly urban and disconnected from everyday subsistence practices.

In the late 1970s Native elders spoke eloquently about the persistence of fishing—commercial and subsistence—in Native life. Roy Bean declared that Tlingit and Haida peoples would "continue on fishing just as long as there is fish to be caught, just as long as the cannerymen wants fish." "Fishing is in these people's blood," explained Ronald Bean Sr., who began seining in the late 1920s. He continued: "If they can make 50–60–80 dollars a day [in] wages, they'll go right out every chance they get to go fishing. And they're at it right now. They got small rigs, you know. And after work, or when they're not working, they go right out and fish salmon and coho and halibut, hand-lining, [and] some of them do good. That's why I say they'll still be at it, even if they have a job." Albert Davis, who also began commercial fishing in the late 1920s, noted that "a lot of our people still rely on trolling for a living and also subsistence. We go out in the winter months. We catch one or two king salmon and that will last us for a couple weeks. So this [fishing] still contributes to our livelihood."[90]

Today Tlingits and Haidas have become increasingly protective of subsistence as a powerful cultural legacy. According to anthropologist Sergei Kan, "Subsistence fishing and hunting continue to be practiced by a much larger group of Tlingit who have argued that for Alaska Natives 'food from the land' remains not only a major source of nourishment but an ideologically and emotionally significant symbolic resource."[91] But given the political, economic, and ecological trends since 1971, how long will the connection between Native peoples and salmon fishing be maintained? Is tradition giving way, or are Native peoples in Southeast Alaska simply creating "new traditions" once again?

THE GLOBALIZED FISHERY: SALMON FARMS AND ENDANGERED FISHERMEN

In his environmental history of the twentieth century, J. R. McNeill writes that "a transition equivalent to the Neolithic agricultural revolution on land is happening in the seas in the late twentieth and early twenty-first centuries."[92] This dramatic revolution is the rapid growth and expansion of global fish farming. In British Columbia, eastern Canada, Chile, Ireland, Scandinavia, and Scotland, aquaculture corporations are producing millions of metric tons of raw salmon for the global marketplace. Reared in giant mesh pens and fattened on feed pellets containing fish meal and fish oil from lower-trophic-level fish, farm-raised salmon is a development, according to writer Terry Glavin, that is "without precedent in the history of agriculture." "At no other time in history," he continues, "have people raised carnivores exclusively for food stock."[93] Salmon farms, in the words of one *Seattle Times* reporter, transform "salmon into livestock that are inoculated to ward off disease and fed pigment-fortified pellets to turn their flesh a pleasing pink."[94] This application of technological mass production to the rearing of domesticated salmon—the Neolithic *and* industrial revolution of the ocean—threatens to destroy both wild fish and small-boat fishermen.

The first threat is ecological: salmon farms have the potential to unleash catastrophe on wild salmon populations. Concentrations of solid waste and nitrogens from farmed-salmon pens could create "algal blooms" that poison marine life. Antibiotics given to the fish could creep into marine ecosystems, promoting the growth of "antibiotic-resistant bacteria."[95] Sea lice infestations in farmed stocks could spread to wild populations with devastating results. A 2001 outbreak in a British Columbia fish farm "was followed by one of the most dramatic and rapid collapses of a wild salmon population known to science, when local pink salmon runs fell, in a single generation, from 3.6 million spawners to 147,000 spawners."[96] A study conducted in 2003 showed that the infection rate of young wild salmon from sea lice, which chew holes in their host's skin, jumped dramatically after the juvenile fish migrated past a salmon farm.[97] Most threatening are new diseases introduced by farmed stocks, which have the potential to unleash a holocaust on wild salmon no less destructive than the virgin soil epidemics that destroyed Native American populations during the Columbian Exchange. Such outbreaks have already devastated wild salmon fisheries in Norway and afflicted British Columbia stocks.[98]

Fishermen, biologists, and environmentalists also worry that salmon farm escapees could overrun wild salmon habitat. By 1999 nearly a million Atlantic salmon had already escaped from salmon farms in Puget Sound and British Columbia. It is unclear if these fish can survive in the wild, but some biologists fear that Atlantic salmon, with their voracious appetites, might simply drive wild stocks to extinction by overgrazing their food supply and destroying their habitat, similar to the ecological imperialism that occurred with the introduction of European livestock and plants to the North American grasslands.[99] "It's like bringing rabbits to Australia," mourns one Alaska fisherman, who wonders if the Canadian government, by allowing salmon farming in British Columbia, is "trying to get rid of the wild fish and the small boat fishermen. It's easier to manage three or four big guys than a few thousand little guys."[100]

The environmental threats posed by industrial fish factories not only imperil salmon ecosystems, but also salmon economies and salmon cultures. The threat is felt most acutely by those whose fortunes have historically been tied to the health of the wild salmon fisheries: small-boat fishermen, Native peoples, and local fishing communities throughout the Pacific Northwest. After Canada lifted its moratorium on salmon farming in 2002, some First Nations peoples in British Columbia embraced aquaculture as a means of economic development. The majority of Natives in British Columbia, however, began to wonder whether their salmon resources—and consequently their livelihoods and cultures—were threatened by salmon farming. "The whole question of salmon resources is fundamental to aboriginal society," says Dave Porter of the First Nations Summit, which has called for another moratorium on salmon farming in British Columbia. If "salmon farms kill a lot of salmon," he says, "then we are looking at a huge impact on the culture of the people who depend on this resource, an impact that would be devastating to say the least."[101]

Yet the economic rather than ecological implications of salmon farming just might prove the most ruinous to small-boat fishermen, whose livelihoods could be rendered obsolete by an efficient system of global salmon mass production. Salmon farms are different than hatcheries, which introduce "wild" stocks of fish into natural ecosystems, hoping they will adapt and thrive. Farm-raised salmon, however, are entirely mass produced, from hatchling to harvest. This gives the new industry numerous market advantages over wild fisheries. The wild fisheries remain incredibly inefficient: fishermen and salmon processors invest large amounts of capital to catch and process an undetermined amount of fish. Investments in processing capacity and labor often exceed the size of fish runs and vice versa, and food quality suffers as production is squeezed into incredibly short seasons. Salmon fishermen can never predict the behavior of salmon, and industrialists can never predict the behavior of salmon fishermen—strikes and boycotts also factor into the costs and instability of the commercial fisheries.

Aquaculture corporations, though, are not dependent on the unpredictable behavior of either salmon or salmon fishermen. Salmon farms control production simply by manufacturing more or less fish and regulating feed. Liberated from the fluctuations of natural salmon runs and the inefficiencies of small-boat fishermen, global fish factories are producing volumes of fresh, "cheap," and high-quality protein for a growing world population,[102] while wild salmon harvests remain subject to the seasonal patterns of fish migrations and the natural fluctuations of wild fish populations. In the 1980s and 1990s the farm fisheries also benefited from "green-minded consumers" who believed that farm-raised salmon were an "environmentally friendly alternative to fishing for salmon in a world where ocean-fish populations are seriously depleted or jeopardized by overharvesting."[103] The rise of the industry was dramatic and, from the perspective of Alaskan fishermen, devastating. In 1980 farm-raised salmon accounted for only 1 percent of the world supply, while wild Alaskan salmon accounted for more than 40 percent; by 2002 farmed salmon had captured over 60 percent of the world market, while wild Alaskan stocks declined to less than 20 percent. Total production of farm-raised salmon grew in the same period from only 15 million pounds to 1.2 million metric tons.[104]

As farmed salmon production grew, world prices for wild salmon plummeted. Between 1988 and 2002 the combined value of all five species of Alaskan salmon fell by 85 percent.[105] The 1990s should have been a prosperous decade for fishermen in Alaska—salmon harvests, in general, were rising to historic levels. Instead, fishermen encountered the perfect storm: competition from farmed fish and record catches of chum and pink salmon pushed prices for those species so low that many fishermen couldn't meet expenses, while at the same time the market for the more lucrative sockeye collapsed as Japan—the major destination for Alaskan salmon—experienced

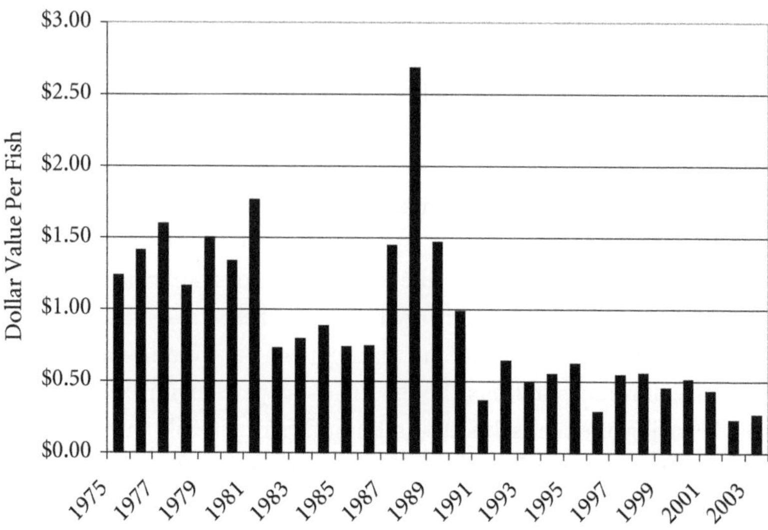

FIG. 5.2 *Price paid to Alaskan fishermen for pink salmon, 1975–2003. The value of wild Alaskan salmon declined dramatically during and after the 1990s as farm-raised salmon flooded the world market. The value of all wild species plunged, with pink salmon reaching the lowest depths—less than fifteen cents per pound paid to fishermen.* SOURCE: *Alaska Department of Fish and Game, "Historical Salmon Catch and Exvessel Values," database.*

a deep recession and Chilean farmed salmon dramatically expanded its Japanese market share.[106]

In the 1990s purse-seiners in Southeast Alaska caught more pink salmon than ever—but earned less (see figure 5.2). Gillnetters and trollers, who targeted higher-value sockeye and king salmon, were also hurting, as catches remained healthy but prices plummeted. In Bristol Bay, Alaska, sockeye catches and prices declined so precipitously that permit prices, which had sold for as much as $200,000 in 1990, dropped to $20,000 by 2001, the same year Governor Tony Knowles declared the region an economic disaster area.[107] Permit values for all the Alaskan salmon fisheries dipped to all-time lows in the early twenty-first century. "As long as you manage to catch five times as many fish as you used to, you can keep going," complained Bob Thorstenson, president of the United Fishermen of Alaska. "If you fish salmon only, it's like the Great Depression."[108] The cover of *Alaska Magazine* in August 2002 read: "Endangered Species: Is Our Salmon Fleet Bound for Extinction?"[109]

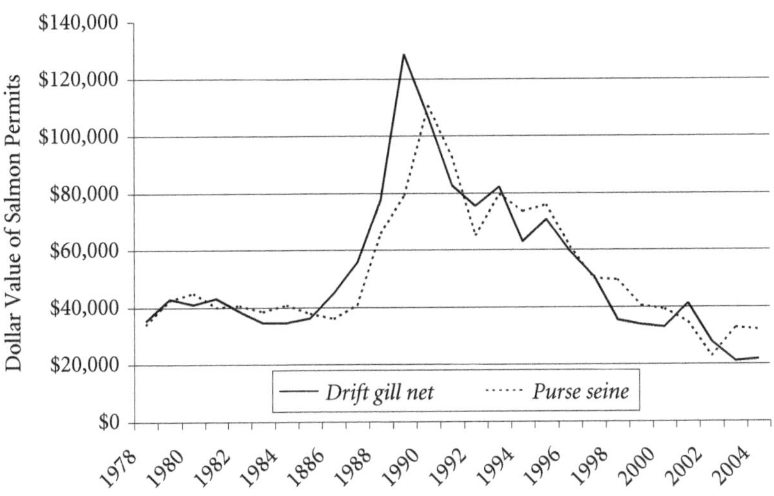

FIG. 5.3 Southeast Alaska commercial fishing permit values, 1978–2004. As prices plunged for wild salmon on the world market, so did Alaskan commercial fishing permit values. SOURCE: *Alaska Commercial Fisheries Entry Commission, "Estimated Permit Value Report"; online at http://www.cfec.state.ak.us/mnu_Research_Commission.htm.*

Alaskan fishermen responded to the specter of fish farms with political activism. In the 1980s the Alaska Trollers Association (ATA) and the United Fishermen of Alaska (UFA) lobbied for a state ban on fish farming, which Alaska's legislature passed in 1990.[110] In 2001, as British Columbia contemplated lifting a moratorium on new salmon farms—which they indeed lifted in 2002—Dale Kelley of the ATA chastised the Canadian government for sacrificing "local fish populations, the environment, [and] artisanal fishermen and their communities" to "multinational corporations based in distant lands." Kelley argued that the Canadian and U.S. governments have "a combined obligation under the Pacific Salmon Treaty to protect BOTH fish and fishermen," a social responsibility that he believed had been sacrificed on the altar of global market capitalism (see figure 5.3).[111]

The protests of Alaskan fishermen like Kelley did not stop Canada from lifting its moratorium, but they did succeed in 2004 (with the help of Alaska senator Lisa Murkowski) in halting a National Marine Fisheries Service (NMFS) plan to promote ocean aquaculture in U.S. federal waters. As with fish traps earlier in the century, Alaska fishermen found it incomprehensible that a federal agency charged with stewarding the fishing industry would support a plan that would drive small-boat fishermen in Alaska to bankruptcy. "We are so opposed to this we've already figured out where we can get a couple of decommissioned navy ships. They can put [farm-fish pens] up anywhere they want and we'll take them down," warned Bob Thorstenson of the UFA. "This is the way Alaskans feel about it."[112]

But how long can Alaskan fishing communities hold out against the power and influence of multinational corporations, who make it their business to encourage, or force, national governments to liberalize new arenas of economic opportunity? How can fisherfolk resist globalization when expanding markets always seem to prevail over the will of local communities? National moratoriums (such as the federal decision in 2004 to postpone ocean aquaculture pending further study) and local bans (such as that imposed by Alaska in 1990, which is already being reconsidered by state politicians) do not stop the global expansion of fish farming; rather, they only serve to keep Alaskans, and Americans generally, out of a lucrative industry that is providing an important protein source for a growing world population. Justin LeBlanc of the National Fisheries Institute, a seafood industry advocate, believes that "marine aquaculture is going to have to develop" in order to "sustain the supply of fish as a protein choice to people."[113]

David Harvey, a Department of Agriculture economist, shares LeBlanc's sense of inevitability with regard to aquaculture, which follows the modern trend toward large-scale industrial organization. "Fishing is sort of the last of the hunting and gathering activities," he has noted. "In almost all other cases, we've gone to industrial agriculture for our food."[114] Is it inevitable also that fishing for wild salmon—with its glaring inefficiencies—will give way to a more rational industrial form of production? Speaking at the British Columbia Aboriginal Fisheries Commission's Fish Farming and Environmental Summit in 2002, biologist Ken Brooks, working for British Columbia aquaculture companies, likewise described the rise of global salmon farming in evolutionary terms: "We are transitioning from buffalo hunting to feeding people using intensive cultivation. . . . If you stand in the way, and think you're going to stop this industry, you're going to get run over, because it's an evolutionary process and we are going, the world is going, to produce more and more of its seafood in intensive systems."[115]

A study published in the journal *Science*, in January 2004, offered temporary hope to fishermen fighting aquaculture on a new front: a "Go Wild" marketing campaign to promote wild salmon as a healthy—and "organic"—alternative to pen-raised salmon. The article—"Global Assessments of Organic Contaminants in Farmed Salmon"—concluded that farm-raised salmon contained "significantly higher" levels of PCBs, dioxins, antibiotics, and pesticides than wild salmon. The authors suggested that eating large amounts of farm-raised salmon—more than one meal per month—could pose serious health risks.[116] Following the publication of the study, American imports of farm-raised salmon dropped temporarily, but by the fall of 2004 the industry had rebounded and was growing as rapidly as ever.[117] The temporary decline and resurgence of farmed salmon in the United States after the highly publicized *Science* findings suggested two important realities. First, consumers in the global marketplace—ever in pursuit of a better bargain—have short memories. The logic of the market, and the lure of cheap consumer products, can turn popular attention away from concerns over the health of humans and endangered wild salmon populations, not to mention the plight of local fishing communities throughout the Pacific Northwest. Second, the aquaculture industry—capital rich, innovative, and market savvy—has the ability to overcome such obstacles. Economist Gunnar Knapp contends that "there are no obvious limits to growth in total world aquaculture production." The problem of feeding millions of carnivores can be solved, he believes, by substituting "vegetable-based feed for fish-based feeds," and environmental and health concerns can be handled by a combination of government regulations and corporate innovation. Knapp suggests that although contaminants in wild salmon cannot be controlled (a fact that smart consumers also realize), contaminants in farm-raised fish can be reduced simply by improving production techniques.[118]

In a trend that is common in the global market economy, what has been a boon for Western consumers has been an economic disaster for local communities. Knapp predicts that "most of the world won't notice or care what happens to the people who make their living from wild salmon."[119] He is undoubtedly correct. Alaskans increasingly realize that the rise of corporate fish farming is inevitable—in his words, "aquaculture is not going to go away" and "globalization is not going to stop." But some, like Knapp, see it as an opportunity rather than a threat.[120] Offshore aquaculture could be a means of creating jobs and economic growth in Alaskan communities that are exceedingly vulnerable to fluctuations in fish stocks and salmon markets. Roger Painter of the Alaska Mariculture Association (AMA) in Juneau wonders if, "in the long run, both fishermen and the communities in which they reside might long for the dependability of supply that fish farms can produce."[121] Another Alaskan, Paul Fuhs of Unalaska, believes that "mariculture" and commercial fishing "can exist side by side." He continues: "Our community is one of the biggest in the commercial fishing industry and is very much a supporter of the [aquaculture] industry."[122] In its 2004 proposals to the secretary of commerce regarding ocean aquaculture, the NMFS wondered if programs could be devised to allow "traditional fishing communities rather than just corporations to benefit from offshore aquaculture operations."[123]

Is the rise of global salmon farming good or bad? What are the costs—environmental and social—of this kind of "progress"? The answer, of course, is complicated and depends on whose perspective one privileges above others. To answer whether it is "good" or "bad," we have to ask, "for whom?" Who will win and who will lose: small-boat fishermen, Native communities, multinational corporations, wild salmon, the environment, consumers, poor people, rich people? Who will benefit and who will pay the "costs"? Aquaculture is a hard sell in Southeast Alaska, with its historical relationship to the wild salmon fisheries. Communities there have lived—and sometimes died—with commercial fishing. Farm fisheries seem an enemy, not a friend, to the persistence of the commercial fisheries: one thrives on the continuation of the wild runs, the other threatens their economic and ecological sustainability; one rests on small fishermen, the other on corporate hierarchies and wage labor. Farmed salmon, however, is moving with the flood tide of history, while small-boat fishers are bucking against it. Has the fishermen's frontier finally come to a close?

TRADITION AND "PROGRESS" IN A GLOBAL WORLD

Limited entry, the continuing battles over Native subsistence and sovereignty, and the rise of farm fisheries all suggest the extent to which the livelihoods of Alaskan fishermen have been, and still are, dependent on political, economic, and ecological factors beyond their control. Sometimes distant forces have helped them, such as cooling water temperatures or the Magnuson Act of 1976, which limited deep-sea fishing by foreign fleets in the North Pacific. Sometimes distant forces have hurt them, such as warming water temperatures (El Niño) or the Pacific salmon treaties between Canada and the United States (in 1985 and again in 1999), which reduced salmon catches for fishermen in southeastern Alaska.[124]

Limited entry has hurt some fishers and helped others. State subsistence policies have challenged the right of Native fishers to claim a privileged place in the fishery. Fish farms have threatened the existence of all salmon fishermen. Despite these political and economic developments, fishing traditions still exist in Southeast Alaska. Humans still interact with nature through work; fishing cultures still pass on their secrets to younger generations. But there is little doubt that the post-statehood transformations of the fishery have made fishing—as craft, occupation, and culture—gravely imperiled. Mostly, fishermen's lives have been changed by the same dynamic forces reshaping lives the world over: technology and global capitalism.

Is this the closing of the fishermen's frontier? Will small-boat fisheries continue to exist in southeastern Alaska or anywhere? If so, they will have to change; salmon managers will have to change; markets will have to change. Gunnar Knapp has suggested that the wild fisheries will have to redesign themselves once again in order to compete with farm-raised fish. This might mean, for instance, reintroducing fish traps or other measures that will restrict access further while increasing economic efficiency.[125] The fishery will once again change—but this is nothing new. The fishery has always been changing, just as society and nature have changed. The question is, When it changes again, will anything be lost? And will anyone care?

Epilogue

ENDANGERED SPECIES?

Alaska is teaming with salmon and fishermen are catching them by the net-full, but the state of the industry remains that of desperation. —*Alaska Fisherman's Journal*, 2003

Most of the world won't notice or care what happens to the people who make their living from wild salmon. —GUNNAR KNAPP, "Implications of Aquaculture," 2005

In 1980, Peter Larkin, one of the world's leading fisheries biologists, tried to assess the present and predict the future of the Pacific salmon fisheries. Paraphrasing Dickens, Larkin contended that 1980 was both the best of times and the worst of times. It was the best of times, Larkin believed, because the price of salmon was at an all-time high, technological transformations had made fishing more efficient, management of the fishery was more sophisticated than ever, and biological knowledge of salmon was greater, as was the capacity to increase salmon populations through artificial propagation. The establishment of a two-hundred-mile limit on foreign fishing—the Magnuson Act of 1976—had "protected substantially many of the fisheries interests of coastal states," and environmental consciousness, manifested in a popular desire to save the salmon, was increasing.[1] It was the worst of times, Larkin argued, because regulation was becoming more difficult as the high prices of salmon attracted an increasingly efficient and competitive fleet of fishermen who could mop up the salmon "in a matter of a few hysterical hours per week." Knowledge of salmon, although vast, was still outweighed by "what we don't know"; technologies for increasing salmon runs had failed as much as they had succeeded; and unresolved tensions between the United States and Canada over salmon harvests persisted.[2]

Looking at Larkin's assessments from the vantage point of 2006, it seems that his "best of times" list would have to be substantially reduced, considering that salmon prices are at all-time lows as is the popular will to actually save the salmon. His "worst of times" list would have to be substantially lengthened, considering that the farm fisheries, so insignificant in 1980, have dramatically reduced the demand and thus the market value for wild salmon. Salmon farming has transformed the wild fisheries in ways that Larkin could not have imagined in 1980. His predictions for the future seem even further removed from the reality of the contemporary fishery because they suggest a kind of technocratic optimism that today seems almost hopelessly utopian. He predicted that oceanographers would be able "to predict broad trends in physical oceanographic conditions as much as a year in advance"; that biologists would come to understand "how salmon find their way around the ocean and eventually back to their home streams" and use such knowledge to dramatically bolster the production of wild salmon; that increasing genetic knowledge of salmon populations would allow biologists to identify the stream of origin of each fish caught and to breed wild salmon even for stocks that had no escapement; and that fish hatcheries would advance to the point where they could enhance "the physiological attributes and behavior patterns relevant to survival" of wild fish stocks. Finally, Larkin predicted that wild Pacific salmon would be successfully transplanted in waterways throughout the world and that "by the year 2020 a modest fishery for pinks, chums, and sockeye will be established in the Atlantic Ocean."[3]

None of this has happened—and little of it seems to be in the works. In fact, scientific advances and their role in shaping the salmon fisheries since the 1980s have paled in comparison to the impact that economic developments, namely the rise of global salmon farming, have had on the wild salmon fisheries. The rise of farmed salmon has even helped to diminish the popular will to steward salmon resources, as consumers—their grocery stores stocked with abundant, modestly priced fresh salmon—are increasingly confounded by the apocalyptic rantings of environmentalists who speak of vanishing salmon. Larkin understood, however, that economic, political, and social factors would ultimately shape the nature of the fishery more than science or nature. In 1980 this led him to predict that small-boat fishermen would continue to dominate the industry. While economic efficiency might "suggest catching most of the salmon harvest with a handful of strategically placed traps," such a suggestion, he admitted, was "simply not socially acceptable, however logical. Like the game of Monopoly, economics has certain rules, imposed arbitrarily by social circumstances."[4]

As an indication of just how much the economic, political, and social landscape has changed since Larkin made his predictions, University of Alaska economist Gunnar Knapp predicted in 1998 that "economic and political pressures" would eventually force the reintroduction of fish traps to the Alaska salmon fisheries. This prediction was influenced primarily by the rise of global fish farming, which, Knapp believed, demanded the transformation of Alaska's hopelessly inefficient small-boat fishers into more cost-efficient producers. Just as industrialization transformed agriculture, forcing small farms to give way to corporate agribusiness, so would the rise of salmon aquaculture compel the reorganization of fishing, with small boats giving way to superefficient modern fish traps.[5] It was not just economists like Knapp proposing such measures. By the beginning of the twenty-first century, some fishermen were also wondering if it wasn't time to reintroduce salmon traps, which might be owned cooperatively by permit-holders.[6] The formerly despised contrivances might save the wild salmon fishery from extinction.

Knapp's other predictions, although pragmatic, were similarly bleak when examined from the perspective of small-boat fishermen and local fishing communities in Southeast Alaska. The cost of producing farm-raised salmon will continue to fall, while the global output of farmed salmon will continue to rise, forcing wild salmon prices into a downward spiral. Wild fisheries will continue to fluctuate from year to year, while farm-raised salmon will grow surely and steadily. In the drive for lower costs and increased profit margins, all but the most efficient harvesters will be forced from the fishing grounds.[7] In Knapp's view this is an inevitable process, but one that opens up new avenues of opportunity for coastal communities, who might seize offshore aquaculture as a stable alternative to wild fisheries.[8] But what are the costs of such a transition from wild fisheries—where local fishing families and fishing cultures still survive—to corporate salmon manufacturing? Economists, like Knapp, are interested in efficiencies and *economic* costs—not *social* costs. Yet the transfer of productive power from individuals and communities to nonlocal corporations entails costs that are not easily quantifiable. The global economy does not distinguish between types of jobs—"any work is all right as long as one gets paid for it."[9] But is there a difference between the work of an "independent" fisherman and the work of a salmon-farm employee? Is something lost when a vocation that traditionally tied communities to the natural world is destroyed by corporate capitalism?

Agrarian writer Wendell Berry has argued that the global free-market economy is "inherently an enemy to the natural world, to human health and freedom, to industrial workers, and to farmers and others in the land-use economies; and . . . to good work and good economic practice." Globalism, in Berry's view, destroys local economies and ecologies by imposing a "total economy"—where everything "has a price and is for sale"—on human communities and the natural world. He defines a total economy as "an unrestrained taking of profits from the disintegration of nations, communities, households, landscapes, and ecosystems." A total economy "licenses symbolic or artificial wealth to 'grow' by means of the destruction of the real wealth of all the world."[10] By embracing corporate fish farms, would Alaskan communities be sacrificing the "real wealth" of healthy wild salmon ecosystems for the "artificial wealth" of mass-produced fish? Would local fishing communities and fishing cultures be enriched, as Knapp suggests—or destroyed, as Berry suggests? Would this transformation "save" communities, who must inevitably adapt to the demands of the global market economy, or culminate, as Berry argues, in the creation of citizens and communities who have "less reverence [and] respect, less gratitude, less local knowledge, and less skill?"[11] Environmentalists often bemoan the loss of biodiversity: industrial agriculture has transformed complex natural ecosystems into highly simplified cash crop monocultures. But what about the loss of human diversity, as distinctive local lifeways are chewed up in the churning gears of global capitalism?

Knapp perhaps has underestimated the ecological and cultural risks that salmon farms pose—but Berry perhaps has overestimated the destructive power of the global economy while romanticizing the value of "traditional" communities and local economies. Fishers in southeastern Alaska, from precontact to present, have never been bound by a fixed "tradition." Rather, they have always adapted and innovated and changed with their surroundings. Their lives have always been shaped by "outside" forces—ecological, economic, and political. Salmon farms in this respect represent just one more external factor to which fishing communities will inevitably adapt. Environmentally conscious fish farms could in a perfect world even preserve wild fish runs in Alaska by driving fish prices so low that heavily capitalized fishermen, such as those who emerged in the wake of limited entry, will not be able to survive. The fishery once again might be dominated by "lifestyle" fishermen with lower expectations of profit but strong connections to both nature and the vocation of fishing. Small-scale local fishers might exploit "boutique" markets by turning their own moderate catches into "organic smoked salmon" or some other value-added niche product.

More likely, some kind of structural reorganization of the salmon fishery will combine permit buybacks, co-ops "where only some of the permit holders fish but everybody shares the profits," and the implementation of individual fishing quotas and community fishing quotas, which are already used in federally managed deep sea fisheries such as halibut and sablefish.[12] Or perhaps some other deus ex machina will save the wild salmon fisheries—fishermen might combine commercial fishing and charter-boat operations for tourists, or perhaps they will become the stars of next year's reality-TV programming. Utopias may indeed emerge out of the desperation of the modern salmon fishery.

The rise of farm fisheries represents just one more step in the transformation of the relationship between humans and animals from one of intimacy and interdependence to one of alienation and scientific manipulation. Native fishers—although they did not always behave as modern environmentalists—lived in close connection with salmon ecosystems and developed important rituals and lifeways which reflected that intimacy. Even after industrialization, salmon fishing resisted the modern process of separating workers from nature. Fishermen, solitary individuals working on small boats, still bent their backs and pulled a living from the sea. That connection between work and nature began to change in the postwar period as increasing technology and limited entry created a new class of professionalized fishermen. Yet small-boat fishing cultures live on. But will such fishermen become the next vocation destroyed by globalization and the technological manipulation of nature? And would that matter to the rest of us?[13]

Perhaps, like Garrett Hardin's tragedy of the commons, there is "no technical solution" to the problem of both maintaining traditions and increasing economic efficiency and profitability within a rapaciously globalizing world. Traditions—which we've already established are malleable—will change or fade away, while efficiency and rationality will march on until they inevitably meet the physical limitations of a finite world. Remaining static—or looking to the past—is not an option. It would be nice to believe, however, that we might consider alternative ways of moving forward. In this sense discussing the future of the wild fisheries and salmon fishermen in Alaska is no less significant than the debates over farming, wage work, and democracy in the nineteenth century, or even those between Hamilton and Jefferson: they are discussions about what kind of society we want to have, the kind of communities we want to live in, the kind of work we want to do, and the kind of relationships we want with nature.

Notes

INTRODUCTION

Epigraphs: Derek Walcott, "The Sea Is History," in *Collected Poems, 1948–1984* (London: Faber, 1984), 364; and Raymond Williams, *Problems in Materialism and Culture* (London: Verso, 1982), 67.

1. Goble, "Salmon in the Columbia Basin," 230.

2. Ibid.; Lichatowich, *Salmon without Rivers*; Taylor, *Making Salmon*; Cooley, *Politics and Conservation*; and McEvoy, *Fisherman's Problem*.

3. "Pink Harvest Sets Record: Salmon Value Tops $300 Million," *Alaska Fisherman's Journal* 29 (January 2006): 26.

4. Lance Van Sittert, "The Other Seven Tenths," *Environmental History* 10 (January 2005): 106; McEvoy, *Fisherman's Problem*; and Taylor, *Making Salmon*.

5. Taylor, "El Niño and Vanishing Salmon," 437.

6. See, for example, Warren, *Hunter's Game*; Jacoby, *Crimes against Nature*; Spence, *Dispossessing the Wilderness*; White, *Organic Machine*; and Morse, *Nature of Gold*.

7. White, *Organic Machine*, ix, x.

8. Ibid., x. See also White's article "'Are You an Environmentalist or Do You Work for a Living?'"

9. It is not my intention here to survey the vast historiography of the American West, but for an introduction to the debate over the "frontier" in American history, see Faragher, *Rereading Frederick Jackson Turner*; Limerick, *Legacy of Conquest*; Limerick, Milner, and Rankin, *Trails*; and Worster, "New West, True West."

10. Haycox, *Frigid Embrace*, 9.

11. Timothy Egan, "The Race to Alaska before It Melts," *New York Times*, June 6, 2005, section 5, pp. 1, 10.

12. See, for instance, Forbes, "Frontiers in American History"; and Aron, "Lessons in Conquest." Although he does not explicitly deal with "frontiers," Merrell's *The Indians' New World* captures the spirit of what I mean by frontiers as fluid

cultural meeting grounds, where Native peoples adapted and survived the process of colonization. See also White, *Middle Ground*; and Colin Calloway, *New Worlds for All: Indians, Europeans, and the Remaking of Early America* (Baltimore, Md.: Johns Hopkins University Press, 1997).

1 FIRST FISHERMEN

Epigraphs: Wolf and Zuckerman, *Salmon Nation*, 9; Horace Marks, in "The Southeast Alaska Salmon Fishery: Interviews with Men and Women Endangered in Fishing, 1913–1978"; and La Pérouse, *Voyage round the World*, 120.

1. Department of Commerce, Bureau of Fisheries, "In the Matter of Hearing in Respect to the Advisability of Further Limiting Fishery Operations, or of Modifying Existing Limitations, in Certain Waters of Southeastern Alaska East of the Longitude of Cape Spencer, to Include All Streams More Than 500 Feet in Width," November, 25, 1919, in U.S. Department of Commerce, Bureau of Fisheries, "Hearings Conducted by the U.S. Bureau of Fisheries in Regulating the Fisheries of Alaska, 1907–1921," vol. 4, 1919, 18–19.

2. The literature on non-Indian representations of Indian peoples is vast. A good starting point is Berkhofer, *White Man's Indian*. For a good overview of the literature on the Noble Savage and the Indian as early environmentalist, see Krech, *Ecological Indian*.

3. Krech, *Ecological Indian*, 20; see, for instance, Charles A. Eastman, *Indian Scout Craft and Lore* (New York: Dover Books, 1971).

4. Krech, *Ecological Indian*, 21.

5. Martin, "Prehistoric Overkill," 115. For an introduction into the voluminous literature and extensive debates on Native American relationships with the natural world, see Calvin Martin, *Keepers of the Game*; Krech, *Indians, Animals, and the Fur Trade*; Krech, *Ecological Indian*; Overholt, "American Indians as 'Natural Ecologists'"; White, "Native Americans and the Environment"; White, *Roots of Dependency*; White, "Indian Peoples and the Natural World: Asking the Right Questions"; White and Cronon, "Ecological Change and Indian-White Relations"; Cronon, *Changes in the Land*; and Sam D. Gill, *Mother Earth: An American Story* (Chicago: University of Chicago Press, 1987).

6. Krech, *Ecological Indian*, 26.

7. Although they have not focused on southeastern Alaska in particular, environmental historians have examined "salmon peoples" further south and have come to a remarkable degree of consensus on the question of aboriginal conservation. Writing on Native salmon fishers in California, the Columbia River, and British Columbia, historians have overwhelmingly agreed that Indian peoples had the technology and population density to overexploit salmon runs but avoided such calamity by developing a complex web of social restrictions that limited fishing intensity. Mostly these

restrictions flowed from a worldview that demanded humans treat animals with proper respect, but they also derived from constraints imposed by Native property rights. Joseph E. Taylor, writing on the Columbia River Indians, succinctly summarizes recent scholarship by arguing that "aboriginal spiritual beliefs, ritual expressions, social sanctions, and territorial claims effectively moderated salmon harvests" (Taylor, *Making Salmon*, 14). See also McEvoy, *Fisherman's Problem*; White, *Organic Machine*; Harris, *Fish, Law, and Colonialism*; and Newell, *Tangled Webs of History*.

The effect of Taylor's work, as well as that of Arthur McEvoy and Richard White, has not been to promote the stereotype of Indians living in perfect balance with an unchanging nature, but rather to further debunk the notion of idle Indians "gratefully taking the bounty of their mother earth" (White, *Organic Machine*, 18) and replace it with a view of fallible humans living within a dynamic natural world of scarcity and abundance, who over time "carefully adjusted their use of resources so as to ensure the stability and longevity both of their stocks and of their economies" (McEvoy, *Fisherman's Problem*, 21). Nowhere do they suggest that Indian peoples did not have the ability to waste or overtax their natural resources, nor that they were proto-environmentalists. Although they do propose that Native regulators acted in a manner to ensure that "the fishery remained healthy for future generations" (Harris, *Fish, Law, and Colonialism*, 20), they do not suppose that this concern for sustainability was based on a scientific understanding of ecology, nor that Indian peoples were somehow uniquely endowed to live in harmony with the natural world. Unlike popular stereotypes which suggest that authentic Native Americans lived in harmony with "Mother Nature," McEvoy (*Fisherman's Problem*, 21) argues that "being an Indian gave one no special advantage in confronting the problem" of resource management. Taylor believes that "it would be anachronistic to portray Indians as conservationists, in the sense of anticipating the rationale and logic of modern conservation." The "explicit motivation" of Native myths, ceremonies, and religious taboos that restrained fishing was "propitiation, not conservation." He argues that "aboriginal ceremonies and taboos . . . moderated harvest *effectively, if not intentionally*" (Taylor, *Making Salmon*, 36).

Although these historians have premised that Native Americans indeed developed a "spiritual, sacred attitude toward land and animals" (Krech, *Ecological Indian*, 22)—certainly fitting the "ecological Indian" stereotype—they have also portrayed the salmon fishers of the Northwest Coast as complex, imperfect, multidimensional, and historical. If you are looking for a stereotype of the ecological Indian, you will not find it among modern environmental historians of the Northwest Coast salmon fisheries. Popular histories of the North Pacific salmon fisheries tend to echo the basic storyline of environmental historians, although they sometimes project an idealized view of Native Americans. See, for instance, Wolf and Zuckerman, *Salmon Nation*. For excellent popular histories of the Pacific salmon fisheries, see Lichatowich, *Salmon without Rivers*; Montgomery, *King of Fish*; and Netboy, *Salmon*. There is also an extensive anthropological literature concerning Indian fishing on the Northwest Coast. See, for instance, Swezey and Heizer, "Ritual Management of Salmonid Fish Resources in California"; Kroeber and Barrett, *Fishing among the Indians of Northwest California*; Stewart, *Indian Fishing*; Stephen John Langdon, "Technology, Ecology, and Economy: Fishing Systems in Southeast Alaska" (Ph.D. dissertation, Stanford University, 1977); and Hayden, *Complex Culture of the British Columbia Plateau.*

8. Testimony of Sam G. Davis in U.S. Department of Interior, "Hearings upon Claims of Natives of Alaska Pursuant to the Provisions of Section 201.21b of the Regulations for Protection of the Commercial Fisheries in Alaska," vol. 1 (1944), 87–88.

9. Ibid.

10. Testimony of Sha-Ta in ibid., vol. 5 (1944), 859.

11. Mr. and Mrs. George Dalton, interviewed by R. Newton, June 21, 1979. Translated manuscript available at U.S. Forest Service, Juneau, Alaska.

12. Nelson Frank as quoted in Berger, *Village Journey*, 54.

13. Nora Marks Dauenhauer, "Five Slices of Salmon," in *First Fish, First People*, edited by Roche and McHutchison, 103.

14. For my discussion of the evolutionary development of the Pacific salmon, I have relied primarily on salmon biologist Jim Lichatowich, *Salmon without Rivers*, 9–23, and geologist David R. Montgomery, *King of Fish*, 21–38. Both provide excellent and accessible summaries of recent scientific research. See also Quinn, *Behavior and Ecology of Pacific Salmon and Trout.*

15. The best overview of anadromy and salmon life cycles is Quinn, *Behavior and Ecology of Pacific Salmon and Trout.* See also Groot and Margolis, *Pacific Salmon Life Histories*; and Pearcy, *Ocean Ecology of North Pacific Salmonids.* For the most thorough review of the scientific literature related to Pacific salmon, see Taylor, *Making Salmon*, 379–410.

16. Arndt, Sackett, and Ketz, *Cultural Resource Overview of the Tongass National Forest*, 25.

17. Montgomery, *King of Fish*, 31. Montgomery suggests the speciation of Pacific salmon was primarily due to these tectonic alternations, rather than glaciation, as has been previously suggested. On speciation, see McPhail, "Origin and Speciation of *Oncorhynchus* Revisited," 29–38.

18. Montgomery, *King of Fish*, 32; also see Lichatowich, *Salmon without Rivers*, 13.

19. Lichatowich, *Salmon without Rivers*, 14–15.

20. Montgomery, *King of Fish*, 21–38.

21. These are my estimates of run sizes based on historical catch records in the Alaska Department of Fish and Game, Division of Commercial Fisheries, "Historical Salmon Harvest and Value Charts, 1878–2003," Zephyr Database.

22. There is a large and growing literature on natural fluctuations in salmon populations. Recently, scientists have examined variability in historical salmon populations by measuring sediments in spawning grounds for nitrogen-15, which is

released by the carcasses of spawned-out salmon. One of these studies analyzed a number of lakes in Alaska, charting sockeye returns over a three-hundred-year period. The results showed a clear link between the size of salmon runs and water temperatures. In other words long before commercial fishers arrived on the scene, salmon populations fluctuated dramatically due to natural changes in ocean climates. See B. P. Finney and others, "Impacts of Climatic Change and Fishing on Pacific Salmon Abundance over the Past Three Hundred Years," *Science* 290 (October 27, 2000): 795–799; Brown, "Pacific Salmon Run Hot and Cold," 685–686; B. P. Finney and others, "Climate Change, Fishing, Alter Salmon Abundance: Scientists Reconstruct 300 Years of Alaska Sockeye Runs," http://seagrant.uaf.edu/news/00news/10–20–00_Finney.html. An excellent overview of climate-induced impact on salmon, including a discussion of Pacific decadal oscillation (PDO), can be found in Quinn, *Behavior and Ecology of Pacific Salmon and Trout*, 261–265; and Nathan J. Mantua and others, "A Pacific Interdecadal Climate Oscillation with Impacts on Salmon Production," *Bulletin of the American Meteorological Society* 78 (June 1997): 1069–1079. For further studies concerning natural fluctuations and climate, see Taylor, *Making Salmon*, 402–403. The best historical treatment of natural fluctuations caused by changing ocean temperatures is Taylor, "El Niño and Vanishing Salmon," 437–457.

23. See Fagan, *Great Journey*.

24. "Basket Bay History Told by Robert Zuboff," in *Haa Shuká, Our Ancestors*, edited by Dauenhauer and Dauenhauer, 63–71; and de Laguna, *Under Mount Saint Elias*, 230–242.

25. Ames and Maschner, *Peoples of the Northwest Coast*, 123–127; Borden, *Origins and Development of Early Northwest Coast Culture*, 115; and Fladmark, *British Columbia Prehistory*, 53–65.

26. See Lichatowich, *Salmon without Rivers*, 30–33; Price, *Great Father in Alaska*, 4–7; and Arndt, Sackett, and Ketz, *Cultural Resource Overview of the Tongass National Forest*, 1–84. For an alternative view, or at least one that suggests that salmon were not necessarily the primary basis for the intensification of food production, see Kenneth M. Ames, "Intensification of Food Production on the Northwest Coast and Elsewhere," in *Keeping It Living*, edited by Deur and Turner, 67–100.

27. Moss, Earlandson, and Stuckenrath, "Wood Stake Fish Weirs and Salmon Fishing on the Northwest Coast," 148–153.

28. Langdon, "Technology, Ecology, and Economy," 67–105.

29. "Glacier Bay History Told by Susie James," in *Haa Shuká, Our Ancestors*, edited by Dauenhauer and Dauenhauer, 245.

30. For a comprehensive overview of subsistence foods and gathering methods from the point of view of the Tlingit, including a discussion of plant cultivation, see Newton and Moss, *Subsistence Lifeway of the Tlingit People*, and Madonna Moss, "Tlingit Horticulture: An Indigenous or Introduced Development," in *Keeping It Living*, edited by Deur and Turner, 274–295. On the annual cycle of production, see

Oberg, *Social Economy of the Tlingit Indians*, 65–78, and de Laguna, *Under Mount Saint Elias*, 360.

31. Suttles, "Coping with Abundance," 58. See also Deur, "Salmon, Sedentism, and Cultivation," 129–155. For a tremendous overview of aboriginal land use that debunks the "pristine myth" of virginal wilderness by showing how Northwest Coast peoples actively cultivated plants and otherwise transformed their environment in varying ways, see Deur and Turner, *Keeping It Living*.

32. Suttles, "Coping with Abundance."

33. Schalk, "Structure of an Anadromous Fish Resource," 234–235.

34. Ibid., 207–249.

35. For an overview of the characteristics of "complex hunter-gatherer" societies on the Northwest Coast, see Ames and Maschner, *Peoples of the Northwest Coast*, 24–29.

36. Boyd, *Coming of the Spirit of Pestilence*, 227–229, 309–313; George W. Rogers calculates the precontact population in Southeast Alaska at 11,800, in his *Alaska in Transition*, 181.

37. Ames and Maschner, *Peoples of the Northwest Coast*, 26.

38. Hewes, "Aboriginal Use of Fishery Resources in Northwestern North America," 222–223. Commercial statistics are taken from the Alaska Department of Fish and Game, Division of Commercial Fisheries, "Southeast Alaska Salmon, by Species, Annual Catch Report," Zephyr Database, statistics run on May 20, 2004.

39. Petroff's larger number rested on his belief that "fully one-half or more than one-half of the catch is consumed in a dried state, very much reduced in bulk and weight." He believed that "the waste in the drying process is so great that one person can easily eat at a single meal a fish that weighed 20 or 30 pounds when alive." See Petroff, "Report of the Population, Industries, and Resources of Alaska," 69–71.

40. Langdon, "Technology, Ecology, and Economy," 201.

41. Krech, *Ecological Indian*, 123–149.

42. Niblack, "Coast Indians of Southern Alaska and Northern British Columbia," 293.

43. The best source for fishing methods in southeastern Alaska is Langdon, "Technology, Ecology, and Economy," 180–191. See also Hewes, "Aboriginal Use of Fishery Resources," 129–147; and Stewart, *Indian Fishing*. Nearly every anthropological source on Tlingit culture has a section on fishing methods. See especially de Laguna, *Under Mount Saint Elias*, 384–387; and Emmons, *Tlingit Indians*, 102–127.

44. Matilda Gamble interviewed by Madonna Moss in *Subsistence Lifeway*, edited by Newton and Moss, 4.

45. Langdon, "Technology, Ecology, and Economy," 176–177.

46. Charles Webster Demmert as quoted in U.S. Department of Interior, "Hearings upon Claims of Natives of Alaska," vol. 4 (1944), 594.

47. Langdon, "Technology, Ecology, and Economy," 186, 190.

48. La Pérouse, *Voyage round the World*, vol. 2, 109.

49. De Laguna, *Under Mount Saint Elias*, 386.

50. Moser, *Salmon and Salmon Fisheries of Alaska*, 36–37.

51. Moser, *Alaska Salmon Investigations in 1900 and 1901*, 257.

52. Taylor, *Making Salmon*, 20, 13; and Newell, *Tangled Webs of History*, 45.

53. La Pérouse, *Voyage round the World*, vol. 2, 121.

54. Henry Katasse interviewed by Richard Newton, March 5, 1980, in Petersburg, Alaska. Transcript available at the U.S. Forest Service, Juneau, Alaska.

55. Ruby Jackson interviewed by Richard Newton in Juneau, Alaska, August 1, 1980. Transcript available at the U.S. Forest Service, Juneau, Alaska.

56. The best discussion of the Tlingit potlatch can be found in Kan, *Symbolic Immortality*.

57. See Drucker, *Cultures of the North Pacific Coast*, 52, and Kan, *Memory Eternal*, for interpretations of Northwest Coast slavery as a "prestige economy."

58. Donald, *Aboriginal Slavery on the Northwest Coast of North America*.

59. McEvoy, *Fisherman's Problem*, 25.

60. McEvoy (*Fisherman's Problem*), Taylor (*Making Salmon*), and Newell (*Tangled Webs of History*) believe this was the case for Native fishers in California, Oregon, and British Columbia. Economist James Crutchfield has argued that "the Indian fishery was intensive enough to affect abundance in some localities where there was a heavy Indian population." See Crutchfield and Pontecorvo, *Pacific Salmon Fisheries*, 69.

61. Langdon, "Technology, Ecology, and Economy," 192–193.

62. See Harris, *Fish, Law, and Colonialism*, 24. On Native management of fish weirs, see also T. T. Waterman and A. L. Kroeber, "The Kepel Fish Dam," *University of California Publications in American Archaeology* 35 (1943): 49–80.

63. Langdon, "From Communal Property to Common Property to Limited Entry," 311.

64. Kew and Griggs, "Native Indians of the Fraser Basin," 35.

65. See Emmons, *Tlingit Indians*, 104; de Laguna, *Under Mount Saint Elias*, 361–362.

66. Emmons, *Tlingit Indians*, 103.

67. Kan, *Symbolic Immortality*, 50. In the case of the Yakutat Tlingit, burning the salmon bones served the same purpose. See de Laguna, *Under Mount Saint Elias*, 824.

68. White, *Organic Machine*, 20.

69. De Laguna, *Under Mount Saint Elias*, 362.

70. Krech, *Ecological Indian*, 148–149.

71. Beck, *Shamans and Kushtakas*, 25–46.

72. "Legend of an Orphan Boy," told by John C. Jackson, interviewed by Richard Newton, Kake, Alaska, September 17, 1979. Transcript available at the U.S. Forest Service in Juneau. See also Newton and Moss, *Subsistence Lifeway*, 30, for a brief analysis of this myth.

73. Newton and Moss, *Subsistence Lifeway*, 4.

74. De Laguna, *Under Mount Saint Elias*, 383.

75. Garfield, "Research Problem in Northwest Indian Economics," 629–630.

76. De Laguna, *Under Mount Saint Elias*, 233. In other instances of encroachment, property owners forced resolution by inviting the poachers to a feast and literally shaming the unwanted visitors from their territory; see Oberg, *Social Economy of the Tlingit Indians*, 99. Intrusion potentially held more dangerous consequences as well. Kalervo Oberg has noted that "if anyone beside the clansmen or those invited were caught taking fish from clan territories, or if they were caught hunting there, they could be killed" (see Oberg, "Crime and Punishment in Tlingit Society," 215).

77. Hewes, "Aboriginal Use of Fishery Resources in Northwestern North America," 21.

78. Forde, *Habitat, Economy, and Society*, 78.

79. Nelson, "Conservation Ethic and Environment," 211.

80. Cronon, *Changes in the Land*, 33.

81. Lichatowich, *Salmon without Rivers*, 39–40; and McEvoy, *Fisherman's Problem*, 19.

82. Nora Marks Dauenhauer, "Five Slices of Salmon," in Roche and McHutchinson, *First Fish, First People*, 102.

83. McEvoy, *Fisherman's Problem*, 39.

2 THE INDUSTRIAL TRANSFORMATION OF THE INDIAN SALMON FISHERY, 1780S–1910S

Epigraphs: Chief Kah-du-shan, as quoted in Hinkley, "'Canoe Rocks,'" 271; and Burr, *Alaska*, 6.

1. On the Northwest Coast maritime trade, see Gibson, *Otter Skins, Boston Ships, and China Goods*; and Fisher, *Contact and Conflict*. A helpful synthesis of scholarship on the fur trade is Douglas Cole and David Darling, "History of the Early Period," in *Handbook of North American Indians*, vol. 7, *Northwest Coast*, edited by Suttles, 119–134. For a useful, although somewhat dated, overview of scholarship on Native Americans and the North American fur trade, see Peterson and Anfinson, "Indian and the Fur Trade."

2. Dixon as quoted in de Armond, *Early Visitors to Southeastern Alaska*, 14.

3. See Wike, "Effect of the Maritime Fur Trade on Northwest Coast Indian Society," 29–53, for a description of different trading goods and for an explanation of the changing nature of Indian demand.

4. Cleveland as quoted in de Armond, *Early Visitors to Southeastern Alaska*, 72.

5. La Pérouse, *Voyage round the World*, vol. 2, 78.

6. Howay, Sage, and Angus, *British Columbia and the United States*, 12–13.

7. K. T. Khlebnikov, *The Khlebnikov Archive [Electronic Resource]: Unpublished*

Journal (1800–1837) and Travel Notes (1820, 1822, and 1824), edited by Leonid Shur, translated by John Bisk (Fairbanks: University of Alaska Press, 1990), 60.

8. Ibid.

9. See Fisher, *Contact and Conflict*; Krause, *Tlingit Indians*, 11–49; Drucker, *Archaeological Survey on the Northern Northwest Coast*; and Wike, "Effect of the Maritime Fur Trade on Northwest Coast Indian Society." On the expansion of the Native slave trade on the Northwest Coast during the fur trade, see Donald, *Aboriginal Slavery on the Northwest Coast of North America*, 250.

10. La Pérouse, *Voyage round the World*, vol. 2, 81.

11. Portlock as quoted in de Armond, *Early Visitors to Southeastern Alaska*, 45, 48.

12. Cleveland as quoted in ibid., 76.

13. Dixon as quoted in ibid., 17.

14. Ibid., 25.

15. The best overviews of Russian America are Haycox, *Alaska*, 35–156, and Black, *Russians in Alaska*.

16. Menzies as quoted in Vancouver, *Voyage of Discovery to the North Pacific Ocean and round the World*, 172.

17. Bancroft, *History of Alaska*, 401–413; Tikhmenev, *History of the Russian-American Company*, 65; and de Laguna, *Under Mount Saint Elias*, 170–173.

18. Rezanov as quoted in Bancroft, *History of Alaska*, 451.

19. Khlebnikov, *Colonial Russian America*, 4.

20. Bancroft, *History of Alaska*, 451–452; de Laguna, *Under Mount Saint Elias*, 173–176; and Tikhmenev, *Russian-American Company*, 99.

21. Tikhmenev, *Russian-American Company*, 154.

22. Khlebnikov, *Colonial Russian America*, 5.

23. Simpson as quoted in de Armond, *Early Visitors to Southeastern Alaska*, 167.

24. Muraviev as quoted in Wike, "Effect of the Maritime Fur Trade on Northwest Coast Indian Society," 70.

25. Belcher as quoted in de Armond, *Early Visitors to Southeastern Alaska*, 145.

26. Golovin, *End of Russian America*, 27. The Tlingit also attacked British trading posts in Southeast Alaska a number of times throughout the 1840s; see Naske and Slotnick, *Alaska*, 49, and Katherine L. Arndt, "Russian Relations with the Stikine Tlingit, 1833–1867," *Alaska History* 3 (spring 1988): 35–36.

27. See Gibson, *Imperial Russia in Frontier America*.

28. Khlebnikov, *Colonial Russian America*, 53.

29. Gibson, *Imperial Russia in Frontier America*, 214.

30. Langdon, "From Communal Property to Common Property to Limited Entry," 312.

31. Khlebnikov, *Colonial Russian America*, 53.

32. Golovin, *End of Russian America*, 82.

33. Khlebnikov, *Colonial Russian America*, 53–54.

34. Simpson as quoted in de Armond, *Early Visitors to Southeastern Alaska*, 167–168.

35. Golovin, *End of Russian America*, 82.

36. Ibid., appendix 9. The number of salmon per barrel comes from Klebnikov, *Colonial Russian America*, 53–54.

37. Golovin, *End of Russian America*, 82.

38. Moser, *Salmon and Salmon Fisheries of Alaska*, 36.

39. Langdon, "From Communal Property to Common Property to Limited Entry," 312.

40. De Laguna, *Under Mount Saint Elias*, 233–234, 260. See also William S. Hanable, "New Russia," *Alaska Journal* 3 (spring 1973): 79.

41. John D'Wolf as quoted in de Armond, *Early Visitors to Southeastern Alaska*, 102.

42. In 1862 there were still only 424 Russians in New Archangel, with the entire colony, including foreigners, creoles, and Natives, numbering 988. See Gibson, *Imperial Russia in Frontier America*, 26.

43. Kan, *Memory Eternal*, 58, 48.

44. Goldschmidt and Haas, "Possessory Rights of the Natives of Southeastern Alaska," 109.

45. Sam G. Davis, "Man Never Too Old to Learn," *Alaska Fisherman*, September 1932, p. 14.

46. Von Wrangell as quoted in James R. Gibson, "Russian Dependence upon the Natives of Russian America," paper presented at a conference on Russian America, sponsored by the American Historical Association and the Kennan Institute for Advanced Russian Studies, 1980, 13–14. This paper can also be found, in near identical form, as Gibson, "European Dependence upon American Natives," 359–383.

47. Gibson, "Russian Dependence upon the Natives of Russian America," 13–14.

48. Golovin, *End of Russian America*, 38.

49. Richard Collinson as quoted in de Armond, *Early Visitors to Southeastern Alaska*, 199.

50. The Russians depended on native foods because their own methods of storing these foods often proved unreliable. In some years the Russians wasted up to twenty thousand salmon for want of salt with which to cure them. See Gibson, "Russian Dependence upon the Natives of Russian America," 18, 22.

51. Golovin, *End of Russian America*, 38.

52. Emphasis added. Kostilevtsev as quoted in Vladimir Gsovski, *Russian Administration of Alaska and the Status of the Alaskan Natives*, 81st Cong., 2nd sess., 1950, S. Doc. 152, 64.

53. Donald, *Aboriginal Slavery on the Northwest Coast of North America*, 250.

54. Oberg, *Social Economy of the Tlingit Indians*, 61.

55. See Robert T. Boyd, "Demographic History, 1774–1874," in *Handbook of*

North American Indians, edited by Suttles, vol. 7, 141; Arndt, Sackett, and Ketz, *Cultural Resource Overview of the Tongass National Forest, Alaska*, 138–139; Thornton, *American Indian Holocaust and Survival*, 241–242; and Tikhmenev, *History of the Russian-American Company*, 428. Estimates vary on precontact and postcontact Tlingit population. Thornton suggests that the precontact estimate of ten thousand for the Tlingit is too small, and judging from Russian estimates, which range from twenty-five thousand to forty thousand, he could be right. The accuracy of the precontact estimate hinges on how devastating were the epidemics of the 1770s, 1830s, and 1860s on Tlingit populations. Most observers note that these epidemics spread unevenly across southeastern Alaska, affecting each locality differently. As for the postcontact numbers, seventy-five hundred is a fairly agreed upon and conservative estimate for the 1860s. Golovin (*End of Russian America*, 29) estimated the Tlingit population in 1862 at somewhere between fifteen thousand and twenty thousand. But Tikhmenev (*Russian-American Company*, 428) gives a count of 7,674 Tlingit in "well-known settlements" toward the end of the Russian period. The most current demographic synthesis of the Northwest Coast can be found in Boyd, *Coming of the Spirit of Pestilence.*

56. Charles Sumner, "Speech of Hon. Charles Sumner, of Massachusetts, on the cession of Russian America to the United States," in U.S. House of Representatives, *Russian America*, 40th Cong., 2d Sess., 1868, H. Ex. Doc. 177, 179.

57. Nathaniel P. Banks, *Purchase of Alaska: Speech of Hon. Nathaniel P. Banks of Massachusetts Delivered in the House of Representatives, June 30, 1868* (Washington, D.C.: F & J Rives & Geo. A. Bailey, 1868), 14–15.

58. Letter of P. McD. Collins, U.S.C.A., to Hon. W. H. Seward, Secretary of State, New York, April 4, 1867, in "Purchase of the Russian Possessions in North America by the United States: Papers Relating to the Value and Resources of the Country," Beinecke Library, Yale University, New Haven, Connecticut.

59. Sources for quotations in order of their appearance in the paragraph: Robert J. Walker, *Letter of Hon. R. J. Walker, on the Purchase of Alaska, St. Thomas and St. John* (Washington, D.C.: Chronicle Print, 1868), 2; *The Alaskan*, March 2, 1889, p. 1; Banks, *Purchase of Alaska*, 14; *The Alaskan*, June 2, 1888, p.1; Ballou, *New Eldorado*, 148; and Morris, *Report upon the Customs District*, 115.

60. *The Alaskan*, August 6, 1887, p. 2.

61. Swineford, *Alaska*, 224–225.

62. Tingle, *Report on the Salmon Fisheries in Alaska*, 6.

63. Genesis 9:7, *New American Bible.*

64. For a good, succinct overview of the laissez-faire doctrine as it relates to the salmon fisheries, see Merchant, "Fish First!"

65. *Pierson v. Post*, Supreme Court of New York, 3 Cai. R. 175; 1805 N.Y. LEXIS 311, pg. 1. This case provides a classic example of Anglo-American attitudes concerning the relationship between property and wild animals. For an excellent dis-

cussion of this case, and particularly its relationship to the doctrine of laissez-faire as applied to the fisheries, see Goble, "Salmon in the Columbia Basin," 229–231.

66. Tingle, *Report on the Salmon Fisheries in Alaska*, 11.

67. See Hardin, "Tragedy of the Commons"; and McEvoy, *Fisherman's Problem.*

68. U.S. House of Representatives, *Salmon Fisheries of Alaska: Reports of Special Agents Pracht, Luttrell, and Murray*, 406.

69. U.S. Department of Commerce and Labor, Bureau of Statistics, *Commercial Alaska, 1867–1903*, 43.

70. R. D. Hume, "The First Salmon Cannery," *Pacific Fisherman Yearbook* 2 (January 1904): 20. On the rise of the Pacific Coast salmon-canning industry, see McEvoy, *Fisherman's Problem*; Taylor, *Making Salmon*; Friday, *Organizing Asian American Labor*; Carstensen, "Fisherman's Frontier on the Pacific Coast"; Dodds, *Salmon King of Oregon*; Smith, "Evolution of the Pacific Canned Salmon Fishery"; and Gregory and Barnes, *North Pacific Fisheries with Special Reference to Alaska Salmon.* For a history of the canning business, see May, *Canning Clan.*

71. See O'Bannon, "Technological Change in the Pacific Coast Canned Salmon Industry"; and Newell, "Rationality of Mechanization in the Pacific Salmon-Canning Industry."

72. Carstensen, "Fisherman's Frontier," 70.

73. Craig and Hacker, *History and Development of the Fisheries of the Columbia River*, 151.

74. Ibid., 152, 159.

75. Briggs, *Letters from Alaska and the Pacific Coast*, 19.

76. White, *Organic Machine*, 43. White notes here that the one-day record catch for a fish wheel was fifty thousand pounds, set in the 1880s.

77. Cobb, *Salmon Fisheries of the Pacific Coast*, 134–135.

78. Ibid., 141–142.

79. APA, "History, 1891–1904," 15, Alaska Packers Association Records, Alaska Historical Library, Juneau. See also Moser, *Salmon and Salmon Fisheries of Alaska*, 18–21.

80. APA, "History, 1891–1904," 48.

81. Ellen Greenberg, "Historical Note on the Alaska Packers Association," in *A Guide to the Alaska Packers Association Records, 1891–1970, in the Alaska Historical Library*, edited by Phyllis DeMuth and Michael Sullivan (Juneau: Alaska Department of Education, 1983), 2; APA, "History," 86–87.

82. APA, "History," 184; Cobb, *Salmon Fisheries of the Pacific Coast*, 134–135.

83. U.S. House of Representatives, *Salmon Fisheries of Alaska: Reports of Special Agents Pracht, Luttrell, and Murray*, 406. On the colonial nature of salmon canning and other industries in Alaska, see especially Haycox, *Frigid Embrace.*

84. Cobb, *Pacific Salmon Fisheries: Report of the United States Commissioner of Fisheries for 1930*, 572–573.

85. Moser, *Alaska Salmon Investigations in 1900 and 1901*, 279, 293.

86. Kutchin, *Report of the Special Agent for the Protection of the Alaska Salmon Fisheries*, 13.

87. Grinnell, *Alaska 1899*, 339.

88. Moser, *Salmon and Salmon Fisheries of Alaska*, 39.

89. U.S. House of Representatives, *Salmon Fisheries of Alaska: Reports of Special Agents Pracht, Luttrell, and Murray*, 407.

90. Kutchin, *Report of the Special Agent for the Protection of the Alaska Salmon Fisheries*, 65.

91. See White, *Organic Machine*, 44.

92. U.S. House of Representatives, Committee on the Territories, *Hearings before the Committee on the Territories*, 34.

93. Testimony of Powell Charles in U.S. Department of Interior, *Hearings upon Claims of Natives of Alaska*, vol. 3, 462.

94. U.S. House of Representatives, Committee on the Merchant Marine and Fisheries, *Fisheries in Alaska*, part 2 (1922), 99–101.

95. *Pacific Fisherman Yearbook* 6 (January 1908): 27.

96. *Pacific Fisherman Yearbook* 8 (February 1910): 43.

97. Cooley, *Politics and Conservation*, 33–34.

98. Testimony of Powell Charles in U.S. Department of Interior, *Hearings upon Claims of Natives of Alaska*, vol. 3, 462.

99. *The Tlingit* (Sitka, Alaska), August 1908, pp. 2–3.

100. "The Things That Are God's," *Alaska Fisherman*, February 1923, p. 3.

101. Moser, *Salmon and Salmon Fisheries of Alaska*, 32. For other examples, see ibid., 24, 71, 113; see also "Salmon Is Wasted," *Daily Alaska Dispatch*, November 3, 1903, p. 1.

102. Interview with George Dalton in "Southeast Alaska Salmon Fishery."

103. Grinnell, *Alaska 1899*, 351.

104. U.S. House of Representatives, *Salmon Fisheries of Alaska: Reports of Special Agents Pracht, Luttrell, and Murray*, 406.

105. Tingle, *Report on the Salmon Fisheries in Alaska*, 19.

106. Moser, *Salmon and Salmon Fisheries of Alaska*, 43.

107. Kutchin, *Report on the Salmon Fisheries of Alaska, 1901*, 70–71.

108. Emmons, *Tlingit Indians*, 49.

109. Merriman as quoted in U.S. House of Representatives, *Affairs in Alaska*, 2.

110. Demmert as quoted in U.S. Department of Interior, *Hearings upon Claims of Natives of Alaska*, vol. 4, 623.

111. Stuteen as quoted in U.S. Department of Interior, *Hearings upon Claims of Natives of Alaska*, vol. 7, 1173; see 1170–1175 for the entire episode.

112. Statement of Gus Klagney quoted in Goldschmidt and Haas, "Possessory Rights of the Natives of Southeastern Alaska," 41.

113. Remsberg, "United States Administration of Alaska," 193–194.

114. See Remsberg, "United States Administration of Alaska," 328–330; and Lain, "North of Fifty-Three," 142–145.

115. See U.S. House of Representatives, *Alleged Shelling of Alaskan Villages*; and U.S. House of Representatives, *Affairs in Alaska*.

116. *The Alaskan*, July 19, 1890, p. 3; *The Alaskan*, July 12, 1890, p. 3.

117. Coontz, *From the Mississippi to the Sea*, 153. See also Price, *Great Father in Alaska*, 55–56.

118. Coontz, *From the Mississippi to the Sea*, 153–154.

119. Ibid., 155.

120. Moser, *Salmon and Salmon Fisheries of Alaska*, 22–23.

121. William Lewis Paul Papers, Acc. No. 1885, Box 1, Folder 2.

122. All of the quotations in this paragraph are taken from the transcript of the meeting between Tlingit clan heads and Governor Brady as reprinted in Hinckley, "'Canoe Rocks.'"

123. Morris, *Report upon the Customs District*, 131–132.

124. Jackson as quoted in Mitchell, *Sold American*, 105.

125. Miner Bruce as quoted in Porter, *Report on the Population and Resources of Alaska*, 32, 70.

126. Grinnell, *Alaska 1899*, 348.

127. Bruce as quoted in Porter, *Report on the Population and Resources of Alaska*, 25.

128. W. T. Lopp, "Native Labor in the Alaskan Fisheries," *Pacific Fisherman* (November 1914): 16. See also Hinckley, *Canoe Rocks*, 232.

129. Moser, *Salmon and Salmon Fisheries of Alaska in Alaska*, 25.

130. Ibid., 44.

131. Tingle, *Report on the Salmon Fisheries in Alaska*, 19.

132. "Justice for Alaskan Natives," *The Alaskan*, April 7, 1906, p. 2. See also "Independence of the Natives," *The Alaskan*, August 3, 1895, p. 1.

133. Muir, *Travels in Alaska*, 197.

134. Grinnell, *Alaska 1899*, 137–138.

135. Vincent Colyer as quoted in Haycox, "'Races of a Questionable Type,'" 158.

136. "Justice for Alaskan Natives," *The Alaskan*, April 7, 1906, p. 2.

137. U.S. House of Representatives, *Salmon Fisheries of Alaska: Reports of Special Agents Pracht, Luttrell, and Murray*, 447.

138. Brady as quoted in Mitchell, *Sold American*, 261–262. Mitchell gives an excellent discussion of the debate over reservations and Alaska Native policy in general; see pages 252–309.

139. Tingle, *Report on the Salmon Fisheries in Alaska*, 19.

140. Briggs, *Letters from Alaska and the Pacific Coast*, 51, emphasis added.

141. Moser, *Salmon and Salmon Fisheries of Alaska*, 43, emphasis added.

142. Betts and Wolfe, "Commercialization of Fisheries."

143. Moser, *Salmon and Salmon Fisheries of Alaska*, 25.

144. Ibid., 110.

145. McEvoy, *Fisherman's Problem*, 41–62.

3 FEDERAL CONSERVATION, FISH TRAPS, AND THE STRUGGLE TO CONTROL THE FISHERY, 1889–1959

Epigraphs: Petersburg Progressive (February 14, 1914): 3; and George B. Case as quoted in U.S. House of Representatives, *Committee Study Resolution—Alaska Fisheries Hearings*, 76th Cong., 1st sess., part 2, 554.

1. U.S. House of Representatives, *Alaska Salmon Commission*, 2.

2. *Proceedings of a Conference of Governors in the White House, Washington, D.C., May 13–15, 1908* (Washington, D.C.: Government Printing Office, 1909), 3.

3. Ibid., 8–10.

4. Pinchot, *Breaking New Ground*, 326.

5. For a discussion of the tensions between social equality and efficiency in conservation policy, especially as they played out in federal fisheries policy, see Taylor, "Well-Thinking Men and Women." For a more general discussion, see Koppes, "Efficiency/Equity/Esthetics."

6. Grinnell, *Alaska 1899*, 339.

7. Tingle, *Report on the Salmon Fisheries in Alaska*, 6.

8. Grinnell, *Alaska 1899*, 339.

9. Moser, *Salmon and Salmon Fisheries of Alaska*, 34. Moser had been calling for stricter laws and enforcement since 1889. See *The Alaskan*, January 5, 1889, p. 3.

10. U.S. House of Representatives, *Salmon Fisheries of Alaska: Reports of Special Agents Pracht, Luttrell, and Murray*, 447.

11. Ibid.

12. *U.S. Statutes at Large* 25 (1889), 1009–1010.

13. *The Alaskan*, September 24, 1892, p. 3.

14. U.S. House of Representatives, *Salmon Fisheries of Alaska: Reports of Special Agents Pracht, Luttrell, and Murray*, 385.

15. See Cooley, *Politics and Conservation*, 78.

16. U.S. House of Representatives, *Salmon Fisheries of Alaska: Reports of Special Agents Pracht, Luttrell, and Murray*, 418.

17. Evermann and Chamberlain, *Alaska Fisheries and Fur Industries*, 7.

18. See McEvoy, *Fisherman's Problem*, 6–7, for an excellent (and brief) overview of MSY as applied to the fisheries.

19. Bower, *Alaska Fishery and Fur-Seal Industries in 1925*, 103.

20. Bower, *Alaska Fishery and Fur-Seal Industries in 1928*, 256–257.

21. Andy McGregor, Alaska Department of Fish and Game, to David Arnold, April 15, 2005; e-mail correspondence in the author's possession.

22. Herman J. West, "Summary of the Season's Operations," in Folder "West Coast District Stream Survey 1932, Box 17, U.S. Fish and Wildlife Service, Record Group 22, Fisheries Research Data Files, 1904–1960, National Archives and Records Administration—Pacific Alaska Region, Anchorage, hereafter abbreviated as NAPAR. See also John Sewell, "Summary of Season's Operations" and H. F. Swift, "Summary of Season's Operations" in ibid. Both provide similar opaque estimates.

23. McEvoy, *Fisherman's Problem*, 6–7; Taylor, *Making Salmon*, 39–67; Taylor, "Burning the Candle at Both Ends"; and Taylor, "El Niño and Vanishing Salmon."

24. Nowhere was this trend more apparent than in the reports of Special Agent Howard M. Kutchin, who decried overfishing yearly during the 1890s while the Alaskan runs were declining. Kutchin congratulated himself heartily during years of rising productivity, such as between 1903 and 1905, when he triumphantly declared that "the regular and systematic surveillance of Alaska salmon waters for ten years past has been productive of beneficial results." See Kutchin, *Report on the Salmon Fisheries of Alaska, 1905*, 24. For his earlier jeremiads, see Kutchin, *Report on the Salmon Fisheries of Alaska, 1897*, 29. Taylor (in *Making Salmon*, 106–107) brilliantly shows how this dynamic played itself out in the Oregon fisheries with regard to the hatcheries, as fisheries managers "blamed fishing for downturns and credited hatcheries for rebounds when the ocean was probably more responsible in both cases."

25. Kutchin, *Report of the Special Agent for the Protection of the Alaska Salmon Fisheries*, 61.

26. Kutchin, *Report on the Salmon Fisheries of Alaska, 1897*, 5.

27. See Cooley, *Politics and Conservation*, for a thorough overview of Alaska fisheries legislation from 1889 through the 1950s. Cooley demonstrates just how much clout salmon canners had in the U.S. Congress, as they successfully watered down every fisheries bill until 1924 and even then continued to influence the corporate-friendly approach of regulators.

28. *U.S. Statutes at Large* 29 (1896): 317.

29. *U.S. Statutes at Large* 34, part 1 (1906): 478.

30. Taylor, *Making Salmon*, 68. Taylor's book is considered the bible for those interested in the evolution of hatcheries as an essential component of fisheries conservation.

31. Evermann, *Alaska Fisheries and Fur Industries in 1913*, 40–41.

32. Kutchin, *Report on the Salmon Fisheries of Alaska, 1900*, 46.

33. *The Alaskan*, Sitka, March 14, 1890, p. 2.

34. Kutchin, *Report on the Salmon Fisheries of Alaska, 1900*, 48–49.

35. Kutchin, *Report on the Salmon Fisheries of Alaska, 1904*, 26; and Kutchin,

Report on the Salmon Fisheries of Alaska, 1901, 57. His views mimicked the declarations of national and international experts on fish culture. See Taylor, *Making Salmon*, 71–78.

36. Bean, "Report on the Salmon and Salmon Rivers of Alaska," 170, 207–208.

37. Jordan as quoted in U.S. House of Representatives, *Alaska Salmon Commission*, 17–18.

38. Cobb, *Pacific Salmon Fisheries: Report of the United States Commissioner of Fisheries for 1930*, 680. See also Hunt, *History of the Marine Hatcheries of Alaska*, 5–7. The best general overview of hatcheries in Alaska during the territorial period is Roppel, *Alaska's Salmon Hatcheries*.

39. Montgomery, *King of Fish*, 150.

40. On the inefficacy of technical solutions to the decline of the fisheries, see Black, "Tragic Remedies," 37–70. For a stunning critique of bureaucratic efforts to transform both nature and society through science, technology, and rational planning, see Scott, *Seeing Like a State*.

41. Jones, *Report of the Alaska Investigations in 1914*, 52.

42. Department of Commerce, Bureau of Fisheries, "In the Matter of Hearing in Respect to Closing to Fishing Certain Streams of Alaska," October 1, 1915, in U.S. Bureau of Fisheries, "Hearings Conducted by the U.S. Bureau of Fisheries in Regulating the Fisheries of Alaska, 1907–1921," vol. 2, 1915–1917, 4–7.

43. Bower and Aller, *Alaska Fisheries and Fur Industries in 1918*, 14.

44. Bower, *Alaska Fishery and Fur-Seal Industries in 1928*, 233; and Bower, *Alaska Fishery and Fur-Seal Industries in 1934*, Appendix I to the *Report of Commissioner of Fisheries for the Fiscal Year 1935*, 12.

45. "Report of John Hansen—1931. RedFish Bay" in Folder "Juneau District Stream Survey, 1931," Box 17, U.S. Fish and Wildlife Service, Record Group 22, Fisheries Research Data Files, 1904–1960, NAPAR.

46. G. A. S. Anderson, "Summary of the Season's Operations," in Folder "West Coast District Stream Survey, 1932," Box 17, U.S. Fish and Wildlife Service, Record Group 22, Fisheries Research Data Files, 1904–1960, NAPAR.

47. Bower, *Alaska Fishery and Fur-Seal Industries in 1930*, 10.

48. Andy McGregor, Alaska Department of Fish and Game, to David Arnold, April 19, 2005, e-mail correspondence in the author's possession.

49. See Montgomery, *King of Fish*, 17–20, for a discussion of the impact of logjams on salmon habitat.

50. U.S. House of Representatives, Committee on the Merchant Marine and Fisheries, *Alaska Fisheries* (1916), 233.

51. James Wickersham, "Slaughter of 'the Silver Horde,'" *American Conservation* 1 (August 1911): 243.

52. Ibid., 248.

53. Bower and Aller, *Alaska Fisheries and Fur Industries in 1915*, 13.

54. U.S. House of Representatives, Committee on the Merchant Marine and Fisheries, *Alaska Fisheries* (1916), 13–14.

55. Jones, *Report of the Alaska Investigations in 1914*, 6.

56. U.S. House of Representatives, Committee on the Merchant Marine and Fisheries, *Alaska Fisheries* (1916), 191.

57. Colonialism and the fight for home rule looms large in Alaska's history, like other western states, except that Alaska's territorial period spanned more than a hundred years, making the conflict even more central to the state's history. See Haycox, *Alaska*; and Gruening, *State of Alaska*.

58. For an overview of the Alaska Native Brotherhood, see Dauenhauer and Dauenhauer, *Haa Kusteeyí, Our Culture*; Drucker, *Native Brotherhoods*; and Mitchell, *Sold American*, 191–251.

59. Dauenhauer and Dauenhauer, *Haa Kusteeyí, Our Culture*, 88–89.

60. *Alaska Fisherman*, May 1923, p. 16.

61. See, for example, "The Fortunes We Lose," *Alaska Journal*, Juneau City, September 23, 1893, p. 1; "Fishing Industry: Should Be Maintained by Appropriate Legislation," *The Alaskan*, January 10, 1903, p. 1; and "The San Franciscans Preparing for Their Annual Salmon Raid in Alaska," *The Alaskan*, April 7, 1894, p. 2.

62. *Pacific Fisherman Yearbook* 8 (February 1910): 43.

63. Evermann, *Fishery and Fur Industries of Alaska in 1912*, 38; Bower, *Alaska Fishery and Fur-Seal Industries in 1920*, 48–49; and Bower, *Alaska Fishery and Fur-Seal Industries in 1926*, 278–79.

64. Kutchin, *Report on the Salmon Fisheries of Alaska, 1901*, 52.

65. Jordan and Evermann as quoted in U.S. House of Representatives, *Alaska Salmon Commission*, 12.

66. Evermann, *Alaska Fisheries and Fur Industries in 1913*, 40.

67. Ibid., 41

68. Wickersham speech of March 5, 1915, reprinted in U.S. House of Representatives, Committee on the Merchant Marine and Fisheries, *Fisheries of Alaska* (1924), 182.

69. U.S. House of Representatives, Committee on the Merchant Marine and Fisheries, *Fisheries in Alaska* (1922), 96–97.

70. Wickersham as quoted in U.S. House of Representatives, Committee on the Merchant Marine and Fisheries, *Alaska Fisheries* (1916), 265.

71. Chris H. Buschmann, "Trap Fishing," *Pacific Fisherman Yearbook* 2 (January 1904): 19.

72. Evermann, *Fishery and Fur Industries of Alaska in 1912*, 40–42.

73. Bower and Aller, *Alaska Fisheries and Fur Industries in 1914*, 13.

74. Evermann, *Alaska Fisheries and Fur Industries in 1913*, 45, 41.

75. U.S. House of Representatives, Committee on the Merchant Marine and Fisheries, *Alaska Fisheries* (1916), 344.

76. Jones, *Report of the Alaska Investigations in 1914*, 6–8.

77. Jones as quoted in U.S. House of Representatives, Committee on the Merchant Marine and Fisheries, *Alaska Fisheries* (1916), 344.

78. On Progressive conservation, see Hays, *Conservation and the Gospel of Efficiency.*

79. U.S. House of Representatives, Committee on the Merchant Marine and Fisheries, *Fisheries of Alaska* (1924), 346.

80. The important difference between registered trap sites and fee-simple titles was that the bureau held the right to prohibit fishing in certain locations for conservation purposes, and it owed no compensation to trap owners who were subsequently prevented from fishing.

81. U.S. House of Representatives, Committee on the Merchant Marine and Fisheries, *Fisheries of Alaska* (1924), 80–81.

82. Ibid., 309–310.

83. Ibid., 151–152.

84. McCord as quoted in ibid., 141.

85. *Heckman et al. v. Sutter et al.*, Case No. 792, Ninth Circuit Court of Appeals, 119 F. 83; 1902 U.S. App. LEXIS 4641, 3–4.

86. U.S. House of Representatives, Committee on the Merchant Marine and Fisheries, *Fisheries of Alaska* (1924), 345.

87. In such legal arguments trap owners held the upper hand because in fact the common right to fishery had never been absolute. In Alaska—and in the rest of America—the open-access fishery had never been "open" at all times and places. Aboriginal fishers had restricted the rights of outsiders to fish at tribal sites. In Alaska aboriginal fishing rights had often been recognized by white fishermen and canning companies who purchased the right to fish from tribal owners. For example, see Moser, *Salmon and Salmon Fisheries of Alaska*, 22–23; and Tingle, *Report on Salmon Fisheries in Alaska*, 5. The Euro-American fishery was theoretically "open access," but in practice numerous constraints had always restricted or prohibited open access, including state and local restrictions and informal customs. For instance, on the Columbia River, gillnetters recognized "drift rights"—exclusive fishing rights accorded to particular groups of fishermen who cleared snags and other obstructions from their right of way. See Martin, *Legacy and Testament.* Furthermore, according to the Anglo-American legal tradition, wild animals could not be owned until they were possessed, but there were no restrictions on the types of devices—including traps—that could be used to apprehend and possess them.

88. Bower, *Alaska Fishery and Fur-Seal Industries in 1922*, 9. For more on the policy of creating fishery reservations, see Cooley, *Politics and Conservation*, 107–114; and Taylor, "Well-Thinking Men and Women," 372–375. For the significant role that Herbert Hoover played in framing fisheries policy in Alaska and the Pacific Coast, see Taylor, "Master of the Seas?" 40–61.

89. Sutherland, *Looting of Alaska's Resources*, 3–5.

90. U.S. House of Representatives, Committee on the Merchant Marine and Fisheries, *Fisheries of Alaska* (1924), 209.

91. The Commerce Department created four reservations in remote western Alaska, where there was little resident opposition. In southeastern Alaska a previous fishery reserve on Annette Island had been created by executive order in 1916 for the benefit of Tsimshian Indians at Metlakatla. See Bower and Aller, *Alaska Fisheries and Fur Industries in 1917*, 21.

92. Harding as quoted in Bower, *Alaska Fishery and Fur-Seal Industries in 1923*, 49–50.

93. "Native Fishermen Vigorously Protest Reservations," *Alaska Fisherman*, February 1923, p. 1. See also *Alaska Fisherman*, April 1923, p. 1.

94. "What Did Hoover Learn," *Alaska Fisherman*, January 1924, p. 9.

95. *Alaska Fisherman*, February 1924, p. 5.

96. Resolutions and letters reprinted in U.S. House of Representatives, Committee on the Merchant Marine and Fisheries, *Fisheries of Alaska* (1924), 26–28.

97. See, for instance, "Bills Affecting Salmon Fisheries," *Pacific Fisherman* 22 (January 1924): 5–6; "Alaska Fisheries Law in Prospect," *Pacific Fisherman* 22 (April 1924): 16–17.

98. *U.S. Statutes at Large* 43 (1924): 464–466. See also Cooley, *Politics and Conservation*, 115–127; and Taylor, "Well-Thinking Men and Women," 357–387.

99. Bower, *Alaska Fishery and Fur-Seal Industries in 1923*, 88–89; and Bower, *Alaska Fishery and Fur-Seal Industries in 1927*, 114.

100. Taylor, "Well-Thinking Men and Women," 377.

101. *U.S. Statutes at Large* 43 (1924): 465.

102. "Letters to Congress," *Alaska Fisherman*, May 1924, pp. 11–13.

103. Bower, *Alaska Fishery and Fur-Seal Industries in 1924*.

104. Frank T. Bell to William Timson, President, Alaska Packers Association, April 30, 1934, in Alaska Packers Association Records, microfilm reel no. 6, hereafter cited as APA.

105. Frank T. Bell to H. B. Friele, Vice President and General Manager, Nakat Packing Company, November 13, 1934, in Folder "Seine Boat Activities S.E. Alaska, 1935," U.S. Fish and Wildlife Service, Record Group 22, Fisheries Research Data Files, 1904–1960, NAPAR. See also Frank T. Bell to W. J. Brown, October 25, 1934, unmarked folder, Box 18, in ibid.

106. Frank T. Bell to Alaska Packers Association, September 27, 1933, microfilm reel no. 6, APA. See also Frank T. Bell to Alaska Packers Association, October 25, 1934, in ibid.

107. Memo "RE: Regulating Types of Gear," microfilm reel no. 6, APA. See also "Why Traps Should Be Continued in Alaskan Waters," November 6, 1935; William Timson to Frank T. Bell, April 10, 1934; William Timson to Frank T. Bell, May 10,

1934; William Timson to Frank T. Bell, June 25, 1934; and J. N. Gilbert to Frank T. Bell, November 5, 1934, all in microfilm reel no. 6, APA. See also Cooley, *Politics and Conservation*, 137–139.

108. U.S. House of Representatives, Committee on the Merchant Marine and Fisheries, *Fish Traps in Alaskan Waters* (1936), 31, 45–47. These arguments were repeated in the 1939 hearings. See, for instance, U.S. House of Representatives, Committee on the Merchant Marine and Fisheries, *Alaskan Fisheries Hearings*, part 3 (1939), 707.

109. U.S. House of Representatives, Committee on the Merchant Marine and Fisheries, *Fish Traps in Alaskan Waters*, 195.

110. U.S. House of Representatives, Committee on the Merchant Marine and Fisheries, *Alaskan Fisheries Hearings*, part 3 (1939), 710, 745.

111. U.S. House of Representatives, Committee on the Merchant Marine and Fisheries, *Alaskan Fisheries Hearings*, part 4 (1940), 1053, 1119, 1057.

112. Bower and Aller, *Alaska Fisheries and Fur Industries in 1915*, 11.

113. *Alaska Fisherman*, January 1924, p. 11. See also Paul's testimony in U.S. House of Representatives, Committee on the Merchant Marine and Fisheries, *Fisheries in Alaska* (1922), 98–101.

114. Untitled Policy Memo in Folder "Violations, Southeast Alaska, 1930," Box 6, U.S. Fish and Wildlife Service, RG 22, Fisheries and Management Records, 1930–1959, NAPAR.

115. Frank W. Hynes, Warden, to Captain M. J. O'Connor, U.S. Bureau of Fisheries, Ketchikan, Alaska, August 11, 1930, in Folder "Violations, Southeast Alaska, 1930," Box 6, ibid.

116. Carl Haug to Special Agent McLoughlin, July 24, 1931, in Folder "Violations, 1931," Box 6, ibid.

117. Baker to O'Connor, Telegram, October 2, 1930, in Folder "Violations, 1931," Box 6, ibid.

118. "Summary Report of Violations," in Folder "Violations, 1943," Box 8, U.S. Fish and Wildlife Service, RG 22, Fisheries and Management Records, 1930–1959, NAPAR.

119. Paul as quoted in U.S. House of Representatives, Committee on the Merchant Marine and Fisheries, *Alaskan Fisheries Hearings*, part 2 (1939), 447.

120. "Outline of Fishery Regulation to Conserve and Expand the Fisheries of Alaska," Exhibit No. 2, Thirty-third Annual Convention of the Alaska Native Brotherhood and Sisterhood, in accession no. 1885, Folder 32, Box 3, William Lewis Paul Papers, University of Washington Manuscripts and Archives.

121. U.S. House of Representatives, Committee on the Merchant Marine and Fisheries, *Alaskan Fisheries Hearings*, part 4 (1940), 1034.

122. U.S. House of Representatives, Committee on the Merchant Marine and Fisheries, *Alaskan Fisheries Hearings*, part 3 (1939), 693.

123. "Extension of Fishing Season," Resolution No. 18, Twenty-eighth Annual Convention of the Alaska Native Brotherhood and Sisterhood, in accession no. 2076–2, microfilm reel 1, William Lewis Paul Papers, University of Washington Manuscripts and Archives; "Outline of Fishery Regulation to Conserve and Expand the Fisheries of Alaska," cited in note 120, above.

124. U.S. House of Representatives, Committee on the Merchant Marine and Fisheries, *Alaskan Fisheries Hearings*, part 4 (1940), 1038.

125. U.S. House of Representatives, Committee on the Merchant Marine and Fisheries, *Alaskan Fisheries Hearings*, part 3 (1939), 689.

126. Jacoby, *Crimes against Nature*, 48–78. On the moral economy, see E. P. Thompson, "The Moral Economy of the English Crowd in the Eighteenth Century" and "The Moral Economy Reviewed" in *Customs in Common: Studies in Traditional Popular Culture* (New York: New Press, 1993).

127. Interview with Otto Hellen in "The Southeast Alaska Salmon Fishery: Interviews with Men and Women Engaged in Commercial Fishing, 1913–1978." Interviewed by Stephan B. Levy and George Figdor. Audio tapes available at the Alaska Historical Library, Juneau.

128. Bower, *Alaska Fisheries and Fur Industries in 1919*, 21.

129. "Trap Pirates Charged with Perjury," *Pacific Fisherman* 22 (January 1924): 14–15.

130. Bower, *Alaska Fishery and Fur-Seal Industries in 1925*, 89.

131. G. Skinner of the Alaska Pacific Salmon Corporation as quoted in Casaday, "Labor Unrest and the Labor Movement in the Salmon Industry of the Pacific Coast," 297.

132. *Spawn of the North*, produced by Albert Lewin (Los Angeles, Calif.: Paramount Pictures, Inc., 1938).

133. Wadewitz, "Pirates of the Salish Sea," 613.

134. G. Skinner as quoted in Casaday, "Labor Unrest and the Labor Movement in the Salmon Industry of the Pacific Coast," 297.

135. Quoted in *Spawn of the North*, cited in note 132, above.

136. Jones as quoted in Wadewitz, "Pirates of the Salish Sea," 617.

137. Bower, *Alaska Fishery and Fur-Seal Industries in 1926*, 252.

138. *Miller et al. v. United States*, Case No. 2231, Third Circuit Court of Appeals, 242 F. 907; 1917 U.S. App. LEXIS 1963. See also *Pierson v. Post*, Supreme Court of New York, 3 Cai. R. 175; 1805 N.Y. LEXIS 311, p. 1. This case provides a classic example of Anglo-American attitudes concerning the relationship between property and wild animals, ruling that property "in wild animals can be acquired only by possession." For an excellent discussion of this case, and particularly its relationship to the doctrine of laissez faire as applied to the fisheries, see Goble, "Salmon in the Columbia Basin," 229–231.

139. *Klemm v. United States*, Case No. 5039, Ninth Circuit Court of Appeals, 22 F.2d; 1927 U.S. App. LEXIS 3528.

140. "Trap Pirates Charged with Perjury," *Pacific Fisherman* 22 (January 1924): 14–15.

141. "J. R. Heckman Sets Forth Views on Trap Situation," in microfilm reel 6, APA.

142. Casaday, "Labor Unrest and the Labor Movement in the Salmon Industry of the Pacific Coast," 296.

143. Clarence L. Olson, Fishery Supervisor, to William A. Holzhimer, U.S. District Attorney, November 4, 1942, Folder "Violations, 1942," Box 7, U.S. Fish and Wildlife Service, RG 22, Fisheries and Management Records, 1930–1959, NAPAR; *United States of America v. Louis F. Paul, David Howard, Peter Sing, and Louis F. Paul Jr.*, Criminal Case File No. 1381–KB, Criminal Case Files, 1907–1955, Archives Box 37, U.S. District Court for the District of Alaska, First Division (Ketchikan); Records of the District Courts of the United States, RG 21, NAPAR.

144. George W. Folta, Counsel at Large, to the Solicitor, Department of the Interior, May 12, 1943, Folder "Violations, 1942," Box 7, U.S. Fish and Wildlife Service, RG 22, Fisheries and Management Records, 1930–1959, NAPAR.

145. "Complaint" in *Tee-Hit-Ton Tribe of Tlingit Indians, etc. v. Clarence Olson et al.*, Civil Case File No. 5051–A, Civil Cases, 1910–1955, Archives Box 240, U.S. District Court for the District of Alaska, First Division (Juneau); Records of the District Courts of the United States, RG 21, NAPAR, 5–11. See also "Specification of Relief Attached to Summons," in ibid.

146. See Arnold, "Work and Culture in Southeastern Alaska," 156–183; and Arnold, "Putting up Fish," 96–118.

147. "Taku Inlet Closed," *Alaska Fisherman*, June 1926, p. 5. See also "Conservation for Traps," *Alaska Fisherman*, July 1924, p. 4; "The Chilcat Country," *Alaska Fisherman*, February 1925, p. 4; "Misinformation or Politics," *Alaska Fisherman*, March 1925, p. 5; and "The Eldred Rock Trap," *Alaska Fisherman*, May 1925, p. 4.

148. *Alaska Fisherman*, June–July 1925, p. 4.

149. Paul as quoted in U.S. House of Representatives, Committee on the Merchant Marine and Fisheries, *Alaska Fisheries Hearings*, part 2 (1939), 445.

150. For an overview of the Alaska Reorganization Act, see Philp, "New Deal and Alaskan Natives," 309–327.

151. U.S. Department of Interior, Office of the Solicitor, Nathan R. Margold Opinion of February 13, 1942, Folder "Alaska Regulations Ruling, 1942," Box 20, U.S. Fish and Wildlife Service, RG 22, Fisheries Research Data Files, 1904–1960, NAPAR, pp. 1, 27.

152. Nathan R. Margold, Solicitor, to Harold L. Ickes, Secretary of the Interior, March 20, 1942, in ibid.

153. Harold L. Ickes to Francis Biddle, Attorney General, December 1, 1942, Folder "Native Fishing Rights, 1942," Box 26, ibid.

154. William L. Paul to Fish and Wildlife Service, June 7, 1942, Folder "Violations, 1942," Box 7, U.S. Fish and Wildlife Service, RG 22, Fisheries and Management Records, 1930–1959, NAPAR.

155. U.S. Department of Interior, Office of the Solicitor, Warner W. Gardner Opinion of November 11, 1942, Folder "Native Fishing Rights, 1942," Box 26, U.S. Fish and Wildlife Service, RG 22, Fisheries Research Data Files, 1904–1960, NAPAR, pp. 1, 3.

156. "Defendant's Memorandum," *Tee-Hit-Ton Tribe of Tlingit Indians, etc. v. Clarence Olson et al.*, 3.

157. *Tee-Hit-Ton Tribe of Tlingit Indians of Alaska v. Olson, Alaska Fishery Management Supervisor of the Fish & Wildlife Service of U.S. Department of the Interior et al.*, Case No. 11006, United States Ninth Circuit Court of Appeals, 160 F.2d 525; 1947 U.S. App. LEXIS 2634; 11 Alaska 309, 2.

158. "Defendant's Brief," *United States of America v. Cyrus E. Peck et al.*, Criminal Case File No. 2573–B, Criminal Case Files, 1926–1955, Box 81, U.S. District Court for the District of Alaska, First Division (Juneau); Records of the District Courts of the United States, RG 21, NAPAR.

159. "Defendant's Brief," *United States of America v. Peter E. Johnson, et al., United States of America v. Frank Paul, et al.*, Criminal Case File No. 2570–B, in ibid.

160. "Conservation of Alaska Fisheries," Resolution No. 40, Thirty-eighth Annual Convention of the Alaska Native Brotherhood and Sisterhood, in accession 2076–2, microfilm reel 1, William Lewis Paul Papers, University of Washington Manuscripts and Archives.

161. *U.S. Statutes at Large* 43 (1924): 466.

162. "Appellee's Brief," *United States of America v. Steven V. Hotch*, Criminal Case File No. 2565–B, Criminal Case Files, 1926–1955, Box 81, U.S. District Court for the District of Alaska, First Division (Juneau); Records of the District Courts of the United States, RG 21, NAPAR.

163. "Defendant's Brief," in ibid; William L. Paul Jr. to P. J. Gilmore, May 29, 1952, in ibid.

164. "Appellee's Brief," ibid.

165. "Editorial," *Voice of Brotherhood* 2 (November 1956): 2, in accession 2076–2, microfilm reel 1, William Lewis Paul Papers, University of Washington Manuscripts and Archives.

166. Taylor makes this point in "El Niño and Vanishing Salmon."

4 WORK, NATURE, RACE, AND CULTURE ON THE FISHERMEN'S FRONTIER, 1900S–1950S

Epigraphs: White, *Organic Machine*, 41; Köepf, *Fisherman's Son*, 146; and "The Fisherman's Union," *Alaska Fisherman*, May 1926, 4.

1. White, *Organic Machine*, x.

2. Virginia Scharff, "Man and Nature! Sex Secrets of Environmental History," in *Human/Nature: Biology, Culture, and Environmental History*, edited by John P. Herron and Andrew G. Kirk (Albuquerque: University of New Mexico Press, 1999),

40. Scharff calls for a "broader, more nuanced, and far more gender-conscious understanding of work than the fundamentally Marxist formulation embraced by most scholars working in the field" (40). She suggests that "feminist activists, labor historians, and feminist social scientists have demonstrated that industrialization and capitalist development led to the creation of all kinds of nonrationalized, nonmechanized, uncommodified (i.e., unpaid) productive work" (41). Although this chapter, and the entire book for that matter, deals primarily with male work cultures (and commercial rather than domestic production), Scharff's emphasis on "nonrationalized, nonmechanized, and uncommodified" work might also describe the Euro-American and Native American subsistence economies that developed in Alaska alongside of but outside the capitalist market economy. Moreover, her call for broadening the definition of "work," and seeing work, like Richard White, as a point of contact between humans and nature is a central point of this chapter.

3. Interview with Ed Hibler in "The Southeast Alaska Salmon Fishery: Interviews with Men and Women Engaged in Commercial Fishing, 1913–1978." Interviewed by Stephan B. Levy and George Figdor.

4. See Haycox, *Frigid Embrace.*

5. See Miller, *Frontier in Alaska and the Matanuska Colony.*

6. Ibid., 225.

7. This section draws extensively from interviews conducted in the late 1970s as part of the "Southeast Alaska Salmon Fishery" project, cited in note 3, above. Although oral histories are always fraught with interpretive problems, I have used these interviews less as a means of reconstructing historical events, than as a way to gain insight into the mentality and worldview of Indian and white fishermen in southeastern Alaska.

8. See Catton, *Inhabited Wilderness.* Theodore Catton has shown how preservationists in the nineteenth and twentieth centuries viewed the natural landscape in Alaska as a kind of platonic ideal for wilderness: "Alaska wilderness areas, because of their magnificent expanse, had more authenticity than the pocket-sized wilderness areas in the rest of the United States" (215). Like the conservationists in Catton's work, white fishermen saw Alaska as a vast wilderness unsullied by civilization.

9. Casaday, "Labor Unrest and the Labor Movement in the Salmon Industry of the Pacific Coast," 51.

10. White, *Organic Machine*, 33.

11. Interview with Toivo Andersen in "Southeast Alaska Salmon Fishery."

12. Interview with John Bahrt in ibid.

13. Interview with Ed Hibler in ibid.

14. Interview with Lahja Puustinen in ibid.

15. Interview with Otto Hellen in ibid.

16. Interview with Roman Keleske in ibid.

17. Interview with Arthur J. Petraborg Sr. in ibid.

18. Interview with Oscar Otness in ibid.

19. Interview with Peter Larson in ibid.

20. Brookman, *Sitka Man*, 1–11.

21. Ibid., 52–53.

22. Ibid., 86.

23. Ibid., 70.

24. Interview with Al Brookman Sr. in "Southeast Alaska Salmon Fishery."

25. Interview with Ruth Brinkley in ibid.

26. Interview with Ed Hibler in ibid.

27. Interview with Henry Yryana in ibid.

28. Interview with Toivo Andersen in ibid.

29. Interview with Peder Liadal in ibid.

30. Interview with Arndt Peterson in ibid.

31. Interview with John Clauson in ibid.

32. Morse, *Nature of Gold*, 117.

33. Ibid., 124.

34. See interviews with Toivo Andersen and Al Brookman Sr. in "Southeast Alaska Salmon Fishery."

35. Interview with Al Brookman Sr. in ibid.

36. See Catton, *Inhabited Wilderness*, 216, for the Native perspective on Alaska "wilderness."

37. See, for instance, interview with Horace Marks in "Southeast Alaska Salmon Fishery." On the early intrusion of non-Native fishers, he remembers that "everybody that can get a hook or a small net in the river was fishing right out of there in competition with us. Originally it was our area, our lifeblood, in the river. And people from all over began to come, began to bring up Italian fishermen to gillnet the area. These are canneries that brought up, we called them, 'black hairs.' . . . As it turned out they were Italians, and they were fisher people in Europe." For the best example of how Native peoples, by the 1940s, continued to see the marine landscape as one defined by cultural patterns, historical use, and clan property rights, see Goldschmidt and Haas, *Haa Aaní = Our Land*.

38. Almost every Tlingit fishermen interviewed told a story of decline: abundant fish become depleted through poor management, greed, overcompetition, and industrial technology. For good examples, see interviews with Howard Gray, Horace Marks, William Johnson, Dick Hotch, Andrew Johnnie, and George Dalton and Jessie Dalton in "Southeast Alaska Salmon Fishery."

39. Interview with Roy Bean in "Southeast Alaska Salmon Fishery."

40. Dauenhauer and Dauenhauer, *Haa Kusteeyí, Our Culture*, 155–156. Interview with George Dalton Sr. in "Southeast Alaska Salmon Fishery."

41. See Hosmer, *American Indians in the Marketplace*.

42. See also Arnold, "Work and Culture in Southeastern Alaska," 156–183.

43. Bower, *Alaska Fishery and Fur-Seal Industries: 1943*, 26.

44. Interview with Ronald Bean Sr. in "Southeast Alaska Salmon Fishery."

45. Interview with Thomas Jackson Sr. in ibid.

46. Interview with Dick Hotch in ibid.

47. Interviews with Archie Brown Sr., Horace Marks, Albert Davis, and Daniel Paul in ibid.

48. Interview with Daniel Paul in ibid.

49. Interviews with George Dalton, Albert Davis, Howard Gray, and Andrew Johnnie Sr. in ibid.

50. Interview with Dick Hotch in ibid. In this interview Hotch recites, in great detail, the entire story of "salmon boy."

51. Interview with Andrew Johnnie Sr. in ibid.

52. Interview with Horace Marks in ibid.

53. Casaday, "Labor Unrest and the Labor Movement in the Salmon Industry of the Pacific Coast," 30.

54. Ibid., 404.

55. White, *Organic Machine*, 44.

56. See, for instance, *Alaska Fisherman*, November–December 1928, p. 4; "All in the Same Boat," *Alaska Fisherman*, June 1928, p. 7.

57. U.S. House of Representatives, Committee on the Merchant Marine and Fisheries, *Fisheries of Alaska* (1924), 307.

58. Secretary of the Alaska Fishermen's Union to Summer S. Smith, May 18, 1927, Folder 14, Box 112, Alaska Packers Association (APA) Records. "Fooling Congressmen," *Alaska Fisherman*, May 1924, pp. 4–5.

59. U.S. House of Representatives, Committee on the Merchant Marine and Fisheries, *Alaskan Fisheries Hearings*, part 2 (1939), 477.

60. Interview with William Love in "Southeast Alaska Salmon Fishery."

61. Competition and conflict between non-Natives and Natives, outsiders and locals, is a recurring theme in the oral histories of Southeast Alaska salmon fishers. Roy Bean, for instance, remembered that "they [outside fishermen] could get kind of nasty if they wanted to. Because we as a Native people are anxious to do our part, to get our share from the fish. The school that they are watching, sometimes we beat them to it, that's what they don't like, so they make a fuss about it. But we have just as much right as they do to get that fish. We want it too. And we have a family that we want to take care of. . . . I don't think we make as much money as they do them years." See interview with Bean in "Southeast Alaska Salmon Fishery."

62. Deanna Paoli Gumina, "The Fishermen of San Francisco Bay: The Men of 'Italy Harbor,'" *Pacific Historian* 20 (spring 1976): 14–15. George Brown Goode and Joseph W. Collins, *The Fishermen of the United States*, in Goode, *Fisheries and Fishery Industries of the United States*, section 4, 30–36. McEvoy, *Fisherman's Problem*, 65–92.

63. See Martin, *Legacy and Testament.*

64. Moser, *Salmon and Salmon Fisheries of Alaska*, 23.

65. Max Stern, "Fishermen Form Crew on Alaska Salmon Ship," in newspaper series "The Price of Salmon," Max Stern Papers, Bancroft Library, University of California, Berkeley (hereafter cited as MSP).

66. Goode, *Fisheries and Fishery Industries of the United States*, 39. In "Fishermen of San Francisco Bay" (cited in note 62) Gumina notes that the Chinese were also important consumers of Italian-caught fish. In 1864, Italians protested a licensing fee levied on Chinese fishermen and fish peddlers by the San Francisco Board of Supervisors (Gumina, "Fishermen of San Francisco Bay," 14). In other words ethnic relationships were very complex and often reflected real economic issues rather than sheer racial intolerance. See also McEvoy, *Fisherman's Problem*, 65–92.

67. Goode, *Fisheries and Fishery Industries of the United States*, 42. Also see *Constitution and By-laws of the Columbia River Fishermen's Protective Union* (Astoria, Ore.: D.C. Ireland, Book and Job Printer, 1890). On Asian contract laborers in the salmon-canning industry, see Masson and Guimary, "Asian Labor Contractors in the Alaskan Canned Salmon Industry." The definitive work on Asian Americans in the salmon industry is Friday, *Organizing Asian American Labor.*

68. Max Stern, "Hell Ships of the Pacific," 2–5, MSP.

69. Max Stern, "Strong Union Wins Decent Conditions for Fishermen," article 16 in "The Price of Salmon," MSP.

70. See Linda Cook and Karen Bretz, "Kake Cannery," U.S. Department of Interior, National Park Service, National Register of Historic Places Registration, NPS Form 10–900 (September 4, 1997), 7–10. This document is available online at http://www.cr.nps.gov/maritime/nhl/kakecannery.pdf.

71. Max Stern, "Hell Ships of the Pacific," 6, MSP. Although this rumored account is not verifiable, cannery records and newspaper stories do reveal that Asian workers died in much greater proportion than whites did. According to a later narrative account written by the daughter of the captain, when the ship was in certain danger, the whites on board "begged my father to batten [the Chinese] down in the hold like so much cattle to keep them off the decks." Certainly it is impossible to know what really happened on the *Star of Bengal*. However, the persistence and apocryphal character of the tragedy suggests the deep-seated racism that pervaded relations among white ethnic fishermen and Asian-American cannery workers. For an APA account of the *Star of Bengal*, see "President's Report of 1908," in APA *History*, reel 1, p. 394, APA. According to the *Seward Weekly Gateway*, 120 out of 137 perished. See "120 Perish in Wreck," *Seward Weekly Gateway*, September 26, 1908, p. 1. For other articles on the wreck and its investigation, see *Seward Weekly Gateway*, October 3, 1908, p. 4; *Seward Weekly Gateway*, January 30, 1909, p. 2; and Joan Lowell, *Cradle of the Deep*, 110.

72. See Casaday, "Labor Unrest and the Labor Movement in the Salmon Industry of the Pacific Coast," 271.

73. Secretary, Alaska Fishermen's Union to Summer S. Smith, May 18, 1927, Folder 14, Box 112, in APA.

74. "So-Called Alaska Fishermen's Union," *Alaska Fisherman*, June 1924, p. 4.

75. U.S. House Committee on the Merchant Marine and Fisheries, *Alaskan Fisheries Hearings*, part 4 (1940), quotations from pp. 2–3, 42, and 94.

76. Jurich as quoted in ibid., 102–135.

77. Dimond as quoted in ibid., 65–78.

78. White makes this argument in *Organic Machine*, 39–40, as does Warren in *Hunter's Game*, 1–20. For further critiques of Hardin's notion of "the commons," see McCay and Acheson, *Question of the Commons*.

79. Furuseth as quoted in U.S. House Committee on the Merchant Marine and Fisheries, *Fisheries of Alaska* (1924), 311.

80. "President's Report, 1933," reel 3, APA.

81. See "President's Reports" in APA "History," 1928–1934 and 1935–1940, reel 3, APA.

82. See "President's Report, 1936," "President's Report, 1937," and "President's Report, 1939" in reel 3, APA. Throughout the 1930s the company would increasingly complain of labor's "unreasonable demands."

83. Bower, *Alaska Fishery and Fur-Seal Industries in 1930*, 47–53; and Bower, *Alaska Fishery and Fur-Seal Industries in 1939*, 137–138, 146.

84. Kresge, Morehouse, and Rogers, *Issues in Alaska Development*, 31.

85. Mark Kirchhoff, "When Alexander Was Great: The Story of a Southeast Fishing Town," *Alaska Journal* 13 (spring 1983): 26–32.

86. The ATA had also struck in 1928, urging nonmember sympathizers to hold out "for prices which insure more than just an eating wage." Tlingit fishermen were sympathetic to the trollers' demands but were not convinced that their own needs would be met by supporting the ATA. Later that year an article in the *Alaska Fisherman* noted that although the ATA demanded that Indians respect its strikes, it had not placed any Tlingits in positions of authority within the union. This changed in the fall of 1928, when the ATA voted Tlingit Charles Johnson of Kake to its board of directors. In turn, the ANB changed its own tune and urged Tlingits to join with white fishermen, proclaiming that Indian "interests will be advanced by joining the Alaska Trollers' Association." See "Trollers Declare Strike," *Alaska Fisherman*, June 1928, p. 7; "Too Many Trollers," ibid.; and *Alaska Fisherman*, November–December 1928.

87. "The Troller's Strike," *Alaska Fisherman*, July 1931, p. 2; "Trollers Stand Pat," *Alaska Fisherman*, July 1931, p. 8.

88. "Troller's [*sic*] Strike Ends in Compromise," *Alaska Fisherman*, August 1931, p. 8.

89. William Paul to Louis Paul, February 3, 1935, William Lewis Paul Papers (WPP), Folder 30, Box 3, Accession No. 1885.

90. Casaday, "Labor Unrest and the Labor Movement in the Salmon Industry of the Pacific Coast," 514.

91. Friday, *Organizing Asian American Labor*, 134–180, quotations on 171 and 149.

92. See Friday, "Competing Communities at Work."

93. Nelson, *Workers on the Waterfront*, 189, 3.

94. Casaday, "Labor Unrest and the Labor Movement in the Salmon Industry of the Pacific Coast," 441, 438.

95. Report of Local #22, United Fisherman's Union (UFU), and Local #32, UCAPAWA, *All Alaska Labor Convention*, Juneau, January 12–15, 1940, available in the Alaska Historical Library, Juneau.

96. Report for Local #16, UFU, in ibid.

97. Report of Local #22, UFU, and Local #32, UCAPAWA, in ibid., 13.

98. Report of A. E. Harding, *All Alaska Labor Convention*, Juneau, January 28–31, 1941, 8–9, available in the Alaska Historical Library.

99. Nelson, *Workers on the Waterfront*, 242.

100. Ibid.

101. U.S. House Committee on the Merchant Marine and Fisheries, *Alaskan Fisheries*, part 4 (1940), 148.

102. Ernest Gruening as quoted in *All Alaska Labor Convention*, 1941, 29, in *All Alaska Labor Conventions, Proceedings*, Juneau, 1938–1942. Available at the Alaska Historical Library, Juneau.

103. Interview with Toivo Andersen in "Southeast Alaska Salmon Fishery."

104. Interviews with William Love and Arthur J. Petraborg Sr. in ibid.

105. ANB circular, [no date], volume 34, Box 2, Accession No. 4246, William Lackey Paul Papers, Manuscript and University Archives, University of Washington, Seattle (hereafter referred to as WLPP).

106. ANB circular, June 2, 1939, volume 34, Box 2, Accession No. 4246, WLPP; ANB circular, May 20, 1939, ibid.

107. Lawrence Calvert, President, Association of Pacific Fisheries, and Eric Fribrock, President, Northwest Salmon Canners Association, to Harold L. Ickes, Secretary of the Interior, December 28, 1943, in Box 26; Folder "Native Fishing Rights, 1943," U.S. Fish and Wildlife Service, Record Group 22, Fisheries Research Data Files, 1904–1960, National Archives and Records Administration (NARA)—Pacific Alaska Region, Anchorage. On the 1944 "Hanna Hearings," see Philp, "New Deal and Alaskan Natives"; Haycox, *Frigid Embrace*, 66–67; and Mitchell, *Sold American*, 284–291.

108. Statement of W. C. Arnold in U.S. Department of Interior, *Hearings upon Claims of Natives of Alaska*, volume 1, 33–37. These unpublished transcripts are available at the Alaska Historical Library, Juneau.

109. The quotations in this paragraph are from, respectively, "Paternalism for Profit: An Analysis of the Haida-Tlingit Claims," *Pacific Fisherman* 42 (November 1944): 41–42; "Turning Alaska Back to the Indians," reprinted from the *Alaska Weekly*, November 3, 1944, in reel 8, APA; "Paternalism for Profit," just cited, 41; "Protest of the Haines Chamber of Commerce" in U.S. Department of Interior, *Hearings upon Claims of Natives of Alaska*, volume 2, 175–176; and "Protest of Juneau Chamber of Commerce," in reel 8, APA.

110. The quotations in this paragraph are from, respectively, Statement of UTA, Local 57, in U.S. Department of Interior, *Hearings upon Claims of Natives of Alaska*, volume 9, 1457; see also protest of United Trollers 56, ibid., volume 5, 910; J. F. Jurich, "Statement of the International Fishermen and Allied Workers of America," ibid.; and Statement of the Seafarers' International Union, ibid.

111. See, for instance, Minutes of ANB Convention, November 14, 1945, in reel 1, accession 2076–2, WPP.

112. The quotations in this paragraph are from, respectively, Charles Webster Demmert as quoted in U.S. Department of Interior, *Hearings upon Claims of Natives of Alaska*, volume 4, 624; Frank Nix in ibid., volume 2, 207; Demmert in ibid., volume 4, 653; and Powell Charles in ibid., volume 3, 435.

113. "Summary," Box 26, Folder "Native Fishing Rights, 1945," NAPAR.

114. "Aboriginal Rights in Alaska: Opinion of Richard H. Hanna, Examiner for the Department of Interior," Box 7, Folder "Violations, 1942," 17–18, NAPAR.

115. Ibid., 5–7.

116. *Annual Report of the Federal Trade Commission for the Fiscal Year Ended June 30, 1954* (Washington, D.C.: GPO, 1954), 35, 2.

117. For an overview of this debate, see Montes, "Alaska Fishermen and the Anti-Trust Laws"; Rosemary Agnes Shairer, "A Survey of the Alaskan Salmon-Canning Industry in the Post-War Period" (M.A. thesis, University of Washington, 1956), 60–75; Casaday, "Labor Unrest and the Labor Movement in the Salmon Industry of the Pacific Coast," 24–30; and Crutchfield, "Collective Bargaining in the Pacific Coast Fisheries."

118. See Casaday, "Labor Unrest and the Labor Movement in the Salmon Industry of the Pacific Coast," 24.

119. *Columbia River Packers Association, Inc. v. Hinton et al.*, No. 142, Supreme Court of the United States, 315 U.S. 143; 62 S. Ct. 520; 86 L. Ed. 750; 1942 U.S. LEXIS 1166; 5 Lab. Cas. (CCH) P51, 127; 1942, p. 1.

120. See Casaday, "Labor Unrest and the Labor Movement in the Salmon Industry of the Pacific Coast," 28–29.

121. Schairer, "Survey of the Alaskan Salmon-Canning Industry," 63.

122. Casaday, "Labor Unrest and the Labor Movement in the Salmon Industry of the Pacific Coast," 29.

5 THE CLOSING OF THE FISHERMEN'S FRONTIER, 1950S–2000S

Epigraphs: Köepf, *Fisherman's Son*, 285; Judson Brown as quoted in Dauenhauer and Dauenhauer, *Haa Kusteeyí, Our Culture*, 135; and J. R. McNeill, *Something New under the Sun*, 252.

1. Peratrovich as quoted in U.S. House of Representatives, Committee on Interior and Insular Affairs, *Alaska Statehood*, 286–287.

2. Ibid., 247.

3. U.S. House of Representatives, Committee on Interior and Insular Affairs, *Alaska Statehood and Elective Governorship*, 38.

4. See U.S. House of Representatives, Committee on Interior and Insular Affairs, *Alaska Statehood*, 297–368.

5. Ibid., 377, 384.

6. Ibid., 287.

7. The Constitution of the State of Alaska, Article 8, Section 3; ibid., Article 8, Section 15. This document is available online at http://ltgov.state.ak.us/constitution.php.

8. Ibid., Ordinance 3.

9. Ibid., Article 8, Section 4.

10. Cooley, *Politics and Conservation*, 195.

11. Interviews with Toivo Andersen and Roman Keleske in "Southeast Alaska Salmon Fishery." Interviewed by Levy and Figdor. Testimony of N. E. Nelson in U.S. House of Representatives, Committee on the Merchant Marine and Fisheries, *Merchant Marine and Fisheries Problems*, 87; see also the testimony of R. J. Ingle in ibid., 103.

12. *Alaska Statutes*, 16.05.260.

13. *Alaska Statutes*, 16.05.060.

14. Interview with John Enge in "Southeast Alaska Salmon Fishery."

15. Ibid.

16. Adasiak, "Limited Entry in Alaska," 194–195.

17. For good examples of this process, see interviews with John Enge, Roy Bean, Dick Hotch, Adolph Mathieson, Albert Davis, and John Bahrt in "Southeast Alaska Salmon Fishery."

18. Hardin, "Tragedy of the Commons," 1244.

19. Ibid., 1244.

20. Hardin's argument has been unfairly misconstrued by both sides of the political spectrum. The left saw Hardin's argument as a critique of "common property" or "public property," including the National Park system, which Hardin suggested would be destroyed under an open-access regime. Hardin's critique, however, was directed more toward the selfish universal nature of humankind (a debatable point, as I mentioned earlier), which can just as easily be read as a critique of laissez-faire

capitalism, with the antidote for both being increased state regulation, a decidedly liberal solution. Conservatives have used Hardin's argument to advocate for the privatization of common property. Hardin, in a one-sentence provocation, suggests that "we might sell [the National Parks] off as private property," but the balance of his argument focuses on the need for state-sponsored coercion to restrain such problems as pollution, and, most important, overpopulation, which is the focus of his essay. His contention that the "freedom to breed will bring ruin to all" would be unlikely to appeal to conservatives. For critiques of Hardin, see Warren, *Hunter's Game*; McCay and Acheson, *Question of the Commons*; and White, *Organic Machine*, 39–40.

21. Hardin, "Tragedy of the Commons," 1245.

22. Gordon, "Economic Theory of a Common-Property Resource," 130–131, 124, 132.

23. See Scott, "Fishery"; Johnson, "Regulation of Commercial Salmon Fishermen"; Crutchfield and Pontecorvo, *Pacific Salmon Fisheries*; and Tussing, Morehouse, and Babb Jr., *Alaska Fisheries Policy*.

24. Crutchfield as quoted in Cooley, *Politics and Conservation*, 198.

25. Crutchfield and Pontecorvo, *Pacific Salmon Fisheries*, v, 177.

26. See especially Tussing, Morehouse, and Babb Jr., *Alaska Fisheries Policy*.

27. See Thomas Morehouse and George Rogers, *Limited Entry in the Alaska and British Columbia Salmon Fisheries*.

28. Thomas Morehouse and Jack Hession, "Politics and Management: The Problem of Limited Entry," in Tussing, Morehouse, and Babb Jr., *Alaska Fisheries Policy*, 306–320; Constitution of the State of Alaska, Article 8, Section 3; ibid., Article 8, Section 15.

29. See Constitution of the State of Alaska, Article 8, Section 15.

30. [State of Alaska] Governor's Office, "Introduction," *Limited Entry Program for Alaska's Fisheries*, n.p.

31. Ibid.

32. See *Alaska Statutes*, 16.43.

33. See *Alaska Statutes* 16.43.290 (1).

34. See *Alaska Statutes* 16.43.250 (1); *Alaska Statutes* 16.43.250 (2); [State of Alaska] Governor's Office, *Limited Entry Program for Alaska's Fisheries*, 6–7. The commission would also take into consideration "applicants who would suffer significant economic hardship by exclusion from the fishery." See *Alaska Statutes* 16.43.250 (b).

35. Interview with Roman Keleske in "Southeast Alaska Salmon Fishery." See also the interview with Adolph Mathieson in ibid., who makes a similar comparison between traps and limited entry.

36. Interviews with William Love and Arndt Peterson in ibid. See also the interviews with Peder Liadal, Erling Espeseth, Adolph Mathieson, and Roman Keleske, all in ibid.

37. See the interviews with Kathy Pfundt and Henry Yryana in ibid. for other examples of fishermen being excluded from the fisheries by the limited entry commission.

38. Morehouse and Hession, "Politics and Management," 317.

39. Adasiak, "Limited Entry in Alaska," 222–223.

40. *Alaska Statutes* 16.43.290 (1).

41. For permit prices and statistical data on permit transfers, see Tingley et al., *Changes in the Distribution of Alaska's Commercial Fisheries Entry Permits*, 123–124.

42. In 1979, Carl Rosier guessed that an outsider would need around $400,000 investment capital to begin purse-seining in southeastern Alaska. See the interview with Rosier in "Southeast Alaska Salmon Fishery."

43. Interview with William Love in ibid.

44. Interview with Carl Rosier in ibid.

45. Cannery superintendent Jack Brennan noted that fishermen invested in equipment to the point where they had "a Rolls Royce doing a Ford's job. It's not effective. They don't have to have this larger boat and this expensive equipment." See the interview with Brennan in ibid.

46. [State of Alaska] Governor's Office, *Limited Entry Program for Alaska's Fisheries*, 31.

47. Tingley et al., *Changes in the Distribution of Alaska's Commercial Fisheries Entry Permits*, 123–124.

48. Interviews with Jamie Chevalier and Roman Keleske in "Southeast Alaska Salmon Fishery."

49. See McPhee, *Coming into the Country*. The best overview of the rise of alternative, countercultural fishing communities in the early 1970s is Upton, *Journeys through the Inside Passage*, 129–142.

50. Interview with Jamie Chevalier in "Southeast Alaska Salmon Fishery."

51. Interview with Kathy Pfundt in ibid.

52. Interview with Tom Jacobson, Howard Pendell, and John Hancock in ibid.

53. Langdon, *Transfer Patterns in Alaskan Limited Entry Fisheries*. These trends continued past 1980, although according to a later study, since 1987 the "migration of permit holders away from rural local communities" to cities, rather than permit transfers, has accounted primarily for the continuing shift from rural to urban permit holding. See Tingley et al., *Changes in the Distribution of Alaska's Commercial Fisheries Entry Permits*, 15.

54. See especially the interviews in "Southeast Alaska Salmon Fishery" with Dick Hotch, Roy Bean, William Johnson, and Andrew Johnnie, all of whom complained that ADFG managers "don't listen to us."

55. See Dombrowski, *Against Culture*, 36–39.

56. Interview with Archie Brown in "Southeast Alaska Salmon Fishery."

57. Interview with Horace Marks in ibid.

58. Interview with Howard Gray in ibid. For similar statements on the negative

impact of limited entry on Native communities, see interviews in ibid. with Dick Hotch, Albert Davis, Andrew Johnnie Sr., as well as those with Ronald Bean Sr., William Johnson, and Thomas Jackson Sr.

59. Kamali, *Alaskan Natives and Limited Fisheries of Alaska*, 18.

60. Betts and Wolfe, "Commercialization of Fisheries and the Subsistence Economies of the Alaska Tlingit," 286, 288, 292.

61. Robert J. Wolfe and Robert J. Walker, "Subsistence Economies in Alaska: Productivity, Geography, and Development Impacts," *Arctic Anthropology* 24 (1987): 68–69.

62. U.S. Joint Federal-State Commission on Policies and Programs Affecting Alaska Natives, *Alaska Natives Commission Final Report*, , volume 3 (Anchorage, Ak.: U.S. Joint Federal-State Commission on Policies and Programs Affecting Alaska Natives, 1994), 6.

63. See *U.S. Statutes at Large* 85 (1971): 688. For an overview of ANSCA, see Mitchell, *Take My Land*; and Haycox, *Alaska*, 271–287.

64. Catton, *Inhabited Wilderness*, 211; U.S. Joint Federal-State Commission on Policies and Programs Affecting Alaska Natives, *Alaska Natives Commission Final Report*, 12.

65. *Alaska Statutes* 16.05.940 (26).

66. Norris, *Alaska Subsistence*, 93.

67. Catton's *Inhabited Wilderness* is the definitive source on Alaska Natives and National Parks. For a broader perspective, see Spence, *Dispossessing the Wilderness*.

68. See Catton, *Inhabited Wilderness*, 211; *U.S. Statutes at Large* 94, part 2 (1980): 2371.

69. Norris, *Alaska Subsistence*, 88–108.

70. *Alaska Statutes* 16.05.940 (25).

71. Norris, *Alaska Subsistence*, 162.

72. Ibid., 162–177, 242–263.

73. Quoted in ibid., 244. My account of the Katie John case and the assumption of subsistence fishing management by the federal government only skims the surface. For the fullest account, see Norris, *Alaska Subsistence*, chapter 9, "The Subsistence Fishing Question," from which my summary is drawn.

74. Ibid., 245.

75. U.S. Joint Federal-State Commission on Policies and Programs Affecting Alaska Natives, *Alaska Natives Commission Final Report*, 39.

76. The best concise overview of the relationship among Native subsistence, ANSCA, ANILCA, and federalism is Haycox, *Frigid Embrace*, 152–157, which I used to guide me through these issues.

77. Berger, *Village Journey*, 6.

78. Ibid., 9–11.

79. Haycox, *Frigid Embrace*, 154–155; *Alaska, Petitioner v. Native Village of*

Venetie Tribal Government et al., No. 96–1577, Supreme Court of the United States, 522 U.S. 520; 118 S. Ct. 948; 140 L. Ed 2d 30; 1998 U.S. LEXIS 1449.

80. Cornell et al., *Achieving Alaska Native Self-Governance*, D-4.

81. Durbin, *Pulp Politics*, 138. Durbin provides an excellent overview of timber harvesting by Native corporations on pages 52–57, 136–148, and 292–301. See also Haycox, *Frigid Embrace*, 130.

82. Durbin, *Pulp Politics*, 147–148.

83. Ibid., 139.

84. Ibid., 140, 297, 301.

85. The quotation is from "Our Lands," available online at http://www.sealaska.com/page/natural_resources.html.

86. U.S. Senate, *Alaska Native Subsistence and Fishing Rights*, 4.

87. See http://www.sealaska.com/page/our_business.html.

88. Dombrowski, *Against Culture*, 63–66.

89. In any case the future of subsistence fishing in Native societies in southeastern Alaska will most likely be decided by those who have the least direct dependence on it, while those who actually practice subsistence as a function of their everyday lives will have the least amount of formal political power, even within Native institutions and communities. Dombrowski (*Against Culture*, 92) suggests that those who rely upon subsistence fishing and hunting "are also among the more marginal individuals in their communities . . . for reasons that are closely related to their subsistence livelihood."

90. Interviews with Roy Bean, Ronald Bean Sr., and Albert Davis in "Southeast Alaska Salmon Fishery."

91. Kan, *Memory Eternal*, 519.

92. J. R. McNeill, *An Environmental History of the Twentieth-Century World* (New York: W. W. Norton & Company, 2000), 252.

93. Glavin, *Last Great Sea*, 208.

94. Hal Bernton, "Bumper Crops of Farmed Salmon: Price Glut Threatens Wild-Fish Industry," *Seattle Times*, September 2, 2001, p. A1.

95. Marcia Barinaga, "Fish, Money, and Science in Puget Sound," *Science* 247 (February 9, 1990): 631.

96. Hume et al., *Stain upon the Sea*, 13.

97. Richard Monastersky, "The Hidden Cost of Farming Fish," *Chronicle of Higher Education*, April 22, 2005, p. 1 (online edition); Jocelyn Kaiser, "Fish Farm Hazards," *Science* 308 (April 8, 2005): 195.

98. Hume et al., *Stain upon the Sea*, 44–45.

99. Bernton, "Bumper Crops of Farmed Salmon," p. A1; Alexandra Morton and John Volpe, "A Description of Escaped Farmed Atlantic Salmon *Salmo salar* Captures and Their Characteristics in One Pacific Salmon Fishery Area in British Columbia, Canada, in 2000," *Alaska Fishery Research Bulletin* 9 (2002): 102–110.

100. As quoted in Hume et al., *Stain upon the Sea*, 46.

101. Quotations from the Web site of the Salmon Nation Community, at http://www.salmonnation.com/voices/friends.html. The First Nations Summit consists of "a majority of First Nations and Tribal Councils in BC and provides a forum for First Nations in British Columbia to address issues related to Treaty negotiations as well as other issues of common concern." See the Web site of the First Nations Summit, at http://www.fns.bc.ca/about/about.htm. See also the statement of the Musgamagw Tsawataineuk chiefs in "Salmon Farming and First Nations," available at http://www.mttc.ca/pdf/SalmonFarmingandFirstNations.PDF. It is important to note that some First Nations tribes have actually embraced salmon farming as a form of economic development.

102. To consumers, it is "cheap" compared with wild salmon, but what are its costs—environmental and social—that are not factored into the price of farmed fish?

103. Todd Wilkinson, "For Alaska Salmon Fishermen, Price—Not Supply—Rankles," *Christian Science Monitor* 4 (June 2003): 3.

104. Knapp, "Implications of Aquaculture for Wild Fisheries," 31; and Joel Gay, "New Frontiers for Fish Farming," *Alaska Business Monthly* 11 (August 1, 1994): 24.

105. Ned Rozell, "The Salmon Storm," *Alaska* 70 (July 2004): 25.

106. Wesley Loy, "First Salmon Nets of 1993 Haul in Plenty of Worries," *Anchorage Daily News*, May 19, 1993; Helen Jung, "Few Fishermen Rejoice over Near Record Catch," *Anchorage Daily News*, December 31, 1995, p. C4; Wesley Loy, "Salmon Prospects Grim," *Anchorage Daily News*, June 24, 2001, p. E1; Gunnar Knapp, "Farmed Salmon Oversupply Ripples through Wild Fishery," *Alaska Journal of Commerce* 26 (February 10, 2002): 12; and Knapp, "Implications of Aquaculture for Wild Fisheries," 94.

107. Knapp, "Challenges and Strategies for the Alaska Salmon Industry," 132.

108. Thorstenson as quoted in Rozell, "Salmon Storm," 27.

109. See Helen Jung, "Endangered Fishermen," *Alaska Magazine* 68 (August 2002): 24–29.

110. See Chuck Kleeschulte, "Finfish Farming Banned," *Alaska Business Monthly* 6 (July 1990): 35.

111. Testimony of Dale Kelley, Leggatt Inquiry, Vancouver, British Columbia, October 11, 2001. Available online at http://www.georgiastrait.org/Articles2001/Leggatt2.php. See also Wesley Loy, "Alaska Pans B.C. Move to Lift Salmon Farm Ban," *National Fisherman* 83 (December 2002): 13–14.

112. Thorenstein as quoted in Dexter Van Zile, "Farm Buoys," *National Fisherman* 85 (January 2005): 22. See also Elizabeth Bluemink, "Federal Panel Concedes to Alaska on Aquaculture," *Juneau Empire*, August 13, 2004, available online at http://www.mindfully.org/Water/2004/Aquaculture-Moratorium13aug04.htm; and Wesley Loy, "Aquaculture Ban Extension Mulled," *Anchorage Daily News*, March 2, 2005, p. F1.

113. LeBlanc as quoted in Van Zile, "Farm Buoys," 23.

114. Harvey as quoted in Al Ritter, "Farmed Salmon Foe to Fishermen: Aquaculture Lowers Demand for Wild Fish," *Seattle Times*, July 21, 2003, p. B2.

115. Ken Brooks quoted in Schreiber, "First Nations, Consultation, and the Rule of Law."

116. Hites et al., "Global Assessments of Organic Contaminants in Farmed Salmon," 226–229.

117. Knapp, "Implications of Aquaculture for Wild Fisheries," 127.

118. Ibid.

119. Ibid., 134.

120. Ibid., 127.

121. Painter as quoted in Kleeschulte, "Finfish Farming Banned," 35.

122. Fuhs as quoted in Imre Nemeth, "Mariculture: Get in Now or Wait for a Quarter of a Century?" *Alaska Journal of Commerce* 11 (November 16, 1987): 6.

123. Bluemink, "Federal Panel Concedes to Alaska on Aquaculture," 2.

124. On the Pacific salmon treaties, see Shepard and Argue, *1985 Pacific Salmon Treaty*.

125. Some of the measures proposed to address the problems of falling prices and profitability in the salmon fisheries are outlined in "Charting New Courses for Alaska Salmon Fisheries: The Legal Waters," *Alaska's Marine Resources* 9 (November 2003): 1–12.

EPILOGUE

Epigraphs: "Slack Markets for Salmon," *Alaska Fisherman's Journal* 26, no. 1 (January 2003), 22; and Gunnar Knapp, "Implications of Aquaculture for Wild Fisheries: The Case of Alaska Wild Salmon," presentation for Bevan Sustainable Fisheries Lecture Series, University of Washington, Seattle, February 10, 2005, 134.

1. Larkin, *Pacific Salmon*, 7.

2. Ibid.

3. Ibid., 8–14.

4. Ibid., 14.

5. Gunnar Knapp, "Looking Upstream: Economist Gunnar Knapp Predicts the Salmon Industry's Future," *Anchorage Daily News*, November 22, 1998, p. C1. This essay can also be found online as Gunnar Knapp, "The Salmon Industry: Twenty-Seven Predictions for the Future" (June 1998), at http://www.iser.uaa.alaska.edu/iser/people/knapp/. Economist Steve Colt also makes the case for the economic efficiency of fish traps in "Salmon Fish Traps in Alaska: An Economic History Perspective," ISER Working Paper 2000.2, February 15, 2000, available online at http://www.alaskool.org/projects/traditionalife/fishtrap/FISHTRAP.htm.

6. “Charting New Courses for Alaska Salmon Fisheries: The Legal Waters,” *Alaska’s Marine Resources* 9 (November 2003): 9.

7. Knapp, “Looking Upstream,” p. C1.

8. See also Knapp, “Challenges and Strategies for the Alaska Salmon Industry,” 132; and Knapp, “Five Economic Considerations in Thinking about United States Offshore Aquaculture,” paper presented at the Pacific Marine Exposition, Seattle, Washington, November 12, 2004.

9. Wendell Berry, “The Idea of a Local Economy,” in *The Art of the Commonplace: The Agrarian Essays of Wendell Berry*, edited by Norman Wirzba (Washington, D.C.: Shoemaker & Hoard, 2002), 257.

10. Ibid.

11. Ibid., 250.

12. See “Charting New Courses for Alaska Salmon Fisheries,” 2–12.

13. One good sign for local fishing communities: an April 2005 conference in Anchorage, hosted by the Alaska Sea Grant College Program and funded by state and federal fisheries management agencies, focused on “understanding and considering impacts to coastal communities” as “a necessary step in the fishery management process.” See Cullenberg, *Managing Fisheries—Empowering Communities*.

Selected Bibliography

ARTICLES, BOOKS, AND DISSERTATIONS

Adasiak, Allan. "Limited Entry in Alaska." In *Pacific Salmon Management for People*, edited by Derek V. Ellis. Western Geographical Series, volume 13. Victoria, B.C.: University of Victoria, 1977.

Ames, Kenneth M., and Herbert D. G. Maschner. *Peoples of the Northwest Coast: Their Archeology and Prehistory*. New York: Thames and Hudson, 1999.

Arbogast, Dean. "Labor in the Alaska Salmon Industry." M.A. thesis, Columbia University, 1947.

Arndt, Katherine L., Russell H. Sackett, and James A. Ketz. *A Cultural Resource Overview of the Tongass National Forest, Alaska*. Fairbanks, Alaska: GDM, Inc., 1987.

Arnold, David. "Work and Culture in Southeastern Alaska: Tlingit Indians and the Industrial Fisheries, 1880s–1940s." In *Native Pathways: American Indian Culture and Economic Development in the Twentieth Century*, edited by Brian C. Hosmer and Colleen O'Neill. Boulder: University Press of Colorado, 2004.

———. "Putting up Fish: Environment, Work, and Culture in Tlingit Society, 1790s–1940s." Ph.D. dissertation, University of California, Los Angeles, 1997.

Arnold, Robert D. *Alaska Native Land Claims*. Anchorage, Alaska: Alaska Native Foundation, 1976.

Aron, Stephen. "Lessons in Conquest: Towards a Greater Western History." *Pacific Historical Review* 63, no. 2 (May 1994): 125–147.

Ballou, Maturin M. *The New Eldorado: A Summer Journey to Alaska*. New York: Houghton Mifflin Company, 1889.

Bancroft, Hubert Howe. *History of Alaska, 1730–1885*. San Francisco: A. L. Bancroft & Company, 1886.

Beck, Mary Giraudo. *Shamans and Kushtakas: North Coast Tales of the Supernatural*. Anchorage: Alaska Northwest Books, 1991.

Berger, Thomas R. *Village Journey: The Report of the Alaska Native Review Commission*. New York: Hill and Wang, 1985.

Berkhofer, Robert F., Jr. *The White Man's Indian: Images of the American Indian from Columbus to the Present.* New York: Alfred A. Knopf, 1978.

Betts, Martha F., and Robert J. Wolfe. "Commercialization of Fisheries and the Subsistence Economies of the Alaska Tlingit." *Society and Natural Resources* 5 (March 1992): 277–295.

Black, Lydia T. *Russians in Alaska, 1732–1867.* Fairbanks: University of Alaska Press, 2004.

Black, Michael. "Tragic Remedies: A Century of Failed Fishery Policy on California's Sacramento River." *Pacific Historical Review* 64, no. 1 (February 1995): 37–70.

Borden, Charles E. *Origins and Development of Early Northwest Coast Culture to about 3000 B.C.* Ottawa: National Museums of Canada, 1975.

Boxberger, Daniel L. *To Fish in Common: The Ethnohistory of Lummi Indian Salmon Fishing.* Seattle: University of Washington Press, 2000.

Boyd, Robert. *The Coming of the Spirit of Pestilence: Introduced Infectious Diseases and Population Decline among Northwest Coast Indians, 1774–1874.* Seattle: University of Washington Press, 1999.

Briggs, Horace. *Letters from Alaska and the Pacific Coast.* Buffalo, N.Y.: E. H. Hutchinson, 1889.

Brookman, Al, Sr. *Sitka Man.* Anchorage: Alaska Northwest Books, 1984.

Brown, Kathryn. "Pacific Salmon Run Hot and Cold." *Science* 290 (October 27, 2000): 685–686.

Burr, Agnes Rush. *Alaska: Our Beautiful Northland of Opportunity.* Boston: The Page Company, 1919.

Carpenter, Frank G. *Alaska: Our Northern Wonderland.* New York: Doubleday, Page, and Company, 1923.

Carrothers, W. A. *The British Columbia Fisheries.* Toronto: University of Toronto Press, 1941.

Carstensen, Vernon. "The Fisherman's Frontier on the Pacific Coast." In *The Frontier Challenge: Responses to the Trans-Mississippi West,* edited by John G. Clark. Lawrence: University of Kansas Press, 1971.

Casaday, Lauren Wilde. "Labor Unrest and the Labor Movement in the Salmon Industry of the Pacific Coast." Ph.D. dissertation, University of California, Berkeley, 1938.

Case, David S. *Alaska Natives and American Laws.* Fairbanks: University of Alaska Press, 1984.

Catton, Theodore. *Inhabited Wilderness: Indians, Eskimos, and National Parks in Alaska.* Albuquerque: University of New Mexico Press, 1997.

Champagne, Duane. "Culture, Differentiation, and Environment: Social Change in Tlingit Society." In *Differentiation Theory and Social Change: Comparative and Historical Perspectives,* edited by Jeffrey C. Alexander and Paul Colomy. New York: Columbia University Press, 1990.

Christy, Francis T., Jr., and Anthony Scott. *The Common Wealth in Ocean Fisheries.* Baltimore, Md.: Johns Hopkins University Press, 1965.

Coates, Peter A. *The Trans Alaska Pipeline Controversy: Technology, Conservation, and the Frontier.* London: Associated University Presses, 1991.

Colby, Merle. *A Guide to Alaska: Last American Frontier.* New York: MacMillan Company, 1943.

Cone, Joseph, and Sandy Ridlington, eds. *The Northwest Salmon Crisis: A Documentary History.* Corvallis: Oregon State University Press, 1996.

Cooley, Richard A. *Politics and Conservation: The Decline of the Alaska Salmon.* New York: Harper & Row, 1963.

Coontz, Robert E. *From the Mississippi to the Sea.* Philadelphia: Dorrance & Company, Inc., 1930.

Cornell, Stephen, Jonathan Taylor, Kenneth Grant, Victor Fischer, and Thomas Morehouse. *Achieving Alaska Native Self-Governance: Toward Implementation of the Alaska Natives Commission Report.* Anchorage: Institute of Social and Economic Research, University of Alaska, 1999.

Cronon, William. *Changes in the Land: Indians, Colonists, and the Ecology of New England.* New York: Hill and Wang, 1983.

———. *Uncommon Ground: Toward Reinventing Nature.* New York: W. W. Norton & Co., 1995.

Crutchfield, James A. "Collective Bargaining in the Pacific Coast Fisheries: The Economic Issue." *Industrial and Labor Relations Review* 8, no. 4 (July 1955): 541–556.

Crutchfield, James A., and Guilio Pontecorvo. *The Pacific Salmon Fisheries: A Study of Irrational Conservation.* Baltimore: Johns Hopkins University Press, 1969.

Cullenberg, Paula, ed. *Managing Fisheries—Empowering Communities: Conference Proceedings.* Fairbanks: Alaska Sea Grant College Program, University of Alaska Fairbanks, 2005.

Dauenhauer, Nora Marks, and Richard Dauenhauer, eds. *Haa Kusteeyí, Our Culture: Tlingit Life Stories.* Seattle: University of Washington Press, 1994.

———. *Haa Shuká, Our Ancestors: Tlingit Oral Narratives.* Seattle: University of Washington Press, 1987.

Daugherty, Richard D. "People of the Salmon." In *America in 1492: The World of the Indian Peoples before the Arrival of Columbus,* edited by Alvin M. Josephy Jr. New York: Alfred A. Knopf, 1992.

De Armond, R. N., ed. *Early Visitors to Southeastern Alaska: Nine Accounts.* Anchorage: Alaska Northwest Books, 1978.

Deloach, Daniel B. *The Salmon Canning Industry.* Corvallis: Oregon State College, 1939.

de Laguna, Frederica. *Under Mount Saint Elias: The History and Culture of the Yakutat Tlingit.* Smithsonian Contributions to Anthropology, volume 7. Washington, D.C.: Smithsonian Institution Press, 1972.

———. "Some Dynamic Forces in Tlingit Society." *Southwestern Journal of Anthropology* 8 (spring 1952): 1–12.

———. "Tlingit Ideas about the Individual." *Southwestern Journal of Anthropology* 10 (summer 1954): 172–191.

Deur, Douglass. "Salmon, Sedentism, and Cultivation: Toward an Environmental Prehistory of the Northwest Coast." In *Northwest Lands, Northwest Peoples: Readings in Environmental History*, edited by Dale D. Goble and Paul W. Hirt. Seattle: University of Washington Press, 1999.

Deur, Douglass, and Nancy J. Turner, eds. *Keeping It Living: Traditions of Plant Use and Cultivation on the Northwest Coast of North America*. Seattle: University of Washington Press, 2005.

Dodds, Gordon. *The Salmon King of Oregon: R. D. Hume and the Pacific Fisheries*. Chapel Hill: University of North Carolina Press, 1959.

Dombrowski, Kirk. *Against Culture: Development, Politics, and Religion in Indian Alaska*. Lincoln: University of Nebraska Press, 2001.

Donald, Leland. *Aboriginal Slavery on the Northwest Coast of North America*. Berkeley: University of California Press, 1997.

Dorsey, Kurkpatrick. *The Dawn of Conservation Diplomacy: U.S.-Canadian Wildlife Protection Treaties in the Progressive Era*. Seattle: University of Washington Press, 1998.

Drucker, Philip. *Archaeological Survey on the Northern Northwest Coast*. Smithsonian Insitution, Bureau of American Ethnology, Bulletin No. 133. Washington, D.C.: GPO, 1943.

———. *Cultures of the North Pacific Coast*. San Francisco: Chandler Publishing Company, 1965.

———. *The Native Brotherhoods: Modern Intertribal Organizations on the Northwest Coast*. Smithsonian Institution, Bureau of American Ethnology, Bulletin No. 168. Washington, D.C.: GPO, 1958.

Durbin, Kathie. *Pulp Politics and the Fight for the Alaska Rain Forest*. Corvallis: Oregon State University Press, 1999.

Ellis, Derek V., ed. *Pacific Salmon Management for People*. Western Geographical Series, volume 13. Victoria, B.C.: University of Victoria, 1977.

Emmons, George Thornton. *The Tlingit Indians*, edited by Frederica de Laguna. Seattle: University of Washington Press, 1991.

Fagan, Brian M. *The Great Journey: The Peopling of Ancient America*. New York: Thames and Hudson, 1987.

Faragher, John Mack, ed. *Rereading Frederick Jackson Turner: "The Significance of the Frontier in American History" and Other Essays*. New York: Henry Holt and Company, 1994.

Fields, Leslie Leyland. *The Entangling Net: Alaska's Commercial Fishing Women Tell Their Lives*. Chicago: University of Illinois Press, 1997.

Fisher, Robin. *Contact and Conflict: Indian-European Relations in British Columbia, 1774–1890*. Vancouver: University of British Columbia Press, 1977.

Fladmark, Knut R. *British Columbia Prehistory*. Ottawa: National Museums of Canada, 1986.

Forbes, Jack. "Frontiers in American History." *Journal of the West* 1, no. 1 (July 1962): 62–72.

Forde, C. Daryll. *Habitat, Economy, and Society: A Geographical Introduction to Ethnology*. New York: Harcourt Brace, 1934.

Friday, Chris. "Competing Communities at Work: Asian Americans, Euro-Americans, and Native Alaskans in the Pacific Northwest, 1938–1947." In *Over the Edge: Remapping the American West*, edited by Valerie J. Matsumoto and Blake Allmendinger. Berkeley: University of California Press, 1999.

———. *Organizing Asian American Labor: The Pacific Coast Canned-Salmon Industry, 1870–1942*. Philadelphia: Temple University Press, 1994.

Garfield, Viola. "A Research Problem in Northwest Indian Economics." *American Anthropologist* 47 (October–December 1945): 626–630.

Gibson, James R. *Imperial Russia in Frontier America: The Changing Geography of Supply of Russian America, 1784–1867*. New York: Oxford University Press, 1976.

———. *Otter Skins, Boston Ships, and China Goods: The Maritime Fur Trade of the Northwest Coast, 1785–1841*. Montreal: McGill-Queen's University Press, 1992.

———. "European Dependence upon American Natives: The Case of Russian America." *Ethnohistory* 25 (fall 1978): 359–383.

Glavin, Terry. *The Last Great Sea: A Voyage through the Human and Natural History of the North Pacific Ocean*. Vancouver, B.C.: Greystone Books, 2000.

Goble, Dale D. "Salmon in the Columbia Basin: From Abundance to Extinction." In *Northwest Lands, Northwest Peoples: Readings in Environmental History*, edited by Dale D. Goble and Paul W. Hirt. Seattle: University of Washington Press, 1999.

Goldschmidt, Walter R., and Theodore H. Haas. *Haa Aaní / Our Land: Tlingit and Haida Land Rights and Use*, edited by Thomas F. Thornton. Seattle: University of Washington Press, 1998.

Golovin, P. N. *The End of Russian America: Captain P. N. Golovin's Last Report, 1862*, translated by Basil Dmytryshyn and E. A. P. Crownhart-Vaughan. Portland: Oregon Historical Society, 1979.

Gordon, H. Scott. "The Economic Theory of a Common-Property Resource: The Fishery." *Journal of Political Economy* 62 (April 1954): 124–142.

Gregory, Homer E., and Kathleen Barnes. *North Pacific Fisheries with Special Reference to Alaska Salmon*. New York: American Council Institute of Pacific Relations, 1939.

Grinnell, George Bird. *Alaska 1899: Essays from the Harriman Expedition*. Seattle: University of Washington Press, 1995.

Groot, C., and L. Margolis. *Pacific Salmon Life Histories.* Vancouver: University of British Columbia Press, 1998.

Gruening, Ernest. *The State of Alaska.* New York: Random House, 1954.

Hardin, Garrett. "The Tragedy of the Commons." *Science* 62 (December 13, 1968): 1243–1248.

Harris, Douglass C. *Fish, Law, and Colonialism: The Legal Capture of Salmon in British Columbia.* Toronto: University of Toronto Press, 2001.

Haycox, Stephen. *Alaska: An American Colony.* Seattle: University of Washington Press, 2002.

———. *Frigid Embrace: Politics, Economics, and Environment in Alaska.* Corvallis: Oregon State University Press, 2002.

———. "'Races of a Questionable Type': Origins of the Jurisdiction of the U.S. Bureau of Education in Alaska, 1867–1885." *Pacific Northwest Quarterly* 75 (October 1984): 156–163.

Haycox, Stephen, and Mary Childers Mangusso. *An Alaska Anthology: Interpreting the Past.* Seattle: University of Washington Press, 1996.

Hayden, Brian., ed. *A Complex Culture of the British Columbia Plateau: Traditional Stl'átl'imx Resource Use.* Vancouver: University of British Columbia Press, 1992.

Hays, Samuel P. *Conservation and the Gospel of Efficiency: The Progressive Conservation Movement, 1890–1920.* Cambridge: Harvard University Press, 1959.

Hewes, Gordon Winant. "Aboriginal Use of Fishery Resources in Northwestern North America." Ph.D. dissertation, University of California, Berkeley, 1947.

Hinckley, Ted C. *The Americanization of Alaska, 1867–1897.* Palo Alto, Calif.: Pacific Books, 1972.

———. *The Canoe Rocks: Alaska's Tlingit and the Euramerican Frontier, 1800–1912.* Lanham, Md.: University Press of America, 1996.

———, ed. "'The Canoe Rocks—We Do Not Know What Will Become of US': The Complete Transcript of a Meeting between Governor John Green Brady of Alaska and a Group of Tlingit Chiefs, Juneau, December 14, 1898." *Western Historical Quarterly* 1 (July 1970): 269–283.

Hites, Ronald A., et al. "Global Assessments of Organic Contaminants in Farmed Salmon." *Science* 303, no. 5655 (January 9, 2004): 226–229.

Hosmer, Brian. *American Indians in the Marketplace: Persistence and Innovation among the Menominees and Metlakatlans, 1870s–1920.* Lawrence: University Press of Kansas, 1999.

Howay, F. W. *A List of Trading Vessels in the Maritime Fur Trade, 1785–1825.* Kingston, Ontario: Limestone Press, 1973.

Howay, F. W., W. N. Sage, and H. F. Angus. *British Columbia and the United States: The North Pacific Slope from Fur Trade to Aviation.* Toronto: Ryerson Press, 1942.

Hume, Stephen, et al. *A Stain upon the Sea: West Coast Salmon Farming.* Madeira Park, B.C.: Harbour Publishing, 2004.

Hunt, William R. *History of the Marine Hatcheries of Alaska*. Anchorage: Alaska Sea Grant Program, University of Alaska Press, 1976.

Jacoby, Karl. *Crimes against Nature: Squatters, Poachers, Thieves, and the Hidden History of American Conservation*. Berkeley: University of California Press, 2001.

Jensen, Ronald J. *The Alaska Purchase and Russian-American Relations*. Seattle: University of Washington Press, 1975.

Johnson, Paula J., ed. *Working the Water: The Commericial Fisheries of Maryland's Patuxent River*. Charlottesville: University Press of Virginia, 1988.

Johnson, Ralph W. "Regulation of Commercial Salmon Fishermen: A Case of Confused Objectives." *Pacific Northwest Quarterly* 55, no. 4 (October 1964): 141–145.

Josephson, Karla. *Use of the Sea by Alaska Natives—A Historical Perspective*. Anchorage, Alaska: Arctic Environmental Information and Data Center, 1974.

Kan, Sergei. *Memory Eternal: Tlingit Culture and Russian Orthodox Christianity through Two Centuries*. Seattle: University of Washington Press, 1999.

———. *Symbolic Immortality: The Tlingit Potlatch of the Nineteenth Century*. Washington, D.C.: Smithsonian Institution Press, 1989.

Karpoff, Mark. "Entry Limitation and the Market for Limited Entry Permits in the Alaska Salmon Fisheries." Ph.D. dissertation, University of California, Los Angeles, 1982.

Kew, Michael J., and Julian Griggs. "Native Indians of the Fraser Basin: Towards a Model of Sustainable Resource Use." In *Perspectives on Sustainable Development in Water Management: Towards Agreement in the Fraser River Basin*, edited by Anthony H. J. Dorcey. Vancouver: University of British Columbia, Westwater Research Centre, 1991.

Khlebnikov, Kyrill T. *Colonial Russian America: Kyrill T. Khelbnikov's Reports, 1817–1832*, translated by Basil Dmytryshyn and E. A. P. Crownhart-Vaughan. Portland: Oregon Historical Society, 1976.

Knapp, Gunnar. "Challenges and Strategies for the Alaska Salmon Industry." *Alaska Business Monthly* 18, no. 10 (October 2002): 132.

———. "Implications of Aquaculture for Wild Fisheries: The Case of Alaska Wild Salmon." Presentation for the Bevan Sustainable Fisheries Lecture Series, University of Washington, Seattle, February 10, 2005.

Knight, Rolf. *Indians at Work: An Informal History of Native Indian Labor in British Columbia, 1858–1930*. Vancouver, B.C.: New Star Books, 1978.

Köepf, Michael. *The Fisherman's Son*. New York: Broadway Books, 1998.

Koppes, Clayton R. "Efficiency/Equity/Esthetics: Towards a Reinterpretation of American Conservation." *Environmental Review* 11 (summer 1989): 127–145.

Koughan, Helen. "An Account of the Alaskan Salmon Industry since 1978, with Reference to Conservation." M.A. thesis, University of California, Berkeley, 1931.

Krause, Aurel. *The Tlingit Indians: Results of a Trip to the Northwest Coast of Amer-*

ica and the Bering Straits, translated by Erna Gunther. 1885; reprinted, Seattle: University of Washington Press, 1956.

Krech, Shepard, III. *The Ecological Indian: Myth and History*. New York: W. W. Norton & Company, 1999.

———. *Indians, Animals, and the Fur Trade: A Critique of "Keepers of the Game."* Athens: University of Georgia, 1981.

Kresge, David T., Thomas A. Morehouse, and George W. Rogers. *Issues in Alaska Development*. Seattle: University of Washington Press, 1977.

Kroeber, A. L., and S. A. Barrett. *Fishing among the Indians of Northwest California*. University of California Publications in American Archaeology and Ethnography No. 21. Berkeley: University of California Press, 1960.

Kushner, Howard I. *Conflict on the Northwest Coast: American-Russian Rivalry in the Pacific Northwest, 1790–1867*. London: Greenwood Press, 1975.

Lain, Bobby Dave. "North of Fifty-Three: Army, Treasury Department, and Navy Administration of Alaska, 1867–1884." Ph.D. dissertation, University of Texas, Austin, 1974.

Langdon, Steve. "From Communal Property to Common Property to Limited Entry: Historical Ironies in the Management of Southeast Alaska Salmon." In *A Sea of Small Boats*, edited by John Cordell. Cambridge, Mass.: Cultural Survival, Inc., 1989.

———. "Technology, Ecology, and Economy: Fishing Systems in Southeast Alaska." Ph.D. dissertation, Stanford University, 1977.

La Pérouse, Jean François Galaup, comte de. *A Voyage round the World, Performed in the Years 1785, 1786, 1787, and 1788, by the Boussole and Astrolabe*. 3 volumes. London: Lackington, Allen, and Co., 1807.

Larkin, Peter. *Pacific Salmon: Scenarios for the Future*. Washington Sea Grant No. NA79AA-D-00054. Seattle: Division of Marine Resources, University of Washington, 1980.

Lichatowich, Jim. *Salmon without Rivers: A History of the Pacific Salmon Crisis*. Washington, D.C.: Island Press, 1999.

Limerick, Patricia Nelson. *The Legacy of Conquest: The Unbroken Past of the American West*. New York: W. W. Norton & Company, 1987.

Limerick, Patricia Nelson, Clyde A. Milner II, and Charles E. Rankin, eds. *Trails: Toward a New Western History*. Lawrence: University Press of Kansas, 1991.

Littlefield, Alice, and Martha C. Knack. *Native Americans and Wage Labor: Ethnohistorical Perspectives*. Norman: University of Oklahoma Press, 1996.

Lord, Nancy. *Fish Camp: Life on an Alaskan Shore*. Washington, D.C.: Counterpoint, 1997.

Lowell, Joan. *The Cradle of the Deep*. New York: Simon and Schuster, 1929.

Lummis, Trevor. *Occupation and Society: The East Anglican Fishermen, 1880–1914*. London: Cambridge University Press, 1985.

Marchak, Patricia, Neil Guppy, and John McMullan, eds. *Uncommon Property: The Fishing and Fish Processing Industries in British Columbia*. Toronto: Methuen Publications, 1987.

Martin, Calvin. *Keepers of the Game: Indian-Animal Relationships and the Fur Trade*. Berkeley: University of California Press, 1978.

Martin, Irene. *Legacy and Testament: The Story of Columbia River Gillnetters*. Pullman: Washington State University Press, 1994.

Martin, Paul S. "Prehistoric Overkill." In *Pleistocene Extinctions: The Search for a Cause*, edited by P. S. Martin and H. E. Wright Jr. New Haven, Conn.: Yale University Press, 1967.

Masson, Jack, and Donald Guimary. "Asian Labor Contractors in the Alaskan Canned Salmon Industry: 1880–1937." *Labor History* 22, no. 3 (summer 1981): 377–397.

May, Earl Chapin. *The Canning Clan: A Pageant of Pioneering Americans*. New York: Macmillan Company, 1938.

McCay, Bonnie J., and James Acheson, eds. *The Question of the Commons: The Culture and Ecology of Communal Resources*. Tucson: University of Arizona Press, 1987.

McEvoy, Arthur F. *The Fisherman's Problem: Ecology and Law in the California Fisheries, 1850–1980*. New York: Cambridge University Press, 1986.

McKervill, Hugh W. *The Salmon People: The Story of Canada's West Coast Fishing Industry*. Vancouver, B.C.: Grays Publishing, 1967.

McNeill, J. R. *Something New under the Sun*.

McPhail, J. D. "The Origin and Speciation of *Oncorhynchus* Revisited." In *Pacific Salmon and Their Ecosystems: Status and Future Options*, edited by Deanna J. Stouder, Peter A. Bisson, and Robert J. Naiman. New York: Chapman and Hall, 1997.

McPhee, John. *Coming into the Country*. New York: Farrar, Straus and Giroux, 1977.

Merchant, Carolyn. "Fish First! The Changing Ethics of Ecosystem Management." In *Northwest Lands, Northwest Peoples: Readings in Environmental History*, edited by Dale D. Goble and Paul W. Hirt. Seattle: University of Washington Press, 1999.

Merrell, James H. *The Indians' New World: Catawbas and Their Neighbors from European Contact through the Era of Removal*. New York: W. W. Norton & Company, 1991.

Miller, Orlando W. *The Frontier in Alaska and the Matanuska Colony*. New Haven, Conn.: Yale University Press, 1975.

Mitchell, Donald Craig. *Sold American: The Story of Alaska Natives and Their Land, 1867–1959*. Hanover, N.H.: University Press of New England, 1997.

———. *Take My Land, Take My Life: The Story of Congress's Historic Settlement of Alaska Native Land Claims, 1960–1971*. Fairbanks: University of Alaska Press, 2001.

Mohr, Joan Antonson. *Alaska and the Sea: A Survey of Alaska's Maritime History*. Anchorage, Alaska: Office of History & Archaeology, Alaska Division of Parks, 1979.

Montes, Felix Anton. "Alaska Fishermen and the Anti-Trust Laws." M.A. thesis, University of Washington, 1947.

Montgomery, David R. *King of Fish: The Thousand Year Run of Salmon.* Cambridge, Mass.: Westview Press, 2003.

Morehouse, Thomas A., and George W. Rogers. *Limited Entry in the Alaska and British Columbia Salmon Fisheries.* Anchorage: University of Alaska Institute of Social and Economic Research, 1980.

Morse, Kathryn. *The Nature of Gold: An Environmental History of the Klondike Gold Rush.* Seattle: University of Washington Press, 2003.

Moss, M. L., J. M. Earlandson, and R. Stuckenrath. "Wood Stake Fish Weirs and Salmon Fishing on the Northwest Coast: Evidence from Southeast Alaska." *Canadian Journal of Archaeology* 14 (1990): 148–153.

Muir, John. *Travels in Alaska.* New York: Houghton Mifflin Company, 1979.

Naske, Claus M. "Alaska's Long and Sometimes Painful Relationship with the Lower Forty-Eight." In *The Changing Pacific Northwest: Interpreting Its Past,* edited by David H. Stratton and George A. Frykman. Pullman: Washington State University Press, 1988.

Naske, Claus M., and Herman E. Slotnick. *Alaska: A History of the Forty-ninth State.* Norman: University of Oklahoma Press, 1994.

Nelson, Bruce. *Workers on the Waterfront: Seamen, Longshoremen, and Unionism in the 1930s.* Urbana: University of Illinois Press, 1988.

Nelson, Richard K. "A Conservation Ethic and Environment: The Koyukon of Alaska." In *Resource Managers: North American and Australian Hunter-Gatherers,* edited by Nancy M. Williams and Eugene S. Hunn. Boulder, Colo.: Westview Press, 1982.

Netboy, Anthony. *The Salmon: Their Fight for Survival.* Boston: Houghton Mifflin Company, 1974.

Newell, Diane. *The Development of the Pacific Salmon Canning Industry: A Grown Man's Game.* Montreal: McGill-Queen's University Press, 1989.

———. "The Rationality of Mechanization in the Pacific Salmon-Canning Industry before the Second World War." *Business History Review* 62 (winter 1988): 626–655.

———. *Tangled Webs of History: Indians and the Law in Canada's Pacific Coast Fisheries.* Toronto: University of Toronto Press, 1993.

Newton, Richard, and Madonna Moss. *The Subsistence Lifeway of the Tlingit People: Excerpts of Oral Interviews.* Juneau, Alaska: U.S. Forest Service, 1984.

Niblack, Albert P. "The Coast Indians of Southern Alaska and Northern British Columbia." In *Report of the U.S. National Museum under the Direction of the Smithsonian Institution for the Year Ending June 30, 1888.* Washington, D.C.: GPO, 1890.

Nichols, Jeannette Paddock. *Alaska: A History of Its Administration, Exploitation, and Industrial Development during Its First Half Century under the Rule of the United States.* New York: Russell & Russell, 1963.

O'Bannon, Patrick W. "Technological Change in the Pacific Coast Canned Salmon Industry, 1900–1925: A Case Study." *Agricultural History* 56 (January 1982): 151–166.

Oberg, Kalervo. "Crime and Punishment in Tlingit Society." In *Indians of the North Pacific Coast*, edited by Tom McFeat. Seattle: University of Washington Press, 1966.

———. *The Social Economy of the Tlingit Indians*. Seattle: University of Washington Press, 1973.

Overholt, T. W. "American Indians as 'Natural Ecologists.'" *American Indian Journal* 5 (September 1979): 9–16.

Pearcy, William G. *Ocean Ecology of North Pacific Salmonids*. Seattle: University of Washington Press, 1992.

Peterson, Jacqueline, and John Anfinson. "The Indian and the Fur Trade: A Review of Recent Literature." In *Scholars and the Indian Experience: Critical Reviews of Recent Writing in the Social Sciences*, edited by W. R. Swagerty. Bloomington: Indiana University Press, 1984.

Philp, Kenneth R. "The New Deal and Alaskan Natives, 1936–1945." *Pacific Historical Review* 50 (August 1981): 309–327.

Pinchot, Gifford. *Breaking New Ground*. New York: Harcourt Brace, 1947.

Price, Robert E. *The Great Father in Alaska: The Case of the Tlingit and Haida Salmon Fishery*. Douglas, Alaska: First Street Press, 1990.

Quinn, Thomas P. *The Behavior and Ecology of Pacific Salmon and Trout*. Seattle: University of Washington Press, 2005.

Randall, R. L. "Labor Agreements in the West Coast Fishing Industry." *Industrial Labor Relations Review* 3 (July 1950): 514–541.

Remsberg, Stanley Ray. "United States Administration of Alaska: The Army Phase, 1867–1877; A Study in Federal Governance of an Overseas Possession." Ph.D. dissertation, University of Wisconsin, 1975.

Ritter, Kathleen V. "Internal Colonialism and Industrial Development in Alaska." *Ethnic and Racial Studies* 2 (July 1979): 319–340.

Robbins, William G. "The World of Columbia River Salmon: Nature, Culture, and the Great River of the West." In *The Northwest Salmon Crisis: A Documentary History*, edited by Joseph Cone and Sandy Ridlington. Corvallis: Oregon State University Press, 1996.

Roche, Judith, and Meg McHutchison, eds. *First Fish, First People: Salmon Tales of the North Pacific Rim*. Seattle: University of Washington Press, 1998.

Rogers, George W. *Alaska in Transition: The Southeast Region*. Baltimore, Md.: Johns Hopkins University Press, 1960.

Roppel, Patricia. *Alaska's Salmon Hatcheries, 1891–1959*. Alaska Historical Commission Studies in History No. 20. Portland, Ore.: National Marine Fisheries Service, 1982.

Schairer, Rosemary Agnes. "A Survey of the Alaskan Salmon-Canning Industry in the Post-War Period." M.A. thesis, University of Washington, 1956.

Schalk, Randall F. "The Structure of an Anadromous Fish Resource." In *For Theory Building in Archaeology: Essays on Faunal Remains, Aquatic Resources, Spatial*

Analysis, and Systemic Modeling, edited by Lewis R. Binford. New York: Academic Press, 1977.

Schreiber, Dorothee. "First Nations, Consultation, and the Rule of Law: Salmon Farming and Colonialism in British Columbia." *American Indian Culture and Research Journal* 30, no. 4 (2006): 19–40.

Scott, Anthony. "The Fishery: The Objectives of Sole Ownership." *Journal of Political Economy* 63, no. 2 (April 1955): 116–124.

Scott, James C. *Seeing Like a State: How Certain Schemes to Improve the Human Condition Have Failed*. New Haven, Conn.: Yale University Press, 1998.

Scudder, H. C. *The Alaska Salmon Trap: Its Evolution, Conflicts, and Consequences*. Juneau: Alaska State Library, 1970.

Shepard, M. P., and A. W. Argue. *The 1985 Pacific Salmon Treaty: Sharing Conservation Burdens and Benefits*. Vancouver: University of British Columbia Press, 2005.

Smith, Courtland L. "Evolution of the Pacific Canned Salmon Fishery." In *The Fishing Culture of the World: Studies in Ethnology, Cultural Ecology and Folklore*, volume 2, edited by B. Gunda. Budapest, Hungary: Akademiai Kiado, 1984.

———. *Salmon Fisheries of the Columbia*. Corvallis: Oregon State University, 1974.

Spence, Mark David. *Dispossessing the Wilderness: Indian Removal and the Making of the National Parks*. New York: Oxford University Press, 1999.

Steller, Georg Wilhelm. *Journal of a Voyage with Bering, 1741–1742*. Stanford, Calif.: Stanford University Press, 1988.

Stewart, Hilary. *Indian Fishing: Early Methods on the Northwest Coast*. Seattle: University of Washington Press, 1977.

Sutherland, Dan A. *The Looting of Alaska's Resources: Speech of Hon. Dan Sutherland of Alaska in the House of Representatives*. Washington, D.C.: GPO, 1923.

Suttles, Wayne. "Coping with Abundance: Subsistence on the Northwest Coast." In *Man the Hunter*, edited by Richard B. Lee and Irven DeVore. Chicago: Aldine Publishing Company, 1968.

———, ed. *Handbook of North American Indians*. Volume 7, *Northwest Coast*. Washington, D.C.: Smithsonian Institution Press, 1990.

Swanton, John R., ed. *Tlingit Myths and Texts*. Bureau of American Ethnology, Bulletin 39. Washington, D.C.: GPO, 1909.

Swezey, Sean L., and Robert F. Heizer. "Ritual Management of Salmonid Fish Resources in California." In *Before the Wilderness: Environmental Management by Native Californians*, edited by Thomas C. Blackburn and Kat Anderson. Menlo Park, Calif.: Ballena Press, 1993.

Swineford, A. P. *Alaska: Its History, Climate, and Natural Resources*. New York: Rand, McNally & Company, 1898.

Taylor, Joseph E., III. "Burning the Candle at Both Ends: Historicizing Overfishing in Oregon's Nineteenth-Century Salmon Fisheries." *Environmental History* 4 (January 1999): 54–79.

———. "El Niño and Vanishing Salmon: Culture, Nature, History, and the Politics of Blame." *Western Historical Quarterly* 24 (winter 1998): 437–457.

———. *Making Salmon: An Environmental History of the Northwest Fisheries Crisis*. Seattle: University of Washington Press, 1999.

———. "Master of the Seas? Herbert Hoover and the Western Fisheries." *Oregon Historical Quarterly* 105 (spring 2004): 40–61.

———. "Well-Thinking Men and Women: The Battle for the White Act and the Meaning of Conservation in the 1920s." *Pacific Historical Review* 71 (August 2002): 357–387.

Tikhmenev, P. A. *A History of the Russian-American Company*. 1888; reprinted, Seattle: University of Washington Press, 1978.

Thompson, Paul, Tony Wailey, and Trevor Lummis. *Living the Fishing*. London: Routledge & Kegan Paul, 1983.

Thornton, Russell. *American Indian Holocaust and Survival: A Population History since 1492*. Norman: University of Oklahoma Press, 1987.

Tunstall, Jerry. *The Fishermen*. London: Macgibbon & Kee, 1962.

Tussing, Arlon R., Thomas A. Morehouse, and James D. Babb Jr. *Alaska Fisheries Policy: Economics, Resources, and Management*. Fairbanks, Alaska: Institute of Social, Economic, and Government Research, 1972.

Tuttle, Charles R. *Alaska: Its Meaning to the World, Its Resources, Its Opportunities*. Seattle, Wa.: Franklin Shuey & Co., Publishers, 1914.

Upton, Joe. *Alaska Blues: A Fisherman's Journal*. Anchorage: Alaska Northwest Books, 1977.

———. *Journeys through the Inside Passage: Seafaring Adventures along the Coast of British Columbia and Alaska*. Anchorage: Alaska Northwest Books, 1992.

Vancouver, George. *A Voyage of Discovery to the North Pacific Ocean and round the World, 1791–1795*, edited by W. Kaye Lamb, volume 1. London: Hakluyt Society, 1984.

Wadewitz, Lissa. "Pirates of the Salish Sea: Labor, Mobility, and Environment in the Transnational West." *Pacific Historical Review* 75 (November 2006): 587–627.

Warren, Louis S. *The Hunter's Game: Poachers and Conservationists in Twentieth-Century America*. New Haven, Conn.: Yale University Press, 1997.

White, Richard. "'Are You an Environmentalist or Do You Work for a Living?': Work and Nature." In *Uncommon Ground: Rethinking the Human Place in Nature*, edited by William Cronon. New York: W. W. Norton & Company, 1996.

———. "Indian Peoples and the Natural World: Asking the Right Questions." In *Rethinking American Indian History*, edited by Donald L. Fixico. Albuquerque: University of New Mexico Press, 1997.

———. *The Middle Ground: Indians, Empires, and Republics in the Great Lakes Region, 1650–1815*. New York: Cambridge University Press, 1991.

———. "Native Americans and the Environment." In *Scholars and the Indian Expe-*

rience: Critical Reviews of Recent Writing in the Social Sciences, edited by W. R. Swagerty. Bloomington: Indiana University Press, 1984.

———. *The Organic Machine: The Remaking of the Columbia River*. New York: Hill and Wang, 1995.

———. *The Roots of Dependency: Subsistence, Environment, and Social Change among the Choctaws, Pawnees, and Navajos*. Lincoln: University of Nebraska Press, 1983.

White, Richard, and William Cronon. "Ecological Change and Indian-White Relations." In *Handbook of North American Indians*. Volume 4, *History of Indian-White Relations*, edited by Wilcomb Washburn. Washington, D.C.: Smithsonian Institution Press, 1988.

Wike, Joyce Annabel. "The Effect of the Maritime Fur Trade on Northwest Coast Indian Society." Ph.D. dissertation, Columbia University, 1951.

Wolf, Edward C., and Seth Zuckerman, eds. *Salmon Nation: People, Fish, and Our Common Home*. Portland, Ore.: Ecotrust, 2003.

Worl, Rosita. "History of Southeastern Alaska since 1867." In *Handbook of North American Indians*, edited by William C. Sturtevant. Volume 7, *Northwest Coast*, edited by Wayne Suttles. Washington, D.C.: Smithsonian Institution Press, 1990, 149–158.

Worster, Donald. "New West, True West: Interpreting the Region's Past." *Western Historical Quarterly* 18 (April 1987).

Wyatt, Victoria. "Alaskan Indian Wage Earners in the Nineteenth Century: Economic Choices and Ethnic Identity on Southeast Alaska's Frontier." *Pacific Northwest Quarterly* 78 (April 1987): 43–49.

GOVERNMENT REPORTS AND OTHER DOCUMENTS

All Alaska Labor Conventions, Proceedings. Juneau, Alaska, 1938–1942. Available at the Alaska Historical Library, Juneau.

Goldschmidt, Walter R., and Theodore H. Haas. "Possessory Rights of the Natives of Southeastern Alaska." In *Report to the Commissioner of Indian Affairs* (October 3, 1946). Available at the Alaska Historical Library, Juneau, Alaska.

Gsovski, Vladimir. *Russian Administration of Alaska and the Status of the Alaskan Natives*. 81st Cong., 2d sess., S. Doc. No. 152. Washington, D.C.: Government Printing Office (GPO), 1950.

Kutchin, Howard M. *Report of the Special Agent for the Protection of the Alaska Salmon Fisheries*. 56th Cong., 1st sess., S. Doc. No. 153. Washington, D.C.: GPO, 1900.

———. *Report on the Salmon Fisheries of Alaska, 1900*. 56th Cong., 2d sess., S. Doc. No. 168. Washington, D.C.: GPO, 1901.

———. *Report on the Salmon Fisheries of Alaska, 1901*. 57th Cong., 1st sess., S. Doc. No. 138. Washington, D.C.: GPO, 1902.

———. *Report on the Salmon Fisheries of Alaska, 1902*. 57th Cong., 2d sess., S. Doc. No. 113. Washington, D.C.: GPO, 1903.

Langdon, Steve. *Transfer Patterns in Alaskan Limited Entry Fisheries: Final Report for the Limited Entry Study Group of the Alaska State Legislature*. Juneau, Alaska. 1980.

Morris, William Gouverneur. *Report upon the Customs District, Public Service, and Resources of Alaska Territory*. U.S. Treasury Department. Washington, D.C.: GPO, 1879.

Norris, Frank. *Alaska Subsistence: A National Park Service Management History* Anchorage, Alaska: U.S. Department of Interior, 2002.

Petroff, Ivan. "Report of the Population, Industries, and Resources of Alaska." In *Tenth Census of the United States, 1880, Special Reports on Newspaper Periodicals, Alaska, Fur-Seal Islands, and Shipbuilding*. Washington, D.C.: GPO, 1884.

Porter, Robert. *Report on the Population and Resources of Alaska at the Eleventh Census: 1890*. Washington, D.C.: GPO, 1893.

Proceedings of the Fifth Annual Convention of the Alaska Territorial Federation of Labor. Juneau, February 8–13, 1947. Available at the Alaska Historical Library, Juneau.

State of Alaska, Governor's Office. *A Limited Entry Program for Alaska's Fisheries: Report of the Governor's Study Group on Limited Entry*. Juneau, Alaska. 1973.

U.S. Department of Commerce, Bureau of Fisheries. "Hearings Conducted by the U.S. Bureau of Fisheries in Regulating the Fisheries of Alaska, 1907–1921." Volume 2, 1915–1917. Unpublished typed transcripts available at the University of Washington Special Collections Library, Seattle.

———. "Hearings Conducted by the U.S. Bureau of Fisheries in Regulating the Fisheries of Alaska, 1907–1921." Volume 4, 1919. Unpublished typed transcripts available at the University of Washington Special Collections Library, Seattle.

U.S. Department of Commerce and Labor, Bureau of Statistics. *Commercial Alaska, 1867–1903. Area, Population, Production, Railways, Telegraphs, Transportation Routes, and Commerce with the United States and Foreign Countries*. Washington, D.C.: GPO, 1903.

U.S. Department of Commerce and Labor, Bureau of the Census. *Special Reports: Fisheries of the U.S.* Washington, D.C.: GPO, 1911.

U.S. Department of Interior. *Hearings upon Claims of Natives of Alaska Pursuant to the Provisions of Section 201.21b of the Regulations for Protection of the Commercial Fisheries in Alaska*. 16 volumes (1944). Available at the Alaska Historical Library, Juneau.

U.S. House of Representatives. *Affairs in Alaska*. 47th Cong., 2d sess., 1883, H. Ex. Doc. No. 9, part 3.

———. *Alaska Salmon Commission: Message from the President of the United States, Transmitting a Communication from the Secretary of Commerce and Labor Submitting a Preliminary Report of the Alaska Salmon Commission*. 58th Cong., 2d sess., H. Doc. No. 477. Washington, D.C.: GPO, 1904.

———. *Alleged Shelling of Alaskan Villages*. 47th Cong., 2d sess., 1883, H. Ex. Doc. No. 9.

———. *Condition of the Inhabitants of Alaska*. 42nd Cong., 2d sess., 1872, H. Ex. Doc. No. 197.

———. *Russian America*. 40th Cong., 2d sess., 1868, H. Ex. Doc. No. 177.

———. *Salmon Fisheries of Alaska: Reports of Special Agents Pracht, Luttrell, and Murray for the Years 1892, 1893, 1894, 1895*. In *Seal and Salmon Fisheries and General Resources of Alaska*. 55th Cong., 1st sess., 1898, H. Doc. No. 92.

———. *Shelling of an Indian Village in Alaska*. 47th Cong., 2d sess., 1883, H. Ex. Doc. No. 9, part 2.

U.S. House of Representatives, Committee on Interior and Insular Affairs. *Alaska Statehood and Elective Governorship*. 83rd Cong., 1st sess. Washington, D.C.: GPO, 1953.

———. *Alaska Statehood: Hearings before the Committee on Interior and Insular Affairs*. 81st Cong., 2d sess. Washington, D.C.: GPO, 1950.

U.S. House of Representatives, Committee on the Merchant Marine and Fisheries. *Alaska Fisheries: Hearings before the Committee on the Merchant Marine and Fisheries*. 64th Cong., 1st sess. Washington, D.C.: GPO, 1916.

———. *Committee Study Resolution—Alaskan Fisheries Hearings: Hearings before the Subcommittee on Alaskan Fisheries of the Committee on the Merchant Marine and Fisheries*. 76th Cong., 1st sess., parts 1–3. Washington, D.C.: GPO, 1939.

———. *Committee Study Resolution—Alaskan Fisheries Hearings before the Subcommittee on Alaskan Fisheries of the Committee on the Merchant Marine and Fisheries*. 76th Cong., 3d sess., part 4. Washington, D.C.: GPO, 1940.

———. *Elimination of Salmon Traps in the Waters of Alaska*. 81st Cong., 1st sess. Washington, D.C.: GPO, 1949.

———. *Fisheries in Alaska: Hearings before the Committee on the Merchant Marine and Fisheries*. 67th Cong., 1st sess. Washington, D.C.: GPO, 1921.

———. *Fisheries in Alaska: Hearings before the Subcommittee of the Committee on the Merchant Marine and Fisheries on Fish and Fish Hatcheries*. 67th Cong., 2d sess., part 2. Washington, D.C.: GPO, 1922.

———. *Fisheries of Alaska: Hearings before the Committee on the Merchant Marine and Fisheries*. 68th Cong., 1st sess. Washington, D.C.: GPO, 1924.

———. *Fish Traps in Alaskan Waters: Hearings on H.R. 4254 and H.R. 8213*. 74th Cong., 2d sess. Washington, D.C.: GPO, 1936.

———. *Hearings before the Committee on Merchant Marine and Fisheries on H.R. 5476, H.R. 7542, H.R. 8172, H.R. 6690, H.R. 7987, H.R. 7988, and H.R. 8115*. 76th Cong., 3d sess. Washington, D.C.: GPO, 1940.

———. *Hearings before the Subcommittee on Alaskan Fisheries of the Committee on Merchant Marine and Fisheries on H. Res. 162*. 76th Cong., 1st sess., part 2. Washington, D.C.: GPO, 1939.

———. *Merchant Marine and Fisheries Problems—Alaska and Pacific Coast: Hear-*

ings before the Alaska Subcommittee of the Committee on Merchant Marine and Fisheries. 85th Cong., 1st sess. Washington, D.C.: GPO, 1957.
U.S. House of Representatives, Committee on the Territories. *Fisheries in Alaska.* 59th Cong., 1st sess. Washington, D.C.: GPO, 1906.
———. *Hearings before the Committee on the Territories.* 79th Cong., 1st sess. Washington, D.C.: GPO, 1946.
U.S. Senate. *Alaska Native Subsistence and Fishing Rights: Hearing before the Committee on Indian Affairs.* 176th Cong., 2d sess. Washington, D.C.: GPO, 2002.

FISHERIES REPORTS

Bean, Tarelton H. "Report on the Salmon and Salmon Rivers of Alaska, with Notes on the Conditions, Methods, and Needs for the Salmon Fisheries." In *Bulletin of the United States Fish Commission,* volume 9. Washington, D.C.: GPO, 1891.
Bower, Ward T. *Alaska Fisheries and Fur Industries in 1919.* Bureau of Fisheries Doc. No. 891. Washington, D.C.: GPO, 1920.
———. *Alaska Fishery and Fur-Seal Industries in 1920.* Bureau of Fisheries Doc. No. 909. Washington, D.C.: GPO, 1921.
———. *Alaska Fishery and Fur-Seal Industries in 1921.* Bureau of Fisheries Doc. No. 933. Washington, D.C.: GPO, 1922.
———. *Alaska Fishery and Fur-Seal Industries in 1922.* Bureau of Fisheries Doc. No. 951. Washington, D.C.: GPO, 1923.
———. *Alaska Fishery and Fur-Seal Industries in 1923.* Bureau of Fisheries Doc. No. 973. Washington, D.C.: GPO, 1924.
———. *Alaska Fishery and Fur-Seal Industries in 1924.* Bureau of Fisheries Doc. No. 992. Washington, D.C.: GPO, 1925.
———. *Alaska Fishery and Fur-Seal Industries in 1925.* Bureau of Fisheries Doc. No. 1008. Washington, D.C.: GPO, 1926.
———. *Alaska Fishery and Fur-Seal Industries in 1926.* Bureau of Fisheries Doc. No. 1023. Washington, D.C.: GPO, 1927.
———. *Alaska Fishery and Fur-Seal Industries in 1927.* Bureau of Fisheries Doc. No. 1040. Washington, D.C.: GPO, 1928.
———. *Alaska Fishery and Fur-Seal Industries in 1928.* Bureau of Fisheries Doc. No. 1064. Washington, D.C.: GPO, 1929.
———. *Alaska Fishery and Fur-Seal Industries in 1929.* Bureau of Fisheries Doc. No. 1086. Washington, D.C.: GPO, 1930.
———. *Alaska Fishery and Fur-Seal Industries in 1930.* Appendix I to *Report of Commissioner of Fisheries for the Fiscal Year 1931.* Washington, D.C.: GPO, 1931.
———. *Alaska Fishery and Fur-Seal Industries in 1931.* Appendix I to *Report of Commissioner of Fisheries for the Fiscal Year 1932.* Washington, D.C.: GPO, 1932.

———. *Alaska Fishery and Fur-Seal Industries in 1932*. Appendix I to *Report of Commissioner of Fisheries for the Fiscal Year 1933*. Washington, D.C.: GPO, 1933.
———. *Alaska Fishery and Fur-Seal Industries in 1933*. Appendix II to *Report of Commissioner of Fisheries for the Fiscal Year 1934*. Washington, D.C.: GPO, 1934.
———. *Alaska Fishery and Fur-Seal Industries in 1934*. Appendix I to *Report of Commissioner of Fisheries for the Fiscal Year 1935*. Washington, D.C.: GPO, 1935.
———. *Alaska Fishery and Fur-Seal Industries in 1935*. Bureau of Fisheries Administrative Report No. 23. Washington, D.C.: GPO, 1936.
———. *Alaska Fishery and Fur-Seal Industries in 1936*. Bureau of Fisheries Administrative Report No. 28. Washington, D.C.: GPO, 1937.
———. *Alaska Fishery and Fur-Seal Industries in 1937*. Bureau of Fisheries Administrative Report No. 31. Washington, D.C.: GPO, 1938.
———. *Alaska Fishery and Fur-Seal Industries in 1938*. Bureau of Fisheries Administrative Report No. 36. Washington, D.C.: GPO, 1940.
———. *Alaska Fishery and Fur-Seal Industries in 1939*. Bureau of Fisheries Administrative Report No. 40. Washington, D.C.: GPO, 1941.
———. *Alaska Fishery and Fur-Seal Industries: 1940*. Department of Interior, Fish, and Wildlife Service. Statistical Digest No. 2. Washington, D.C.: GPO, 1942.
———. *Alaska Fishery and Fur Seal Industries: 1941*. Department of Interior, Fish, and Wildlife Service. Statistical Digest No. 5. Washington, D.C.: GPO, 1943.
———. *Alaska Fishery and Fur Seal Industries: 1942*. Department of Interior, Fish, and Wildlife Service. Statistical Digest No. 8. Washington, D.C.: GPO, 1944.
———. *Alaska Fishery and Fur-Seal Industries: 1943*. Department of Interior, Fish, and Wildlife Service. Statistical Digest No. 10. Washington, D.C.: GPO, 1944.
———. *Alaska Fishery and Fur Seal Industries: 1944*. Department of Interior, Fish, and Wildlife Service. Statistical Digest No. 13. Washington, D.C.: GPO, 1946.
———. *Alaska Fishery and Fur Seal Industries: 1945*. Department of Interior, Fish, and Wildlife Service. Statistical Digest No. 15. Washington, D.C.: GPO, 1948.
———. *Alaska Fishery and Fur Seal Industries: 1946*. Department of Interior, Fish, and Wildlife Service. Statistical Digest No. 17. Washington, D.C.: GPO, 1948.
———. *Alaska Fishery and Fur Seal Industries: 1947*. Department of Interior, Fish, and Wildlife Service. Statistical Digest No. 20. Washington, D.C.: GPO, 1950.
Bower, Ward T., and Henry D. Aller. *Alaska Fisheries and Fur Industries in 1914*. Bureau of Fisheries Doc. No. 819. Washington, D.C.: GPO, 1915.
———. *Alaska Fisheries and Fur Industries in 1915*. Bureau of Fisheries Doc. No. 834. Washington, D.C.: GPO, 1917.
———. *Alaska Fisheries and Fur Industries in 1916*. Bureau of Fisheries Doc. No. 838. Washington, D.C.: GPO, 1917.
———. *Alaska Fisheries and Fur Industries in 1917*. Bureau of Fisheries Doc. No. 847. Washington, D.C.: GPO, 1918.

———. *Alaska Fisheries and Fur Industries in 1918*. Bureau of Fisheries Doc. No. 872. Washington, D.C.: GPO, 1919.

Cobb, John N. *Pacific Salmon Fisheries: Report of the United States Commissioner of Fisheries for 1916*. Bureau of Fisheries Doc. No. 839. Washington, D.C.: GPO, 1917.

———. *Pacific Salmon Fisheries: Report of the United States Commissioner of Fisheries for 1921*. Bureau of Fisheries Doc. No. 902. Washington, D.C.: GPO, 1921.

———. *Pacific Salmon Fisheries: Report of the United States Commissioner of Fisheries for 1930*. Bureau of Fisheries Doc. No. 1092. Washington, D.C.: GPO, 1930.

———. *The Salmon Fisheries of the Pacific Coast*. Bureau of Fisheries Doc. No. 751. Washington, D.C.: GPO, 1911.

Cobb, John N., and Howard M. Kutchin. *The Fisheries of Alaska in 1906*. Bureau of Fisheries Doc. No. 618. Washington, D.C.: GPO, 1907.

Collins, J. W. "Report on the Fisheries of the Pacific Coast of the United States." In *Report of the Commissioner for 1888*. Washington, D.C.: GPO, 1892.

Craig, Joseph A., and Robert L. Hacker. *The History and Development of the Fisheries of the Columbia River*. Department of Interior. Bureau of Fisheries Bulletin 32. Washington, D.C.: GPO, 1940.

Evermann, Barton Warren. *Fishery and Fur Industries of Alaska in 1912*. Bureau of Fisheries Doc. No. 780. Washington, D.C.: GPO, 1913.

———. *Alaska Fisheries and Fur Industries in 1913*. Bureau of Fisheries Doc. No. 797. Washington, D.C.: GPO, 1914.

Evermann, Barton Warren, and F. M. Chamberlain. *Alaska Fisheries and Fur Industries in 1911*. Bureau of Fisheries Doc. No. 766. Washington, D.C.: GPO, 1912.

Goode, George Brown. *The Fisheries and Fishery Industries of the United States*. Prepared through the Co-operation of the Commissioner of Fisheries and the Superintendent of the Tenth Census. Washington, D.C.: GPO, 1887.

Jones, Lester E. *Report of the Alaska Investigations in 1914*. Washington, D.C.: GPO, 1915.

Kamali, Nasser. *Alaskan Natives and Limited Fisheries of Alaska: A Study of Changes in the Distribution of Permit Ownership amongst Alaskan Natives, 1975–1983*. Alaska Commercial Fisheries Entry Commission Report No. 84–8. Juneau, Alaska. 1984.

Kutchin, Howard M. *Report on the Salmon Fisheries of Alaska, 1897*. U.S. Treasury Department Doc. No. 2010. Washington: GPO, 1898.

———. *Report on the Salmon Fisheries of Alaska, 1898*. U.S. Treasury Department Doc. No. 2095. Washington, D.C.: GPO, 1899.

———. *Report on the Salmon Fisheries of Alaska, 1903*. Department of Commerce and Labor Doc. No. 12. Washington, D.C.: GPO, 1904.

———. *Report on the Salmon Fisheries of Alaska, 1904*. Department of Commerce and Labor Doc. No. 35. Washington, D.C.: GPO, 1905.

———. *Report on the Salmon Fisheries of Alaska, 1905*. Department of Commerce and Labor Doc. No. 53. Washington, D.C.: GPO, 1906.

Marsh, Millard C., and John N. Cobb. *The Fisheries of Alaska in 1907*. Bureau of Fisheries Doc. No. 632. Washington, D.C.: GPO, 1908.

———. *The Fisheries of Alaska in 1908*. Bureau of Fisheries Doc. No. 645. Washington, D.C.: GPO, 1909.

———. *The Fisheries of Alaska in 1909*. Bureau of Fisheries Doc. No. 730. Washington, D.C.: GPO, 1910.

———. *The Fisheries of Alaska in 1910*. Bureau of Fisheries Doc. No. 746. Washington, D.C.: GPO, 1911.

Moser, Jefferson F. *Alaska Salmon Investigations in 1900 and 1901*. Bulletin of the United States Fish Commission. Washington, D.C.: GPO, 1902.

———. *The Salmon and Salmon Fisheries of Alaska: Report of the Operations of the United States Fish Commission Steamer Albatross for the Year Ending June 30, 1898*. United States Fish Commission Bulletin for 1898. Washington, D.C.: GPO, 1900.

Rich, Willis H., and Edward M. Ball. "Federal Fishery Laws and Regulations Affecting the Salmon Fisheries in Alaska, 1889–1924." In *Statistical Review of the Alaska Salmon Fisheries*. Bureau of Fisheries Doc. No. 1041. Washington, D.C.: GPO, 1928.

Thompson, Seton H. *Alaska Fishery and Fur-Seal Industries: 1948*. Fish and Wildlife Service Statistical Digest No. 23. Washington, D.C.: GPO, 1952.

———. *Alaska Fishery and Fur-Seal Industries: 1949*. Fish and Wildlife Service Statistical Digest No. 26. Washington, D.C.: GPO, 1952.

———. *Alaska Fishery and Fur-Seal Industries: 1950*. Fish and Wildlife Service Statistical Digest No. 29. Washington, D.C.: GPO, 1953.

———. *Alaska Fishery and Fur-Seal Industries: 1951*. Fish and Wildlife Service Statistical Digest No. 31. Washington, D.C.: GPO, 1954.

———. *Alaska Fishery and Fur-Seal Industries: 1952*. Fish and Wildlife Service Statistical Digest No. 33. Washington, D.C.: GPO, 1954.

———. *Alaska Fishery and Fur-Seal Industries: 1953*. Fish and Wildlife Service Statistical Digest No. 35. Washington, D.C.: GPO, 1955.

———. *Alaska Fishery and Fur-Seal Industries: 1954*. Fish and Wildlife Service Statistical Digest No. 37. Washington, D.C.: GPO, 1956.

———. *Alaska Fishery and Fur-Seal Industries: 1955*. Fish and Wildlife Service Statistical Digest No. 40. Washington, D.C.: GPO, 1957.

Tingle, George. *Report on the Salmon Fisheries in Alaska, 1896*. U.S. Treasury Department Doc. No. 1925. Washington, D.C.: GPO, 1897.

Tingley, Al, Nancy Free-Sloan, Stefanie Moreland, and Kurt Iverson. *Changes in the Distribution of Alaska's Commercial Fisheries Entry Permits, 1975–2000*.

Alaska Commercial Fisheries Entry Commission Report No. 01–1N. Juneau, Alaska. 2001.
U.S. Fish and Wildlife Service, Fisheries Research Data Files, 1904–60, Record Group 22. National Archives and Records Administration, Pacific Alaska Region, Anchorage, Alaska.
U.S. Fish and Wildlife Service, Fisheries and Management Records, 1930–59, Record Group 22. National Archives and Records Administration, Pacific Alaska Region, Anchorage, Alaska.
Criminal Case Files, Records of the District Courts of the United States, Record Group 21. National Archives and Records Administration, Pacific Alaska Region, Anchorage, Alaska.

INTERVIEWS AND ORAL HISTORIES

Dalton, Mr. and Mrs. George. Interviewed by Richard Newton. June 21, 1979. Petersburg, Alaska. Transcript available at the U.S. Forest Service, Juneau, Alaska.
Davis, George. Interviewed by Richard Newton. June 21, 1979. Hoonah, Alaska. Transcript available at the U.S. Forest Service, Juneau, Alaska.
George, Lydia and Jimmie. Interviewed by Madonna Moss. May 13, 1981. Angoon, Alaska. Transcript available at the U.S. Forest Service, Juneau, Alaska.
Jackson, John C. Interviewed by Richard Newton. September 17, 1979. Kake, Alaska. Transcript available at U.S. Forest Service, Juneau, Alaska.
Jackson, Ruby. Interviewed by Richard Newton. August 1, 1980. Juneau, Alaska. Transcript available at the U.S. Forest Service, Juneau, Alaska.
James, Billy and Martha. Interviewed by Richard Newton. March 4, 1980. Petersburg, Alaska. Transcript available at the U.S. Forest Service, Juneau, Alaska.
James, Chester. Interviewed by Richard Newton. August 9–10, 1979. Kake, Alaska. Transcript available at the U.S. Forest Service, Juneau, Alaska.
Johnson, Minnie. Interviewed by Richard Newton. June 26, 1979. Angoon, Alaska. Transcript available at the U.S. Forest Service, Juneau, Alaska.
Katasse, Henry. Interviewed by Richard Newton. March 5, 1980. Petersburg, Alaska. Transcript available at the U.S. Forest Service, Juneau, Alaska.
"The Southeast Alaska Salmon Fishery: Interviews with Men and Women Engaged in Commercial Fishing, 1913–1978." Interviewed by Stephan B. Levy and George Figdor. Audio tapes available at the Alaska Historical Library, Juneau.

MANUSCRIPT COLLECTIONS

Alaska Packers Association Records, 1891–1970. Alaska Historical Library, Juneau.
Brady, John G. Papers. Beinecke Rare Book and Manuscript Library, Yale University, New Haven, Connecticut.

Emmon's Family Papers. Beinecke Rare Book and Manuscript Library, Yale University, New Haven, Connecticut.

Garfield, Viola. Papers. Manuscript and University Archives, University of Washington, Seattle.

Matsen, Iva L. Papers. Manuscript and University Archives, University of Washington, Seattle.

Paul, William Lackey. Papers. Manuscript and University Archives, University of Washington, Seattle.

Paul, William Lewis. Papers. Manuscript and University Archives, University of Washington, Seattle.

Price, Robert E. Collection. Alaska Historical Library, Juneau.

Smith, Harold H. Papers. Manuscripts and University Archives, University of Washington, Seattle.

Stern, Max. Papers. Bancroft Library. University of California, Berkeley.

NEWSPAPERS, MAGAZINES, AND TRADE JOURNALS

The Alaskan, Sitka, 1885–1907.

Alaska Fisherman, Ketchikan, 1923–1932.

Alaska Fisherman's Journal, 1977–2006.

Alaska Fishing News, Ketchikan, 1940–1944.

Alaska Labor News, Anchorage, 1916–1917.

Alaska Weekly, Seattle, dates vary.

Daily Alaska Dispatch, 1900–1919.

Ketchikan Alaska Chronicle, 1920–1926.

Pacific Fisherman, 1903–1955.

Pacific Fisherman Yearbook, 1904–1955.

Petersburg Progressive, Alaska, dates vary.

Index

WEYERHAEUSER ENVIRONMENTAL BOOKS

The Natural History of Puget Sound Country by Arthur R. Kruckeberg

Forest Dreams, Forest Nightmares: The Paradox of Old Growth in the Inland West by Nancy Langston

Landscapes of Promise: The Oregon Story, 1800–1940 by William G. Robbins

The Dawn of Conservation Diplomacy: U.S.-Canadian Wildlife Protection Treaties in the Progressive Era by Kurkpatrick Dorsey

Irrigated Eden: The Making of an Agricultural Landscape in the American West by Mark Fiege

Making Salmon: An Environmental History of the Northwest Fisheries Crisis by Joseph E. Taylor III

George Perkins Marsh, Prophet of Conservation by David Lowenthal

Driven Wild: How the Fight against Automobiles Launched the Modern Wilderness Movement by Paul S. Sutter

The Rhine: An Eco-Biography, 1815–2000 by Mark Cioc

Where Land and Water Meet: A Western Landscape Transformed by Nancy Langston

The Nature of Gold: An Environmental History of the Alaska/Yukon Gold Rush by Kathryn Morse

Faith in Nature: Environmentalism as Religious Quest by Thomas R. Dunlap

Landscapes of Conflict: The Oregon Story, 1940–2000 by William G. Robbins

The Lost Wolves of Japan by Brett L. Walker

Wilderness Forever: Howard Zahniser and the Path to the Wilderness Act by Mark Harvey

On the Road Again: Montana's Changing Landscape by William Wyckoff

Public Power, Private Dams: The Hells Canyon High Dam Controversy by Karl Boyd Brooks

Windshield Wilderness: Cars, Roads, and Nature in Washington's National Parks by David Louter

Native Seattle: Histories from the Crossing-Over Place by Coll Thrush

The Country in the City: The Greening of the San Francisco Bay Area by Richard A. Walker

Drawing Lines in the Forest: Creating Wilderness Areas in the Pacific Northwest by Kevin R. Marsh

Plowed Under: Agriculture and Environment in the Palouse by Andrew P. Duffin

Making Mountains: New York City and the Catskills by David Stradling

The Fishermen's Frontier: People and Salmon in Southeast Alaska by David F. Arnold

WEYERHAEUSER ENVIRONMENTAL CLASSICS

The Great Columbia Plain: A Historical Geography, 1805–1910 by D. W. Meinig

Mountain Gloom and Mountain Glory: The Development of the Aesthetics of the Infinite by Marjorie Hope Nicolson

Tutira: The Story of a New Zealand Sheep Station by Herbert Guthrie-Smith

A Symbol of Wilderness: Echo Park and the American Conservation Movement by Mark Harvey

Man and Nature: Or, Physical Geography as Modified by Human Action by George Perkins Marsh; edited and annotated by David Lowenthal

Conservation in the Progressive Era: Classic Texts edited by David Stradling

CYCLE OF FIRE BY STEPHEN J. PYNE

Fire: A Brief History

World Fire: The Culture of Fire on Earth

Vestal Fire: An Environmental History, Told through Fire, of Europe and Europe's Encounter with the World

Fire in America: A Cultural History of Wildland and Rural Fire

Burning Bush: A Fire History of Australia

The Ice: A Journey to Antarctica